‘Good Women do not Inherit Land’

# 'Good Women do not Inherit Land'

## Politics of Land and Gender in India

*by*

Nitya Rao

Routledge
Taylor & Francis Group
LONDON AND NEW YORK

First published 2018
by Routledge
4 Park Square, Milton Park, Abingdon, Oxon OX14 4RN

and by Routledge
605 Third Avenue, New York, NY 10017

First issued in paperback 2023

*Routledge is an imprint of the Taylor & Francis Group, an informa business*



Publisher's Note
The publisher has gone to great lengths to ensure the quality of this reprint but points out that some imperfections in the original copies may be apparent.

Print edition not for sale in South Asia (India, Sri Lanka, Nepal, Bangladesh, Afghanistan, Pakistan or Bhutan).

*British Library Cataloguing in Publication Data*
A catalogue record for this book is available from the British Library

*Library of Congress Cataloging in Publication Data*
A catalog record for this book has been requested

ISBN 13: 978-1-138-50192-8 (hbk)
ISBN 13: 978-1-03-265298-6 (pbk)
ISBN 13: 978-1-315-14461-0 (ebk)

DOI: 10.4324/9781315144610

Typeset in Plantin 10/13
by Eleven Arts, Delhi 110 035

SOCIAL
SCIENCE
PRESS

This book is dedicated to
Susheela, Mariam and the many Santal women who
inspired me with their everyday struggles for survival and dignity

# Contents

*Acknowledgements* xi
1. Introduction 1
2. A Personal Journey 35
3. Faces of Poverty: The Villages Profiled 54
4. Reinventing Tradition: Agrarian Movements in History 109
5. Land as a Productive Resource 146
6. Locating Identities 175
7. Women's Claims to Land 201
8. Custom and the Courts: Bargaining with Modernity 232
9. Development Interventions: Does One Size Fit All? 256
10. Reframing the Debate: Challenges and Dilemmas 283
Annexure 1: Profile of Sample Households 303
Annexure 2: Regional Demographic Indicators 310
Annexure 3: Land and Production 314
Annexure 4: Types of Land Disputes 320
*Bibliography* 328
*Glossary* 343
*Acronyms* 346
*Index* 348

# Tables, Figures and Photographs

## TABLES


3.1: Some Well-being Indicators, 1991 and 2001 (in per cent) 62
3.2: Characteristic Features of Chuapara and Bagdiha 107
3.3: Women's Rights and Responses in Chuapara and Bagdiha 108
4.1: Changes in Land Holdings by Gender in Chuapara 128
4.2: Changes in Land Holdings by Gender in Bagdiha 128
4.3: Land Distribution in Dumka Subdivision, Dumka District, 1998–99 137
5.1: Total Land in Acres 168
6.1: State versus Indigenous Constructions of Identity 177
6.2: Chuapara: Land Holdings by Ethnic Group during Four Settlements 180
6.3: Bagdiha: Land Holdings by Caste during Four Settlement Periods 186
6.4: Historical Shifts in the Construction of Male Identities 191
7.1: Women's Land Holdings in Chuapara and Bagdiha 207
7.2: Households by Marital Status 218
7.3: Historical Shifts in the Construction of Santal Female Identities 227
9.1: Pensions for Widowed Women in Chuapara and Bagdiha 262
9.2: Caste-wise Distribution of Employment and Ration Cards 264

9.3: Targeting: Excluding the Poor or Including the Rich? 266
9.4: House Allotment in Chuapara and Bagdiha 275

## FIGURES

5.1: Paddy Output of Sample Households (per acre) 150
5.2: Rice Consumption during Different Seasons in Some Sample Households 156
6.1: Changes in Ownership of Land by Quality: Bagdiha 189
7.1: Family tree of the Marandi Clan 209

## PHOTOGRAPHS

3.1: The Chuapara school in disrepair. Breeding a generation of non-literate children. 66
3.2: Her *kurram* plot. Nati gives her Children some maize. 80
3.3: Women selling tubers. 82
3.4: Pounding rice on the *dheki*. A joint activity. 89
3.5: An overcrowded bus. Seasonal labour migrants to Bardhaman. 97
3.6: To the Gando *haat*. Carrying liquor for sale. 99
4.1: Statues of Sidho and Kanhu in Dumka bazaar. 111
5.1: Ploughing remains a man's job. 152
5.2: Threshing paddy. Women as equal participants. 153
8.1: The revenue court. Waiting to be heard. 247
9.1: Digging a well. A typical employment generation scheme. 271

## ON THE COVER

Sheila Marandi, 18 years old, the eldest daughter of Mary and Chura, our hosts in Chuapara. She was a key support to her parents in the paddy fields and within the home. Married in 2000 and now a mother of two, she remains a strong worker and mainstay of her family. She got no share of her father's land.

# Acknowledgements

This book is a result of many years of work with women and women's organizations struggling for change, for recognition, for equality. Successes were celebrated; failures were used as grounds for learning. The battles were not easy and led to a process of reflection, both collective and individual. As a woman, participating in the struggles of other women, I realized that many of these struggles were my own too though the context was different. The futility of dichotomous divisions between 'us' and 'them' struck me strongly; it also brought out the hypocrisy of middle-class life. As women, we were willing to compromise in our daily lives, but this seemed unacceptable, a sign of powerlessness in relation to poor women.

Over the last decade I have worked with Santal women in different capacities—as a trainer, a researcher and a friend. Their literacy levels may be low, but living and working with them, witnessing their courage first-hand, has given me the inspiration to write this book. I had undertaken some capacity-building training with a group of Santal women field-workers belonging to several local non-governmental organizations (NGOs) in the region over a three-year period during the mid-1990s. The stated purpose was women's empowerment. At the end of this period, the women started asking questions and demanding more control over the projects from the concerned NGOs, but they were firmly told that this was not possible. The next thing I knew most of them had left these organizations. They were jobless, and though committed, were left with no resources to carry forward their work.

They recognized and accepted their role-defined identities—of being mothers, wives and home-makers, as well as cultivators and NGO workers, but beyond this, they also saw themselves as women in their own right, as full social persons, with dignity and status. Their perception of their identities as women seemed much clearer than that of many urban middle-class women. This was a very powerful insight, guiding this book, as it made me realize, that though poor in material terms, these women would not compromise their basic identities and principles for small resources from NGOs or the government. Not understanding this is perhaps the one main reason why a lot of group initiatives with women have failed to deliver.

Rather than an experiential outpouring, I decided to research and analyse these struggles and assertions of identity in a more rigorous manner. The School of Development Studies at the University of East Anglia provided me financial assistance for conducting my PhD research and a supportive home and academic environment for my writing. While most of the material for this book was collected as part of my PhD work in 1999–2000, it has been updated during subsequent extended visits in 2004 and 2006. I am grateful to the Rockefeller Foundation for awarding me a one-month residency at the Bellagio Study Centre in February-March 2004, where I began the writing of this book. The analysis has been developed and strengthened through extensive discussions with a range of people—academic colleagues, friends and the women named in the book. Some of the material has been published in international journals and I have benefited from the comments of the anonymous referees.

While it is not possible here to thank each person who has contributed to this book, I cannot but mention a few. I should start with Kumar Rana, who introduced me to the Santal Parganas in 1996 and developed in me a passionate desire to work in the area. He helped me gain some insight into Santal masculinities and has always been willing to share information and ideas. Amit Mitra helped me work through many of the ideas in this book, always willing to give feedback, engaging in debate, and encouraging me to keep writing at times when I almost gave up. Financial support for a photo-documentation project on the lives of women in the Santal Parganas was provided to us by the Friedrich Ebert Stiftung, New Delhi; I am grateful for their support. Some of the pictures taken in the study villages are reproduced here.

To Pushpa Murmu, my interpreter and constant companion in the field, I owe much of the credit for this book; also for giving me a window into the lives of the local women, many of whom speak no Hindi. Her cheerful personality contributed greatly to establishing a rapport in the villages. She never complained, despite the hard schedules I sometimes set for our work. I could not have gathered several of the intricate details and participated in informal talk, without her support. In the villages, I particularly want to acknowledge the affection and support of Mariam Tudu and Chunda Marandi, as well as Susheela Hansdak and Hemant Hembrum, who readily provided us a place to stay in their homes. Apart from the many men and women, the children, wanting to engage in stories, games and songs, provided me a break from my questioning, and also constantly reminded me of the realities of daily life on the ground.

I would like to especially specially thank my friends in a local women's NGO, Ayoaidari Trust, for not only providing me a home and companionship in Dumka, but also discussing with me my research and understanding of Santal women's perspectives on land. I am also grateful to other NGO leaders in the region, in particular, Satyender Singh, who discussed their views with me. Several lawyers and missionaries gave me their time generously. I am also fortunate to have been able to talk with key political leaders in Jharkhand, to understand their thoughts and positions on the legitimacy of women's land claims at a time when the Jharkhand movement, built on the basis of ethnic and class identities, was at its peak. Sibu Soren, Stephen Marandi, Ram Dayal Munda, N.E. Horo and A.K. Roy all made the time to meet me. Several officers, both at the block and district levels, and across departments, shared with me the problems they faced and their views on possible solutions. I wish to thank them all for their cooperation. In particular, I would like to thank the then Deputy Commissioner of Dumka district, who provided me access to the District Record Room, archival research which deepened my insights into the continuities between colonial and post-colonial administration on the ground.

Amongst academic colleagues, I would like to specifically thank Cecile Jackson at the School of Development Studies for not only commenting on my original PhD work as one of my supervisors, but for her willingness to discuss ideas and provide support thereafter too. I would like to also thank Narayan Banerjee and late K.S. Singh in Delhi, Ann Whitehead and Ben Rogaly at Sussex, Barbara Harriss-White in Oxford and Gunnel Cederlof in Uppsala , for their thoughtful comments on parts of this material, which have been presented at seminars at different places over the last few years.

My family has been a source of immense strength and support, and I am grateful to all of them for this. My daughter Anandi has grown up from a little girl to a young adult during this period, and watching her develop her own independent personality has egged me on to complete this book. I would never have been able to do this work without the unstinting love and support of my parents—from physical care when I was sick to intellectual engagement and comments—also for their inspiration through their own commitment to the removal of hunger and poverty and the empowerment of women in India.

Last but not least I would like to sincerely thank Social Science Press for their encouragement, support and hard work in making this book a reality.

May 2008
University of East Anglia
U.K.

CHAPTER

# 1 Introduction

Rimani Marandi has hardly a moment to sit and relax. Working in the fields, going for wage labour, brewing liquor for sale, cooking and looking after the children ... the list goes on. From difficult beginnings in a poor family, where she toiled at home while her brothers went to school, hard work inured her to life's uncertainties. But now her husband lives with another woman. He wanted to bring her in as a second wife, but Rimani put her foot down. She also refused to divide the property, as she is looking after the two children. To make her give in, her husband harasses her constantly: harvesting a little paddy from her fields clandestinely, coaxing Jeevan Soren to demand back the paddy he lent her, pressurizing the village council to make her agree to a partition of the land or just shouting obscenities at her.

Sheela Hansdak, a primary school teacher of four decades standing, is married to a former *mukhiya* of Bagdiha. They are not in want. They have considerable land. Yet, as a woman, she has had a difficult life. Her father had four wives, and she was the eldest daughter of the second wife. Her mother left her father and won a maintenance suit. Her father was a low-paid schoolteacher with a large family. Despite the burden of paying alimony, her father sent Sheela and another half-sister to the Moharo Mission School. When they came home for vacations, she had to work a lot, yet listen to the grumbling of her stepmother who resented the Rs 20 being paid monthly for her education. She grew up hating her mother, missing not just the love, attention and care, but also holding her responsible for the ensuing struggles in her life. Admiring her father's commitment to education, she resolved to be a teacher and dedicate herself to educating girls. She married, had children and despite the arduous task of home-making without any support, she got a government schoolteacher's job. There was no crèche in the school. Her students' parents would bring her a *charpai* on which she would lay down her baby. This concern kept her going and energized her to work hard at school and home. She retired in 2002 after teaching for 37 years.

Sona Tudu, 44 years old, with six daughters and a son, lost her husband in October 1997. Two of her daughters were already married then, living in neighbouring villages, so her sons-in-law helped to plough her two acres of land. Her hard work and independence irked her husband's brother and male cousins. The death of a child in the family emboldened them to call Sona a witch, holding her responsible for this death. The harassment continued. When she could bear it no longer, she filed complaints with the panchayat at Gando and the police. A notice was sent to the kin and things quietened down. But now in times of need she lacks any social support. Her daughter died of tuberculosis in December 2000 as Sona was unable to raise sufficient resources for her treatment.

Struggles to assert one's identity keep women alive and comprise the very essence of their womanhood. This reality struck me on a hot summer day in 1999, while 'interviewing' Rimani of Bagdiha village in Jharkhand's Santal Parganas. A woman is not just a mother or a home-maker, or even a cultivator; she is all of these, and more. It is this coexistence of multiple identities that is seen in the differential use of the terms *Orahor* (or home-makers), *Chasahor* (or cultivators), and *Gogohor* (or women). In the use of these terms, the Santals acknowledge and recognize that women have role-based identities, but also identities beyond these roles, as women.

Rimani did the unheard thing of saying 'No' to her man and others around her. She refused to acquiesce to the norms of her society or the demands of her husband. She refused to leave the house, partition the land, or allow her husband to bring home another woman. She refused to succumb. Rimani, thin, emaciated, hardly looking her 37 years, feeding her children with difficulty but ensuring that they did not miss school even for a day, went through life with a stoic smile. She taught me that asserting one's identity becomes possible only when we learn to say 'No', something that women in middle-class urban India often dream of doing but do not find the courage to do.

Sona doesn't fit the stereotype of an Indian widow. She is young, she is active, and she is independent. She works hard to feed and educate her children. She has the reputation of being a hard worker, and is often called for jobs, big and small, agricultural and non-agricultural. Observing no restrictions, she was also made the secretary of a woman's group organized by the government, in the village. This recognition, however, comes with a price. It provokes jealousy and leads to threats.

The struggles, and more important, the strategies of the women I met in the two villages of Santal Parganas, Bagdiha and Chuapara, gave me a new understanding of life, and over time, became the driving force for writing this book. By the word 'strategies' I do not mean manipulative actions, but a set of thoughts and actions that seek to achieve a possible set of outcomes. In 1999–2000, I met these women frequently while collecting data for my thesis. Subsequently, I have continued to visit them regularly; it is not only a second home to me, but also a place that has contributed to my own intellectual and emotional development as a person and as a woman.

Their contexts and lives are different: there is hard work, pain, frustration, but also a sense of control and power. Rimani, in our very first meeting, spoke candidly to me about her failed marriage, her husband taking up with another woman, and how she now proposed to get him back. Being able to talk about her marital relationship, and her sexuality openly and without apologies, was perhaps itself an empowering experience, a process of sharing that was also affirming her own identity. It was a valuable strategy for me, although my 'middle-class' upbringing and the academic socialization that instilled in me the need not to get too involved with the 'subjects' of one's research, prevented me from opening up totally to these women. They understood, and strong bonds were created between us.

Ultimately, it was a question of identities and of how one's self was valued. I constantly struggled with the question of what really constitutes the identity of a person, of a woman. Society recognizes women as daughters, wives or mothers, and as working women too, who are supplementing the household income. But what about the person, her aspirations as a human being, her choices of careers or even the number of children she wants to have? Pursuing her choices would render her selfish, uncaring and individualistic, in the eyes of the society. Indeed, asserting one's identity through making such choices would mean confronting the disparagement of the family and the local community. I was not at all clear how women distinguish between the roles attributed to them on account of their physical and social location, and the identity gained through this (or objective identity) and their own 'subjective' identity, as 'persons'. I never faced a loss of identity, and nor did any of the women in these villages. Rather it is the threat to the identity, to our self-worth that the struggles and strategies are all about, taking different forms according to contexts, and changing over time.

Self-valuations are based on gender, but at the same time, differences arise due to ethnicity, class position, particular subject positions within the family and the stage in the life-course (Whitehead, 1984). Identities, of all these women, and perhaps of every woman, are based on such self-valuations. These identities influence the experience of subordination, the sense of loss of identity, and as a result, the nature of struggles.

The key to finding oneself as a person, something as true in my life as of these Santal women, was to stay within the system and fight it. This very act of resistance leads to a sense of being, and also begins transforming the system itself. Women are proud of being mothers and wives, and cherish their reproductive roles, but would like this to be one element only, albeit an important one, of their identities as persons. The objective dimension is important, but so is the value dimension. It is the recognition of only one facet, as a mere cog in the wheel of production and reproduction, that makes women fight back to exercise the freedom of choice, and negotiate the realm of possibilities. As the mother of a growing child, my activist and academic pursuits often led to the opprobrium of being a 'non-caring' person, even a 'bad' mother. For the Santal, this attempted conversion to a non-being sometimes takes the brutal form of being labelled a '*dain*' (a witch). The '*dain*' is attributed with magical powers that endow her with the ability to do evil and wreak havoc. This transformation takes the form of being accused of having sucked the blood (read life) out of one's nearest, including children and husbands. In urban India, women may not be called '*dains*', but are, very often, attributed the same qualities when they seek to assert and establish their identities.

## ISSUES AROUND IDENTITY

There is considerable theorizing on identities, particularly its linkage with notions of property and resources. Identities do have a material basis, they are located and established within one's particular material context. But they also have a more intangible, discursive element, reflecting the ways in which people are spoken about, in many ways equally important to one's sense of personhood and well-being. How does one tell whether someone is just giving in to domination or deliberately doing something differently? I was left wondering, and still wonder whether Rimani really needed Solomon, her husband, back? Why did she draw on the Christian morality of monogamy to get him back? Was it to demonstrate her sexual subservience and loyalty to her husband, or was it a way in fact of asserting not just her sexuality, but her ability to make decisions and her identity as a person? Her strategy in this case was carefully chosen—faithfulness to her husband and responsibility towards her children gave her the moral high ground to retain control over her husband's landed property. But more, she was able to publicly demonstrate that she still had a hold over his emotions, even though she knew the day he had left with the other woman, that their emotional bonding had been shattered. She could demonstrate that she had lived up to the image of the 'good woman' and 'good wife'. Solomon returned to her in 2001. Thus, while grounded in and informed by the material politics of everyday life, her discursive strategies, that is, the way she presented her case, comprised a central site of contestation. Discourse then is another means of establishing one's identity as a person.

Globally, land is a key element in the identities of indigenous people. Many of their struggles for recognition begin with land, which takes on multiple meanings. More than a material resource, it becomes a metaphor for their culture, language, social and community norms, and indeed, their very identity. Rimani refused her husband a share of the household land, even though the land title was in his name. It meant more to her than just a few fields on which paddy could be grown. It meant her recognition as an individual, with rights in the children, household and the community, and her right to resist being relegated to the objective role of a wife. It meant pointing to the unity among the productive, reproductive and symbolic values of land. She was setting the framework within which she wanted to be assessed, while challenging the patriarchal framework that set the terms of evaluation only as a good wife. She held that the man had failed in his performance of his objective roles as husband and father. She turned the tables on the community leaders, who were earlier inclined to a partition of the land between Rimani and her estranged husband. They now had no other choice but to accept Rimani's claims.

Her strategy has found support in the larger context wherein women's rights to land are now centrally located in the national policy agenda. While the original demand for equal property rights lay in the discourse around gender equality, this is now seen as a key strategy to enhance food production and food security, in a situation when men are often absent from the rural areas (Rao, 2006). The translation, however, of such policy statements into practice remains weak, precisely due to the underlying assumptions which link it to the performance of particular roles, rather than seeing it as one element of a holistic identity. While earlier women were labelled as home-makers, now they are categorized as producers. And as became obvious during the course of this research, women were refusing to be labelled, one way or the other, but wanted space to assert their identities. As Mary Tudu, the 40-year-old spouse of Chuapara's Chura Marandi, with whom I lived for several months, often said to me, 'We may be physically able to manage the plough, but this is not something we want to do, let the men do at least this task.' Women sought not to deny men their roles, responsibilities and identities, but recognition for themselves, not just in relational terms, but also as individuals.

Unravelling the major strands of the debates around land, and around gender and indigenous or ethnic identities raises many questions. Can land really be understood as only an individual, productive asset or does it need to be viewed as a socially embedded resource too, tied to notions not just of wealth, but dignity, status and power? What are the contradictions and complementarities between statutory titling (an abstract system representing 'modern' institutions) and customary tenures (a face-to-face mode of 'traditional' regulation), or between individual and collective rights? How far do inheritance laws, by creating a disjuncture between production and reproduction, not merely deny women rights to land, but also question their identities as 'full beings'? And finally, how should land rights be positioned within the larger context, not just of gender equality, but also globalization, as patriarchy does not operate in a vacuum, but adapts to contextual variations and shifts over time?

Some of these tensions and questions, emerge from a separation of the two discourses, one around rights to landed property and the other around identities and gender equality. These have been addressed in this book, through a detailed study of the shifts in property relations amongst the Santals—who account for more than 35 per cent of the total Scheduled Tribe population of Jharkhand—in two different agro-ecological contexts of Dumka district. I attempt to analyse the validity of the Marxian axiom that property relations are fundamentally social relations; that is, not relationships between people and objects, but between people and other people. Struggles over land are not just about material change or redistribution of a resource, but also about shifts in power relations between different groups, about asserting one's identity. Adopting an undifferentiated approach to land as just a physical category can then divert attention from women's struggles to be valued and recognized as equals in society.

## *ADIVASI* IDENTITY AND LAND

Hindu hucksters settled upon various pretences, and in a few years grew into men of fortune. They cheated the poor Santal in every transaction. The forester brought his jars of clarified butter for sale; the Hindu measured it in vessels with false bottoms: the husbandman came to exchange his rice for salt, oil, cloth, and gunpowder; the Hindu used heavy weights in ascertaining the quantity of grain, light ones in weighing out the articles given in return. The fortunes made by traffic in produce were augmented by usury (Hunter, 1996[1868]: 158).

Historical records present a case of exploitation and displacement of the *adivasis*[1] during the colonial period, to construct a strong

[1] While there is considerable discussion on the terminology (see, for instance, Baviskar 1995, for a good summary), *adivasi* (or original inhabitants) is the term generally used to refer to the Scheduled Tribes as recognized by Article 342, Part XVI of the Constitution of India. Such notification made them eligible for special provisions to promote their educational and economic interests.

argument for 'protecting the primitive' as part of the civilizing mission. These notions prevailed in the Indian state after independence. Recognition that the *adivasis* had been historically exploited and marginalized led to the demarcation of their habitats as Scheduled Areas to be governed by separate legislation, at least as far as their resources were concerned.[2]

While protection was consciously made a policy, displacement has continued apace, in terms of land alienation by landlords and moneylenders, deforestation in both colonial and post-colonial times and more importantly, by large-scale government development projects post-independence. Fernandes and Paranjpye (1997) claim that government development projects, mainly dams, mines and industries, have displaced almost 16.4 million people since 1951. Close to 38 per cent of the displaced are *adivasis* and only 25 per cent of them have been rehabilitated. Though constituting only 8 per cent of the country's population, this disproportionate representation amongst the displaced, speaks for their deprivation. Apart from material consequences in terms of insecurity, uncertainty and physical mobility, this has led to a change in their social status and identity, from cultivator to labourer. It has also meant a loss of cultural autonomy, knowledge and power. Both these major streams of discourse—protection and displacement—tend however to construct the *adivasis* as passive victims of alienation from their land and forests.

A further problem lies in understanding the meaning of resources to *adivasis*. Land as a resource itself has been divided into two distinct domains in contemporary social research—the 'natural' domain of environmental studies, and the 'cultural' domain of production relations in agriculture (Agrawal and Sivaramakrishnan, 2000). Environmental studies, preoccupied with mountains, forests and tribal populations, focus on the relationship between people in mountainous and forested regions in the context of deforestation and environmental change, and almost entirely leave out the agrarian context. Though recognizing the close relationship between the material and cultural,

[2]The Santal Pargana Tenancy Act was passed in 1949, the Chota Nagpur Tenancy Act, 1908, continued despite the existence of the Bihar Tenancy Act, in present-day Jharkhand.

this approach glosses over gender and other differences in portraying homogenous indigenous communities.[3] Studies on agrarian relations, on the other hand, ignore the role of changing forest and common property relations—the larger environmental context—in shaping social and economic identities and relations.[4]

The passivity, homogeneity and unidimensionality of resource use implicitly attributed to the *adivasis* in the above views are questionable. First, as Béteille (1991) has pointed out, caste and race are not only about inequality, but also about collective identity. Intense and widespread livelihood crises lead to mass-based resistance movements. There has been a long history of resource-based resistance movements in the region, culminating finally in political autonomy for Jharkhand.[5] This is discussed in detail in Chapter 4.

Second, relationships of domination and subordination cannot be sustained unless accompanied by processes of mutuality and negotiation. If domination is perpetrated without façades of caring, then the dominated are likely to either die of starvation and neglect, migrate in search of greener pastures or rise in revolt, thus destroying the very objective of the exploiter. Such facades often take the form of expressions of benevolence and speak of the 'ingratitude' and the ineptness of the subordinate. The subaltern studies school of historiography sought to correct this prejudice by giving voice to the subordinated. Although in this process, the attempts to demonstrate unity and homogeneity of the subordinate overshadow the recognition of contested understandings of rights and identities, the strength of subaltern analysis lies in opening up space to rethink sociality itself.

[3]See for example Banuri & Marglin (1993). Gadgil and Guha (1992, 1995), while dividing society into the 'ecosystem people' and 'omnivores', do recognize the issue of scarcity and conflict over resources within the community.

[4]Essays on land and labour by Bardhan (1984), Bernstein (1977), Byres (1977), Athreya et al. (1990) are examples.

[5]The Santal *hul* of 1855, the Sardar and Kherwar movements in the 1870s and 1880s, the Birsa movement (1898–1900), and the Tana Bhagat movement in the 1920s are remembered even today. More recently, the Naxalite movement has been raising some of these issues, concentrated as it is in the tribal-dominated regions of central India. *Adivasi* movements for land persist in other states as well, particularly Maharashtra, Andhra Pradesh and Kerala.

Individual and collective agency is situated in daily practices, and gaps and silences are found in the dominant views of history. It helps focus on multiple perspectives, multiple truths, and everyday forms of resistance.[6]

Third, in all these approaches, gender has not been a major axis of analysis. While women may be excluded from authority in the male order, particularly in terms of resource control, they exercise varieties of informal power in daily practice, adopting several everyday resistance tactics. More formal and public resistance through lawsuits have also been used to negotiate their land claims. At the same time, not all men necessarily have authority in the public sphere. In fact, the critical role of women in the production process and their consequent exercise of informal power have often meant a perceived devaluation of male identity, even leading to alcoholism and abuse. Neither men nor women then form a homogenous category, but respond to and align themselves differently in different contexts.

Fourth, research on *adivasis* continues to focus on forests and common property resources rather than private land-holdings and agrarian relations. In fact, *adivasi* areas have plains as well as hill-tracts, forests as well as barren lands. Amongst the Santals, as other Scheduled Tribes in India, agriculture is the main source of livelihood and land is an essential element of identity. Collective rights and community control are seen as hallmarks of this identity, guaranteed by the Fifth and Sixth Schedules of the Constitution of India. In principle, collective land rights can promote gender equality by guaranteeing all members of the community access to land. In practice, however, it doesn't necessarily work in this way, as landed property has historically been linked with male identity. Women's demand for rights to land is seen by many *adivasi* men as disrupting the struggle to establish a collective identity and gain collective rights, in a context of overall marginality.

This becomes obvious, in the context of a judgment of the Supreme Court of India in May 1996, in response to two writ petitions—*Madhu Kishwar v. State of Bihar* 1982 and *Juliana Lakra v. State of Bihar* 1986, filed on behalf of two women. The court, while clarifying that it had

[6]Pioneering work has been done in India by a number of subaltern studies historians such as Ranajit Guha, David Hardiman, Partha Chatterjee, Arvind Das, Shahid Amin, Ajay Skaria, and others.

no intention of interfering with customary law, granted the concerned women rights to land in keeping with the fundamental right to life guaranteed to all citizens, irrespective of sex, creed or caste, by the Indian Constitution. *Adivasi* leaders in Jharkhand condemned the judgment. They felt that initiating a discussion on individual rights, counter to their claims to community rights, based on the principles of mutuality and responsibility was an attempt to create divisions within *adivasi* society. They pointed out that women had a much better position, greater respect and autonomy in *adivasi* society, and the issue of rights to land could not be examined in isolation from the overall social context and cultural practices (Abhiyaan, 1999). They feared that women would become the channel for the intergenerational transfer of land to the wealthy, mainly the *dikus* or outsider-traders.[7] The discourse of 'community' was used to deny women access to land as 'individuals'.

Similar struggles were being fought around the same time by women in other communities too. Mary Roy challenged Syrian Christian inheritance practices[8] and Shah Bano, the Muslim inheritance and maintenance laws.[9] In both cases, self-appointed male leaders of these communities mobilized protests against the state's interference in their 'culture' and 'identity'. Male leaders and politicians used women as symbols to defend what they defined as the identity of the community, albeit at the cost of women's own identities.

[7]Explanation and discussion of the *adivasi-diku* relationship is in Chapter 3. The word *diku* is from the Hindi work *dikkat* (meaning trouble), and literally means 'one who gives trouble'.

[8]Mary Roy filed a Public Interest Litigation in the Supreme Court in 1984 challenging the Travancore Christian Succession Act, which denied daughters any share in intestate property, as a violation of the Fundamental Right to Equality under Articles 14 and 15 of the Constitution. The Supreme Court struck down the Act in February 1986 creating a hue and cry in the church, legislature and media.

[9]Shahbano, a Muslim woman in her seventies, divorced by her husband, applied for maintenance under Section 125 of the Criminal Procedure Code. A Constitution bench of the Supreme Court upheld her right to maintenance. This created an uproar amongst Muslim religious leaders, who saw it as an attack on Muslim Personal Law. They demanded the exclusion of Muslim women from Section 125 of the CrPC, and despite considerable initial opposition from all quarters, a bill to this effect was introduced in Parliament and passed as the Muslim Women's Maintenance of Rights on Divorce Act, 1986. Women's groups protested that the government was sacrificing the interests of women for the sake of electoral politics, but to no avail.

Yet there can be other ways of staking one's claims. In 2000, I met women like Dibri, then 25 years old or Bahari, then 35, in Chuapara, who had secured cultivating rights through negotiation with kin or community leaders rather than through overt assertion. This strategy was also supported by several *adivasi* women leaders, many of them aligned to the Jharkhand Mahila Mukti Morcha, a network of local women's organizations, who found it strategic to negotiate their rights within marriages and the community rather than demand independent land rights for women. While they recognized that the mainstream discourse of the Jharkhand movement that non-*adivasi* men could use women's independent land rights to exploit them and to alienate their lands, was often used to counter women's interests, they realized the strategic potential of the movement to bring substantial material gains to the group as a whole. By supporting the movement and its discourse of the community, they exerted moral pressure on the village leaders and obliged them to support women's claims as a means of establishing their own credibility as guardians of community rights—the normative basis of the movement. Such demonstration became important also for the leaders in the face of a seemingly progressive state framework that ensures equal rights to men and women. Possible opposition from them to women's land claims was neutralized in this process.

The tension between respecting the collective land rights of indigenous communities and guaranteeing individual rights to women is not unique to the Santals, but can actually be seen in several parts of the world. An indigenous woman in Ecuador has been reported to say: 'Indigenous women do not have their own demands, as women, for we are not separate from our people ... We ... have not organised ourselves with the goal of creating an organisation apart from that of men, but rather, we have seen the necessity for women to work jointly with men to address the conflicts we confront' (quoted in Deere & Leon, 2001: 247/253). Issues of identity here gain precedence over redistribution. Tribes and castes continue to be strong markers of identity, despite the existence of hierarchical and often exploitative relationships, including those that are gender-based, within these categories. The lesson appears to be to strive to transform the system from within, rather than quit, as the grass on the other side is likely to be less green, especially for *adivasi* women, who are often stereotyped as being promiscuous and sexually available due to their relative mobility as women.

Women have been an integral part of the movement for political autonomy in Jharkhand, since the 1960s (discussed further in Chapter 4), but the issue of their independent land rights has been actively opposed, more so, in the last decade. Women publicly asserting their rights to land have been branded as '*dains*', harassed, and killed (Mishra, 2003). The assertion by the women is a demand for recognition, but is construed as a challenge to male authority. It is seen to be disruptive of the social order and hence needs to be controlled. While land was important to Sona as an essential resource for her survival and also recognition of her value as a cultivator and worker, for Rimani, land was an instrument to establish her identity as a valued being vis-à-vis her husband, then staying with another woman. For Sheela, land was not an issue, yet she had to struggle to retain her identity. It became increasingly clear to me that, for these women, the issue really was protecting their identity, which in fact, is their most valued possession.

Land is a necessary condition for the fulfilment of women's aspirations, but this alone is not enough. Social acceptance and legitimization as full-fledged workers is key to the use and control of land, as it is to the realization of one's identity. Without social acceptance, even women with rights to land, are unable to make them functional. Soha Marandi in Chuapara, for instance, has a land title, but is unable to cultivate it due to physical threats to both her and her husband from her male cousins. As a result, she has been forced to leave the village with her husband (further details in Chapter 6).

## POWER AND THE NEGOTIATION OF IDENTITIES

The use of multiple strategies for asserting rights starkly raises the role of power in the negotiation of identities. While largely excluded as political actors, both from the dominant discourses and counter-narratives in the public arena, women try to achieve their goals by investing in certain identities or roles over others, as a strategy for transforming the unequal power relations in society. Of course, there are differences amongst women; they do not all face the same tensions and conflicts, nor do their struggles take the same forms. Yet the question of securing their identities remains.

This involves not just open challenges, such as going to the police station or the local courts. More often, it means enlisting the support of other marginal groups, in this case, male *adivasi* leaders, to their cause, building coalitions across different axes of injustice. The Santals as a group are socially underprivileged, and the Santal male leaders have also to fight for their collective rights. Wherever possible, therefore, they make common cause with struggles of other marginalized groups, as they have with women struggling for control over land. Similar experiences of mutual support between traditionally unequal groups has been discussed by Harriss (1982) in relation to patron-client ties in rural Tamil Nadu.

The understanding of inequality, gender inequality in particular, and the consequent avenues for solidarity to negotiate one's identity, are not uniform across societies, or even within societies. While the specific roles of reproducers and home-makers are assigned to women, as roles of providers and protectors are to men, these identities are not static. They change over the life course, with different roles dominating at different stages of life. Apart from these shifts in objective, role-defined identities over time, women's subjectivities change with context and experience, often leading to simultaneous negotiations on several fronts. For instance, Sheela's going to school carrying her young children with her, was a negotiation to keep her job as a teacher, even though the material contribution of her salary to the household was not significant. But seen as a good mother, she was also perceived to be a role model for her students. She made her point and even though for a while it meant being overworked, she was eventually able to garner the necessary support for performing her multifarious tasks. Today, although she has retired, her pension forms a significant part of the household budget.

Seeing power as operating in everyday social practices, as Foucault does (Gordon, 1980), can help understand the nature and form that strategies of resistance take. Often women's resistance is reflected in a range of daily negotiations, and only when their lives or livelihoods are seriously threatened, does it take more public and overt forms.

This brings to the fore the feminist insistence that the 'personal is political', highlighting the importance of the exercise of power in the domestic realm alongside its more public forms. Only by identifying both kinds of power, those that women do exercise and those from which they are excluded, and how these change and are negotiated over time, can we understand the nature of gender relations and inequality.

Consciousness, as any psychologist would say, runs deep, with only a small element expressed at any time. However, submerged elements in the consciousness surface in response to contextual triggers and different elements are expressed independently or in conjunction with others at different moments. Thus identity itself is not a singular. The 'person(s)' with whom one is interacting and the context of interaction become critical in defining the dominance of a particular identity. Women's agency can thus be direct or indirect, operating through both consent and resistance and can only be understood in relation to the material contexts, institutional norms and ideological structures which they confront.

As the examples at the beginning of this chapter reveal, the specificity of the manifestation of gender relations in historically and culturally contextualized forms helps clarify why all women may not have similar interests in matters of land. So while some women support women's rights as central to their economic survival, others oppose them, depending on their perceptions of what they have to gain or lose. The mother-in-law daughter-in-law relationship in the Indian context, exemplifies the reality of differences amongst women and the varying nature of relationships between them. There is an antagonism built into their relationship for control over a man: a son and husband simultaneously. For both, he figures crucially in the perceptions of future security. Competing for control, the identities of these two women either dominate or get subordinated in response to their individual and specific life situations.

Accepting a dynamic concept of power in the everyday interactions of individuals and institutions helps unravel the complexities of domination and empowerment, and is a core idea explored in this book. For instance, the belief that government policy supports land titling in women's names, makes local leaders more sympathetic to women's land claims, at least in their discourse. It becomes a means to demonstrate their concern for women, and thus, reinforce their own authority in the community and vis-à-vis the state. Yet when women in reality assert their claims to land, demonstrating their power in the process, the local community response is to label them '*dains*'. This is not just a male response, but also of women, whose interests, along with their husbands and children, are likely to be adversely affected.

Power does not operate in a vacuum, but is embedded in social practices, related closely to both the material and symbolic reproduction of societies. Critical theorist, Jurgen Habermas (1987, 1989) uses this distinction to classify activities. For example, he sees paid work as constituting material reproduction, while child-rearing and socialization activities as constituting symbolic reproduction. Given that most activities, whether paid work or child-care, encompass both material/biological and social/symbolic meanings, the distinction is only a pragmatic one. Yet it helps focus attention on the idea that each activity can have several meanings, irrespective of where it is conducted, even though only one may appear significant at a particular moment in time. The economy and state (system institutions) often seem to be engaged primarily in material reproduction, while symbolic reproduction is seen to be primarily located in the family or 'private' sphere (what he calls 'life-world'). For women in particular, aspects of the material and symbolic are merged in the work they do, and are hard to separate from one another. Separating these strands and then allocating different values to them, has often contributed to the subordination of women. Habermas points to the cross-connections between these elements, highlighting the existence of a plurality of interests as well as sites of engagement, allowing for a more nuanced analysis of the informal uses of power alongside collective political action to change outcomes at different levels.

In the case of land relations, an understanding of the multiple and interacting sites of engagement as well as multiple interests becomes critical. Within the family and kin-group, inheritance rights are fiercely contested, not only for material reasons, but also for status and honour, drawing on kinship ideologies and marriage practices, as well as state policies and market mechanisms to support claims. Land becomes a means of asserting one's identity as a full member of the community. In this process of assertion, social norms and customs are challenged, with individuals using discourses from one level to strengthen their voice in another, using also those spaces—family, community, or state—that are most supportive of them. The contestation across multiple institutional sites is discussed in Chapter 8.

Such a conceptualization of identities allows for a rethink of the public sphere. This is a space not only for contesting the state, but also for staging conflicts against other forms of domination, whether of gender, racial-ethnic or class, opening up the idea of competing 'publics' as against one 'public' (Fraser, 1989). Several examples exist, of how women, blacks and other marginal groups, excluded from official institutions, have created and used alternate spaces, whether women-only voluntary associations or black churches, to contest the exclusionary norms of the public sphere, elaborating alternative forms of political behaviour and public speech (Arendt, 1958). Marginality or exclusion itself can then offer grounds for resistance and resource claims, as in reality, people are in relations of both inequality and interdependence (Tsing, 1993).[10]

In an illuminating comment, one of the village headmen, Manglu Marandi, mentioned that women were excluded from the village decision-making council as they narrated incidents and actions in great detail, often leading to considerable embarrassment for the men concerned. It was therefore considered wiser to allow them to speak their minds in private, rather than in public, where saving face might become difficult. Discourses and people's narratives of themselves and of others are important in understanding how social identities are fashioned and altered over time, how the cultural hegemony of the dominant is both secured and contested and the prospects for emancipatory social change and political practice. To quote Foucault:

> We must not imagine a world of discourse divided between accepted discourse and excluded discourse, or between the dominant discourse and the dominated one; but as a multiplicity of discursive elements that can come into play in various strategies ... discourse can be both an instrument and an effect of power, but also a hindrance, a stumbling block, a point of resistance and a starting point for the opposing strategy (1990[1976]: 100–1).

[10]This is clearly seen in the functioning of vote-bank politics in much of South Asia, as also caste politics in India, where people are simultaneously included and exploited.

What this also implies is that poor material conditions may not automatically lead to the formulation of policies or actions seeking to reverse the situation. As Dreze and Sen (1995) ask in their essay on the political economy of hunger, what are the political forces and interests that determine the public provision of entitlements such as the public distribution system, health care, public employment, relief, subsidies or productive inputs? How have the needs of the poor been defined, and by whom? Over the last decade in India, there has been a strong emphasis by the new social movements, particularly Dalit and Backward Caste movements on advocacy at the macro level, to secure special benefits from the state, alongside grassroots action at the micro-level.[11] The struggle for Jharkhand state is an example of the successful politicization of a collective identity, though the ultimate creation of the state itself was perhaps a trade-off between different political parties seeking electoral gains and brownie points for their commitment to the *adivasi* cause! Yet, in a context of economic liberalization and political decentralization, the ability of the *adivasi* groups to speak out and make themselves heard in the larger political space, has enabled them to make larger claims on limited material resources.

Political contestation then seems critical for securing both one's material needs and social identities. It is a struggle over cultural meanings, over modes of subjectification—positioning people as specific sorts of people with specific capacities and needs—and over the power to construct both authoritative definitions of social situations and legitimate interpretations of social needs (Fraser, 1989: 107). The importance of a new vocabulary,[12] a re-description of social life that allows for contestatory interactions between competing publics is crucial to this process, especially as it has consequences for garnering access to material resources. To quote E.P. Thompson, '... every contradiction

[11]Examples include the Dalit movement in Uttar Pradesh under the leadership of the Bahujan Samaj Party (BSP) and the Backward Castes in Bihar under the Rashtriya Janata Dal (RJD).

[12]The concept of developing new vocabularies for pressing claims, comes from Richard Rorty, when he says 'nothing can serve as a criticism of a final vocabulary save another such vocabulary; there is no answer to a re-description save a re-re-description.' (1989: 80).

is a conflict of value as well as a conflict of interest ... every class struggle is at the same time a struggle over values' (1978: 231).

Whitehead (1984) has pointed out that the ability of individuals, men or women, to act in relation to land, is determined by their own positionality within particular sets of material, ideological and legal practices that structure their society. So we are not free-floating individuals, but socially embedded, and this shapes our capacity to act. While this understanding does take into account positionality at particular moments in time, what it misses is the multiple meanings that can be attributed to each of these acts and practices. What may appear to be submission could, in fact, also be construed as an act of resistance; acting dumb is an example. These meanings are expressed at the interface, and hence are specific to each particular interaction. Further, the meanings attributed to particular positions and actions themselves change over time. So for instance, while a mother-in-law in the Indian context may be a powerful character in the early years of her daughter-in-law's married life, she ceases to be as powerful once she is widowed. She may in fact be subordinated by the daughter-in-law in the later years of her life, although she would still attempt to find ways to retain some control. The power equation alters because the daughter-in-law has grown comfortable in her role as wife, mother and home-maker and has thus, expanded her sphere of influence. This brings one back to the point about boxing people into particular categories and roles and valuing them in relation to these parameters. If it is recognized that one's consciousness shifts with context, and at the same time that each activity can reflect multiple meanings and multiple negotiations, both objective and subjective, then clearly the parameters for valuing different individuals as social beings would change.

Gender is not a clear-cut group identity, yet it is inscribed within all other identities. The vocabularies for contesting gender identities though likely to be more fluid and contextual, nevertheless exist. If the goal is improving one's material condition and social position, the struggles need to be both material and ideological. While for men, their ideological superiority is established within the patriarchal context of their own society, it is challenged vis-à-vis other social groups which see themselves as superior. This simultaneous existence of power and powerlessness makes them wary of any challenges to their authority internally. They therefore tend to oppose any claims made by women that pose a challenge to their authority. And this is where land comes in—while material production is recognized as being jointly authored, the transmission of prestige, or symbolic production, through the inheritance of both name and property, is exclusively male. A struggle over land then combines the two struggles, for a material resource, and the ideological value of being a recognized member of the social group.

## GENDER AND PROPERTY IN DEVELOPMENT DISCOURSE: CONTOURS OF THE DEBATE

Land, as a means of claiming identity as 'full persons', helps put the discussion around gender and property rights in a clearer perspective. For example, Engel's influential essay, the 'Origin of Family, Private Property and the State' (1972 [1884]), traces a direct link between private property, class formation and the subordination of women. He linked the transformation of women from equal, productive members of society to dependent wives to the shift from community ownership and production for use to private ownership under the control of men and production for sale. While the division of labour remains unchanged, the ideological valuation of roles changes, prioritizing men who generate surpluses in the market over women engaged in housework. Engels therefore called for the abolition of private property and for women to join the labour force, along with a socialization of housework and childcare responsibilities, in order to emancipate women.[13]

Feminist scholars, arguing that gender relations are not egalitarian even in property-less households, have critiqued Engels theory. According to Mary Evans, 'the entry of women into social production without an accompanying change in the ideology of gender and the socialisation of the sexual division of labour institutionalizes the

[13]The Report on Women's Role in the Planned Economy of the National Planning Committee of India, 1947, reproduced this view, saying 'Private property is the root cause of many inequalities', hence arguing for a different system of ownership. This was however qualified by stating that 'so long, however, as the very foundation of society is based on a system of private property, women cannot claim equality with men unless she has the same rights as men to hold, acquire, inherit and dispose of property' (quoted in Saradamoni, 1983: 154).

double shift that women work' (1987: 82–3). Sacks further says, 'although property ownership seems important for women's domestic position vis-à-vis a husband, the exercise of domestic power, particularly in class societies, is limited by whether or not women have adult status in the social sphere' (1974: 222). Theoretically, domestic labour can be performed by anyone, but ideologically it is seen as part of a woman's role, thus mediating and restricting her choice of and control over paid labour, as well as her participation in the public realm of decision-making—the basis for social adulthood. A change in production relations that socially values men's work, but domesticates women's, often with support from the state legal system and ideology as in the case of land being recorded in the names of men, influences the relations of power and authority between men and women.

Despite the multiplicity of feminist discourses, each prioritizing somewhat different factors as the root causes for women's subordination, the women and development discourse till the early 1980s focused primarily on changing production relations, particularly employment and labour force participation to make women's work visible and valued. It did not question the meaning of paid work or indeed property rights and the 'legitimacy of the distinction between the private and the public' (Evans, 1987: 87).[14]

In a rural and primarily rice-growing area such as the Santal Parganas, there are considerable overlaps between production and reproduction. It is often not clear which aspects of women's involvement in these processes contribute to an enhancement of their power and status in the household and community. This makes it difficult to predict whether it is property rights, women's involvement in the labour process, or an attention to cultural meanings, be it in terms of revaluing domestic work, that will provide the key to gender equality. Women prioritize each of them at different moments of time to claim recognition for their identities as they see it then. And perhaps that is why no one strategic intervention is likely to be able to mobilize all women to struggle.

[14]Radical feminists in the 1970s and 1980s, through campaigns such as 'wages for housework', politicized women's contributions, seeking to change the ideology of worth that devalued domestic work, and also secure greater mutuality and balance in the gender division of labour. See Young et al. (1981), Moore (1988), Ramazanoglu (1989), Beneria and Sen (1981) on the domestic labour debate.

The issue of land rights for women gained visibility in development discourse with the dramatic statement at the UN Women's Conference in Copenhagen in 1980 that women owned only one per cent of the world's resources, while constituting 50 per cent of the world's population. The exclusion of women from the ownership of land has thereafter remained on the global agenda, especially with the strengthening of women's movements all over the world during the UN Women's Decade (1975–85). The UN Convention on the Elimination of All Forms of Discrimination Against Women (CEDAW), 1979, included specific clauses on the equal treatment of women in agrarian reform and similar rights for both spouses in the ownership, management and disposition of property. Yet, the discourse seems to have shifted from one of equal rights as persons within CEDAW, to a more instrumental one in terms of poverty reduction and agricultural growth in recent years—reflecting a shift from a normative to a materialist underpinning. The World Development Report 2000–01, for instance, states, 'In most developing countries titles to land are normally vested in men. Since the great majority of the world's poor people live in agrarian settings, this is a fundamental source of vulnerability for poor women ... So women face disadvantages not only in land ownership, but in gaining access to the resources and information that would improve yields ... For Burkina Faso analysis of household panel data suggests that farm output could be increased 6–20 per cent through a more equitable allocation of productive resources between male and female farmers' (World Bank, 2001: 118–19). The New Agricultural Policy in India, 2000, makes an explicit link between women's rights to land and household food security, especially the nutrition of children (Tenth Plan, Section 4.1.60).

A major reason for this shift in policy is the increasing visibility of women's participation in the agricultural labour force. In India as in most rural societies of Asia and Africa, with rising populations and growing pressure on land, the diversification of livelihoods has become essential for survival. Men have moved into non-farm activities or migrated, leaving women to tend the land. This is because women have a disadvantage in terms of lower literacy levels, restrictions on mobility and responsibilities for children and household maintenance. In India, 85 per cent women and 71 per cent men are agricultural workers as per National Sample Survey data of 2004–5. In such a context of apparent domination of the rural sector by women, individual tenures in the names of males become a hindrance to growth, by creating a range of practical difficulties in production—the inability to access credit, inputs and extension services all linked to land-holdings.

While individual titles existed in many parts of India in the pre-colonial period, land could not be alienated to pay arrears of revenue, nor could the title-holder unilaterally alienate the land, compromising the interests of heirs and the larger community. During the colonial period, individual titles became a strategy for revenue collection and enhancement by the colonial government, with defaulters effectively losing their land. Individual land titling has continued post-independence, particularly at the instance of the World Bank since the mid-1970s,[15] as a strategy for agricultural growth and development. The philosophy of production now being exclusively one of individual profit, rather than of collective identity and satisfaction of basic human needs, there has been a rapid 'invisibilization' of the multiple uses and users of land, and consequently, the denial of a range of rights. Land then gets allocated to those seen as being the most efficient users of this resource, rather than those most in need. Apart from women's rights, use rights over the commons and grazing lands too have got invisibilized and consequently alienated. In addition to the local struggles to control the commons, in cases of displacement by large development projects such as dams and mines, these are not compensated for, even though the commons constitute a vital element of local livelihood resources.

After India's independence, agrarian reform and land distribution programmes were initiated in recognition of the fact that land distribution was highly skewed and had enhanced insecurity for those without land. The principle of individual rights and control was however maintained. Yet, given the inefficiencies of state bureaucracies, what also emerged was a growing gap between rights as reflected in the land register and those practised by the local communities. A low caste landless labourer in India, for instance, may have received a plot of land under the aegis of state-led land reform, yet he is unable to cultivate

[15]The Bank's land reform policy paper in 1975 recommended formal land titling and the promotion of land markets as a precondition to modern development. This led to titles being exclusively in male names.

it on account of hostility from the local elite, who are often the patron and only form of insurance, in times of crisis. Women face a similar hurdle, often from their own male kin. In tribal areas, most of the officially 'landless' people are traders, ex-servicemen and other groups, not necessarily the poorest, or even dependent on land for their survival. Yet they have received a disproportionate share of the redistributed land—in Dumka district, this amounts to 18.5 per cent of the total land distributed while they constitute only 10 per cent of the population (Records of the Assistant Collector, Land, 2000). The *adivasis* see this as a state strategy to deprive them of land and allocate it to the 'big' people, those with material and political clout.

The persistence of high levels of hunger and malnutrition in the rural areas, particularly amongst women and children, has shown however that the increasing vulnerability of the poor to food insecurity is not just due to production constraints or landlessness. Dreze and Sen (1995) point out that chronic under-nutrition is related not just to food intake, but also to access to education and health care, employment opportunities and the provision of social security as a back-up against entitlement failures within society. The need for social support and strengthening a range of entitlements is increasingly emphasized. Within the women's movement too, land rights are today no longer a priority agenda, despite the successes in terms of resource access made in the previous decades. The focus now is on issues of violence against women, health and reproductive rights alongside equal employment opportunities. Even in countries like Brazil, which has active rural unions of women workers, land rights seem to have disappeared as issues in relation to social security benefits or recognition as workers (Deere, 2003: 267–8). While this shift may be strategically useful from a livelihood perspective, it remains strongly materialist, viewing land as just another resource, useful for making a living. It ignores the symbolic meanings of land to the construction of identities, or how ownership of land is used discursively by one group against the other, by men against women.

These larger discussions on the failure of the state to eradicate poverty and hunger, a persistent agenda in the global discourse, now represented by the Millennium Development Goals, point to the 'limits of the centralized state in terms of its knowledge about the complex, functioning social orders' (Scott, 1998: 7). This has led to a shift in growth and development strategies in favour of market-led production systems on the one hand, and to the use of participatory and local negotiation methods to give voice to local and customary knowledge on the other, for making administration more effective. In disputes relating to the partition of family property, court proceedings are in any case often the last resort. They are lengthy and expensive, and court officials are also seen not to have enough knowledge of the local context to give justice (Srinivas, 1962). Decentralized dispute resolution can mean the possibility of discussions with all the concerned parties with a view to obtaining a fair outcome and also maintaining social interactions. While customary practices should not be romanticized given the social reality of differentiation, there is considerable practical evidence to show that customs are not static but are continually being adapted to new ecological and social circumstances. To quote Scott, 'Customary systems of tenure..are usually riven with inequalities based on gender, status and lineage. But because they are strongly local, particular, and adaptable, their plasticity can be the source of micro-adjustments that lead to shifts in prevailing practice' (1998: 34–5).

Yet, feminist lawyers, academics and activists point to the weaknesses of customary law in protecting women's rights, embedded as it is in male-dominated power relations and social structures. Agarwal (1994) and Deere and Leon (2001) strongly recommend the need for explicit state policy and gender-progressive laws including land titling for women based on their respective reviews of land policies in South Asia and Latin America. They see this as a strategy to empower women economically and also strengthen their position to challenge other social and political inequalities. So do several African feminist lawyers, despite their reservations about the implementation of statutory law (Butegwa, 1991). They call for the correction of a major source of subordination—the lack of land rights—through legislative action. Following them, the Report of the International Fund for Agricultural Development (IFAD) argues that 'the strength of custom and male power make it difficult to identify practical changes to land systems that will improve women's land rights '(2001: 87). By locating the source of subordination in custom or patriarchy, it becomes possible to fix responsibility for women's exclusion. The problem of land distribution is then presented as a struggle for control between men and women, or between modern and customary law. Neither custom nor patriarchy are static across time and space, and ground realities contribute to shaping them. In fact, tribes such as the Santals, though patriarchal, are seen as being supportive of women and their rights.

While the push for retaining the emphasis on rights is justified as an affirmation of women's identities, such dichotomization between gender or legal frameworks, each presented as internally united and homogenous, is however problematic. The functioning of the village community or indeed, the household, begins with the experience of being both included and excluded. Communities such as the Santals are part of the state as citizens, yet remain at its periphery as a remote, marginal group. While the woman is initially an outsider in her husband's home, and treated as such—a person with divided loyalties—she becomes central as the mother of his heirs, to the reproduction of the patrilineage, and in this role, a complete insider. At the same time and despite this, she continues to be excluded from certain forms of decision-making and control.

Just as gender relations are not just based on unilateral male domination, but on how women react to and deal with this, separations between statutory and customary tenure systems too are now being rethought. Modern institutions do not just embed themselves into a life-world, to use Habermas' term, but are also affected by how laypersons, deal with these systems in their day-to-day life. This simultaneous inclusion and exclusion at various levels, and the ambivalence it implies in terms of social relations can also provide new strategies and ways of negotiation, gaining support for one's struggles often from unexpected quarters. Santal women, such as Rimani or Soha, have been quite successful in enrolling the support of male village leaders for their land claims. They also confided in me as an outsider, and by this very act, were able to shame their men to take some action in their favour.

Either way, it is important to recognize that women's land claims have always been different from those of men, as it is they who move both spatially and socially at the time of marriage. The spatial movement from one village to another in a patrilocal context and the shift in belongingness from one family to another can lead to a crisis of identity in more ways than one. Struggles follow to establish oneself as a wife, a mother, a worker, but most critically, a person. The role-specific identities are often easier to establish, with the maintenance of the home, the production of children and contribution to cultivation. It is establishing one's personhood that is perhaps most difficult for women in their new context. Land, given its stability, is perhaps one way of reclaiming this identity as a person, of gaining status and recognition as a valued member of a new community, of becoming an 'insider' able to participate in decision-making processes in the marital home. At the same time, claiming inheritance rights to land in the parental home is also a way of retaining one's status and identity in the home of one's birth, and not just being treated as a transitory visitor or '*paraya dhan*' (another's wealth).

The issue of inheritance of parental property has been recognized by the amendment to the Hindu Succession Act (1956) in August 2005, and is a demand that is gaining ground amongst women in middle-class, urban India. Amongst the Santals, however, the claims to marital property continue to dominate in the current context, though interestingly, contextual claims to natal property, '*taben jom*' as it is called, as a back-up, emergency resource, are also being articulated. This is discussed in greater detail in Chapter 7.

## CHANGING DIMENSIONS OF EQUALITY: THE STATE AND SOCIETY

Most modernist analyses of agrarian change tend to focus on commercialization, technology, institutional regimes and state policy as the main sources of rural transformation, ignoring questions of power and politics at the local level. Critiques of such approaches have raised the need to understand local processes of struggle over access to and control over resources and people, as well as power relationships, within a larger global context of state policies.[16] Social change is a dynamic process, not just about inequalities, but the negotiation and re-negotiation of relationships and identities between multiple

[16]Brass (1984: 114) reflects that material issues become irrelevant without reference to political and ideological considerations at given historical conjunctures, and the manner in which these structure the balance of class forces and struggles.

actors—peasants and elite classes, traders, officials and local strongmen—across genders and generations and at multiple levels.

The role of law and a supportive legal framework have been emphasized in recent poverty strategies, and there is no doubt that the very existence of favourable policies can be used to leverage resources in political struggles. In India, there is considerable legislation to support women's rights and policy statements of the central government in favour of both women as well as other marginalized groups providing the space, both legal and administrative, for making claims.[17]

Béteille (1991) has used the example of the Indian Constitution, however, to illustrate the tension between equality as a right and as a policy. Articles 14, 15 and 16 make equality before the law and equal opportunities irrespective of race, caste, sex and religion, the Fundamental Right of every citizen of the country, enforceable by courts of law. In recognition of the reality of a hierarchical society and the subjection of certain groups of people to severe disadvantages, however, the Directive Principles of state policy provide a framework for redistribution of resources. The two major tools of redistribution have been agrarian reform and quotas for education and public employment for the marginalized. Both of these have been challenged and continue to be contested in the light of the Fundamental Rights. The demands for equality can be conflicting, as the claims of some would be recognized over others, in a context of limited resources.

Yet, with the introduction of reservations in local government institutions for women and Scheduled Castes, who constitute a majority of the poor, better access to political power, information flows and resources, have led them to realize that their conditions of poverty need not be permanent. A similar situation is found in relation to gender equality. A question however remains: is having exactly the same resources and opportunities as men the way forward for women or is it necessary to create a facilitating environment to better negotiate gender relations?

A key issue in a welfare state is the basis for entitlements—are these determined on the basis of need (means-tested), deserts (return for work) or citizenship (universal)? While one can argue for need-

[17]The Scheduled Tribes (Recognition of Rights) Act, 2006, is one of the most recent ones that recognizes the rights of *adivasis* to forest resources.

based entitlements in terms of being the most redistributive, it can stigmatize the needy, but worse, given the biases and inefficiencies in implementation, it can miss out the needy. In the identification of Below Poverty Line (BPL) households, for instance, I found that the poorest were often excluded and the better-off secured the benefits (see Chapter 9 for discussion). One also finds a clear pattern of patronage and corruption here, based on an underlying sub-text of 'dependence' (Fraser, 1997). Seen as a negative moral trait (an individual, often psychological problem) rather than a structural problem in recent years, the poor are blamed for their poverty and the commitment to redistribution amongst the field-level bureaucracy appears low. In Dumka, I was often told by the generally upper caste Hindu bureaucrats that Santal men are lazy, often drunk and do not work hard, that is why they continue to live in such poverty. For any benefit granted, therefore, a proportion is extracted as commission. The issues, however, being both structural and ideological, struggles are then required with the state and the economic system, not only for welfare services, but also over norms and meanings of work.

The second basis for entitlement is more exclusionary, often defined and implemented in relation to public employment, hence limited in scope. However, there is now an increasing movement in India for a change of legislation to recognize the range of informal sector work situations, dominated by women, as work, and link them to social insurance programmes. Following the Report of the Second National Labour Commission (2000), the Unorganised Agricultural Sector Workers (Conditions of Work and Livelihood Promotion) Bill, 2007, the Unorganised Non-Agricultural Sector Workers (Conditions of Work and Livelihood Promotion) Bill, 2007 and the Unorganised Workers Social Security Bill, 2007, have been drafted. None of them have yet been passed by Parliament. Household work, however, continues to remain out of the pale.

The third form of entitlement, citizenship, deals with public services such as the provision of basic education and basic health to all citizens. The proper functioning of these services is key to gender equality. However, in line with the policies of adjustment and liberalization, there is an increasing trend towards privatization, with visibly negative consequences for girls and women. The village school is perceived to be useless, and parents who want to give their children a fair education, struggle hard to get them into private, fee-paying schools, often residential. In Bagdiha over the past decade or two, several families, especially widows, have converted to Christianity, a major reason being the ability to access better health care facilities run by the missions. Each of these justifications for entitlements has its strengths and weaknesses, but what needs to be remembered is that outcomes will vary for differently situated people.

Most development policies are centrally determined, but governments are not monolithic entities. Individual bureaucrats at different levels, according to their own ideologies, interpret state policies. Ethnographies of the state in India are few, yet they do show that actual outcomes of projects are influenced by the everyday practices of bureaucrats and field workers who live between national policies and local realities (Goetz, 1997, Corbridge et al., 2005). People too have local ways of resistance and of continuing negotiations on the ground.

Tribes similarly are often constructed as homogenous and bounded communities, but are, in fact, complex mosaics of cultural groups and social classes, products of diverse agrarian histories and interaction with the state. To glorify the past or speak of traditions in a unitary way is fraught with the danger of reflecting the voices of the then dominant; tensions and differences are not modern-day inventions. Such politics often carry within them notions of accentuated masculinity, an exclusionary relationship with land and even ethnic purity (Skaria, 1999: 299). The case of Jharkhand clearly demonstrates that calling on tradition is itself a political discourse ridden with power relations, using a particular construction of historical identity to seek a shift in political organization and social relationships.[18]

Social change can then be understood as a complex, continuous and multi-dimensional process, playing out both in people's material lives as well as in the contestations over meanings, cultural constructions and symbolic representations. Rather than a radical break, it spans the gulf between the old and the new, between invention of new traditions and the application or manipulation of existing norms and practices, between conflict and cooperation. It works both at the micro-level of

[18]Martin Orans (1965) has illustrated in the case of Jharkhand, the construction of a distinct socio-cultural identity as a justification for political power.

an individual agent as well as in the macro-context, as a collective struggle against structures of oppression. The example of land as a central resource in negotiating social relations and identities is used in this work to illustrate this complexity and gain some insight into the directions and dimensions of change.

While identities are constantly being renegotiated, this process seems to be intensified in situations of economic necessity and environmental change, and in this case, the wider negotiations of meaning and power as represented by the struggle for a separate Jharkhand state. The expression of rights and needs have implications not only for understanding self-images that are embedded in gender, ethnicity and political status, but also for material circumstances and resource flows. Simplification and uniformity need not necessarily serve the cause of equality and redistribution. A more nuanced understanding of gender relations and social institutions, livelihoods and resources, moving beyond dualisms, can help us take a broader view of equality and address the larger issues of development and well-being.

Gramsci was perhaps one of the first thinkers to conceptualize politics as extending to all spheres of life, and not just the state. The notion of difference and historical conjuncture were central to his politics, as was the need to construct a unity out of differences (Simon, 1982). This contradiction is being confronted by feminist writers today, and is a recurrent tension in this book—the need to recognize difference amongst women, without losing the space and legitimacy to share common ground and advocate for positive change.

## STRUCTURE OF THE BOOK

Having provided a conceptual framework for understanding the dynamics of asserting and negotiating one's identity and personhood in different spheres of life and particular points in time, I recount in a little more detail in the next chapter, my own personal journey that motivated me to write this book. I also briefly discuss the methodology adopted.

As I have said earlier, this book is a result of participating and sharing in women's struggles over the last two decades. Priorities differ with context and it was important for me to understand the reasons underlying this difference. While arguing for women's land rights as a general principle, I found that this was not necessarily being practised even within my own extended family. My granduncle had divided all his land between his two sons, rather than giving his two daughters a share in it as well, when from the material standpoint at least, my two aunts could perhaps be seen to be in greater need of that resource than their brothers. Additionally, it was they who were primarily performing the care function in relation to their parents, despite officially having 'shifted loyalties' at the time of their marriages. Yet they themselves never articulated any sense of discrimination.

In the middle-classes, it is increasingly recognized that daughters continue to give affection and care to their parents until later in the parents' lives, by which time the sons have become independent of the parents. It was important for me then to also understand how such social discourses could be used to change the ability to act and reshape social practices to acknowledge women as insiders rather than outsiders in both the natal and marital home, as persons in their own right. In my own experience, during my postgraduate years, when I topped the class in mathematics, several of my classmates, especially those studying science, went out of their way to find explanations as to how this may have happened. It could have been, according to them, hard work, or more likely, partiality or even nepotism! I started then, though perhaps not consciously, to think about how strategies of resistance in daily life play out within relationships of interdependence, each contributing in its own way to the recognition of one's identity as a woman, but more importantly, a person.

In Chapter 3, I move on to profile in some detail, the villages studied and their distinctive livelihood systems, raising issues of diversity and change, the key role of social relations and networks in livelihood security, the meanings of different livelihood choices to men and women of different categories and in different settings. This chapter highlights these contextual differences against the background of a few key well-being indicators, such as literacy, sex ratios and work participation of women, over time, in Dumka district, Jharkhand State and in relation to India as a whole. Data for Scheduled Tribes is also analysed at these three levels. While indicators for Scheduled Tribes women are more favourable than for women in general, except for literacy, trends suggest a decline in the status of women post-independence, and provide a context for examining women's growing claims to land in public arenas.

In Chapter 4, I discuss the historical and contemporary political, economic, legal and policy context in the region based on an analysis of land tenure policies and resistance movements following the advent of colonialism. The roots of the discussion on women's rights to land go back to the early twentieth century and the granting of individual titles in male names, which, with one stroke, dispossessed women and masculinized land relations. I highlight the role of the agrarian movement in the Santal Parganas in the 1960s and 1970s to regain alienated land and its repercussions on women's land claims. This is compared with land movements in other parts of India and the world, with a focus on the successes and failures of women's struggles to gain rights to land.

Chapter 5 focuses on the material value of land in people's livelihoods. How much food is produced, in what circumstances and under what rules land is used in exchange transactions, in emergencies and to improve one's social and economic position, are some of the issues addressed. How do production relations in agriculture shape women's identities as cultivators and producers, and how do they impact on the negotiation of gender relations? The chapter also explores the general agricultural scenario in the region, and the varying patterns of intensification of land use, relating this both to the distinctiveness of the two different social and geographical settings and the gendered politics of labour use and resource access.

Chapters 6 and 7 provide a detailed analysis of identities and social relations, based on ethnicity and gender, using both archival (land records) and ethnographic material. Changes in social and kinship relationships and hierarchies seem to respond simultaneously to changes in land ownership patterns and to the symbolic meanings attached to land by different groups and genders. After exploring the meaning of land for Santal masculinities in a context where they are marginalized by both state and market institutions in Chapter 6, I turn to the implications of these changing constructions of male identity on women's land claims as daughters, sisters, wives and widows in chapter 7. This chapter also looks at how women manipulate patriarchal land inheritance in their favour, and the role of sons in this process.

Carrying forward this discussion, I examine in Chapter 8 the multiple arenas in which these divergent claims and meanings are contested. It becomes clear that women in different subject-positions use different arenas to contest their needs, from household to community, revenue bureaucracy and legal courts. There is also discussion here of a more open, social arena, wherein non-state players such as NGOs, missionaries, revivalist and political groups also engage in the discussion. The choice of arena is linked both to the sense of legitimacy they carry as well as their accessibility in terms of both material and human resources. Discourse here plays a critical role in legitimizing particular identities and roles.

In Chapter 9, I briefly examine state policies to see how far the state, itself a differentiated social institution, understands women's land claims in terms of a network of related needs rather than as an isolated particular need. How far do policies respond to the ongoing processes of contestation over rights to land and the meanings attached to this? Acknowledging different social and cultural constructions of women and men in terms of their livelihoods, particularly land relationships, and paying attention to practical demands as well as discursive claims, could lead to more sensitive and responsive policies and in turn, to positive development outcomes.

The final chapter seeks to bring together some of the issues raised in the book in relation to the struggles around land and the construction of gendered identities. It points to the dynamism of this process and the interconnections between the different struggles. Within such a framework, it becomes clear why without acknowledging the linkages between materiality and sociality, linear, technical policies are likely to fail to meet their objectives.

CHAPTER

# 2 A Personal Journey

Everywhere women get beaten, humiliated and victimized, physically and mentally. Despite this reality of subordination, we have an extraordinary capacity to resist and fight for our dignity. Not every act of subordination goes unchallenged, and women do strategize to retain self-respect. As a woman researcher it was imperative for me to recognize elements of helplessness and subordination as well as agency and resistance, and develop a methodology to represent and reflect both. In my attempt to do so, the biggest challenge I faced and continue to face is dealing with the notion of love. The realm of love is a major site for the exploitation of women, making them feel somehow responsible, and therefore guilty, for what goes wrong within relationships, conjugal, filial or sibling. Even if they are not directly guilty of marring a relationship, women appear to bear the burden of setting it right. Coloured by emotions, resistance becomes difficult.

Mary, with whom I lived for the first few weeks of my stay in Chuapara, for instance, was unhappy from the time I first met her in 1999, with her husband Chura's philandering. Occasionally he was also violent. Though angry, she was helpless to do anything at that point in time. She told me how she was waiting for her daughters, then 18 and 13 years old, to get married before creating a fuss. In 2005, with both daughters married, she did leave him, after yet another violent episode. She was not indifferent; she still loved him, loved life and wanted to live it well. So she went to their local pastor and asked him to intervene. A date was fixed for both parties to meet at the Church. Chura, her husband, did not turn up. The pastor then came to the village, gathered a few elders, and asked both Mary and Chura to narrate their stories. The differences were resolved and a compromise was reached with Chura publicly promising not to hit her again. She returned home, for it was her home too. She had helped make it. Mary never suffered from any false consciousness, yet there were moments when she was helpless.

While women do exercise agency, the forms vary, reflecting changes in women's positions over time. Giving in perhaps was the appropriate strategy at this moment, as she had raised the issue publicly and succeeded in reaching a negotiated settlement. She too was attached to her home and her life built over twenty years, hence leaving it was not an easy option. She is not the only one to suffer domestic violence. Domestic violence is said to have increased across all social categories in India going by the latest National Family Health Survey data 2005/6[1] and is a global problem affecting all classes and racial groups. At least Mary has raised her voice against it.

This insight reflects my own journey of self-recognition. When I first visited the Santal Parganas in 1995, I was involved with a network of feminist NGOs in the region. I believed that women needed to speak out, to resist the injustices they faced. And these occurred at multiple levels—they were violated by the state, by contractors, and within their own homes. Women's groups had been organized as solidarity groups, and also to provide women livelihood resources that would strengthen their capacities to act and exercise choice. To confront material poverty, investments were made in wasteland development and tree plantation; and credit provided for small livestock. Training was provided to enable women to work together in groups. Yet, real headway was not apparent in terms of poverty reduction and livelihood security. Women were prepared to organize exclusive groups for particular, functional activities, such as accessing credit, but land was a different matter. It was not just that it had critical importance to their livelihoods and survival, but their very identities and closest relationships were implicated in any land claims they made. They had to tread carefully.

While the NGO-supported group could be a tool in the process of negotiating their rightful share of resources, there were several problems with it too. First, it organized women around particular activities, treating

[1] Physical mistreatment by husband is said to have increased from approximately 25 per cent in 1998–9 to 35 per cent in 2005–6 (NFHS 3).

them as autonomous individuals, rather than as social beings. It was also premised on a 'deficit' model, providing women with resources and skills that they 'lacked' and which could help 'empower' them. The groups were hence an add-on, and not an integral part of their lives. They met only when the NGO facilitator visited the village, rather than serving as solidarity groups.

Second, women recognized the symbolic and historical significance of land to *adivasi* identity in general, and kin identity in particular. Twenty-five-year-old Dibri of Chuapara was hesitant to register the land in her own name, even though she was the only claimant. She had no resources for the land transfer, but given the lack of immediate challenge, she also felt it worthwhile to adhere to kin norms. Similarly, 28-year-old Dhaki and her widowed mother Shaniwari in Bagdiha were unwilling to break completely from their kin-clan network. They were being exploited and harassed by their own kin-group, who had appropriated a part of their land. Still, they perceived some benefits in retaining their kin identity and links. If their rights had to be practicable, the kin had to accept them as legitimate and this meant negotiating their rights within this framework rather than exclusive of it, through group or state structures. Were these women suffering from some form of false consciousness to invest in identities that were disadvantaging them materially? It made me think about relationships in middle-class homes, where there is a continuous 'giving in' by the woman as wife, even though to the public view, she is an independent, 'empowered' woman. Clearly there is a similar process of negotiation going on in both sites, but we tend to evaluate them against different parameters. We see the rural woman not claiming her right to land as a sign of subordination alone. This may be the case, but it is simultaneously a conscious act, an investment being made by her towards a different future.

The assumptions behind projects, both of NGOs and the state, construct rural women, especially *adivasi* women, as being passive and not fighting for their rights. They are then almost told what they need to do. Apart from being patronizing, it is also an affront to their identities as persons. This realization led me to examine some of the processes through which particular 'needs' were identified. Were watersheds or trees, being pushed by the NGOs or the state, really the crucial needs named by the local women? I found women talking about abusive clients when they sold products in the weekly market, of sexual abuse by contractors and employers on the worksite, of problems of accessing clean drinking water, of poor health and educational services, but rarely of watersheds. While this is not to deny the importance of the latter in potentially enhancing productivity, I learnt however, that naming one's experience itself is both a public and a political act. It is difficult as it often involves what could be interpreted as 'letting down' or an 'act of treachery' by one's patrons, even one's nearest. Its legitimacy therefore needs to be established, it is not a given. The possibility of other interpretations also makes it open to contestation. This sense of threat, of potential challenge, of being shamed in public, can stop one from speaking out. Such experience is not particular to the Santals. Silences do speak, yet in the short-term, they may result in a loss of identity, of self-worth, for the women concerned.

A specific problem faced by Santal women relates to the culture of state institutions, including the civil justice system that renders them 'inarticulate' on account of their illiteracy in the state language, Hindi. They are not, however, lacking in knowledge, confidence or courage. For instance, to respond to my questions on agriculture, Karuna Hembrum of Bagdiha, wife of a community leader, first called her husband. I was an outsider and she felt it appropriate that her husband should be the one to interact with me. It was only after a few months, when I was less of an outsider, and also after she had realized that I did not expect 'technical' responses, that she started explaining in detail, the various processes involved in agriculture, from bunding and manuring, to planting and weeding. She compared these tasks to the flutter of birds, constantly flying in and out of their nests to find food for their young ones. She conveyed her point adequately. Speech and articulation are linked to language, to the subject and the audience, rather than constructed in a vacuum, hence linking silence and the inability to articulate to either ignorance or lack of agency can be a methodological fallacy.

While the problems they confront are several, only few get prioritized and articulated within state structures. 'Voice' or the right to articulate priorities here has got linked with financial resources and money, whether margin money to be deposited for a construction project, or a small bribe for a personal benefit. This denies the resource-deprived effective voice, and is aggravated in the case of women by a largely male development bureaucracy, themselves uncomfortable in dealing with poor women, but conveniently putting the blame on women and their relative lack of mobility. So even when women are prepared to speak, they are not heard. Dinu's 40-year-old wife, dissatisfied that with the monsoons approaching the contractor had left the construction of her house incomplete, said, 'I am not afraid of anyone. I am prepared to complain to the highest officials. But they do not understand me.' In Chuapara, houses under the Indira Awas Yojana, a government scheme for the provision of houses to those below the poverty line, were being constructed in the names of women.[2] Yet when the government functionaries visited the village to check on the construction, they only spoke to the men, even though the women were physically present in the village.

Women's identities are negotiated at different levels—within the household and in the community, but also by the bureaucracy and political leaders. Though each of these negotiations influence and reinforce the other depending on the relative power of the concerned parties, one or the other of these interpretations gains predominance at a particular point in time. These often become stereotypes, with women expected to perform certain roles and not others. People start believing in these stereotypes, even though they may be far from reality, as the purpose is clearly to justify certain actions and policies. But this also creates a crisis of identity, most clearly represented for me in my research assistant, translator and friend, Pushpa Murmu, a local woman who stood on the boundaries of the educated world. A graduate, and active in organizing women's groups in her own village, she was never acknowledged as such by the bureaucracy. They would listen to her when she was with me, but refused to entertain her in my absence. The question remains as to how women negotiate this process of labelling, giving in to certain expectations and resisting others, to assert their own sense of being?

It is not so different for men either. *Adivasi* men have been constructed as lazy, drunken and indigent, thus justifying the state's paternalistic

[2]Please see Chapter 9 for further discussion on government policies and schemes.

policies, with power in the hands of the non-*adivasis*. Poverty is attributed to these individual characteristics rather than shifts in the political economy. Historically, British administrators had represented the Santals as simple and industrious people, having brought them into the region as settlers, to clear the forests and make them cultivable. Santals had also helped the British develop the tea gardens of the neighbouring state, Assam. O'Malley however noted that the Paharias or the 'hill people' lived in poverty 'owing largely to their drunken habits and idleness'(1910: 196). They had resisted the British inroads into the area, and the Santals were perhaps also brought in to balance the Paharias' power.

The stereotype image of an *adivasi* as being lazy and drunken still holds. It is true that, among *adivasis*, drinking has social sanction and is widespread. On recent visits since 2003, after the formation of Jharkhand, I noticed liquor being sold everyday and not only on *haat* (market) days, several men drunk all the time and unable to work, and women more angry and more vocal in their criticisms. On a recent research project, one of my male research assistants, Gunda Hembrum, would end up getting totally drunk every time I gave him some money. Clearly alcoholism is turning into a social problem, yet its possible relationship with frustration due to malnutrition and unemployment, hostility towards the better-off turned inwards, is never considered. The structural causes of poverty—unequal markets, lack of capital and lack of basic facilities of education and health—are today getting further intensified, with the focus of the state on industrialization and growth. With land holdings shrinking over generations and the total neglect of investment in agriculture and irrigation, men are increasingly unable to fulfil their roles as providers/cultivators or *chasa hor*. Educated men like my assistant, Gunda, are neither able to cultivate land nor find a suitable job. Many go in search of wage labour, but cash incomes quickly disappear—the demands on them are many. People are not 'lazy' or 'backward' by nature, but choose strategies, both of production and consumption, which enable them to retain some level of dignity as persons. Drunkenness is often the result of a failure to perform their roles as providers and live up to their expectations, it helps them forget that they have failed their identities. The same can be said of the 'passivity' of women—it is not a natural trait—there is in it, an element of social conditioning, but also a studied element of conscious choice.

The Santals, both men and women, seek to establish their identity in relation to and often in opposition to, the dominant constructions. Much of the debate that goes around development projects is, in fact, about negotiating one's identity. One finds 'status quoist' positions held by the dominant, including the local elite, confronted by 'oppositional' challenges from those seeking to assert their identities. The service providers, seen as 'experts', whether from the government or NGOs, often step in to play a bridging role from an administrative standpoint (Fraser, 1989). This is often a compromise position, and not really meeting the needs of the 'beneficiary' or 'project participant'. Such understanding can explain, to some extent, project failure, but development is a political project and unless a clear stand is taken in favour of any one group, project goals are unlikely to be met. Middle paths don't work.

I started this book with profiling a few Santal women. They and others like them in the villages where I stayed changed me for life. They showed me that while perhaps not literate in a formal sense, they are conscious of their problems, have thought through sets of possible solutions within their context, and strategize, both as individuals and groups, to assert their identities. Their struggles revealed to me that despite their material poverty, or perhaps because of it, they were vigilant in ensuring that their identities were protected, that they could not be taken for granted. Support and service could not be one-way at all times, mutuality had to exist. Yet, they also loved and gave of themselves freely; their lives were not constituted only of demands and struggles. Their courage was inspiring, as such articulation brings with it threats of violence and abandonment, but as they showed me, rather than giving in, holding on to one's conviction and acting upon it when required, helps to diffuse the threats. Better still, the result is usually positive. Garma's wife in Chuapara going to the police or Sona to the panchayat office when harassed as '*dains*', were able to make their opponents back off. Stray instances of '*dains*' being killed do exist, but such cases are few and far between.

The research was grounded in the recognition that many of our experiences were shared, despite different contexts, and so were our struggles, leaving little justification for the use of different parameters to understand the lives of Santal women and those of urban women like myself. Ultimately we were both seeking a life of dignity and claiming recognition of ourselves as persons, using whatever means were available to us and relevant in our respective contexts.

This recognition influenced both my methodology and the methods used. While my research was conducted over a period of 18 months between June 1999 and December 2000, rather than staying continuously in the villages over the period, I moved to and from my home in Mumbai. This helped create a distance, essential for reflection. Staying continuously in the field, as anthropologists tend to do, perhaps would not have made the comparison across contexts as stark. When cultural contexts are so different, anthropologists often try to gain acceptance as an 'insider' by immersing themselves in the local context. Only such acceptance is seen to produce 'authentic' knowledge, but this experience is then treated as distinct from one's own. What the experience brought to me however was not just the stark difference in material contexts and day-to-day living reality, but the commonalities at the emotional and ideological levels as well. The movement across contexts helped me understand better the contextual imperatives, and also some of the more universal dilemmas and strategies that women confront. It led to the conviction that reason and emotion are interdependent and together form the roots of any analysis, just as the well-accepted linkages between subjectivity and objectivity in much of anthropological research (c.f. Heggenhougher, 1992). The fieldwork has resulted in a concrete product in the shape of this book, but as a process it has had many intangible outcomes. While their material realities have not changed substantially, the ability to share their feelings and articulate their aspirations have led to a sense of self-worth and recognition for all the women involved.

## AN INSIDER VIEW?

> To take sides is inevitable. We can never again pretend to be impartial, since we recognise that neutrality itself is partial ... We need first and foremost to be open and honest about our partiality, especially to the people with whom we work (Caulfield, 1979: 315).

The research essentially focused on two villages, living and participating in their social life. Participant observation however took a new meaning. While clearly I was not an 'insider'—I came from urban India, spoke a different language, was brought up in a different material context—I wished to represent the perspectives of Santal women in relation to land, but also their daily life struggles, and made this clear in all my discussions with different people. As Ellen (1984: 220) has pointed out, a 'neutral observer' would get only traditionally accepted responses that confirm established norms, because there are always things that people do not say publicly or do not even know how to say. They live them as their common experience. Bolder and often more challenging reactions and responses emerge if one takes sides.

And this did happen. I became aware of my own multiple identities and positions—as a woman, a mother, an educated person, a researcher, a Hindu—and realized that different people responded to each of these identities in different ways. The data I collected depended upon which of my ascribed statuses I was perceived to be occupying at that particular time. While this had some advantages for my research, it also made me aware of inherent conflicts and contradictions.

Taking sides was essential. It was impossible to develop the same level of closeness with different actors. With some of the women, I shared many daily tasks, as well as numerous little stories of travel, of family life and of my working life, the experience of working alongside bringing up a child, of the support I had in the range of reproductive and home-making activities, and the choices I had to make. Women here too had multiple positions and had to choose between different actions, balancing the performance of roles with activities they enjoyed. During my early days in the village, when I tried to talk to Mary and her 18-year-old daughter Sheila about their lives, they soon lost interest. They felt a distance, as I was educated and from a different culture, and they were not sure of what I wanted of them or what I did when I was not in the village. They however asked me to come with them to the river to have my bath, wash clothes and collect water, and learn about their lives through sharing these very personal moments. They also took me to their paddy fields to teach me how to transplant. I was a poor student, slipping several times in the mud, my planting skills clumsy! This became the source of much laughter, and also of bonding. Life here was not just about questions and answers, but a lot of confiding and joking too. We were different, yet at this basic level, we shared a common struggle for survival with dignity. The bonds built through such experiences, albeit small, have persisted. Despite our different work and lives, when we meet, we still share a sense of closeness. Soon children had begun to drop in, and I would spend the afternoons playing games or telling them stories.

The local moneylenders and traders initially tried to draw upon my identity as a Hindu to build a degree of proximity. When they found me living in a Santal home, they invited me to stay and eat with them. Given the norms of pollution and purity, they felt that I should not eat with the Santals. When they discovered that I did not care, I lost the advantage of being a Hindu in my discussions with them. Though polite, they could not trust me, and hence the interviews and talks were always guarded. I found the social distance between the Hindus and Santals so great, that it was impossible to establish intimate relations with both. I had chosen to live with the Santals, and in so doing, I had tacitly made my social and political choice. It was with only one Hindu woman, ostracized by her own community, could I develop a close friendship.

Many of the educated Santals, particularly men, were active in the public sphere and in the political struggle for the separate state of Jharkhand, then reaching its peak. As part of their political ideology, they presented to me a unified view of their community, one however, that was represented only by men. To establish their difference from mainstream society, they also rejected several progressive ideas, especially in relation to women's rights, claiming that they, in fact, treated women better than mainstream Hindu society, where women had many legally sanctioned rights, but few real ones. On the basis of my discussions with several women, facing violence, abandonment, the threat of living with a co-wife, it was clear that in spite of the high ideals they professed, practice amongst the Santals, or tribes more generally in a contemporary context, was not significantly different from the larger society, in the realm of women's status and rights. When I challenged their assertions on the basis of my experience, they persisted in trying to gain my support for their position. It was obvious that they viewed my education and ability to access the district bureaucracy as sufficient grounds for their sustained effort.

Discussions with such men helped me deepen my insight on the nature of prevalent contestations, forcing me to acknowledge the marginality of these men also in the larger context, and their own struggle to establish their identity as equal citizens. I began to understand why they were opposing women's independent land claims. In the experience of several of them, especially those in urban and peri-urban contexts, often in salaried employment, they found a large number of their non-Santal male colleagues married to Santal women. They recognized that these Santal women aspired to better material lives, and how this pointed to their own inability to provide such lifestyles. They interpreted such marriages then as clever ploys by the non-Santals to gain access to Santal land and resources. Discussions around identity, whether nationalist or religious, regard women as guardians and transmitters of identity. When identities are perceived as being under threat, the first act is therefore to enhance control over women. While as an educated person, I thus gained some insight into male views and perspectives, this could never be a complete picture. As a woman, I was not permitted to participate in the agricultural rituals that were exclusively male spaces at the village level—a site for men to share their insecurities and devise strategies to retain their identities.

All these interactions made me see, and accept, that I too was an actor in the shaping of local discourses, with my subjectivities both influencing responses and being challenged by them. I could not write myself out of the story. There are many ways to organize knowledge, in fact representation is a 'way of speaking relative to the purposes of the discourse' (Tyler, 1984: 328, quoted in Strathern, 1988: 18). Discourse itself is a reflection of people's hopes and imaginings, of what they would like to see, their fantasies of power, rather than what constitutes their life as it is. Women and men therefore often told me their stories of negotiation, of resistance, of subversion, rather than of subordination and powerlessness. As in my own life, for them too, compliance with and resistance to particular roles, ideologies and structures, were simultaneously, responses to structural constraints and conscious strategies to change, even slightly, the existing unequal power relations. We do not always struggle, but also compromise, to maintain harmony in the short run, and possibly gain materially, in the longer term. The hypocrisy in development policy and practice became clear to me as while forgetting or perhaps ignoring the compromises we make in our own life for the sake of both love and harmony, these women were expected to constantly struggle for rights in their own households and communities. Recognizing this contradiction led to a change in my thinking and in my life. We need to grant women, particularly poor women 'agency' and 'knowledge', asking them what works and what doesn't and the practical possibilities for change, rather than assuming always that we know best.

## FIELD SITES AND METHODS

Villages have been regarded as 'conjunctures of much wider processes and relationships' (Harriss, 1982: 17), a reflection of a complex world at a micro-level. I decided to study two villages in Dumka district as a starting point for my analysis of wider social processes in relation to negotiating both land and identities. The two villages, in contrasting agro-ecological zones, one forested, hilly, remote and inhabited exclusively by *adivasis*, called here as Chuapara, and the other Bagdiha, different in each of these respects, were selected in order to facilitate the study of different trajectories of change. Differences in settings could also be used to explore possible differences in women's struggles over land and over their identities.

I did not go to the villages with a pre-planned and preconceived research design, which would give me all the answers in a neat and clean fashion. Even today I probably have more questions than answers! It is, in fact, the constant questioning that enables one to break new ground. As I sat and chatted with people in both villages, I decided to first focus on a few households to get a deeper insight into their lives, livelihoods and processes of assertion as well as mutual love and support. I finally selected 24 households for detailed study, 11 in Chuapara and 13 in Bagdiha. These households reflect a wide spectrum of household types—monogamous and polygamous, widowed and separated, residing in the man's village or his wife's, small-holder and medium-holder. They also represent a wide range of personalities: some tragic, some comic. The names of the people and villages have been changed to protect their identities. A list of selected households is provided in Annexure 1, with some details of each. I interacted with these households over an extended period of time to gain a dynamic view of household behaviour as well as the social context.

In terms of research methods, this was primarily an ethnographic study. While I did conduct a village survey towards the end of my stay to gain an understanding of the extent of the problem in terms of food and livelihood insecurity as well as conflicts over land, it was through qualitative research that I could develop an understanding of the nature of deprivation, poverty and the complexities of the domestic economy. People tend to offer information depending on the purpose of the study. If it has implications for state benefits, they tend to overplay their poverty; while if it is an issue of status and identity, they may well underplay or even hide it. A few households, such as Chura Marandi's, who treated me as their guest, were until the very end, ashamed to tell me that they too were indebted. I was in the village when even the best house was leaking due to heavy rains, several houses collapsed, the source of drinking water disappeared and there was no food cooked in the village. It was my extended stay and direct observation that provided insights into elements of poverty and seasonality, the realities of people's lives that perhaps could not have been captured through quantitative surveys alone.

Material lives are also complex in other ways. Land-holding size as an indicator of poverty, for instance, has no meaning in a hilly terrain unless we know its quality, the labour available with the household for cultivating it and the access to water. Cash income similarly cannot be used as an indicator of well-being, as people often manage with minimal cash; staggered harvesting makes it difficult to make an accurate estimation of output. Surplus is not sold in bulk in the markets, but often exchanged in weekly markets a little at a time for other essentials, throughout the year. The fluidity between survival and stability makes it difficult to generalize about livelihoods, though varying livelihood strategies, gendered in nature, can be identified, and are further discussed in Chapter 3.

Despite a focus on these two villages, a village does not really constitute a significant boundary for an analysis from a woman's perspective. Women's kin links extend beyond the village boundaries, as it is they who generally move residence at the time of marriage in a patrilineal society. If one is talking about inheritance of parental property, then the spatial dimension, the distance of the marital village from the natal one, becomes crucial. In order to understand the discourses around land, therefore, I explored the issue of women's land claims in a larger cluster of villages within the two panchayats (unit of local government) where my study villages were located. Contacts in the other villages were usually made through women's kin links.

At the same time, I was talking to other groups of people, significant in shaping the discourse around land and carrying much more voice than the village men and women in the field of politics, such as political leaders, lawyers, missionaries and NGO leaders. I tried to understand the functioning of a range of institutions including the settlement courts, law courts, revenue and development bureaucracy, and village institutions. Government policies and schemes, legal orders, NGO projects and the ideologies and perspectives they carry, do influence gender and other social relationships at the village level. For instance, Dhiru Kol of Chuapara, illiterate and not economically secure, is sought out by other people in the village due to his contacts with block-level officers and an understanding of their ways of functioning. Far from being self-contained and egalitarian 'little communities', interactions of *adivasi* villages with the outside world, have influenced their ways of living and being.

I also spent some time in the District Record Room of Dumka going through the land revenue records of these two villages. Such historical research, including an analysis of the shifts in land policies over the last 135 years or so, allowed me to make some links between micro and macro levels of analysis.

## CRITICAL ISSUES IN RESEARCH

In a village, everyone has a place and a contribution to make—one cannot remain in a purely information extracting capacity, as an outsider, even as a researcher. A role was found for me as a mediator, to communicate with government personnel, to read documents, help draft letters and advise in the event of disputes. Some started seeking me out to help them in their struggles, both personal, and with the government. For instance, complaints to me about food pilferage from the child-care centre served as a threat to the concerned worker, with the hope that it would function better.

For me, this was a key ethical issue—how far could I address, both through my research and my presence in the village, not only the basic concerns of the people like livelihood insecurity, political oppression, indebtedness, physical and mental harassment, ill-health and illiteracy, but also the struggle for dignity and recognition.

And here, my experience of the two villages was contrasting. In Chuapara, people were totally unaccustomed to outsiders, especially someone like me, an educated woman from a city, wanting to stay for a length of time. They were suspicious, even though I had been accepted by one of the village leaders, Chura Marandi, and had initially stayed in his home. I explained the purpose of my stay in the village and my research in a village meeting, yet people found it hard to believe. Various rumours were floated—that I was a government officer who had come to survey landholdings which might later be acquired for the building of a dam or coal-mining, as such prospecting work was, in fact, going on in the region. I was able to establish a degree of trust with a majority in this village through a process of mutual sharing, yet some element of suspicion remained until the very end. When I went back in the summer of 2003, I found their fears were not ill-founded; the people of the next panchayat were up in arms against displacement from their homes—their land had been acquired for the mining of coal.

I was often asked, especially by the educated youth in Bagdiha, my second study village, how they would benefit. Would they get good drinking water, a functional health centre or jobs? They were used to people coming to the village, doing surveys, promising things and leaving, never to be seen again. So here, people would answer my questions, and in some ways they were more friendly and open. They were also practical, safeguarding their own interests and on the lookout for what they could get from me. I have tried, therefore, to write about our shared experiences and feelings, rather than treating them as the 'subject', the 'other'. I go back at least once every year to visit these people, especially those with whom I spent many hours talking, who shared with me their lives and thoughts. I have not contributed materially to their lives, but valuing our relationship, this friendship, which cuts across divisions of class, education and ethnicity, and making the time and space for this, is valuable.

It was impossible for me to engage in pure research, especially in Chuapara. Daily living itself was so difficult, no drinking water, no electricity, and no access to essential commodities or medicines for a long distance. There was a primary school in the village, but no teacher. In my early enthusiasm, I asked the village people to organize around some of these issues and approach the relevant officers in Dumka. There was no response. I soon realized that they had made several complaints, but these had not been attended to. Each visit to Dumka meant a five-hour walk to the road, a three-hour bus ride, an overnight stay and considerable expense. They just did not have such surpluses to spend. I helped with an application to the District Education Officer and on subsequent visits to Dumka, tried to follow up with the authorities about the school. Several months later, in January 2000, a teacher was finally appointed. This experience demonstrated to me, first-hand, that policies were not made or implemented in response to material needs, they were a result of power relations and relative ability to negotiate by the groups concerned. It was a big lesson on the workings of power and knowledge in real life—one that was reinforced on several occasions thereafter. I once asked the Education Officer for some information for my research and informed her that Pushpa, my research assistant, would come and collect it. But each time Pushpa went, she was turned away on some excuse or the other and asked to come another time. On my next visit, I was handed over the information. There were several issues at play. Pushpa was considered insignificant in terms of her relative power, but more perhaps was to be gained by a direct interaction with me. By doing me a 'favour', I would be obliged to return it if required. In many ways, unravelling this nexus between power and knowledge, and the shifts in behaviour in response to gender and ethnicity, became a central focus of my research.

The lack of health care services hit me harder, especially due to my own helplessness in this field. I had my supply of chloroquine tablets for malaria, widely prevalent in the region. One day, while chatting with 30-year-old Marangkudi in Chuapara, I found that her five-month-old baby daughter was sick with malaria. This was a particularly poor family, with four young children. They had no resources to go to the private hospital, 10 kilometers away, or the state-run primary health centre, even further away. The sub-centre was closer, but the Auxiliary Nurse Midwife (ANM) visited only once a week. There was a so-called 'private doctor' in the village, a quack really, but his rates were too high, Rs 150 for one injectible dose. I gave the baby the first dose of the anti-malarial tablet and asked Marangkudi to come the following morning for the next dose. She didn't. I was worried that something had happened to the baby, so rushed to their house. I found that the baby was better and I gave her the second dose. When I asked her why she hadn't come, she said she'd stayed away because she had no money to pay me. That year there was a malaria epidemic in the region and several hundreds died, including 10-year-old Sahib and 4-year-old Mistri—children of Nati Hansdak and Karu Tudu, my neighbours in the village. The health care system was neither functional nor accountable. Widespread protests followed across the state and efforts were made to enforce attendance at the health centres by the doctors and ANMs, yet the impact was short-lived. One expected some positive shifts after the formation of Jharkhand in 2000, yet progress has been slow.

## MOVING ON

While my research techniques come from a well-established toolbox of research methods, I have tried to adapt the ways in which I have used them in this research. I made a political choice in terms of representing the perspectives and voice of Santal women, but in the process, discovered the commonalities in our experiences as women and our struggles to gain recognition as persons in the larger society. While I narrate their stories, they are not my 'subjects'. This is my interpretation, filtered through the lens of my own ideology and positionality, alongside the conceptual and methodological toolbox available to me.

When one is struggling for one's identity, each act takes on multiple meanings, both objective and subjective at the same time. Irrespective of the outcome, the struggle itself then becomes important, in terms of asserting one's sense of self. While for the purposes of analysis, I have tried to disentangle the material and the symbolic meanings of each act in the following chapters, this is hard to do in real life. Food security, for instance, may imply adequate calorie intake in an objective material sense, but it also implies status, fulfillment of masculine roles, recognition of joint production and mutuality in the conjugal relationship, at a more subjective level. The simultaneity of these meanings is what constitutes one's identity, and these are constantly being renegotiated on the ground. The element of time is crucial in this process. I have tried to capture the shifts in positions and meanings even within a short time frame. Actions may appear to be contradictory and lack consistency, but this reflects the dynamism of the process of change, influenced by the interactions between many people and multiple institutions.

I started my research with the quest to explore the contours of the land debate and the elements of power and knowledge implicated in the process of negotiation and contestation of rights to land. In the field I discovered that this was not only a manifestation of the debate around identities and gender but also ethnicity and caste. The ideologies of power and domination remained, though their forms changed over time, often in response to the public discourse of equality. The markers of change were those of the administrator, rather than the local people. Performance vis-à-vis institutions of the state, whether land revenue settlement or the village school, become the standards to assess well-being, though these same institutions could be a source for the perpetuation of inequities. The story usually follows the official perspective. My study area lies within one of the most 'backward' states in India; and one of the villages could be classified as being extremely backward, with low levels of income, low literacy rates and high mortality rates. While these material indicators of well-being cannot be denied, the story can be told differently, from the perspective of the subordinate, identifying ideologies and structures, embedded in institutions of state and society that perpetuate such subordination.

It may appear that, as a researcher, my emotions and subjectivity are taking precedence over facts, with the 'truth' being dismissed as mere detail. Epistemologically, the question remains: what is the truth? As I have tried to establish in this chapter, each act can be interpreted in multiple ways—it reflects a material fact but also carries within it an emotional reality. It is only when the two are taken together can one understand people's lives and actions, and the responses to the subtle playing out of power and knowledge in daily life.

In the chapters that follow, I attempt to tell the story of the villages where I lived from the perspective of the local people, in particular Santal women. How did they think about their work and resources, about infrastructure and services, or about leadership and voice, in relation to their own identities? I thereafter explore the links within a larger framework, at once dynamic and challenging.

CHAPTER

# 3 Faces of Poverty

## The Villages Profiled

My clothes clung to my body. I was bathed in sweat and a dull headache formed as the overcrowded bus ground to a halt after a bumpy three-hour ride from Dumka along a road that was a necklace of potholes connected by strings of macadam. It was a cacophony of screams and shouts, with children crying as more passengers pushed into the bus, a converted Dodge truck, at Gopikandar, the block headquarters. Would I be able to survive the remaining few kilometres to Durgapur, I wondered, as a sack of rice fell on my shoulders.

It was June 1999. We pushed our way out of the bus at Durgapur, a few tea stalls near the bus-stand, otherwise quiet and sleepy. It is different on a Saturday, buzzing with activity as the site of one of the largest local *haats* (markets). My 28-year-old research assistant, Pushpa Murmu, and I started on our 17-kilometre walk on a mud path through the forest, grazing lands and fields, and several streams that lay dry. I learnt of the fury of these streams in September, when a continuous heavy downpour for three days literally cut us off from all humanity. The streams on all sides were flooded then, the water flowing at a high velocity. But for now, we trudged along, stopping frequently to rest and drink water. On the roadside we saw huge fruit trees, and in the heat of the summer, the juicy jamuns and mangoes provided some refreshment. We passed the old *Damin* bungalow[1] at Silingi overlooking the Bansloi river and finally reached Chuapara, hot and tired. Five-year-old Daud, the son of the *anganwadi* worker,

[1] The *Damin-i-koh*, or 'the skirt of hills' as the British rulers called it, was an area 'reserved' for direct rule by the colonial rulers.

Teresa Baskey, met us just outside the village. He took us to the home of Chura Marandi, his uncle, and a village leader, with whom we were to stay.

Daud soon became a part of our household, giving us little bits of information, picking fruit, fishing for us, providing insights into the life of his family, the difficulties, the violence, the negotiations that were constantly going on between his mother and usually drunk father. All the Santals have land, but often in the uplands or forests, hence this is not a guarantee of security. Both drought and excessive rains can push households to the brink of poverty. They pull through by engaging in several other trades: wage labour, making and selling liquor, cutting and selling timber, taking fruits and berries to the market. Still, during my stay, most households were indebted to the moneylender. Death was an everyday event, so was disease.

We moved to Bagdiha two weeks later, just as the rains were starting. A much shorter walk of 5 kilometres from the main road, but with hardly any trees or shade, it proved to be an equally exhausting journey. Hectic activity was underway on both sides of the road: paddy saplings were being transplanted in the fields. Here, too, we stayed with one of the village leaders, Harnath Hembrum and his wife, Sheela Hansdak, a primary schoolteacher and the central figure in her home. My first impressions in Bagdiha were very different. With better infrastructure, roads and water, daily tasks seemed easier to perform. Closer to an urban centre, and more exposed to education and the educated, in many ways the life experiences of some of the women were closer to my own. Despite all that, the subordination of the Santals to other caste groups and institutions of the state and market appeared intact.

Yet one cannot assume that life here has stayed static. The people, their houses and animals, their language may have remained the same, but the forests are now confined to the surrounding hills, having disappeared from the village in one generation. At the same time, new varieties of paddy are grown and marketed. These are not insignificant changes. In Chuapara, dramatic changes have occurred in the last six years with the construction of a road under the World Bank-funded Bihar Plateau Development Project (BPDP). Completed in June 2000, the stated objective of this 47-kilometre long road running through the remote, hilly parts of Dumka district was to facilitate connectivity of the people to markets and services (health and education). I was returning to Chuapara in a hired jeep, on the newly inaugurated metalled road at the end of June 2000. As the jeep raced forward, so did my thoughts. I was moving not just through physical space and time, but mental and metaphysical space as well!

Later that year, I spoke to the concerned project manager at the World Bank, New Delhi (Interview, 4 December 2000). Talking about the benefits of the road, he said, 'As production increases people want to market their output, and in market centres they can get 10–15 per cent higher prices than in the village.' But, according to the manager at Ranchi, there had been many constraints in the process of road construction. 'In remote villages people want to stay in isolation, they are afraid of exploitation, so don't cooperate whole-heartedly. Being uneducated, they don't understand the importance of roads for taking their produce to the market.' (Interview, 14 December 2000).

Was the project manager right, or would the fears of the villagers come true? What in fact happened? As I heard from Chura, appointed as a contractor, and tasked with collecting the labour required, supervising their work and making the payments, the contract for road construction had been given to a private company from outside the district. Wage employment was provided to the local villagers, but lasted only as long as the stretch of road near their village was being constructed. Thereafter people from other villages nearer the site got employment. Only few people got longer-term jobs in the camp set up for the drivers, engineers and other company staff, all coming from outside.

Wages were calculated and dispersed on a weekly basis. Men had more cash in their hands than ever before, but few were able to save. They purchased some food and clothes, and spent the rest on liquor. Teresa told me, 'I prevented my son from going to work on the road. When he earns a cash wage, he is tempted to drink with the other men, and then gets into fights. He stole a cycle and for this we had to pay a big fine' (16 March 2000). Still, the road had its benefits. Even though Chura was drinking a lot and abusing his wife Mary, his daughter Sheila and sister Naina got work on the road-site for several days. For them, the objective was to save for Sheila's forthcoming wedding. They earned Rs 3000, and therefore, did not have to borrow much for the wedding. Similarly, working on the road enabled Garma Kol's son to earn enough to pay for his own treatment and his father's without getting indebted.

Teachers are now more regular in attending schools, coming on their motorbikes, and boys like Daud, about 12 years old in 2006, are able to cycle to the middle school at Silingi.

While the road was planned as a positive intervention in terms of improved accessibility, it enhanced the fear of exploitation. Buchanan's topographical survey of the region from 1807–10 had indicated the existence of rich mineral deposits, particularly coal and iron (Oldham, 1930). Correspondence from 1844–9 relates to the application to mine coal by two parties, Messrs Duncan and Sweetland, to James Pontet, the then Superintendent of the *Damin-i-koh*, or 'skirt of hills' as the area was called. Pontet in turn had recommended the construction of a road, in a letter in July 1844, to support coal mining in the area. The mine was to be located in the Bargo area, close to Chuapara (21 July 1849, File 7). The fear of displacement due to coal mining was expressed by the locals when I first attempted to collect land-related information in the village. This was compounded by the fact that geological survey work was underway, and the process of land acquisition for coal mining had started in a neighbouring panchayat. The local people were up in arms to save the lands they had inherited from their ancestors. By 2005, the resistance was broken by a combination of coercion and incentives; money and liquor were liberally distributed, and work started on the site. Administrators who opposed the move were quickly transferred (Rao, 2005a). Tractor-loads of labour were brought everyday to the site from other areas to counter local opposition—the road itself enabling such large-scale movement of labour!

The first visible impacts of the road seem at best mixed. Earlier, every Saturday morning, one found groups of women carrying head loads of products to the Durgapur *haat*. Now trucks and vans enter the villages, collecting produce such as jackfruits at much lower prices, with the transactions generally being settled by the men. One trader set up shop in Silingi, buying *sal* leaf plates at the rate of Rs 0.75 per 20 plates, as against Rs 1–1.25 in Durgapur, a cut of more than 25 per cent. Yet many started selling him the plates. There are advantages: groups of girls can go to Silingi on their own and return home early, the time and effort spent on carrying things to Durgapur is saved. Rather than finding better markets for the villagers' produce as the project manager BPDP claimed, improved connectivity seems to have increased extraction and lowered prices. Badka Tudu has a jackfruit tree beside the road. Earlier they consumed some of the fruit and sold some in the weekly *haats*, keeping up a small stream of income for several weeks. In 2000, Badka sold the entire produce of the tree to an agent, who came one day with his truck and harvested the entire lot. They got nothing to keep, and the one-time cash payment of Rs 500 quickly disappeared. Alternately, men carry the fruit or other produce to Durgapur on their cycles. While they do buy and bring home the daily necessities, they also spend money on liquor and other expenses. Women appear to be the losers, losing the discretionary control they earlier had over such income.

While resource extraction has increased, the inflow of information on government schemes and benefits has not. Visits from government functionaries remain few and far between, thus keeping intact the power and knowledge hierarchies between the petty bureaucrats, the local mediators and the village people. With the coming of the road, however, cycles have increased, making communication somewhat better for men, who can go more easily to the block headquarters or other places. The women, on the other hand, seem further alienated from the mainstream, dependent more and more on men for information and goods—the *haat*, a good source of information, is now only occasionally visited. By July 2004, lacking maintenance, the road had broken in parts. The single bus service to Amrapara, which had become a lifeline, especially for women, the elderly and the sick, was discontinued.

The road has a history, reconstructed in this case, from the archives. Villages have a history too, sometimes written on paper or palm-leaf, sometimes retained in people's memories. But here in Chuapara, as in Bagdiha, the past is hazy and the picture is unclear and does not extend beyond a single generation. The forest bungalow at Silingi, constructed by the British in 1909, is a visible reminder of colonial rule. Congress volunteers supposedly burnt this during the freedom movement, but there is no written or oral record of this incident. One imagines that Chuapara was settled before 1850; it resembles, in many ways, Richard Carstairs' lucid village story entitled *Harma's Village* (1935), wherein the village leader Harma was a central figure in the Santal hul of 1855 discussed in Chapter 4. Chura and his brother Samli could roughly recount upto three generations of their ancestors in name, but only about the present, their parents' lives and their own childhood, in any detail. Only one old man, recounted seeing the District Commissioner, W.G Archer, sometime around 1944–5, distributing food during the famine of that time. The history recounted to me was of day-to-day negotiations, of local conflicts, of administrative actions, and to some extent, of Christianity and its influence. It was a narrative of the workings of power, both of domination and resistance, in everyday life.

Before moving to this day-to-day account of the two villages, I briefly point to the status of well-being and employment in Jharkhand, distinguishing between the 'achievements' of the Scheduled Tribes and the total population. While global indicators of work participation, literacy and mortality are undeniably useful indicative guides to inequality, the yardstick for assessment is from an administrative standpoint.[2] They do not tell us much about the diversities stemming from social, political, cultural and economic factors, about relative freedoms and securities, deprivations and vulnerabilities, or about local measures of well-being, both absolute and relative. In a study on well-being I conducted in the same locations in early 2006, I found reciprocity in social relationships, including emotional support and care emerging as the single most significant factor in the perception of well-being, across genders and generations. This was followed differentially by food security, education, health and status considerations.

Scheduled Tribes in India are subject to multiple and overlapping inequalities due to both their physical and social locations in the larger political economy, what the Scheduled Tribes and other traditional forest dwellers (Recognition of Forest Rights) Act 2006 terms as 'historical injustice'. Marginality based on their ethnic identity has, therefore, been used as the organizing principle in order to make claims on the nation-state. All other axes of difference, especially gender difference, have been subordinated in the public, political discourse. That women are resisting this process of marginalization was evident

[2]The Human Development Indicator based on GDP (Gross Domestic Product), per capita, educational achievements and life expectancy, factors seen to enhance human capabilities and life choices, is used to monitor progress across the world's nations. In 1995, to mark the fourth World Women's Conference at Beijing, gender differentials in outcomes were incorporated into this index.

during the Assembly elections in 2000. Rupi Kisku, wife of Sibu Soren, a founder leader of the Jharkhand Mukti Morcha and in the forefront of the struggle for Jharkhand, was the candidate from Dumka. Despite the following her husband had, Rupi lost. She had campaigned as Rupi Soren, in an attempt to capitalize on her husband's name, but this worked against her in the local context. Marriage within a clan (group having the same title) is considered incest, so she was seen as a 'bad woman' by the local people. Women here pride themselves on retaining their own maiden surnames, a mark of their independent identity. They saw Rupi's act of taking on her husband's surname as a sign of weakness, a lack of confidence as a woman and a person, and as a result, did not vote her to power.

Understanding the context and its history is critical to an analysis of the exercise of power in the domestic domain and the struggles for the assertion of identities by women. While women's agency is not lacking, it is located within the realm of what is possible for them at a particular point in their lives. Land ownership, settlement histories, occupational patterns, education and health provision, access to markets, interactions with the government, transport and communication and religion, all contribute to the patterning of gender relations. So do politics and the role played by political parties. By pointing to the dominant narratives, it becomes possible to also unravel the process through which alternate narratives of women's role and status are constructed, where ethnicity is implicated as much as gender.

## JHARKHAND STATE AND DUMKA DISTRICT

On 2 August 2000, the Parliament approved the bill for the reorganization of Jharkhand as a separate state, after an extended period of struggle. The marginality of the tribes of Jharkhand within the state of Bihar was the major official justification for separation; it was believed that this would facilitate the development of the region and its people. On the ground, the struggle was ostensibly for the upliftment of the 'community', though the leadership and control were exclusively male. Here, a 'tradition' in the guise of community participation, control and decision-making was being 'invented', to use Hobsbawm and Ranger's phrase, as a counter to the official frameworks, yet it mirrored these same frameworks in terms of its hierarchical structures and male bias.

Dotted with hills and plain tracts, rich in forests and coal deposits, Dumka district in the Santal Parganas lies in the northeastern part of the state of Jharkhand.[3] The Santals are the largest tribe in Jharkhand, forming 35 per cent of the *adivasi* population of the state, a large number concentrated in the Santal Parganas, to which they give their name. The first chief minister of the newly formed state was a Santal belonging to Dumka district. While politically important, and named the second capital of Jharkhand, the people of Dumka have continued to remain materially deprived. There are other paradoxes too. Census data on female work participation and sex ratios reveals favourable trends for *adivasi* women, but literacy and life expectancy are both highly unfavourable. *Adivasi* women are seen and valued as good workers, but only for manual, unskilled work. These paradoxes point to the contradictions within measurements of development, including the human development indicators, which ignore the ideologies and structures of subordination within society. At every level, protest and resistance continues in the newly formed Jharkhand, underlining this truth.

Work participation rates for *adivasi* women in Jharkhand are much higher in comparison to that for the general female population in the state or even for India as a whole (Table 3.1). While in India 74 per cent of women were classified as non-workers in 2001, the ratio at 65 per cent is much lower for Dumka district, 40 per cent of whose population is *adivasi*. For the Scheduled Tribes, women classified as non-workers are even lower: 59 per cent for Jharkhand and only 53.5 per cent for Dumka. Interestingly, the Census of 1991 ranked Dumka third in terms of female work participation rates in the then Bihar State, following the districts of Gumla and West Singhbhum, both with *adivasi*-majority populations (Census 1991, Series 5 Bihar, Part II-B(I)).

Women here, especially the Santals, are recognized as active participants in the workforce, a point further clarified by examining the occupational status of men and women in agriculture during the

[3]Other districts include Godda, Sahebganj, Pakur, Deogarh and Jamtara, the last created in 2002.

Table 3.1: Some Well-being Indicators, 1991 and 2001 (in per cent)

| | India | | | Jharkhand | | | Dumka | | |
|---|---|---|---|---|---|---|---|---|---|
| | M | F | Total | M | F | Total | M | F | Total |
| Main workers | | | | | | | | | |
| 1991: | 51 | 16 | 34 | 47.6 | 13 | 30.7 | 53.4 | 17.6 | 36 |
| 2001 | 45 | 15 | 30.5 | 37 | 10 | 24 | 40.5 | 12.5 | 27 |
| Marginal workers: | | | | | | | | | |
| 1991 | 0.6 | 6.3 | 3.4 | 0.7 | 10.8 | 5.4 | 0.8 | 18 | 9 |
| 2001 | 6.5 | 11 | 8.6 | 11 | 16 | 13.5 | 13 | 22 | 17.5 |
| Non-workers: | | | | | | | | | |
| 1991 | 48 | 78 | 62.5 | 50.5 | 76 | 62 | 45.5 | 64.5 | 55 |
| 2001 | 48 | 74 | 62 | 52 | 73.5 | 62 | 46 | 65 | 55.5 |
| Literacy Rate: | | | | | | | | | |
| 1991 | 64 | 39 | 52 | 45 | 20 | 33 | 49 | 18 | 34 |
| 2001 | 76 | 54 | 65 | 68 | 39 | 54 | 63 | 33 | 48 |
| Sex Ratio: | | | | | | | | | |
| 1991 | | | 927 | | | 922 | | | 955 |
| 2001 | | | 933 | | | 941 | | | 961 |
| Juvenile sex ratio: | | | | | | | | | |
| 1991 | | | 945 | | | 979 | | | 985 |
| 2001 | | | 927 | | | 967 | | | 976 |
| Infant Mortality Rate (1991) | 91 | 101 | – | *75* | *104* | – | 86 | 85 | – |

| | India STs | | | Jharkhand STs | | | Dumka STs | | |
|---|---|---|---|---|---|---|---|---|---|
| | M | F | Total | M | F | Total | M | F | Total |
| Main workers | | | | | | | | | |
| 1991: | 53.7 | 30 | 42 | *53* | *23* | *38* | | | |
| 2001 | 43.5 | 24 | 34 | 38 | 17 | 27.5 | 41.5 | 18 | 30 |
| Marginal workers: | | | | | | | | | |
| 1991 | 1 | 13.7 | 7.2 | *1* | *16.4* | *8.6* | | | |
| 2001 | 10 | 21 | 15 | 14 | 24 | 19 | 15 | 28 | 21 |

*(contd.)*

*Table 3.1 (contd.)*

| | India STs | | | Jharkhand STs | | | Dumka STs | | |
|---|---|---|---|---|---|---|---|---|---|
| | M | F | Total | M | F | Total | M | F | Total |
| Non-workers: | | | | | | | | | |
| 1991 | 45 | 56 | 50.6 | *35* | *30* | *33* | | | |
| 2001 | 47 | 55 | 51 | 48 | 59 | 54 | 42 | 53.5 | 48 |
| Literacy Rate: | | | | | | | | | |
| 1991 | 40.6 | 18 | 29.5 | *30* | *11* | *20* | 35 | 10 | 22.5 |
| 2001 | 59 | 35 | 47 | 54 | 27 | 41 | 49.5 | 22 | 36 |
| Sex Ratio: | | | | | | | | | |
| 1991 | | | 972 | | | 975 | | | 975 |
| 2001 | | | 977 | | | 987 | | | 992 |
| Juvenile sex ratio: | | | | | | | | | |
| 1991 | | | 984 | | | 989 | | | |
| 2001 | | | 972 | | | 979 | | | 981 |
| Rate of surviving children (1991) | | | – | 89 | 85 | 87 | 90 | 87 | 88 |

*Source:* Various Census Tables, 1991 and 2001.
*Note:* 1991 work participation, literacy and sex ratio figures for Jharkhand; STs in italics refer to STs in Bihar.

last 100 years. Until 1961, women and men in the Santal Parganas appear to have almost worked at par with each other, both as cultivators and agricultural labourers (See Annexure 2, Table 3). Many men in the villages narrated how they were unable to cultivate land without the help of women. Sunil Marandi of Bagdiha was one such man. Despite his wife Agnes begging him not to take additional land on lease, he did, yet provided her no extra support. Exasperated and totally exhausted, she left for her parents' home in the middle of the planting season. There was no option for him but to leave the land fallow.

Fewer women as main workers in the census data reflects a definitional problem in data collection that has led to the invisibility of women's work post-1961, with women being counted mostly as marginal workers. To clarify, any work done for less than 180 days in a year is defined as marginal. Most women's work is thus treated as marginal. But it is interesting that men are counted as cultivators, even though their agricultural activity too constitutes less than 180 days of work. What seems to count here is both the ownership of land and male identity as cultivators. If the categories of main and marginal workers are added, however, then the pre-1961 estimates continue to hold true even today.[4] Yet the political leadership in particular uses these classifications discursively to portray women as dependent home-makers rather than workers.

Santal men use this political-administrative stereotype of women to resist women's claims in a context where their own identities are under threat. The Census Report of 1951 as well as the District Gazetteer of the Santal Parganas, 1965, point to the overwhelming dependence of close to 91 per cent of the population on agriculture. The proportion of owner-cultivators was high due to historical factors such as legal restrictions on land transfers, which prevented the growth of a class of landless labour. Until 1961, agricultural labour constituted only 10–11 per cent of the labour force engaged in agriculture in the Santal Parganas as compared to around 30 per cent for Bihar (Census, 1961, Vol. IV, Bihar). In the 1991 Census this had gone up to 17 per cent and in 2000, to 20 per cent in Dumka district (DAO, 2000).[5]

Landlessness and near-landlessness are growing, yet Santal men see their identities as cultivators rather than labourers. Increasingly pushed towards labour work, they struggle to retain control over land and thus, to their identity as cultivators. In matters of land ownership, therefore, even better off women are now being forced into relationships of dependency with their male kin. For instance, 26-year-old Dhaki Marandi of Bagdiha, comes from a reasonably well-off family, with over 5 acres of land. She was married, but returned to her natal home

[4]Visaria (1996) uses NSS data to show that female work participation rates have remained fairly stable at around 32–4 per cent for rural women from 1951 onwards. It is 54 per cent for rural men. He further shows that while there is a decline in the proportion of rural male workers in agriculture from 83.7 to 74 per cent from 1961 to 1993–4, the proportion of women has dropped only marginally from 89.7 to 86.1 per cent during this period (Table 4: 730).

[5]Visaria (1996: 334) based on NSS surveys shows an increase of the proportion of male agricultural workers from 21 to 26 per cent from 1961 to 1987–8, and women from 24 to 33 per cent.

when her husband took a second wife. She lives now with her mother Shaniwari Murmu, who looks older than her 55 years. Dhaki has been unable to cultivate her land properly due to lack of male labour for ploughing her fields. This has made her adopt several strategies. She has virtually gifted a part of the land to her male kin to silence their objections to her cultivating the remaining small plot with the help of hired male labour. But to secure this labour, she maintains three heads of cattle. She looks after the cattle through the year, but allows the plough-man to use them for his fields.

Despite access or even ownership, women's relationship with land as an asset is different from that of men, on account of the social taboo on ploughing. This reflects a valuation of what is appropriate for different statuses and genders, within households and societies, and is legitimized by the classifications of work at the national level as main, marginal or non-work.

Mass poverty persists amidst apparently plentiful resources. While the average land holding was estimated at two hectares per household in 1985–6 (DSO, 1986), this includes different qualities of land, not all of which may be suitable for paddy cultivation. Most of the households in my study had about one hectare of paddy land rather than two, after partition and division, and hence with average paddy yields of 1500 kg per hectare (DAO, 2000), this meant a rice output of 1000 kg (1kg paddy = 0.66 kg rice). This means that a family of five, consuming a basic diet of about half a kilo of rice per head per day should have just enough for consumption (fieldwork data). Collection and sale of forest produce and some wage labour provide cash for additional expenses like oil, spices and occasionally vegetables or meat. On the face of it, this suggests the possibility of fairly secure livelihoods. Yet this was not the case. Hunger and malnutrition were rampant. During the monsoon months, there was no rice to eat. Money and food was borrowed, to be repaid twice over in six months' time. Resource endowments then, did not necessarily improve production possibilities due to a range of other deprivations, education and health care on the one hand, and cultural-historical and political factors on the other (Geertz, 1968).

Women's relatively higher work participation rates, while linked to poverty, also reflect higher levels of mobility and economic independence. This is confirmed by an analysis of gender development indicators in eastern India that reveals that gender backwardness here is more due to economic and social deprivation than gender discrimination (Rustagi, 2002).[6]

The education scenario provides a good example. While general literacy rates in Jharkhand and Dumka lag far behind the country as a whole, these are even lower for the Scheduled Tribes. The causes of illiteracy seem to lie in the supply of education to the *adivasi* communities, particularly in remote areas, both in terms of access and quality. When I first got to Chuapara, I was horrified to see the primary school. A broken down building with a caved-in roof, it housed two cows, but no children! A walk to the outskirts of the village took me to the children, playing games and singing songs, while the cattle were grazing in the open fields below the hills. Both girls and boys were engaged in *guppi*,[7] and there seemed to be no difference in their capacity to manage the

3.1: The Chuapara school in disrepair.
Breeding a generation of non-literate children.

[6]See also Agnihotri (2000) on the 'prosperity effect' in reducing women's status.
[7]Refers to the task of grazing the cattle in Santali.

animals. Coming back to the school, on the records, it had a Santal teacher, and several children on the rolls. The teacher, however, was rarely seen in the village. He lived with his wife, an ANM at the Kolha health sub-centre nearby, and his children in Dumka. After several months of representation and struggle another teacher was finally appointed in January 2000. A Muslim from Amrapara, a small town 5 kilometres beyond Durgapur on the Dumka-Pakur road, and not fluent in Santali, he had tremendous problems in settling down here. There are only a few men in the village who can speak Hindi and he clearly lacked company. Also because he had to leave his family behind, he was away frequently.

A new building was built in 2003. Following the Supreme Court of India's judgment on provision of mid-day meals in all primary schools, in 2005, I found Dibri Hansdak, one of the poorest persons in the village in 1999, appointed as one of the cooks in the school. Her children too were now in school. The mid-day meal was regularly served. There was an additional teacher, though he too was a non-Santal. Both teachers lived at Amrapara and came to school on their motorbikes. The school was at least functioning and the children came regularly. A few had gone on from primary school to the middle school in Silingi, 3 km away. Boys such as Daud and Nunka now shared a cycle ride to the middle school. But the older girls, like Detmai and Pahi, 13 and 12 in 1999, were embarrassed to attend school with children much younger than themselves and missed the chance of acquiring even a basic education. They also had substantial household responsibilities by this time. Detmai was married in 2004, and became a mother a year later.

With schools functioning, literacy rates are likely to rise by the next decadal census. Yet learning is abysmal and children go through primary school understanding precious little of what is taught. Apart from teacher absenteeism and unfilled vacancies, rote learning of a standardized curriculum, mostly irrelevant to their context, and taught in Hindi, a language foreign to them, is responsible for this. In Dumka district, 1200 posts of schoolteachers at the primary and middle level have been vacant since 1995. Also, when teachers do take classes, there is no accountability; they are not held up to scrutiny if examination results are poor. There is a District Education Officer (DEO) and Block Education Officers (BEOs) to keep a track of the functioning of the government schools and teachers, but they too, are lackadaisical about the education function of the schools. A decade of non-functioning schools and non-literate children!

In January 2004, the government appointed 276 teachers, but there was still a considerable backlog. A large number of educated youth were appointed as para-teachers in 2006. 'Para-teachers' are expected to perform all the functions of a teacher, the major difference being in terms of recruitment procedures and training. They are local youth selected through the recommendation of the panchayat rather than through a public selection process. While often well-educated, they lack pre-service teacher training. These young men and women, untrained and underpaid, are dejected and worried about their future prospects, having invested hugely in their own education, hence are constantly looking for alternative, more lucrative opportunities. While committed no doubt, it seems unfair to demand accountability from these youth, while the regular teachers are let off scot-free! Lack of adequate number of teachers is compounded by teacher absenteeism and the 'multi-tasking' required of teachers. For instance, state and district government machinery often requires teachers to help in administrative tasks like vetting the electoral rolls, collecting Census data and other periodic data collection and verification. Recent Education Survey data, collected in part or whole by teachers themselves, points out that more than 32,000 schools in rural India have no teachers!

In 2006, young Santal children were studying Sanskrit, a classical language, in disuse even by the elite. Neither student nor teacher had any clue what to do. Yet the children were meticulously examined in the subject, and, not surprisingly, failed. Their failure however, did not mean that they were not intelligent. I had interacted with the same children in 1999–2000. We would read stories and play games all afternoon. A favourite game was collecting leaves and berries and classifying them by the number of uses each had. The knowledge of these 6-year-olds was much more than mine. Yet, now at age 12, they were 'failures' in school, thanks to the curriculum.

Medium of instruction is another big issue. In 1999, two of the 1523 primary schools in the district, and three of the 308 middle schools used Santali as the medium of instruction. This includes blocks such as Gopikandar and Kathikund, where more than 80 per cent of the population is Santal, and neither parents nor children understand Hindi. Census 1991 recorded 60 per cent of men and 76 per cent of women as being monolingual (in Santali). But it was only in December 2003 that Santali was recognized as a major Indian language and adopted in the Eighth Schedule of the Constitution, opening the possibility for some change in the future.

In the school at Chuapara meanwhile, with two male teachers, one Muslim, the other Hindu, the school culture is now more masculine. Earlier, during *guppi*, it was difficult to distinguish young girls from boys. Now the standards are different, and often the change is very subtle. Before serving the mid-day meal, the girls were busy washing the plates of all the children—one little boy even got angry with a girl for refusing to wash his! It is not surprising then, that the gender gap has barely improved from 31 to 30 percentage points in Dumka in the last decade, and has, in fact, increased from 23 to 28 percentage points for the Santal Parganas as a whole (Annexure 2, Table 4). As mentioned above, the proportion of middle to primary schools is roughly one to five. Middle schools are more distant and not as easily accessible as primary schools. The lack of middle and higher schools for girls, especially in the remote areas, leads to higher dropout rates among girls. While boys go to the middle school on their cycles, girls stay at home. Of the 71 high schools with residential facilities in the district, only seven are for girls. Scholarships are provided but are not sufficient to cover the cost of education. Higher education for girls involves considerable difficulty for the household in terms of accommodation and safety, apart, of course, from the domestic labour lost. In October 2003, the government launched a special programme for girls' education to reverse this trend. Residential bridge schools are being set up in each block to help girls through the middle school years in a compressed time frame of a year. In each of these schools, 100 girls are accommodated, a small proportion of those aspiring to a better education. Bicycles are also given to all girls reaching class 8, to enable them to continue their higher education. Results, however, are yet to be seen.

Turning to sex ratios, often seen as a proxy indicator for women's well-being, these are still 'balanced' in Dumka,[8] and higher than the total population sex ratio, even though the trend seems to be declining. This could be a result of worsening diets, malnutrition and growing susceptibility to disease. Sevati Tudu in Bagdiha recounted how the forests had disappeared over the last 30 years, especially in the 1970s, at the instigation of both the *mahajan*s and the Forest Department.[9] While in Chuapara, jackfruit, mangoes, berries and dates, apart from a range of greens and mushrooms, supplemented diets, at least to a small extent, this was missing in Bagdiha. Rice and potatoes constituted the staple, greens were occasionally collected, but fruits were more or less absent.

Even firewood is a problem and has to be collected from distant hills. Coming down the hill with a head load of wood, Sevati, already about 55 years old, slipped and fell. Her leg was fractured. There is a sub-centre of the Primary Health Centre (PHC) located close to her home, but the health service is non-existent. A 'private doctor' treated her at much expense. Seven years later, I found her able to walk slowly, and was informed that until then she had been crawling on all fours.

Official records show a gradual improvement in health infrastructure particularly post-1970. Apart from a civil hospital at Dumka, there are 14 PHCs and 386 health sub-centres in the district (Pratichi Health Report, 2005). It is another story that I never found the sub-centre in Bagdiha open. The village leaders complained several times to the Health Department. Finally they requested that the centre be officially closed, so that state money is not wasted any more! This too has not happened. A few are able to go to Dumka for treatment while the Christians prefer the Mission Hospital at

[8]Agnihotri (2000) has defined 'balanced' sex ratios as between 960–980 females per 1000 male.

[9]After *hul* Jharkhand, the *mahajan*s could not recover their loans by taking over the land, so they asked the Santals to sell their trees and repay the dues. While 560 out of 1630 *bighas*, almost a third of village land was classified as village and government forests during the Gantzer settlement in the 1930s, only 2.89 hectares out of a total land area of 292.72 hectares in Bagdiha is now listed as forestland.

Mohulpahari. In fact, health care was a prime motivating factor for several of the households here to convert to Christianity. The majority however still depend on the quacks—untrained 'doctors', who live in the villages and are, therefore, accessible during a crisis. Given the lack of competition, they charge large sums of money for treatment. Usually the sons or nephews of the local *mahajan* (moneylender), they also arrange the loans required for this. In return, land is mortgaged, or labour tied, often indefinitely, to the father or uncle of the 'doctor'. Despite the expense, lack of proper diagnosis and care has meant that diseases such as malaria and diarrhoea continue to be major causes of mortality.

The health situation is no better in Chuapara, if anything, worse. The ANM, Bibi Kisku, living in Gopikandar, the block headquarter, is responsible for the Silingi health sub-centre. She has no assistant, and therefore, the sub-centre is usually closed, except on her weekly visits to Silingi. The only health provider is the quack, Ram Dey, who lives in a rented room in Chuapara, and starts each morning to roam the villages on his cycle, with a little steel box of medicines. He worked as an assistant to a compounder in Dumka for a few months, and that has entitled him to now play doctor with the villagers. During the malaria outbreak in 1999, he strongly resented my helping the villagers with anti-malarial tablets. He promised quicker relief and soft loans to keep his custom intact. Many died that year.

The Civil Surgeon's version is different. I went to meet him after the outbreak of the malaria epidemic. I myself had been hit by falciparum, a virulent form of malaria that attacks the brain leading to death or some form of permanent hearing or vision impairment, if not treated very quickly. I had taken over three months to recover, with good medical care and a healthy diet. The Civil Surgeon told me, '... the main reason for high morbidity amongst the *adivasi*s is their low level of health awareness. Where there is any illness, they go to the *ojha* (traditional healer) rather than the PHC.' He never once referred to the condition of the PHCs; that not only were they ill-equipped, both for diagnosis and treatment,[10] but also that almost half the posts lay

[10]The ANM of Silingi sent 17 slides for malaria testing in June. It took more than six weeks for the report to return from Dumka.

vacant.[11] The Gopikandar PHC, for instance, had one dirty bed and a pile of hay stacked inside, hardly conducive for the treatment of sick people! Lack of any transport facility from the village also made the PHC difficult to access—a possibly futile expedition in any case.

The Report of the Independent Commission on Health in India states, 'there are significant differences in patterns of mortality and morbidity within regions and states, that are hidden in the aggregate statistics. The more remote, sparsely populated and resource-poor an area is, the greater chances of its neglect, in terms of the availability and effectiveness of health services. For example, the stretch of tribal areas, extending from West Bengal to Gujarat ... remain underserved, ignored and forced to accept a lower quality of life' (1997: 7). In Bihar, the Report identified all the districts constituting the Santal Parganas within the top ten vulnerable districts.

The poor state of the health system contributes to the general state of deprivation, but does not explain the reason for declining juvenile sex ratios in 2001, which could be the early signals of a decline in women's status. A possible explanation could lie in the tightening control of outsider-traders, mostly Bengali, over markets in forest and agricultural produce, intensified in the Chuapara area with the coming of the road. This has reduced women's control over forest produce and, in turn, their bargaining power. Nati complained that her husband Karu Tudu had sold wood in her absence to a passing *paikar* (trader), and then spent the money received on liquor. Though the work participation rates for *adivasi* women continues to be higher than that for all women, declining economic control in the markets combined with exclusive male inheritance of landed property, may be strengthening a preference for male heirs amongst the Santals. Additionally, the political struggle for Jharkhand has led to a focus on ethnicity and a subordination of women's rights, especially to property. With a masculinization of social relations in the public sphere, there is a simultaneous devaluation of women's social role and identity.

Some of these descriptors of well-being and their influence on social relations are brought to life in daily activities and social practices, as

[11] 81 out of 191 (42 per cent) sanctioned posts for doctors were vacant in Dumka district in 2005 (PHR, 2005).

well as in the difficulties faced by different groups of men and women in the study villages. I focus particularly on elements of work and livelihoods, of physical and social infrastructure and of political leadership, as these are key variables involved in the negotiation of gender relations and ultimately, survival itself.

## VILLAGE DESCRIPTIONS: MARKING DIFFERENCES

### Chuapara: Resources and Livelihoods

Surrounded by hills and forests, Chuapara, with 52 households, gets its name from the stream, *chuin* in Santali, which forms its eastern boundary, and provides the source of water for washing, cleaning, and drinking. After crossing the stream, a kilometre or so along the road, was the broken school building on the right, and a small group of houses—*latar tola*—or the lower hamlet. This group had 18 houses that included the Santal sub-clans of Murmu, Tudu, Hansdak and Hembrum, not part of the dominant group.[12] A path leads south to *tala tola*, with 19 households, most belonging to the Marandi sub-clan, said to be the founders of the village. They collectively control the largest proportion of village land and also positions of authority. Two of their men, Samli Marandi, Chura's brother, and his son Theophil, have completed high school and a few others are educated upto middle school. Only one woman, Mary, Chura's wife, has completed primary school, and serves as an assistant at the *anganwadi* centre that runs in the house of Chura's cousin, Manuel Marandi. Five of the households in this *tola* have converted to Christianity. Across the *bari* (homestead) behind Chura's house is *chetan tola* or the upper hamlet inhabited by 11 Kol and two Paharia households in addition to two Santal houses. A few more Paharia households live in the surrounding hills, but are not classified as part of the village community. The Santals however do interact with them, paying them a small amount of money to cultivate crops, maize and black eye beans, on the hill-slopes during the winter. The Kols and Paharias are currently

[12]The Santals are divided into 7 major and 5 minor sub-clans. The major sub-clans are Marandi, Murmu, Hembrum, Hansdak, Tudu, Kisku and Soren.

in dispute with each other over land cleared on the boundaries of the village.

Chuapara has had no official *majhi* (headman) since 1950, so for purposes of revenue collection, it is a *khas* (government-administered) village.[13] According to some, after the death of the last *majhi*, his son started using the common property of the village for his personal gain, so the village leaders asked for his dismissal. The *majhi*'s son, however, claims that since there is hardly any *pradhani jote* (land allotted to the headman in lieu of services) in the village, he was not interested in the post. In addition to revenue collection, this involves entertaining petty bureaucrats like the revenue and development functionaries when they came to the village. The discourse around the *majhi* and his role, in fact, reflects a questioning of the meaning of the community itself, particularly its responsibility in relation to land. Is he a representative of the people, or of the administration? Is land valued symbolically for its history and the power this entails, or is it just another resource, a number in a book of records?

There is no *majhi*, but the village has sought to create its own sense of community. It recognizes a group of elder men (mostly Marandis, though it also includes Badka Tudu and Lakhan Murmu from *latar tola*) and seeks their counsel in the event of any dispute. Women are not represented amongst the village leaders, and while not debarred from attending the hearings, they generally do not do so. Petty thefts and minor disputes are resolved locally, though land disputes are increasingly turning to the courts for resolution. One reason for selection of Chuapara as a study village was that it had recorded a case of witch killing. When I first came to the village, I thought this would be a hot topic of conversation, but it wasn't. The woman in question was old, she had been sick for several months, and had apparently died a natural death. Her son, Chetan Murmu, was poor. The Prevention of Witchcraft Act had just come into existence in 1998 and Chetan Murmu tried to use this occasion to make some money by filing a case of witch killing against his better off cousin,

[13]The major disadvantage is that in order to get settlement of village wastelands they have to go to the SDO court. If there is a *pradhan*, he is authorized to do so as per sections 27–28 of the SPTA, 1949.

Lakhan Murmu. The latter is not rich. He had just been sanctioned a loan from the bank for a pair of buffaloes and had some cash at hand. Chetan was trying to extract some of this. But by filing a case with the police, the money was ultimately spent in defending the case, going to Dumka for the hearings, and both parties were worse off by the time the case was dismissed. The village leaders were annoyed with Chetan for not consulting them or taking their advice. Later when he apparently raped a woman in the village, and again refused to accept their decision or punishment, the village leaders had their revenge by getting him arrested. There is some sense here not only of the struggle of these men to maintain their own identities as leaders, but also project an imagined community against the larger powers of the state and its machinery.

Above the *majhi* is the *parganait*—the leader of a group of villages. The *parganait* for Silingi panchayat with 23 villages is Samli Marandi of Chuapara.[14] Post-independence, the *parganaits* have become redundant in terms of their official authority. Yet they continue to be socially influential and their support is sought for a range of activities, not least in asserting rights to land and voicing protest against possible development displacement. The Bharat Jan Andolan, a national NGO, sought the support of the *parganait* for organizing a protest against the construction of the road through this region. In the neighbouring panchayat, the *parganait* has mobilized the villages against acquisition of land for coal mining (PUCL, 2003). Samli's household is relatively prosperous, the only one to possess a transistor, having been able to take advantage both of education and contacts in the government and other villages to enhance their livelihoods. Theophil, in fact, now engages in petty contracting work.

As part of the PESA (Panchayati Raj Extension to Scheduled Areas Act, 1996), local political leaders and parties have been demanding recognition for the *majhi-parganait* system, claiming this to be the 'traditional' administrative system in the area. This raises a question about 'tradition' itself, its invention and reinvention in response to colonial and state domination, as I argue in Chapter 4. It is clear, here

[14]His father too was the *parganait* and had a regular contract signed by the DC, W.G. Archer, in 1945.

too, that the *majhi* and *parganait* were appointed and given recognition by the colonial rulers in order to perform certain tasks on behalf of the government, to help administer the region and collect revenues. The system functioned at the pleasure of the government. If the *majhi* defaulted on revenue payments, he could lose his benefits and post. This seems the case in Chuapara, with Paul's son being dismissed as *majhi* by the state, which then took over direct responsibility for revenue collection. The freedom to act for these village officials is circumscribed by state norms and rules rather than representing any 'pure' form of indigenous culture. All discourses then are socially constructed, reflecting the interplay of forces of domination and resistance.

I have spoken already about the road. This has brought in the traders, but not amenities like electricity, or pump sets for irrigation and mills for grinding paddy. These tasks remain manual and laborious. Before food can be cooked, paddy has to be pounded in the *dheki* (hand-pounding device), for which two people are needed. It is energy-intensive and not a task that can be handed over to younger children. But by the time they are 12 or 13, girls like Pahi and Detmai do start assisting their mothers—in the first case, the woman is a widow and in the second, her husband is usually drunk. Men otherwise are seen helping their wives at the *dheki*. Clean drinking water has been identified as a basic need and the state is apparently making efforts to universalize its provision. Four hand-pumps had been installed in Chuapara. None were functional. Complaints were made, but the government functionaries never responded. The villagers once got them repaired on their own, but they are non-functional yet again. Chura got his daughter married to a man familiar with mechanical repair work, hoping he could help. But the issue of the cost of spare parts remains. In 2006, there was but a thin trickle from the hand-pump beside the primary school. The only source of drinking water is a little spring beside the stream. This was covered by the overflowing stream during the monsoons, leaving people with few options. Another spring was discovered 3 kilometres upstream, but the walk was treacherous, through slippery mud and slush. Men took on the task of bringing drinking water at this time, but as the water in the stream receded and the old spring was visible again, women reverted to this source. Disease due to polluted drinking water was rampant—diarrhoea, jaundice, body aches.

A majority of the houses are now built of brick and tile, replacing the earlier mud and thatch ones. Constructed with state support under the Indira Awas Yojana,[15] they do not necessarily provide better protection from the rains. In September 1999, all the huts were leaking. We were not able to sleep at night, as we kept moving about in search of a dry spot. Sometime during the night we heard a loud thud. The neighbouring hut had collapsed. The lack of rainproof housing meant that there was no dry wood to cook food. Most families remained hungry, and so did we. We exhausted the little kerosene oil that we had, there was no shop in the village to get some more and we could not go to the next village to buy it, as the stream was flooded. A man was reportedly washed away in its fury. The roof tiles could potentially have protected us from the rain, but these are liquid assets, sold to repay debts. When Naina's husband left without warning, she needed money to cultivate her fields, so she sold a few tiles. When Dibri Hansdak was hospitalized and could not return home until the medical bills were paid, her husband Mantu sold off their tiles, apart from mortgaging some land.

When the rain finally stopped on the fourth day, we all emerged from our huts, cramped, our bodies aching, and stomachs empty. The children went out into the fields, and soon found a pig in one of the fields. They threw sticks and stones at it, caught it and killed it. The harvest was not yet in, and the pig should not have been in the field. But the issue was now not one of a lack of responsibility, but rather of hunger. A fire was lit, the pig was skinned and roasted, and shared by a large number along with some maize gruel. But this was not enough. Two more pigs were killed that evening and consumed. There was a sense of immediate relief, although the rains had destroyed most of the early ripening paddy (*sathi* or the 60-day variety). A bad harvest, of course, meant several days more of hunger, of advancing malnutrition and ultimately, death. In the aftermath of the rains, water collected in pools, mosquitoes multiplied and malaria spread. No spraying, no doctors or nurses, no medicines and most of all, no food. The image of children eating a few grains of rice floating in a bowlful

[15] 71 per cent of the households have got houses sanctioned under the Indira Awas Yojana, which gives special priority to the *adivasis* and Scheduled Castes.

of water is still vivid in my mind. Several died, including Saheb and Mistri, my neighbour's children. It was painful, but not surprising.

The state was nowhere in sight during this crisis. Everyone was starving. More than half the households in the village have ration cards that entitle them to cheap food grains from the public distribution system, yet they rarely get any rations. The Santal dealer in Kolha village mentioned that it was too expensive for him to procure the rations, as he lacked adequate capital to make advance payments to the Food Corporation of India. So he only got some kerosene oil, which he distributed amongst the cardholders. Some of the villagers claimed that he sold it in the open market for a profit, rather than spending additional money to transport the grain to the villages. Women of a neighbouring village had protested against him.

Rice is the staple; land is the main productive resource. All the Santal households have some paddy land, up to three acres. Forests, are still substantial, almost half the land area of the village as per the records,[16] and even now people are able to clear land from the forests for cultivation and get *pattas* (titles) for them. In 1999, at least three households cleared fresh plots of land. Located in the hills, with abundant rainfall, the irrigation system in the village is good. The fields lie in line with the gradient, so water can drain out from one into the next. In 1996, a check-dam was constructed upstream and channels cut through the fields, making the fields beside the stream suitable for double cropping. This cannot however be taken for granted, due both to constraints of capital and labour, and the technical problem of the check-dam not actually holding water, resulting in low productivity and output insufficient for survival as discussed further in Chapter 5.

Above the check-dam on the hill-slopes, live several Paharia households. They cultivate small *bari* or homestead plots, but depend primarily on *kurram* or shifting cultivation and on wage labour. *Kurram* is seen now as an illegal activity by the Forest Department, often subjecting the people to bribes in the form of rice, chicken or cash in

[16]Out of a total area of 246.74 hectares, 121.40 is classified as forests and 106.07 as cultivated land during the present settlement.

return for such cultivation. As per Rule 10(i) of the Santal Pargana protected forest Rules (1894), Paharias do have legal rights to *jhum*, not just in unsettled areas, but also in settled villages in the areas which have been set apart for the purpose by the Settlement Officer. Further, all people with occupancy rights were entitled to privileges in the protected forest granted by Regulation III of 1872, which included the removal of trees of any unreserved species for their own use from forest areas within their village boundaries (O'Malley, 1984[1910]: 179–83). Clearly there is a legal anomaly here in terms of existing rights to forestlands. While the rules remain legally valid, they are ignored by the staff of the Forest Department in enforcing the Forest (Conservation) Act, 1980 that seeks to keep the *adivasis* completely out of the protected forests. It is hoped that this situation will change with the adoption of the rules framed under the Scheduled Tribe and Other Traditional Forest Dwellers (Recognition of Forest Rights) Act, 2006, which allows forest-dwellers to self-cultivate forest land under their occupation (with a ceiling of four hectares) as well as collect, use and dispose of non-timber forest produce in order to meet their livelihood needs.

The issue of forests has been conflict-ridden, especially as it forms an important livelihood resource, essential for everyday survival. Apart from firewood, both men and women are engaged in the collection of forest produce, though what they collect is quite different. Men, including Dibri and Marangkudi's husbands, mainly collect *kath* (poles) for house construction, each sold in the market for Rs 15–20, depending on the season. What women gather changes with the season, though the collection of the broad-leafed *asan* (*terminalia tementosa*) for making leaf-plates is carried out throughout the year, except in the monsoon. In March, rings of fire are visible on all the surrounding hill-slopes—forest floors being cleared for collection of *mahua (bassia latifolia)*, a big income earner, and the basic ingredient for making liquor. *Mahua* trees are prized property, noted in earlier land records, with rents on *mahua* in fact being one of the major causes of resistance in the 1870s and 1880s. During the *mahua* season, women and children leave their homes before dawn, with little baskets to collect the flowers as they fall to the ground. They return home at noon to eat their meal and spread the *mahua* in their courtyards to dry. Income from the

3.2: Her *kurram* plot. Nati gives her children some maize.

sale of *mahua* carries them through the hot summer months, when food stocks are beginning to run low.

Forests are important to Santal lives, but their management is a contentious issue. According to Samli Marandi, earlier when the *majhi* was responsible for the forest, if there was a fire, he would take all the people to put it out; if anybody was found cutting wood illegally they would be fined, and this protected the forest. Badka Tudu reminisced about the thick forests in Chuapara when he was a little boy, and their gradual destruction over the last 30 years, due in part to the corrupt practices of the forest guards. It was not surprising then that my neighbour, Karu Tudu, started shouting at me when I returned to the village after a gap of a few months in January 2000. Apparently the forest guard had visited the village asking about me. I was not there, but he extracted some rice and chickens from the local people. Karu was furious. He threatened to drive me out of the village if I was associated in any way with the Forest Department or any of its officials. It took Pushpa and me a while to calm him down and reassure him of our credentials. In the realm of the forests and their control, one can see power at play at three levels—between the state, the community of *adivasis* and women, the primary users.

Forest produce occupies a major place in the weekly *haat* at Durgapur, and this niche is occupied by the Santal women. On the *haat* day, hundreds of women come to sell fruits, leaf plates, berries and fuel wood apart from liquor. They negotiate a price with the traders, mostly men, from local towns as well as trading centres of Bengal. They have to sell their produce and return home walking a long way, and also need to purchase essentials for the home. They have no time, and no facilities for storage or transport. This makes their bargaining position relatively weak and they often end up fixing a price lower than expected. Sheila, Chura's daughter, said one evening, after returning from Durgapur, 'I was expecting at least Rs 25 for the fruit, but finally got Rs 15. The market was flooded with jackfruits. They had to be sold' (24 June 1999). The purchasers not only have capital and transport, but are often the sellers of clothes, grains and cosmetics, all objects which women need to purchase from the market. This points to the politics of markets that disadvantages *adivasi* women (White, 1993), apart from the prices that quickly fall in response to increased supply. Santal men trade in relatively high-value forest products such as construction material and small livestock, including goats and pigs. While they too are disadvantaged, their products are in the market only occasionally rather than being a regular source of income.

Women's high participation in the markets points towards their greater dependence on forests as a livelihood earning asset and a source of identity, but simultaneously to their relative disadvantage in terms of land ownership. Incomes may be small, yet engagement with product and labour markets, gives women economic independence, and also a productive identity. The shutting out of forests can then disproportionately disadvantage women, contributing to a decline in both status and identity.

## The Travails of Making a Living

Poverty amidst plenty, it is said, and so it is here. Everyone has land, yet no one has enough food. There is no homeless person, yet shelter is fragile. Almost everyone has been assessed by the government to

3.3: Women selling tubers.

be 'below the poverty line' (BPL) and has been provided ration cards for subsidized food, yet this is not a reality. Clean drinking water, primary education and primary health care are seen as basic needs, but the public provisioning is not worth its name, definitely not of a level to provide a sense of security.

Credit and capital here are life and death issues, not just technical matters. Several households have received bank loans with subsidy for cultivation of crops or for the purchase of bullocks, essential for ploughing and hence establishing the status of a man as a cultivator, yet these have failed to serve their purpose. With loans pending against most, institutional credit for further use is not often an option. The only way to survive then is through social support. Kin networks are, in fact, the first call, and borrowing from kin, both for daily consumption and special occasions such as marriages, is widespread. As Minu Dehri said, 'There is no food, but I don't want to borrow from the moneylender. Last year I borrowed some money from my sister, and once the *ghanghra* (black-eyed beans) was harvested and sold, returned it with interest to her. I prefer to do the same this year as well' (14 September 1999).

The story of Karu Tudu and his wife Nati, my neighbours in Chuapara, provides a painful example of reliance not just on kin networks, but broader social networks, to make a living; even these fail at times. Karu inherited considerable land, about 2 acres of *dhani* (paddy land) and 2.75 acres of *bari* (homestead land). A few years ago, he was sick and all the paddy land was leased out to meet the medical expenses. They had to borrow food for consumption, thus extending the land mortgage year after year. Karu drinks a lot of liquor and is usually in poor health. With four children, Detmai (13), Saheb (10), Nunka (7) and Mistry (4), it fell upon Nati to feed the family. She used to go for wage work when available locally, or collect forest produce and grow some maize in the hill slopes, with the help of her little children.

In 1999, her *kurram* crop of *ghanghra* (black-eyed beans) failed. She could not even repay the seed loan. There was no more land to be mortgaged. The children were her only remaining assets. Detmai was sent to work in the house of the man who gave them the seeds in a neighbouring village, while Saheb was to mind the cattle belonging to Lakhan Murmu of *latar tola*. The children received no wages, their only remuneration being daily meals; they were expected to work an entire year to repay the debt. Saheb sometimes came home in the afternoon, after his meal at Lakhan's house. He would want to join in our games, and we often timed them so he could be there.

Despite the different activities Nati undertakes, there are days when there is nothing to eat in the house. On such occasions, Nati uses the goodwill she has with the households where her children are working. When she asks for a little paddy or rice, they cannot refuse. Her mother lives in a neighbouring village. Nunka went to stay with her for a large part of the year, helping with her cultivation. In return, Nati's mother brought them some paddy. These social relationships not only contributed towards meeting their basic food needs, but also helped them gain a level of security. Several village leaders, for whom either she or her children worked, sought to help her by making Karu the *gudit* (community messenger). This position entitled him to collect 2.25 kg paddy and 40 heads of maize from each household after harvest for his service to the village. Even then they paid the price; by the end of 2002, severely malnourished, both Saheb and Mistry had succumbed to malaria. In 2003, Nati had another baby boy, whom she called Master.

Childhood here is short and children shoulder responsibilities early. While a few children like Karu's are employed, others engage in agricultural tasks and grazing cattle from an early age. Many, particularly girls, also assist in household tasks. Pappu's blind mother Jhumri said, 'The planting is delayed this year. My daughter-in-law sold some *tendu* leaves and *sal* leaf plates, but she couldn't do much as she was alone. The children are still young. Once they start helping in all these activities, the condition of the household will improve' (25 June 1999). The situation is indeed a little more comfortable in households with grown-up children.

Apart from relatives and better off villagers, the moneylender is a crucial figure in the lives of most *adivasis*. Much has been written about the exploitation of moneylenders, the exorbitant interest rates they charge and unfair practices they engage in (c.f. Hardiman, 1986), yet they do provide money when it is most needed. Dhiru Kol, a petty contractor himself, said, 'We borrow to keep up the relationship. Only if he knows us, will he lend to us when we are in desperate need.' In a remote village with no government presence, the comment by the *parganait* follows a similar line. 'We heard of the *hul* Jharkhand, when people were forcibly cutting the crop and taking back their land from the *mahajan*. But we did not try to do so. After all, we have borrowed money; so let him cultivate the land. If we need money in the future, he will continue to give it to us. Where else can we go?' (20 March 2000). Small loans serve not only to pass over seasonal troughs, but also maintain contact with the lender, so he will help them when they are desperate.

But with cultivation alone unable to provide security, based as it is on uncertain rainfall and few inputs, increasingly, there is a turn towards non-agrarian economy for employment. Broader social networks become important for facilitating this process. People who have gone to work in Assam, for instance, follow a friend or someone who knows a recruiting agent. For government jobs, contacts are even more important, though in addition, they need to be 'bought'. Chura,

Theophil and Dhiru invest a lot of time in other villages, building up suitable 'infrastructure-type' projects such as repairing a road, building a pond or a check-dam, for taking on petty contracts. This activity has intensified since 1995–6, following the government norm that all contracts in *adivasi* areas would be given to residents of the local panchayat.

Dhiru Kol has taken several contracts in the past few years for the construction of structures ranging from a cross-dam to a tank and residential houses under different employment and development schemes of the government. Several people in the village had complained about him. I was expecting to meet a typical contractor, corrupt and arrogant. On the contrary, Dhiru is poor, illiterate, and apparently sincere. Silingi is a remote, *adivasi*-dominated panchayat, with a few educated men and even fewer educated women. What happens in such a situation is that the contract is given in the name of a local *adivasi* as per the state norm, but is actually controlled by a *diku* from outside the community (Amrapara or other towns). This 'partnership' is necessitated not only because the need for maintaining accounts requires some basic educational skills, but also the need to put up some capital as earnest money. As Dhiru said, 'How can I do this on my own, neither do I have the capital to make the deposit, money to pay the bribes, nor the required contacts with the decision-making authorities. If I can earn Rs 500 or Rs 1000, that is enough for me.' The *diku* contractor keeps the accounts and promises to divide the savings from the project, but Dhiru usually receives nothing. His strategy is to constantly change his partner, hoping that someone will give him a fair deal. While his partners have prospered, he himself is still dependent on the moneylender for his survival, borrowing at least one or two sacks of rice each year.

Another 'contractor' from the same village is Chura Marandi. He had the contract for constructing a road through the village. Though educated up to class 7 and priding himself on this, Chura too undertook the project in partnership with a *diku* from Amrapara. He also talks of the commissions to be paid, but he further analyses the flimsiness of the project, 'This road ideally requires boulder pitching, but that will require another project. Projects are sanctioned in such a way that enable all concerned people to repeatedly make money, not out of concern for the needs of the local people. If another project is made for the boulder pitching of this road, the people sanctioning it can once again earn money.' While not fitting the stereotype of an 'exploitative contractor', given the relatively little differentiation in terms of land-holdings or access to land, it is these social contacts that lead to differences of class position and gender inequality.

Several references have been made to the term *diku* and some clarification may be appropriate here. Deriving from the Hindi word *dikkat* or 'trouble', it literally means 'one who gives trouble'. There is thus nothing inherent in the term to imply non-*adivasis*, outsiders or even moneylender-traders, for whom this term is commonly used. Yet, embedded within a history of exploitation, breach of trust and antagonistic relations, the term has a political and symbolic significance, evoking strong emotions of both pain and anger, often at their own helplessness to resist. While the Santals cannot do without the *dikus*, they resent this dependence, as they see it as being strictly one-sided. For instance, while Dhiru Kol partners with *dikus* for construction projects, he curses them too: 'We will do our own development. We don't want the Bengalis here. I will drive this Bengali out of our village.' There is a contradictory, love-hate relationship between the Santals and the *dikus*—the Santals see the *dikus* as privileged and need their support to access resources, especially from the state, yet they think this privilege has been acquired through unfair means. In fact, in present times, there are exploiters amongst the *adivasis* too, what Mahapatra (1976) has termed 'the insider diku', but they are not considered *dikus* in the local context. In this text, therefore, the term *diku* is used in the way the Santals use it, referring to outsiders, all potential troublemakers.

In the last decade, social capital has been identified as the 'missing link' in development, the explanation for project failures. Rather than propagating technocratic solutions for livelihood insecurity, the discourse is moving in the reverse direction. Policy-makers at global levels in particular seem to suggest that the 'reasons for poverty have to be understood through detailed analysis of social relations in a particular historical context: between those with land and without land, for example; between rich and poor households; between men and women …' (Murray, 2001: 1). The analysis of resources and technologies is not enough. Ellis, in his framework for understanding livelihoods, recognizes that the 'translation of a set of assets into a livelihood strategy… is mediated by a great number of contextual social, economic and policy considerations' (2000: 37). While this is true, the problems lie not just in the local context and local power relations. A view from below suggests that macro power relations as reflected in state policies may be the major constraint. The better off in Chuapara are only slightly more secure than the worse off. In periods of crisis as during the heavy rains, no one ate, not even the wealthiest in the village.

How far can they withstand the forces that commodify land, that eventually make them give it up by neglecting investment for decades? Market liberalization is seen as an opportunity to improve lives, yet how far is it an opportunity when the playing field is not level? Do people, women in particular, depend on their kin who may be exploiting them, out of choice, or for the lack of options? Emphasizing social capital as the way to 'fix' development, while ignoring structural inequalities, is unlikely to lead to secure livelihoods. It appears as a way of 'depoliticizing development' to borrow the title of the critique of this concept by John Harriss (2001). Sara Berry's (1993) comparative study of changing patterns of resource access and use across four agrarian systems in Africa during and after the colonial period, demonstrates the role and interplay of multiple factors in understanding this process. It is not just relative factor prices, as market sensibilities would lead us to assume, or local rules and norms governing the definition of property rights, or even the nature of contracts, that shape resource access and use. It is rather the exercise of power and knowledge and the terms in which rights and obligations are defined not just in relation to kin and community, but also to outsiders, including the state, that plays a significant role in shaping livelihoods.

While the social relations and contacts developed by men have been emphasized in the preceding paragraphs, women too have a role to play. They may be left out of government-related domains and from agricultural rituals in the community, yet they are not only economically active, but also have considerable social freedom, to meet their friends, visit relatives or simply chat. They not only cooperate with one another in the use of domestic resources, such as the sharing of *dhekis* for pounding rice, but also in taking products to the market, in agricultural operations, sometimes even sharing food. Given that there are no rice mills in the vicinity, and only a dozen *dhekis* in the village, friendships, to a large extent, are seen in the sharing of such assets. Women's contacts also cross the boundaries of the village, given that they move from their natal village after marriage, and are called upon in times of crisis, whether material or emotional. When talking of their lives, it emerged that many of the women had exercised the option of exiting from their marriage when they found that their husbands did not care much about them or attempted to restrict their mobility, an issue further discussed in Chapter 7. They do not easily tolerate marital violence, even if they have children to support. Their confidence to survive economically seems to place them in a stronger bargaining position within the household, though this varies with household forms and structures. Yet their message is clear: they want a life of dignity, even if this means greater hardship.

## Domestic Labour

The engagement with production is however closely linked to reproduction and domestic labour. In a place like Chuapara, where a large part of women's time is spent on tasks that are indispensable for daily survival, it is difficult to fix the boundaries between production and reproduction. The gender division of labour is then flexible, and shifts across seasons in light of the work burdens in paddy cultivation or social demands on time. Income-earning or income-saving strategies may be chosen, shared and divided amongst different members of the household—husband and wife, two adult females or parent and child.

In general, men seem to take on a smaller share of domestic labour, about a fourth. In the monsoons, things change and their contribution increases. In July, paddy is being transplanted. Women return from the fields at dusk, tired, having uprooted the seedlings in the morning and planted them in the afternoon. If men do not work with their wives to pound grain on the *dheki,* the meal cannot be prepared. During my stay, the spring was flooded and a new source of drinking water was found further upstream. It was a much

3.4: Pounding rice on the *dheki*. A joint activity

longer walk, so men collected the water too. In households with young children, men spent considerable time in childcare. The only activities they did not engage in were washing utensils and clothes. When the peak period recedes, male contribution again gets more unpredictable.

In terms of the reliability of support for household tasks then, women prefer to rely on a second adult woman, be it a daughter or a sister. Mary, when she is away for the pulse polio campaign, for instance, is sure of a hot meal, cooked by her daughter or husband's sister, when she returns. While her husband Chura does help occasionally, as an aspiring government contractor, he spends considerable time networking in other villages and the block headquarters, hence his support cannot be relied on. Also, aspiring to a higher status, there is an attempt to copy upper caste Hindu practices, where performing domestic labour is perceived as demeaning for a man. Yet, even Chura, during the transplanting period, did not hesitate to pound paddy regularly on the *dheki* with Mary. While considerable negotiation seems possible in terms of the allocation of tasks in practice, reproductive work is normatively seen as the responsibility of the woman—*ora hor*—or person of the house. She can arrange the labour to perform these activities, but ultimately if the work remains undone, she shoulders the blame.

Things are different in the case of a woman-headed household like Bahari's. When she had a high malarial fever, she took an injection from Ram Dey and as soon as her fever subsided, she was at the river fetching water, and later in her maize plot. When asked why she did not rest, she answered, 'My daughter is only 11 years old. She does a lot of work, but hasn't yet learnt how to plant the maize. Also, as a mother, I feel bad to put the entire burden of work on her. She is willing, but I feel guilty' (12 June 2000). In women-headed households particularly, the contradictions between the multiple roles of women as mother, worker, provider and nurturer,[17] often become glaring. Bahari wistfully recounted the happier times when she had the support of her husband. This is not because she did not work on the fields earlier, but because the responsibility for planning and farm management was his. The emotional strain that sole responsibility for all activities puts on women is a factor not often taken into account in the discussion of poverty and livelihoods. The notion of autonomy and empowering women through independent work and income needs to be balanced with the ethics of care and culturally valued notions of appropriate roles and behaviour in a context where state support services are largely absent. What such women are looking for is recognition of their value, rather than a demonstration that they are capable of performing all tasks independently.

Women here are economically and socially active, yet rather than total autonomy, they seek responsibility, love and mutuality from their

[17]Oppong and Abu (1987), discuss the seven roles of women. They are: parental, occupational, conjugal, domestic, kin, community and individual.

men. Gradual exclusion from increasingly competitive and unfair markets, from education as well as government projects, may have a negative impact on their identities as persons in the future, with implications for gender relations too. Not having a land title has barely had a material impact on them at present, though it is likely to become an issue, if indeed they continue to be excluded from public life. This seems to already be the case in Bagdiha, which I turn to next.

## BAGDIHA: DIVISIONS IN THE COMMUNITY

In contrast to Chuapara, Bagdiha in Dumka block, lies in the plains, 17 kilometres from Dumka and 5 kilometres from the main Dumka-Rampurhat road. A daily minibus service to Dumka is run by one of the *mahajans* of Bagdiha. At other times, one needs to walk to the road-head to get a bus. Paddy fields are visible on both sides of the road; there are few trees to provide shade, and no forests in sight.

Bagdiha has 235 households living in seven *tola*s, more dispersed and diverse than Chuapara. When coming from Dumka, we first enter an exclusively Hindu *tola*, *mahajan tola* or *kumhar para* (potter's locality), with about 45 households. The name demonstrates its character, accommodating the moneylenders or *mahajans* belonging to the trading castes of *telis* or traditional oil-pressers on the one hand, and the potters, an occupational category servicing the needs of the peasants, on the other. As one enters, there are a few large, double-storeyed brick houses, belonging to three brothers, *telis* by caste, who own a rice mill, several grocery stores, a truck and a minibus. They are recognized as major paddy and rice merchants in the region. After these big houses come the houses of poorer relatives, some engaged in agriculture, or actually wage labour (several having mortgaged their land to their richer relatives), though a large number engage in petty trade of different sorts, travelling from village to village on their bicycles selling their wares. Some have taken up other businesses like running grocery stores that sell on credit, tailoring or medical shops or just hawking in villages. With electricity coming to the village in 2005, some even have fridges and sell chilled liquor! While there are visible differences amongst the *adivasis* as well, class and gender divisions seem starker amongst the Hindus, and litigation on matters of land is not uncommon. It was methodologically important to recognize the internal differences and conflicts within each of these communities, especially as one is constantly presented with unifying and homogenous images, with conflict apparent only between communities, such as the Santals and *dikus*, or the Santals and Paharias.

This is not to say that social relations do not exist between the *dikus* and Santals in Bagdiha. Many have close interactions, such as the Hindu widow Mira Gorain, who has been struggling against her wealthy kin, and has been actively supported by Santal leaders including Harnath Hembrum. But the general feeling is that of mutual antagonism and mistrust. Their homes are physically separated not to mention the caste boundaries drawn by the Hindus, who see the Santals as lowly, though lying outside the caste structure. The politicization of religion post-2000 and the construction of Hanuman temples in several villages across the district have reinforced the idea that *adivasis* are like Hanumans—the monkey-god ever present in the service of Lord Rama (the *dikus*). They are seen as simple people, loyal and obedient, yet lacking in intellect, hence incapable of enterprise. They are not credited with qualities of leadership, rather their role is seen as providing labour and services to the Hindu castes.

Half-way through the *mahajan tola*, begins the settlement of the *kumhars* or potters, the only common element between the two being their Hindu religion. The present *mukhiya* or elected headman of the village panchayat being a *kumhar*, has ensured members of his caste group access to several state benefits. A third of eligible Hindu widows receive a pension from the state in contrast to only one in every ten Santal widows. While 50 per cent of the *kumhar* households have a ration card, only 24 per cent of the Santals have one. Better access for the Hindus here clearly reflects imbalances in power, not only due to income differences, as there are several poor households among the Hindus too, but also command over information and social networks.

Following straight on from the *mahajan tola* is *sadhu tola*, an *adivasi* hamlet of about 40 households, where Pushpa and I lived with Sheela Hansdak, her husband Harnath Hembrum, and her widowed cousin, Varsha Tudu. Their son is employed in the army, and two daughters are married. It was here that I developed my closest relationships, and understood the nuances of identity and status, the distress caused to Sheela, for instance, by the elopement of her only son with a poor, illiterate girl from the same village. It went against her every instinct—she had stood up for education all her life and struggled for this cause—yet had a daughter-in-law who was totally illiterate. There was Rimani on the other hand, struggling for daily survival, but who made sure that her two children regularly went to school. So many others like Sona and Dhaki, Agnes and Karuna, who made me realize that not only did they have aspirations as individuals, but equally in relation to their children.

Further north is the *majhi* (headman) or *chetan* (upper) *tola*, somewhat larger in size, but not better off. While the former *patta majhi* (revenue headman) of the village, appointed by the government, is resident here, he no longer has any powers, this being a *khas* village now. While there is no official headman, each *tola* except the *mahajan tola* has at least one *majhi*, popularly called *handi majhi* (liquor headman), fulfilling social and ceremonial roles in the village as well as coordinating and leading the process of dispute resolution at the local level.

Near the primary school is a small hamlet, called the school *tola*. While the health sub-centre is totally dysfunctional, the primary school works, with all except the Hindu children going to school, the latter studying with a private tutor in their own *tola*. Dharam Marandi, the *pradhan* during *hul* Jharkhand, lives close to the school and said that he keeps an eye to see that the teachers attend the school regularly and that it functions smoothly. He joked, 'The teachers usually don't like a posting in Bagdiha, as they know that here they will have to work.' There are three other *tolas*—road *tola,* which is near the road, *palas para,* which has a huge *palas (butea frondosa)* or flame of the forest tree and *hissa tola,* or the hamlet at the end. All these hamlets are largely inhabited by *adivasis*, the Santals and the Kols (152 households), though there are a few Scheduled Castes, the Rajwars and Doms, the latter primarily wage labourers. There are no Muslims in the village.

Here too, the absence of a clear hierarchy of village leadership has meant a more democratic functioning of the mechanisms for dispute resolution. All adult males can participate, and freely give their views, thus potentially creating an internal pressure for abiding by the judgments pronounced. A majority of cases coming to Manglu Marandi, the *majhi* of *sadhu tola*, involved women and property—a widow's rights, an abandoned woman, the share of the first wife in a polygynous relationship, the inheritance of a daughter or the claims of a separated sister, discussed further in Chapter 8. Yet increasingly cases are being taken to the *thana* (police station) and courts of law by the male kin, despite considerable time and expense. This is perhaps a delaying tactic, in the hope that desperate women would resort to other means of living during the period of the court hearings and eventually give up their claims through non-attendance and lack of information. Such a view, however, points to the fragility of the very notion of the 'community', raising questions about its roles and responsibilities, and the legitimacy of its moral authority. This is especially true in the context of a mixed caste village, where disputes with the Hindus are, in any case, taken to the courts rather than being resolved locally.

## Livelihood Resources: Land and Labour

While Chuapara was part of the 'old reserve' or *Damin*, Bagdiha was part of a *zamindari* estate ruled by a Paharia king. Killed during the Santal *hul* of 1855, his son retained the *zamindari*, that is, the right to manage the land and responsibility to pay the rent. Some British officials felt that the propaganda of the Congress Party, prior to the first provincial government elections in 1937, had made the leaders defiant and was, thus, responsible for their refusal to pay their rents. Yet they also recognized that roads, wells, schools and other public amenities had been neglected (Tour Diary of Davies, DC, 1936–7).

In the perception of the villagers, it was during this period, when the third land survey and settlement operation took place that more land was registered in the name of the *dikus*, primarily to make good rent arrears. The Bagdiha land records do not tell this story—the Santals retained control over 77 per cent of the land throughout this period, at least on paper. Informal transfers were however rampant, and it was this land that was repossessed by the Santals during the agrarian movement, which started in Bagdiha and in which most households participated, in the 1960s.[18]

[18]Called *hul* Jharkhand, please see Chapter 4 for a detailed discussion.

Here, too, most of the *adivasis* have land and see themselves as farmers, yet unlike Chuapara, there are a few large landowners and a few near-landless. There are also a large number of women who have inherited land, either because they had no brothers or because their fathers wanted them to stay in the same village and hence, gifted them land. In *sadhu tola* itself, out of 40 households, ten were women landowners, whether *gharjawaes* (resident husband),[19] widows or inheriting sisters. Bullocks, essential for cultivation and a sign of male identity, are also maintained by single women such as Dhaki as a tool for negotiating male labour for ploughing her lands. Despite this, in recent years, women's rights are increasingly being contested.

Choti Tudu, the younger widow of Girish Soren, had been accused as a witch soon after his death ten years ago. The harassment persists. As Girish did not have a child by his first wife, Munni, he married Choti. She has two daughters. After his death, while Munni leased out her land, Choti tried to cultivate her share, but constantly faced difficulties in getting the land ploughed on time. Last year she got her 13-year-old daughter, studying in middle school, married to a *gharjawae*. With the help of her son-in-law she was able to cultivate the land. Still, their situation is very difficult. She goes out for labour, sells liquor in the *haat* and migrates to Bengal with her younger daughter, while Munni looks after the house. They still have had to borrow some money, cut consumption and harvest a part of the crop early. They have a ration card, but rarely use it, as the quantity of grain is insufficient, and also they do not have lump sum cash available for the purchase.

There is no river in Bagdiha, but about 40 wells were dug during the *jal hai jaan hai* ('Water is Life') campaign for irrigation purposes in the early 1990s. Water is thus available for a *rabi* (winter) crop, but its use is labour intensive; it has to be drawn and the fields irrigated manually. Further, cash crops, generally grown in the winter, need fertilizers, hence access to capital is important for their cultivation. Finally, community arrangements for cattle management during the *rabi* (winter) season have broken down post-1970s, making it difficult

[19]Son-in-law who stays with wife's family. Detailed discussion in Chapter 7.

for a few to cultivate, if the rest do not co-operate. Hence, there is hardly any *rabi* production in the village, with a majority of people migrating to Bengal for agricultural wage work, seen as providing better returns.

Labour is a key resource in Bagdiha, with limited land and virtually non-existent forests. An estimated 100,000 people migrate from Dumka to Bardhaman district of West Bengal for paddy transplantation and harvest work during the *boro* season,[20] and somewhat fewer for the *kharif* (July-August for planting and November-December for harvest, known as *aman* in Bengal) crop. From Bagdiha, almost 75 men and women from 152 Santal and Kol households migrated for the *boro* transplanting (February) and harvest (May), while none of the *telis*, *kumhars* or Scheduled Castes from the village did so. This is also a period when there is no work at home, since there is no second crop. They go in small groups either with a contracting agent who comes to the village to collect labour, by prior arrangement with a cultivator in Bardhaman, or then, to the labour market there in search of a suitable employer. A smaller number go for the *aman* harvest in December, after finishing their own harvest work quickly, or leaving it to some other member of the family. If at all there is a choice in terms of deciding whether to migrate or not, it is at this time, as some harvest labour work is also available locally. Wheras for harvest work, men and women seem to be employed almost equally, for transplantation work, women are preferred. Jeevan Soren recounted that migration had increased over the last two decades due to the introduction of the *boro* crop in West Bengal with the rapid spread of tube wells post-land reform.

Working days, inevitably, are long, and living conditions poor. Ten to fifteen adults are often piled together in a tiny, dark cattle shed. There is no window, no light and hardly any space to move. Mud *chulhas* (stoves) are temporarily constructed outside the shed for cooking food. Toilets are a problem, and women in particular, have to get up before daybreak to go out into the fields, as there is little privacy. They work in the fields from early morning to late evening and are paid a wage of Rs 30 in addition to daily rations of rice, salt, oil and potatoes.

[20]This refers to the irrigated later winter or early summer crop in West Bengal. Numbers of migrants during 1999–2000 were estimated by me and for subsequent years by Kumar Rana.

3.5: An overcrowded bus. Seasonal labour migrants to Bardhaman.

Yet they return year after year. The main advantage over local wage work appears to be the lump sum payment that they receive at the end, which can be used for the purchase of clothes and other assets, or for repairing houses and repaying debts. They would never be able to earn enough locally for these purposes.

Migration however works differently for different people. Choti Tudu, migrated to Bengal with her daughter for the *aman* harvest in December. Hard work and cold weather made her ill. She could not work for six days and for these six days of absence, she was neither paid a wage nor given her rations. She brought back only Rs 400. At home, her older daughter had also been sick and her co-wife had mortgaged a silver ornament for Rs 200 for her treatment. With her meager earning, they released the ornament, bought some rice, and the money was gone. She decided not to go for the *boro* planting even though she had no other source of income. She reasoned, 'My daughter and co-wife are both sick. If I go and something happens to them, what is the use?' (15 January 2000). She started brewing liquor and engaging in casual wage work locally instead. Chronic illness, due to prolonged under-nutrition and hard work, not only leads to high debt burdens, but also reduces the capacity to work itself. While it is true that migration can enhance women's earnings, the trade-offs in terms of social costs can be high.[21]

The story of Rimani, who had been migrating for several years with her husband Solomon, is more positive. Their land had been mortgaged, they had no cattle, so they went to Bengal, taking their two young children along. Rimani at one point said, 'We have land, why don't we try and save money, buy cattle and start cultivating? The children's education is disturbed by going away repeatedly' (16 January 2000). This was about eight years ago. It was by gradual hard work that they rebuilt their house, and were able to educate their son Vinod, who completed high school in 2002. They were able to use migration to change their livelihood trajectory to one of stability, though at the time of this research, Solomon had left Rimani and was living with another woman. There are other positive stories too. Money saved from migration is often invested in purchasing cattle, as in the case of Jeevan Soren, who served both as a labourer and a labour contractor for over 20 years. Not only has this helped him improve his own cultivation, but he is also able to lease in additional land. Not migration per se, but the forms of migration and the conditions under which it takes place determine its outcomes in terms of agricultural development or poverty reduction. In Bagdiha, most households now cultivate high yielding varieties of paddy on at least some of their land, having seen the differences in productivity during their migrations.

There is also an issue of identities. Unlike the Hindu castes that tend to withdraw female labour as a sign of status, among the Santals, men prefer to stay away from wage-work and let women engage in it. This is clearly visible in the household of Panthi Marandi, married to a *gharjawae* and owner of her land. She is now an old woman, living with her three sons, two of whom are married with children of their own. Her daughter, a second wife to a man from a neighbouring village, also lives with them, with her two daughters. They cultivate their own lands, 5.14 acre of *dhani* (paddy land), but with so many mouths to

[21]Karlekar (1995) includes economic and sexual exploitation, lack of childcare and education, and increased workloads as social costs. At subsistence levels, issues of autonomy can become irrelevant.

3.6: To the Gando *haat*. Carrying liquor for sale.

feed, this is not sufficient. Her daughter-in-law, daughter and granddaughter migrate to make up for the shortfall, while her sons stay behind. While Panthi owns the land, her sons will inherit it. In the case of her daughter and daughters-in-law, therefore, the lack of assets, poverty and casual wage labour are linked. They see migration as contributing to the houschold's subsistence—to its food supply, clothes and for an unmarried girl, to her dowry.

Men, seeing themselves primarily as cultivators, perceive wage labour as a loss of status. Seasonal agricultural migration therefore is represented by them in terms of the need to protect their women, subject otherwise to sexual abuse by employers at the destination. Other migration decisions are projected as an adventure to see new places, or a strategy to build capital for investing in their own land. As a result, they prefer long-term migration to distant locations. The main employer is the Border Security Force and recruitment takes place annually in Dumka. They usually leave after ploughing the land for the monsoon paddy and return before the next planting season. Some men do send money back home, but many bring back a lump sum when they return at the end of the contract, usually six to eight months. While male income contributes towards meeting large expenses (such as house construction or debt repayments), the entire physical and financial burden for daily maintenance falls on women, leading to overwork, poor health, indebtedness and harassment. Even though the women undertake all other agricultural operations, it is the men who, through the act of ploughing, assert their control over the land and their identity as cultivators. Migration patterns thus reveal the interactions between the micro-context relating to the individual's ability to choose between alternate courses of action, and the macro-context, including the political, economic, socio-cultural and resource relationships that constrain such decisions. With shifts in external factors and changes in life cycle, the chosen strategies also change. As with other livelihood decisions, migration processes are also deeply embedded in social roles, expectations and relationships.

Unlike Chuapara, women in Bagdiha mostly go to the bi-weekly *haat* at Gando, barely a kilometre away, to purchase essentials. If they have no cash, they trade in some paddy. There is no forest produce, so the only other product sold by women is liquor. All the liquor-sellers are women, both Santal and Hindu, many being from women-headed or women-only households, while the drinkers are mostly men. The women have to often bear the brunt of lewd male jokes. In the absence of Solomon, Rimani had taken to brewing liquor. She complained, 'My son does not allow me to sell liquor in the *haat*. He says if you sell liquor to men, someone may fight, some will drink and not pay, some may abuse you, so I only sell it from home' (16 January 2000). Though not a regular seller, the old widow Malati Kisku, makes and sells liquor whenever she needs cash. She receives a government pension for widows, amounting to Rs 100 per month, but often this does not arrive on time. She saves most of it to pay the labour to cultivate her land, and a little for oil and spices. The liquor market is an interesting picture of gendered power relations, bringing to light the generally low social status and lack of alternatives for women, the sellers. At the same time it provides space to them to earn an income and reduce indebtedness. Though not in the *haat*, Hindu women, mostly widowed, both *teli* and *kumhar*, such as Mira, make and sell puffed rice, carrying it on their heads from door to door through the surrounding villages.

## Social Alliances and Household Work

March and April are the months of leisure and celebration. There is an annual fair at Gando, with a range of stalls selling cloth, food and liquor. Football matches and other sporting events are held during the day and films are screened at night. Their own harvest is done, the migrants have returned from Bengal and leave again for the summer harvest only in May. Other men too are back home until the next rains. There is a sense of fulfillment, of festivity. This is the time when weddings take place and new alliances are arranged, a major site for this being the *haat*.

Engaging in wage labour markets seems the key to survival here. Yet this implies a reliance on the individual's capacity to work and earn. If this fails for any reason, then there is a crisis, as unlike in Chuapara, social support networks have virtually broken down. Sona Tudu, a widow, has five *bigha*s (1.6 acres) of land. With ploughing support from her son-in-law after her husband's death, she made sure they had enough food to eat and clothes to wear. She engaged in wage-work for food supplements and sometimes sold liquor in the market to finance the purchase of household goods. She collects firewood and her children collect greens. Her hard work had ensured that she was never in debt. One of her daughters was suffering from tuberculosis of the bone. After prolonged local treatment, which failed, she was finally admitted to the hospital. Her leg would have to be amputated if she had to be saved. Sona borrowed money for the operation as none of her husband's kin would help. They perhaps resented her independence, complaining that she never had time to socialize with them. They had also charged her with being a witch a few years ago. She parted with her land, yet the girl died. The large amount of loan required and her weak social networks have meant that she is being charged exploitative and excessive rates of interest. She is now dependent on wage-work alone for survival, until she is able to reclaim her land.

The critical role of labour is visible also in the gender divisions of work and the decision-making around the use of time. While men and women both contribute almost equal time to family agriculture, the seasonal patterns of wage earning, essential for survival in a cash-driven economy, are different. In July and September women are more focused on their household agriculture and it is the men who look for wage labour (in ploughing), but from December to March, it is women who engage in wage work. This is partly explained by migration, particularly for paddy transplanting to Bengal in the month of February. Local wage labour is also required for cleaning and applying mud to houses during the festive occasions of *sohrai* (harvest) and *baha* (spring), in January and March respectively. Earning cash incomes, which they control, is important to women, and perhaps one reason why a second cash crop under men's control does not seem an attractive proposition.

This pattern of labour is mirrored by sharp seasonal shifts in the performance of household maintenance tasks. Collection of fuel wood from the distant forests is entirely women's work, concentrated in the dry, winter months, as also cooking, cleaning and washing. Bagdiha, however, has several wells used both for drinking water and for washing and other purposes. These are close to the houses, so collection of water is not a big issue. The tasks of cooking, washing utensils and clothes are done whenever women find the time for them. Several hand-pumps have been installed, but as in Chuapara, here too, they do not work. While the women are away, having migrated to Bengal, men contribute to household tasks, but refuse to do these tasks when the women are present. Mahani, the daughter of Jeevan Soren, who came back from her husband's house when he took another wife, noted, 'Mother can't walk, so the entire burden falls on me, both of work in the fields and at home. When I was in Bengal, my brothers used to help my mother—they would fetch the water, sweep the floors, clean the utensils and assist with cooking. But as soon as I returned, I was expected to take over all the tasks' (10 January 2000).

Despite this, one finds that women still find some leisure for chatting with friends and neighbours. This is perhaps on account of the better access (than in Chuapara) to essential facilities such as water, a shop in the village for daily requirements, and a mill for grinding paddy, that runs on a diesel generator.[22] These amenities reduce the drudgery

[22]Electricity has been available since August 2005, but the voltage is low and the service irregular.

involved in household maintenance tasks and also make them less time-consuming than in Chuapara. Yet, in a market-driven context, it doesn't help people, especially women without cash. Binoti Kolin, a widow, living with her son who is currently working on a stone-crusher in Bengal, and separated daughter, has little cash to spare. She is one of the few women in this village who continue to hand-pound small quantities of grain on a *dheki*, every day. She also does not have the minimum amount of grain that can, in fact, be ground in the mill.

Household work is thus both elastic and context-sensitive, based on notions of need and valuations of work in different environmental contexts and particular relationships. In better off households, women may not go out for wage labour, but their domestic work is endless—managing labour, post-harvest processing and storage, apart from entertaining guests and maintaining a larger home.

While the physical burden of work may be lighter to some extent due to the easy access to services in Bagdiha, the gender division of labour itself is more rigid, influenced also by status considerations in a mixed caste context, so that performance of certain household tasks by men is seen to negatively influence their status. In terms of perceptions of well-being, however, many women still find this situation preferable. As Mahani said, 'I was married in a forest village near Kathikund, with no facilities. The work burden there was endless and I constantly fell ill. My husband failed to get me medical treatment, their family was poor, so ultimately I returned home to my parents. Here somehow the work seems less arduous.'

For men here, accessing government officers and benefits is seen as a source of power and status. The Hindu castes in the *mahajan tola* have an advantage in accessing government resources, not only on account of language, but also cultural and social affinity with the petty bureaucracy, most of whom are Hindus. Their *tola* is the first when one enters the village from Dumka, hence the first stop for all visiting functionaries. Most of the *adivasi* men, however, have cycles to facilitate communication with Dumka and the block headquarters and two even have motorcycles.[23] They try to build relationships of familiarity

[23]In 2004, upon her retirement, Sheela bought a motorcycle, the first woman to do so, though she uses a driver to take her to and from Dumka.

through frequent visits to various government offices. Though there is no NGO working in Bagdiha, a group of Santal boys influenced by NGOs in nearby villages have set up a Savings Club. Clearly, engaging with government/service institutions is seen as a status symbol for men, while domestic labour is not.

## MULTIPLE CONTEXTS, LIVELIHOODS AND RELATIONSHIPS

The little stories and daily occurrences that one experiences when living in a village emerge in different forms throughout this book. It is important however to highlight at this stage, following from the above descriptions, that even remote villages do not fit the stereotypes of isolated and homogenous islands of amiable and peaceful social relationships—a happy-go-lucky *adivasi* life as we are often given to believe. The contextual data may seem to be homogenizing, and sometimes this is necessary for policy-making and political purposes. One needs however to guard against simplistic conclusions and generalizations about social and cultural relationships in any society. A range of actors have reciprocal or hierarchical relationships with the Santal men and women in the village, changing with time and space. There are the Hindu caste groups that include the landless Scheduled Castes, many of them also oppressed by the *mahajans*, the artisan castes and the money lending and trading class. The relationships range from one of class solidarity to class hatred. The two villages selected for this study, apart from differences in their ecology, size and settlement patterns, also reflect different trajectories of change.

Most households have a basic strategy based on household farming of paddy, the staple food, together with arrangements for individual economic activity. While land is clearly the most important wealth-generating asset in an agrarian society, it cannot be cultivated without cattle, some capital and labour power. The deployment of these assets is influenced not only by factors of immediate survival, but also by negotiations within the household, by emotional and social bonds and relationships, and valuations of alternative strategies. Women's attempt to control their own labour and the earnings from it, following the monsoon paddy crop, for example, is a strategy to assert their own identity. Yet their approach remains inclusive, as in the case of Rimani hoping that the return of her husband would somewhat improve their standard of living. Elizabeth Francis, writing about Kenya, notes 'people respond to opportunities provided by the resources they have to hand, by market demand, by the vagaries of cross-border trade or by social networks' (2000: 21).

While recognized as central economic actors in Santal society, women, moving as they do across villages at marriage, derive their economic identities from a more diversified resource base—from land, forests, labour and small livestock. While these provide them some flexibility in the use of the different resources, the absence of direct control over land also exerts more pressure on them to engage in alternate activities for household subsistence. Sometimes these livelihood choices are unfavourable options, reflecting the inability of women to successfully negotiate their land claims. A study in Dumka district found that most firewood head loaders were widowed or abandoned women, with weak social networks and unable to cultivate their lands. The work is tough, with heavy loads to be carried for long distances, the markets are exploitative and they are subject to harassment both by forest guards and villagers protecting their forests (Rao, 1999). Nati, in Chuapara, is a good example of this strategy. Yet, her vulnerability is so great that she had to send her children out to work, two of whom she was unable to save from illness. While she is a strong woman, a knowing subject and economic actor in her own right, she operates within structures that constrain her choices. She is unable to control her husband's consumption of liquor or his clandestine sale of the wood that she has collected. With several children, she has to continue to work for survival, yet negotiate with him, in the hope that one day his land will be retrieved, and their lives will improve.

The interaction with the government, particularly the revenue and development bureaucracy, has become a significant element in making one's living. Those who have access to them are able to access information, and this becomes a powerful weapon in negotiating social hierarchies. Even at the cost of a lower output, Chura and Dhiru of Chuapara spend a lot of time outside the village in activities seen as building social capital. Women lose out here, not so much due to their own constraints of language or mobility, as the perceptions of the petty bureaucracy, about women and women's roles. These often closely follow the Hindu norms of restricted mobility, and most of the petty bureaucrats, essentially Hindu and male, even on village visits, rarely speak to the women. Despite the fact that it is the women who primarily engage with both labour and product markets, especially for forest produce, the Block Development Officer of Gopikandar (where Chuapara is located), said, 'Most schemes are given to men as they have to go around to collect materials and labour, and women can't do this.' While women may have economic control over wages and incomes, it has not necessarily led to a higher social status. Declining sex ratios seem to suggest the opposite. High levels of mobility and participation in markets in fact have led instead to the creation of a negative stereotype of Santal women as being 'loose'.

At the margins of poverty, it must be recognized that the concept of security in livelihoods is fluid. There are movements between the states of survival, stability and growth (Grown and Sebstad, 1989), but these are not unidirectional. An illness, a death, a marriage, a poor crop or even just the withdrawal of tenancy, can push back households. During crisis periods, households and individuals often rely on work intensification and expenditure saving methods such as cutting food consumption, switching to poorer quality of food, drawing on savings, selling valuables, borrowing and engaging in marginal and illegal activities. Children, kin and friendship networks are important contributors in this process. Yet even such support can erode under extreme conditions of poverty, illustrated by the cases of Sona, Choti and other such women-headed households, in the face of resistance to culturally accepted notions of appropriate behaviour. Both of them held on to their share of land and this resulted in their being branded as witches.

In a general context of vulnerability and the struggle for survival, land is valued for its enduring quality, the stability and identity it provides, even more than perhaps for its capacity to produce. Policies to strengthen rural livelihoods need to understand that sources of risk facing different kinds of households, and women within them, are not always material, and respond accordingly.

Tables 3.2 and 3.3 summarize the contrasting features of the two villages.

Table 3.2: Characteristic Features of Chuapara and Bagdiha

| Feature | Chuapara | Bagdiha |
|---|---|---|
| Distance from Dumka | 74 km | 17 km |
| Distance from Road-head | 18 km | 5 km |
| Population features | *Adivasi* (Santal, Kol and Paharia) | Mixed castes (Santal, Kol, Teli, Kumhar, Rajwar) |
| Size of settlement | 52 households | 235 households |
| Total Population (1991) | 267 | 1144 |
| Total Workers (1991) | 77 Male, 79 Female | 328 Male, 197 Female |
| Present administrative status | *Khas* village | *Khas* village |
| Ecology | Hilly and forested | Plains |
| Cultivated land area* | 192.86 acres | 524.67 acres |
| Forest land area | 291.36 acres | 16.62 acres |
| Livelihood | Agriculture (settled and shifting), forest produce | Agriculture (settled), wage labour and migration |
| Migration | Rare | Widespread |
| Women's literacy | Very low (8 female, 23 male) | Moderate (110 female, 231 male) |
| Infrastructure in village | Primary school, *angan-wadi* centre | Primary school, ration shop, rice mill, tailor |
| Infrastructure within 2 km | None | Bank, Post Office, market, middle school |
| Electricity | Not available | Connection in 2005 but irregular |
| Drinking water | Stream | Wells |
| Communication | Poor | Fair |
| Access to bureaucracy | Low | High |
| Settlement history | *Damin-i-koh*, local administration and revenue privileges | Zamindari estate, subject to revenue demands of administration |

*(contd.)*

*Table 3.2 (contd.)*

| Feature | Chuapara | Bagdiha |
|---|---|---|
| Land-holding Pattern | Marginal to medium farmers | Marginal to large farmers |
| Participation in contemporary land struggle | No | Yes |

*Note:* * from Settlement records.

Table 3.3: Women's Rights and Responses in Chuapara and Bagdiha

| Features | Chuapara | Bagdiha |
|---|---|---|
| Women's economic base | Forest, *kurram, bari* | *Bari*, labour |
| Marital mobility | High | Restricted |
| Polygyny | Absent | Present |
| Legal registration of women's land rights | Marginal | High |
| Dispute resolution | Social negotiation | External mediation through lawyers and courts, and bureaucracy |

CHAPTER

# 4 Reinventing Tradition
## Agrarian Movements in History

30 June 1855:

On this full moon day, a grand assemblage of over ten thousand Santals, fully equipped with bows and arrows, swords, battle-axes and drums, was held at Bhagnadihi, a little village in the heart of the Barhait valley. A call was given to the Santals to rise, throw out the oppressors and start a *raj* (kingdom) of their own. One of the leaders, Sidho, said, 'I have been complaining for five years against the mahajans and until now no investigation has been made.'[1]

7 July 2000, Bhagnadihi:

The podium constructed for the celebrations on 30 June had just been dismantled. After hectic activity, the village was now quiet. While the annual ritual persists, the character of Bhagnadihi is no longer the same. An all-Santal village, in the heart of the *Damin-i-koh* (in 1855), it now has 130 Muslim trader and moneylender households as against 70 Santal families. The descendants of Sidho and Kanhu are themselves indebted, their children unable to go to school. On this day in 1855, the rebellion took a violent turn, with the killing of Mahesh Dutta, the *daroga* of Dighee, not far away in Panchkattia. Today the family is unable to release their mortgaged land (Personal Diary).

Sidho and Kanhu, the accepted leaders of the Santal *hul,* as the rebellion was called, remain symbols of the struggle against oppression. They represent an image of the 'primitive rebels', honest

[1]Judicial Proceedings, 8 Nov 1855, no. 25–26, Government of Bengal, Sidho's deposition before Ashley Eden, the Assistant Special Commissioner for the Suppression of the Santal Insurrection.

and chivalrous on the one hand, and armed with bows and arrows prepared to loot and kill in their fight for freedom from domination, on the other. Theirs was not only a struggle against economic oppression or political control, but also for ideological freedom, to legitimize a culture and an alternative way of life, based on emotional attachment to their land. This image has persisted in the minds of both the local *adivasis* and the administrators, telling a story of subordination, contestation and change.

The image however is neither static, nor singular. The Judicial Proceedings quoted above present a romantic picture of the event of a single night, coincidentally, a full moon night. But was it, in fact, a rebellion, a sudden outburst or a movement for the expression of suppressed interests? The *hul* was not a one-day affair; it was, on the other hand, fired by the unchanging and intense subjugation, and the day-to-day suffering of many thousands of people. It provided a voice to *adivasi* aspirations, achievements and collective existence—a choice between a new world without poverty and hunger, based on a radical rejection of existing hierarchies, or an adaptation to a modern capitalist economy over which they might have little control. A similar situation persists even today as more land gets privatized and the meanings accorded to it change. But ambiguities remain and the symbolism of land in relation to life itself has become a major site for contestation and resistance. For the state, the images symbolize a possible violent backlash which needs to be prevented through reformist policies, protective legislation and special development programmes. Arvind Das (1993), in an incisive comment, viewed land reform itself as a response to peasant discontent, rather than being unilaterally introduced by the ruling elite as a move towards social justice.

Following the formation of Jharkhand as a separate state, there has been not just the installation of statues of Sidho and Kanhu all over the Santal Parganas, but also the renaming of public and private institutions after them. They represent a social idea of equality and justice, of a movement in response to chronic uncertainty and enduring suffering, not a backlash against particular policies or actions. The images represent a point of decision, where the choice lies between fighting back to change the system and continuing to suffer. The *hul* clearly was seen as the successful result of a long-drawn out struggle.

4.1: Statues of Sidho and Kanhu in Dumka bazaar.

The symbolisms of the struggle, however, have changed with the times, keeping abreast with the changes in the nature of the state and the governance system itself. Today's India is a free nation with a legal framework designed to protect and promote *adivasi* livelihoods. Yet land is alienated both legally and extra-legally. Besides redefining the relationship with land, the present-day movements need also to reconceptualize the meanings of citizenship and personhood. Yet certain symbols and images are repeatedly drawn upon to arouse emotions, and construct solidarity.

Lessons from the past are adapted to the new circumstances and contexts of people's lives, and traditions are reinvented (Hobsbawm and Ranger, 1993), rather than preserved. A graphic illustration comes from the life of the leader of the Jharkhand Mukti Morcha (JMM),

Sibu Soren, who became a folk hero in the 1970s, like Sidho and Kanhu. Apart from land occupation, he presented an agenda for agricultural modernization through collective action. Today he stands accused for murder and the use of violence, not acceptable within a democratic system.[2] Another example of adaptation is of the Santal leaders speaking out in favour of women's rights to inherit land as a response to the state trying to take over control of land distribution and dispute resolution. Traditions can then be seen as 'a means of handling time and space, which inserts any particular activity or experience within the continuity of past, present and future, these in turn being structured by recurrent social practices' (Giddens, 1990: 37). They represent a creative process of identity formation.

Yet the administrative response often fails to take note of the change, mistaking an ideal, almost-static belief system for reality. Tradition and custom are reified in the minds of administrators as 'backward' and an impediment to 'development'. State laws and policies are then constructed in opposition to 'tradition', failing to recognize their elements of pragmatism and responsiveness. It is widely acknowledged that 'custom' itself was invented as a response to colonial rule and policies in most parts of the world. With globalization and consequent changes in the economy, the nation-state and day-to-day life, traditions and norms are rapidly being reformulated. Gender relations too have been transforming, yet these shifts are not easily acknowledged.[3] There are several commonalities between the positions of *adivasis* and women in Indian society—both are citizens in as far as they cast their votes, yet both are marginalized and sought to be controlled. Progressive ideas are floated for their equality, yet 'tradition' becomes the excuse for keeping them subordinated.

Everyone has multiple interests and commitments. One may not actively participate in every protest movement, yet an absence need not necessarily imply a lack of participation, as support is possible through everyday actions in many different ways. Inaction too is a way

[2]Sibu Soren has been acquitted after a higher court overturned the judgment of the lower court. He was sworn in as Chief Minister of Jharkhand on 28 August 2008.

[3]There is a growing body of work on women's agency and everyday negotiation in the patriarchal societies of South Asia. See, for instance, White (1992) and Kabeer (2000) for Bangladesh, Kapadia (1995) for India.

of exercising power and resisting domination (Lukes, 1974). Resistance in its everyday forms is an important tool for bargaining and exercising power, taking either more public, overt forms or remaining covert and local. This is particularly visible in the case of women manoeuvring between a discourse of rights and the reality of everyday subordination. Their decision is not just defined by the social context of the times, but also varies with the position of the individual or group within that society, making for 'everyone's forms of resistance'.

Aspects of resistance are particularly visible in the negotiations around the meanings of land to different individuals and groups. The struggle here gets extended to include broader issues of life and livelihoods, of governance and control over resources, of gender relations and identity itself. While the state has used the statues of Sidho and Kanhu to first placate the *adivasis* and then celebrate their victory, in this visible glorification, the daily struggles of the people and women amongst them have been forgotten. Neither *adivasis* nor women have been given control over the land, despite policy statements in favour of women for over a decade, including the most recent Scheduled Tribes (Recognition of Forest Rights) Act, 2006. Such laws and statements, whether practised or not, do however make a difference, if only symbolically, giving weightage to the long-standing demands and struggles of these groups. Any action or inaction, then, carries within it multiple layers of symbolism and meaning, and without going into these, it is difficult to make sense of the struggles over land.

India has had a long history of land struggles, supported largely by the Left political parties post-independence. The 1940s and 1950s saw intense struggles in southern India, in traditional rice areas that had seen rapid capitalist penetration in agriculture. While this had led to loss of land for the poor, the employment picture is not so clear, with Gough (1981), for instance, describing a decline in regular, male contracts, while labour opportunities for women, in fact, increased. Protest followed, land being crucial to the identities and social standing of peasants, small and marginal farmers or even tenant-farmers. The Telengana people's struggle (1946–51), the Thanjavur movement in the 1950s and 1960s, or the Tehbhaga movement in Bengal are well- known in this regard. Their demands, however, did not look beyond 'class'—giving land to the 'tiller'. The aggrieved was always construed as a man, although women actively participated both in agriculture and the struggle (Kannabiran and Lalita, 1990; Shivaraman, 1973). The point is not just of visible, physical participation, but the recognition that these changes affected women as much as their men.

The experience of most Latin American countries is similar, with a period of peasant discontent followed by land reform. Membership of production cooperatives or ownership rights to land ended up in the name of the head of the household, usually a man, although a few women mostly widowed or separated, were also included. Cuba was perhaps an exception, as not only was cooperative membership opened up to all adult members of the household, but the peasant unions (ANAP) along with the women's organization (FMC), ensured that women did actually join these units. Only in the late 1990s, with the growing strength of the women's movement globally, and the consequent rise in local women's groups and supportive women within government, has there been enhanced pressure to recognize women in the process of land reform and titling (Deere and Leon, 2001). As mentioned in Chapter 1, a push to include women in land titling programmes has also emerged from an efficiency perspective, given the rapidly shifting sectoral distribution of the working population, with women dominating the rural scene.

While certain aspects of feudal oppression, that included not just economic exploitation, but also the sexual exploitation of women, were addressed by these social movements, gender-specific issues such as the ownership and control over land, division of labour, decision-making and intra-family relations were avoided. The male leaders of the Jharkhand movement, in fact, opposed women's rights to land, framing this as an avenue for further exploitation of *adivasi* women by non-*adivasi* men! This does indeed point to the biases of the Left political parties, as Agarwal rightly points out (1994: 442), as well as to the difficulties of mass organization as a strategy to change gender inequities at the household level. Apart from differences in class, caste and religion, women's motivation to participate in mass resistance to secure rights to land, however, is likely to be influenced by negotiations within the household and community, political manipulations and the fact of social embeddedness of their land claims. If men deny them plough labour, for instance, they would be forced to leave their land fallow. Further, for a large number of women, their identities are located within their marriage and families, and security here is often a prime consideration in their decisions.

The first land struggle in India to explicitly take up the issue of women's land rights was led by the Chhatra Yuva Sangharsh Vahini in Bodhgaya district of Bihar. After three years of intense struggle, in 1981, when a part of the land was to be distributed, the titles were all made in the names of men, with the exception of some widows. Despite lists with the names of women being drawn up for several villages, the local government functionaries refused to give them the title on the pretext that they were not the 'head of the household'. The women felt it was unjust, and persisted with their claims, leading ultimately to their gaining the titles, countering multiple tiers of resistance, from the family and the community, including male activists, the state and the bureaucracy in the process (Manimala, 1984).

Agarwal (1994), analysing the variables responsible for this victory, highlights the role of women's struggle, the growing solidarity among women and the involvement of some middle-class feminist women activists. Clearly, the spread of the women's movement and feminist consciousness did contribute to the process of debate and analysis in Bodhgaya, lacking in earlier movements. At the same time she underplays the role of male support that was crucial in this success, though recognizing that the petty bureaucracy agreed to give the land titles in the names of women only after the 'firm refusal by the villagers (both men and women) to take land in male names' (Ibid: 449). So while there was indeed a collective struggle for women's land rights, it could not have succeeded without the support of the village men and outside activists.

Another positive story comes from the western Indian state of Maharashtra. The women's front or Mahila Aghadi of the Shetkari Sangathana—a farmer's organization formed under the leadership of Sharad Joshi in Maharashtra in 1980—passed a resolution at Amravati in 1989 that called upon all male members of the Sangathana to give a portion of their land to their wives.[4] This was subsequently endorsed

[4]The Shetkari Sangathana has led a number of agitations for remunerative prices of onions and other crops, against hike in electricity tariffs, for liquidation of rural debts and state dumping in domestic markets; *http://www.angelfire.com/in/swatantra*, as on 18/2/08.

by a huge rally of male farmers. Lakshmi Mukti, as the programme was named, called upon men to voluntarily transfer a piece of their land in their wife's name. The movement drew upon the Ramayana and the fact that Sita, the loyal and dutiful wife of Lord Rama, had been left destitute upon Rama's return to his throne. The movement gained momentum, with men who transferred land to their wives being honoured with certificates (Kishwar, 1997). In this case, the men not only supported, but actually took pride in their support of women's rights. Realizing the goals of emancipatory politics, in this case transforming gender relations, often depends on incrementally enhancing the spaces women have for action and control, rather than gaining absolute, autonomous rights. Here it meant gaining support from the privileged (men) to reform the existing system rather than making a radical break. Choices have to be made between diverse strategies, and not all of them need be 'public', nor necessarily antagonistic. Women in Bodhgaya were perhaps more 'overtly active' than the women in Maharashtra, yet both ultimately managed to win some control over land.

From each of these examples one can find multiple, often divergent representations of an 'objective reality'. The meaning derived from them by different groups also varies according to their own values, ideology, knowledge of context and understanding of history (Barthes, 1977). Returning to the imagery of Sidho in Jharkhand, he can thus be, at the same time, a 'bloodthirsty savage' (in the eyes of the Hindu moneylenders), 'barbaric yet chivalrous' (in the eyes of the European officers) and a 'divine messenger' or 'suba thakur' (in the eyes of the Santals) (Hunter, 1996 [1868]: 174). Whatever the case, he provided the vision of a different society and could not be ignored.

To understand the different systems and levels of meaning related to gender and land, the historical context of land relations and the shifts in institutions of management and control, will be briefly recounted setting out the established *doxa*[5] that is being challenged. Colonial land revenue policy converted shared fields into the property of an individual, usually a male, ignoring the nuances of women's rights. In one stroke they were converted into legal dependants of their male relatives. The call to restore 'community' control in present-

[5]*Doxa is* a term used by Bourdieu (1977) to represent everyday activities and practices that are taken for granted in daily life (this would include shared beliefs).

day Jharkhand still refers to a group of male patriarchs as the 'community'. The meaning of land as a form of property and gender relations, then, are not just closely interlinked, but also shift with contextual changes.

## A HISTORY OF RESISTANCE AND CHANGE

Although the Santals give their name to the Santal Parganas, the Paharias are said to be the original inhabitants of the region. Their livelihoods involved a combination of forest produce collection, hunting and *kurram* or shifting cultivation. When the British came here in 1765, they were keen to encourage settled agriculture and a process of peasantization in order to enhance future revenues. Cleveland, the Collector of Bhagalpur from 1779–84, sought to facilitate this process by establishing peace in the Rajmahal area, a major trading centre located on the river Ganga, by giving administrative responsibility to the Paharia chiefs. Following the Permanent Settlement of Bengal in 1793, the need for revenues intensified. Rewards were instituted for successful farmers and for loyalty. The Paharias, however, instead of obliging, actively opposed the colonizers (Bradley-Birt, 1990).

In 1818, the *Damin-i-koh* was constituted as a *khas mahal* (government estate) and the Santals were encouraged to reclaim and settle land for cultivation in this region. By 1836, over 427 Santal villages were established in the *Damin*. James Pontet, originally an indigo planter, was appointed the Superintendent in 1837. Writing to the Commissioner of Bhagalpur of the settlement of new villages and the problems that emerged as soon as rents had to be collected, he noted, 'As they leave cultivated lands behind them, I do not consider it policy to follow them for arrears of revenue as we shall be for many years dependent on this industrious race (the Santals) to bring these forests into cultivation. Many villages would have broken up and people moved away from the village in a night' had he insisted on payment when the crop had failed (File 7, 1844). The process of enhancing revenue collection had to be a gradual one and balanced with the need to clear and settle new land for cultivation, as clearly, the *adivasis* did not fit into the role of model, yeoman farmers.

Yet rents were enhanced, leading to a demand for cash to pay rents on the one hand and for scribes to maintain records on the other. There was an influx of non-*adivasis*—moneylenders and record-keepers—into the region, and their exploitative practices led to mounting social discontent. By 1845, Pontet's reports to the Commissioner started reflecting signs of growing oppression and paupersiation. The Bengalis, he says, don't want to settle in one place, but continue to take advantage of the needs of settlers for salt, seed and their ignorance of weights. In the hilly tracts near the Bansloi river (where Chuapara is located), there were complaints that the *mahajan*s were seducing the Santals with drink and not allowing them to go to the *haat* with their produce. They monopolized all produce, used larger measures for claiming repayment and purchase than for sales and loaning and charged exorbitant interest on debts taken. If the Santals were unable to pay, they lost their cattle and land. Several complaints were made and the *Naib Sezawals* (or Indian officers) were asked to investigate, but they did nothing. Several of them, mostly Bengali, were known to have amassed large sums of money through illegal extortions far in excess of the rent and other dues to be collected (Datta, 1988).

By 1854, the growing discontent fuelled by starvation and penury reflected itself in little acts of resistance. When the *mahajans* came to collect the harvest, people refused to pay. These dissidents were called 'dacoits' and punished, but not the *mahajan*s. In 1854, Pontet felt that 'the objective of my appointment by government being accomplished that is the clearing of the forest, civilising the hill race and lastly bringing in a handsome revenue.' From Rs 6,682 in 1837–8, the revenue increased almost nine times to Rs 58,033 by 1854–5, mainly through the process of new settlement (Sinha, 1991: 15). The railways, work on which started in the early 1850s, was a new source of oppression, with the rulers acquiring land without proper compensation as well as harassing the *raiyat*s for free supplies. The breaking point appears to have been the 'alleged forcible abduction of two Santal women by Europeans employed on the railroad' (Datta, 1988: 50).

Modern society, as represented by the colonial government, was based on depersonalized, abstract systems of governance, underpinned by professional expertise. Lack of alternatives made people accept these systems (Giddens, 1990). Yet, the hegemony of the system could not be maintained just by force. Reassurance that it worked and was reliable, was needed, particularly at the 'access points'. When this started breaking down, the petty bureaucrats—the first points of access—turned exploiters, and the higher regulatory authorities failed to act, people were deprived of their livelihoods, and as a result, lost faith in the system. The only option left to them was direct action to change the system of governance. A call was given for an open, armed struggle.

The Santal's hatred of the *mahajan*s was shown by the murder of a large number of them, starting with Mahesh Dutta at Panchkattia in 1855,[6] who, after 20 years in service, was found to have amassed enough wealth to leave his widow Seetalbati and two infant daughters in 'easy circumstances'. The cry was then 'death to the moneylenders, the police, the civil court officers, the landlords and the railway subordinates' (MacPhail, 1922: 55). The enemies were clearly identified in the domain of '*sarkar, sahukar aur zamindar*' (state, moneylender and landlord)—elements of economic exploitation legitimized by the political superstructure (Guha, 1983: 27).[7]

The stories, folktales and testimonies collected by Norwegian missionaries, provide an interesting insight into the *hul*, though pointing often to barbaric acts and tales of suffering (Soren, 1999), setting the ground for 'saving the natives' in the future. God is said to have presented himself to Sidho and Kanhu as a white man though dressed in the native style, a signal to the missionaries to help the Santals! The official sources of information are the judicial and police records, maintained with a view to repression, of 'policing' local communities (Dirks, 1997). These tend to present the Bengalis as the local oppressors, rather than the Europeans or their revenue policies.

It is not surprising that the testimonies from the Santal prisoners, Indian officers and European *zamindars* differ in their identification of causes of the rebellion. While Sidho complained of the oppression

[6]In the *hul*, 50 Bengali traders were killed in Barhait itself, according to the report of Captain Sherwill. Descriptions and analysis of the *hul* have been provided by Orans (1965), Man (1983), MacDougall (1985) and Pontet in his letters to the Commissioner.

[7]See Hauser (1983), Baviskar (1995), Das (1993) and also Scott's (1976) description of peasant rebellions against the exaction of moneylenders, landlords and the state, when left with less than a minimum subsistence. O'Malley notes a yearning for independence, to have total control over their land and resources, and not be dependent on any masters as another reason for the *hul* (1910: 48).

of the *mahajans* and 'railway sahibs', Mr Charles Barnes, an indigo planter, traced the outbreak to religious fanaticism; Mr Grant, a European *zamindar*, to the exactions of the *Naib Sezawals* and an Indian government pleader to the Santals' fanatic disposition (Sinha, 1991). While often presented as a Santal versus Hindu struggle, the Santals were supported by the poorer Hindu castes, the milkmen, blacksmiths and others, the enemy being the rich Bengalis. Class oppression formed the context, though millenarian symbolism—obeying the command of God—helped organize the masses.[8] The ideological and material-pragmatic considerations clearly worked jointly to shape the movement. There is the need, therefore, to interpret records carefully, questioning the nomenclatures of revolt and resistance on the one hand, while recognizing the perspectives of the administrator-writer, or missionary, on the other.

Women's role in the *hul* and later movements has been acknowledged, yet is invisible in colonial and post-colonial accounts. In the past few years, however, there has been a deliberate attempt by the women's movement in Jharkhand to highlight women's active participation. Phulo and Janho have been claimed as sisters of the leaders Sidho and Kanhu, fighting hand-in-hand in the Santal *hul*. The purpose perhaps is to resist marginalization by demonstrating women's equal role in society and social movements, on par with men, both in their daily struggles for survival and in the more overt and violent rebellions. One needs to understand this portrayal in the context of the struggle for a separate state, based on the logic of a different social organization that seeks to counter the marginality experienced by the *adivasis* vis-à-vis the mainstream state and society. In presenting such a unified community, however, it has ignored gender inequalities.

I have not found any evidence in the records or folklore to support this claim, though there is mention of a sister named Lilmuni.[9] According to the narrative of Chotrae Desmanjhi, a 14- or 15-year-old boy during the *hul*, Sidho and Kanhu ordered all women to be married to avoid violation, and in fear, people obeyed (Skresfrud, 1928). There seems

[8]The essence of millenarianism, as reflected in the new millennium, is the hope of a complete change in the world, to make it a world without deficiencies.

[9]*Sido Kanhukin Hullet' Katha* (SKHK) gives the names of six persons: Sido, Kanhu, Cand, Bhaero, Podo Kuar and Lilmuni; Ms. 8vo 1448, in vol. M (Santalia: 0381) or Ms. Fol. 1686-V-1 (Santalia: 2468) Oslo Collection.

evidence from anonymous narratives in the Norwegian mission's Santal archives that when they came to power, Sidho and Kanhu themselves took beautiful girls, daughters and wives of other men, and rapes were common (Anderson, 2005: 40). The order, however, points not just to the physical risks facing unmarried women but to other elements of women's role in the struggle and society as well. Men could not constantly be on the move and in battle without the support of women to look after their homes and cattle. When men attacked particular households, the women went with them to collect the loot, mostly grain, landing many women too in jail (Guha, 1983). But more, the giving of this order reflects the need to control women's sexuality, an articulation of women as a form of property—to be protected, just like land.

## AFTERMATH OF THE *HUL*: THE BEGINNING OF LAND SETTLEMENTS

The *hul* lasted over a year and was suppressed by the use of force, killing more than 10,000 Santals including the leaders Sidho and Kanhu. Yet, it had been successful in highlighting at least some of the elements of exploitation and harassment of the local people, and also the significance of land, both economic and spiritual, to the Santals. Attempts at conciliation followed. A separate district of the Santal Parganas was formed.[10] The Santals got back their lands, some found their cattle and for others, wage employment on the railways helped earn and save money (Hunter, 1996[1868]: 176). The aim of the new administration was to establish direct communication between the people and their rulers and render the appointment of Bengali intermediaries superfluous. The Santals were to be their own police, lawyers were to be excluded from the courts, and the court procedures were to be simplified (Man, 1983). While supporting the image of the Santal as a 'noble savage' and as an 'industrious race', the creation of a district named after the Santals was also a way of undermining the power of the Paharias, who continued to oppose the colonial rulers.

While the structure of government changed, the guiding principles continued to be the same, based on the characteristics of the Santals

[10]The Act XXXVII of 1855, making this a separate district, removed it from the ambit of the general laws and regulations.

identified by Francis Buchanan (1810–11) namely, 'their contempt of Hindu prejudices, their superstitious belief in witchcraft and their strong communal instincts' (McPherson, 1909: 31). The first led to a form of protectionism of the Santals and Paharias from the rapaciousness of the Hindu moneylenders and even petty officers such as the *amins,* reflected both in the subsequent land settlements and in the restoration of authority to the Santal village headmen. The second prepared the way for missionary activities of 'civilising the savage mind', leading to the setting up of the Lutheran Mission in Benagaria in 1871 by Lars Skresfrud, a Norwegian, barely 22 years old at that time. He soon put together not just the rudiments of Santal grammar and a dictionary, but also a collection of traditions and customs. This was completed by his successor Rev. P. O. Bodding, who arrived in 1890 and led the mission from 1910 when Skresfrud died, until 1922, after which he focused entirely on scholarly tasks, including the collection of Santal folk-tales.[11] The third principle in many ways guided the general administration systems, both civil and criminal. The society was seen as simple and homogenous, and the complex inter-relationships already in existence between different groups were ignored. The headman or *majhi* was given responsibility for revenue collection, and settling forest and waste tracts for cultivation. This, however, was conditional on the regular payment of rents. The accountability of the *majhi*, whether as a representative of the people or of the state, became ambiguous, and the contradictions have persisted to the present day, as seen in the last chapter.

A few years after the Santal *hul*, rents were again enhanced, with non-payment leading to the eviction of headmen from their office and lands.[12] Moneylenders used the courts to gain legal title over their debtors' possessions (MacDougall, 1985). Signs of resistance were visible again. Large meetings were organized, crowds gathered to complain against the *zamindars*. Property disputes peaked in 1861

[11]Much information on *adivasi* language and culture in Jharkhand is derived from missionary work and records. Bodding's contribution vis-à-vis the Santals, especially the Santal dictionary, or Hoffman's Encyclopaedia Mundarica, a detailed account of the Mundari language, has yet to be surpassed. Of course, one needs to remember that their documentation of customs and traditions was interpreted from their own perspective as Christians, and as missionaries in India.

[12]Act X of 1859 allowed for the enforcement of all laws passed by the Governor General of India, unless the Santal Parganas were especially exempted from their operation.

(Report of the Administrator of Criminal Justice, Calcutta). Bengalis started panicking and leaving the district.

To avoid a repeat of 1855, the government passed the Santal Pargana Settlement Regulation III in 1872. Apart from making the Santal Parganas a Non-Regulation district, that is, exempt from the general laws, this sought to limit interest rates on credit to 24 per cent, and restored headmen to their positions. It also recommended that a land survey and settlement be conducted. Browne Wood, who was responsible for this, was born in Calcutta in 1822, had joined the civil service and risen from the ranks to become the Deputy Commissioner (Santal Parganas) in 1860. He held the joint office as Settlement Officer from 1873–9.

The first land settlement in the region, the Wood settlement, demarcated village boundaries, identified forest, irrigation and grazing rights, and listed the number of houses and ploughs. An 'eye measurement' of land was conducted, class by class, based on the principle of an honest guess rather than accuracy (as the operation needed to be done cheaply). The rent was fixed in consultation with and negotiated by the headman for a period of 7 to 10 years. The task of distributing the land and the rent payable amongst the *raiyat*s was left to the headman, the concept of communal control thus left untouched. The *majhi* got a 1 per cent commission from the rent collected or land in lieu thereof, for his services.

With the stability of tenure and fixity of rent provided by this Settlement, occupancy and cultivating rights became valuable. Following the famine of the early 1870s, however, a majority of Santals were indebted to the *mahajan*, having borrowed money and grains for consumption as well as payment of rents. To overcome the usury laws of Regulation III and the cap on interest rates to 24 per cent, moneylenders starting demanding land in repayment of debts. Between 1873–87 about half the cultivable land in the non-*Damin* portion of the Santal Parganas was sold. In the annual report for 1882, the Divisional Commissioner (DC) (from 1879–84) Mr W. B. Oldham observed that 'the bazar traders of Dumka had gradually absorbed all the Santal settlements in the vicinity ... and that a considerable portion of the lands of cultivators ... had passed into the hands of creditors' (McPherson, 1909: 45). The dispossessed party could file a suit through the *zamindar* or headman, but this rarely happened. The economically strong *dikus* could bribe the headman into silence. Many migrated to Assam, taken by labour contractors to clear the forests and develop tea plantations in that region.

The period following this settlement saw considerable internal differentiation amongst the Santals, with the *majhis* often settling land of those who had left the village in dire circumstances with their own kin, or even with moneylenders, in return for a payment, giving rise to new problems and tensions. As in other colonial contexts such as El Salvador, the change from communal to individual tenure was seen as a way to enhance production and, in turn, land revenue. However, this enabled wealthy landowners to expand their holdings, and led to a decline in the commons as well as a proportional rise in near-landlessness (Pearce, 1985). In many ways, it is the same today and those with money power control not just information, labour and product markets, but also the means of violence, particularly visible vis-à-vis women claimants, as discussed in detail in Chapter 7. One needs to recognize here that adapting to a process of modernity is not easy and often involves periods of compromise and internal struggle. The headmen in this case, were under pressure to pay the rents, and as the Report of the Santal Pargana Enquiry Committee of 1938 revealed, many headmen too lost their land during this period.

The response to widespread dispossession from their lands came in the form of diverse and broad-based resistance. The experience of the Santal *hul* had led to the recognition that militancy could not work against the military strength of the rulers. During the famine of 1874–5, a Santal village headman Bhagirath started a movement against the payment of rent, particularly on *mahua* trees (a major safeguard against famines), seized alienated lands and wrote petitions complaining to local officials about their renewed oppression.[13] In 1881, another faction of the Kherwars, as they were called, under Dubia Gossain, organized against the Census survey operations (MacDougall, 1985). These leaders gave a call for religious revitalization when they sensed

[13]For four years when they didn't pay rent, it got accumulated and finally they had to mortgage their lands. Called the Sardar Movement in Chota Nagpur, Birsa Munda drew much of his inspiration, content and format from this. He gave it a messianic form with considerable religious content (Singh, 1966).

a real threat to *adivasi* solidarity from various quarters: growing activities of the missionaries, migration to the plains of Bengal for paddy harvest work as well as the tea gardens of Assam and the increasing powers of the bureaucracy and courts vis-à-vis the headmen. They sought to adapt traditional beliefs and customs to the new circumstances, perceiving a threat both to their authority and beliefs by the cultural dominance of the Christians as political rulers and Hindus as the economic exploiters. Yet not only did the Kherwars assume the rituals and symbols of Hinduism (a reference point in terms of status), but also the emergence of a new leadership was based on the political consciousness imparted through education in Christian mission schools. Interestingly in the search of identity and recognition, the symbols of the oppressor often become the tools, and sometimes, the end itself.

In this movement, domination was seen not just in economic and agrarian terms (rents charged even during the famine), but also felt in political and religious spheres, with insults and sexual abuse used to injure people's dignity and social standing. Resistance was guided by the vision of an alternate social order based on social dignity and respect. The imagery of Sidho and Kanhu was invoked, and the idea that they had been instructed by the Supreme God (*marang buru*) to protect their community was asserted, even though militant action was largely avoided. The demand this time, had shifted from state protection to political power, but drew strategically on the notion of community identity, an 'imagined community' to use a phrase of Anderson's (1983), prevalent in the ruling discourse.

Writing about peasant movements in Andalusia, Spain, in the late nineteenth century, the well-known historian, Eric Hobsbawm, notes that the rise of revolutionism was not just a result of bad conditions and economic distress, nor a reflection of outside political movements such as the general strikes led by the Bolsheviks. It was also linked to the abolition of feudalism in 1813 and the introduction of capitalist legal and social relationships, driven by the markets and thus controlled by the wealthy. The ideology of the new peasant movement tried to counter this marginalization, economically, through a programme of common ownership, and politically, through anti-authoritarian, local governance structures. Rather than a 'precise set of economic and political demands, they were for a new moral order' (1971: 82) based on justice and freedom.

This element of identity formation based on an alternative morality was strong amongst the Santals, leading to the conscious building up of a distinct tradition by the leadership, what Gautam (1977) has called the process of 'Santalization'. The *Adivasi* Mahasabha, formed in 1938 by Jaipal Singh in Ranchi, to improve the status of the *adivasis* and lead the fight against the *dikus*, emerged as a full-fledged political party in 1951. An appeal for a separate state was made to the States Reorganisation Commission in 1956, but this was rejected on several grounds: that the *adivasis* formed a minority in the region, they did not have a common language and finally, that the economic balance of the region would be disturbed. It thereafter grew into a separatist movement, taking the form of a mass party, including both *adivasis* and other working classes settled in the region over several generations. It led a mini-renaissance, concentrating on the development of the script, literature and an independent identity for the region, to bolster its struggle for a separate state. It is perhaps the confidence in a new world and faith in their identity that made the modern movement for Jharkhand politically effective and ultimately successful, even though the present administrative reality does not stand up to the test of this strategy. But as in other nationalist movements, in the process of making political claims, the role and rights of women become more and more circumscribed.

## Detailing Land Rights: Surveys and Settlements

The Wood settlement, as already mentioned, rather than bringing stability in land tenures, led to rapid transfers of land, growing economic differentiation and renewed resistance. Mr Richard Carstairs, who remained DC for 13 years from 1886–1900, made an elaborate enquiry in 1886, leading to the passage of Regulation II the same year to stop all transfers and mutation of land.[14] After 1887, therefore, no further sales took place, but transfers continued in other forms, with *mahajan*s

[14]Mr Carstairs spent almost half his career (1872–1903) in the Santal Parganas. He gave a sympathetic account of the *hul* in his novel *Harma's Village* and left a detailed account of his life as a district officer.

gaining a foothold in many villages, supported by the police and civil administration. While overtly the settlement sought to placate the demands of 1855, the need for revenues and for cheap labour remained; nor did the structures of colonial rule change. The gains for the Santals could, therefore, at best be partial.

In 1898, a new survey and settlement operation was initiated by Hugh McPherson, appointed as the Settlement Officer.[15] Local men, a number of them Santals, were trained as field staff for the survey. Rules were prepared for the disposal of illicit alienations, rent settlement, preparing the village record of rights and duties (including a statement of custom) and for appointment of headmen. Village lists recorded every holding, and where these had emerged after the last settlement also indicated the form of acquisition, whether purchase, mortgage, sub-lease, gift or reclamation (McPherson, 1909: 58). While the earlier settlements had not touched the arena of individual rents, this was now done, as it was felt that rent enhancements would otherwise adversely affect those *raiyats* who had invested in extending or improving their lands. Individual rents were not to be increased by more than 50 per cent (33 per cent in the *Damin*), except in cases where the present rents were so low that an 'increase would cause no hardship' (Ibid: 68–70).

McPherson wrote in the Annual Report of 1904, 'thirty years after the first settlement ... three-fourths of the *raiyati* lands of the tract are still in the hands of old *raiyats* and their heirs, while one-fourth has been the subject of transfer, legal or illegal . ... We have interfered with nothing that was ... not prima facie objectionable, e.g., the passage of the lands of bonafide cultivators, aboriginal or non-aboriginal, into the hands of the foreign *mahajan* class' (McPherson, 1909: 79). Earlier in 1901, the DC of the Santal Parganas from 1900–6, Mr C.H. Bompas had suggested the need for relaxing the rules in relation to land transfers, as 45 per cent of the population of the district as *diku*. Though this was not done, and the discourse of protectionism persisted, the pressure for revenue collection often led to the opposite in practice.

It was Mr Bompas who drafted a note on the subject of partition, inheritance and marriage, which formed the basis for the formulation

[15]It was assumed that the task would be completed in 18 months, consisting of both a traverse and cadastral survey. In reality, the first phase took till 1904, and was continued in 1907–8.

Table 4.1: Changes in Land Holdings by Gender in Chuapara

| Caste | McPherson (1898–1908) | | | | Current (1978-the present) | | | |
|---|---|---|---|---|---|---|---|---|
| | F. No. | Total | F acre | M acre | F.No. | Total | F acre | M acre |
| Santal | 0 | 13 | 0 | 95 | 1 | 14 | 2.9 | 149.1 |
| Kol | 2 | 6 | 4.5 | 30.5 | 0 | 6 | 0 | 38.2 |
| Total | 2 | 21 | 4.5 | 127 | 1 | 22 | 2.9 | 189.6 |
| Per cent | 9.5 | 100 | 3.4 | 96.6 | 4.5 | 100 | 1.5 | 98.5 |

*Source:* Land Records, Chuapara.

Table 4.2: Changes in Land Holdings by Gender in Bagdiha

| Caste | McPherson (1898–08) | | | | Gantzer (1924–29) | | | | Current (1978-the present) | | | |
|---|---|---|---|---|---|---|---|---|---|---|---|---|
| | F.No. | Total | F acre | Macre | F.No. | Total | F acre | Macre | F.No. | Total | F acre | Macre |
| Santal | 1 | 31 | 3.4 | 290.1 | 2 | 38 | 4.7 | 411.1 | 6 | 52 | 12.3 | 402 |
| SC | 2 | 11 | 1.2 | 10.6 | 1 | 8 | 1.2 | 21.5 | 2 | 8 | 1.1 | 18.6 |
| *Teli* | 1 | 11 | 5.2 | 22.1 | 1 | 9 | 11.6 | 24.4 | 5 | 23 | 6.6 | 36.3 |
| *Kumhar* | 0 | 11 | 0 | 25.6 | 0 | 12 | 0 | 41.4 | 8 | 26 | 1.9 | 18.6 |
| Muslim | 0 | 1 | 0 | 4.3 | 0 | 1 | 0 | 7.2 | 3 | 1 | 3.1 | 4.1 |
| Total | 4 | 74 | 9.8 | 365.2 | 4 | 76 | 17.6 | 520.8 | 24 | 118 | 25 | 514.6 |
| Per cent | 5.4 | 100 | 2.4 | 97.7 | 5.2 | 100 | 3.3 | 96.8 | 20 | 100 | 4.6 | 95.4 |

*Source*: Land Records, Bagdiha.

of the settlement rules. He noted that daughters did not inherit a share of land, even though McPherson had found many women in cultivating possession of land (Ibid: 123). As many men were absent, having migrated to Assam in the preceding two decades, the names of women left behind to cultivate, were in fact recorded in this survey. The recording of women in the McPherson Settlement (See Tables 4.1 and 4.2 for data on the study villages) has often been attributed to McPherson's ignorance of Santal law. Whether intended or not, this gave the woman in question an absolute title for life.

This settlement was a turning point in both property and gender relations. A complex system of shared family control was replaced by the privileging of an individual, usually male. Women's voices and rights were abruptly erased as men's were recorded. The logic for this derives from modern capitalist ideas where land is seen as a commodity, under private and determinate ownership. Revenue payments could be fixed on every plot of land and collected in regular instalments from identifiable proprietors. Men were preferred as proprietors, as it was believed that women could not interact easily with the legal and administrative machinery, an assumption based on the roles and expectations from women in nineteenth-century English society. While the task of protecting and defending the land had indeed been a part of male identity, production and the control over produce had always been shared. In fact, land was best controlled and managed in the plurality of relationships, the example from McPherson himself confirming this, with women cultivating when their men migrated.

Alongside this shift to individual titles, a key change from the point of social control was the setting up of the settlement court as the final court of appeal for all objections. That contestation was widespread is evident from the fact that more than 55,000 objections and 5000 appeals were filed. The significance of this step was that it set up, for the first time, an alternative mechanism for dispute resolution, distinct from the authority of the *majhi* and village council, thus officially initiating a process of undermining their authority in mediating land use and transfer.

Delayed by the war, the next settlement was initiated in 1922 under the charge of Vincent Ellis Davies as Settlement Officer and J. F. Gantzer as his assistant. During this Settlement, there was a much more rigid interpretation of Santal laws of inheritance, and consequently, a refusal to record women. Their authority undermined by the establishment of settlement courts to resolve disputes in relation to land inheritance, as well as the granting of individual land titles by the state rather than themselves, the *Parganaits, Desmanjhis, Sardars*[16] and other community leaders organized a meeting in Dumka on 15 February 1916. They sought to reinterpret tradition to make provision for the security of women alongside male kin-groups. They identified clear rights for both daughters and widows (Bodding et al., 1942). As Gantzer comments,

> the rules against female succession among Santals ... are changing owing to the force of public opinion ... the change which is occurring is in the direction

[16] *Parganait* refers to a head of a cluster of villages, *desmanjhi,* his assistant in the cluster, and *sardar*, a village headman, known also as *majhi.*

of ameliorating the condition of women and giving them a more assured footing in the family. During the course of the revision settlement operations, the daughters of a deceased Santal have sometimes been recorded as his heirs not only without opposition from the agnates but at their request (quoted in Archer, 1984[1946]: 685).

Following consultations with the Santal male elite in 1916, exceptions came to be allowed. The settlement operations were completed in 1935, with 62,787 objection suits and 5528 appeals having been filed during the process (Gantzer, 1936). This vast number was a clear sign that protectionism wasn't working, and that there were loopholes in the agrarian laws that were being exploited by different interests. But more important, it reflected a move by the male leadership to reassert their moral authority by demonstrating that individual titling was an alien concept in a society based on principles of community support and shared control. This last entailed a support to women's land rights and explicit recognition of their critical roles in both production and reproduction. Interestingly, while several writers have noted the existence of individual rights, even if circumscribed by accountability to the community (Roy Burman, 1992), the communitarian image has nevertheless persisted, enhanced by the propaganda of the Jharkhand movement, seeking to provide an institutional alternative to the liberal, individualistic, market-driven one.

The Santal Pargana Inquiry Committee, set up shortly afterwards to review the problems encountered during the Gantzer Settlement, received a large number of representations regarding the settlement operations, seen as 'defective owing to numerous errors of fraud and negligence' (1938: 32). While not yielding to the demand to contest the entire settlement in the civil courts, the Committee recommended the setting up of a tribunal for correction of errors in the records. Following its recommendation on the need to codify tenancy law, the Santal Pargana Tenancy Act (SPTA) was passed soon after independence in 1949. It carried on the legacy of protectionism by re-stating the non-transferability clause (Section 20), yet in terms of women's rights, it also carried forward the flaws that had emerged in Gantzer's account. Women's land claims were recorded as gifts rather than rights, their interests subsumed under those of their male kin.

## THE SECOND *HUL*: DID INDEPENDENCE MAKE A DIFFERENCE?

7 July1966, Bagdiha:

One adult from each house reported at Manik Marandi's fields early in the morning, with some paddy seedlings in his/her hands. More than 100 people had gathered to plant his land. On paper, Manik owned a lot of land, yet this was all with the *mahajans* and he had nothing to eat. The actions were repeated the following day on Jhina's land. The struggle had started.

In 1966, a movement evocatively called the *hul* Jharkhand (Jharkhand rebellion) was launched from Bagdiha. It aimed at releasing land as well as securing debt relief. It raised the issue of *adivasis'* rights as citizens of an independent India. Despite the presence of the SPTA, in the decades after independence, exploitation by *mahajan*s, in collusion with the official machinery, had increased. While the Tribal Sub-Plans had been introduced to provide coordinated services to the *adivasis*, with limited budgets and lack of commitment on the ground, they appeared as mere statements of concern rather than real tools for development, largely failing in their objective to improve the conditions of the *adivasis*. They did not help transform the unequal social and economic structures, developed over 200 years of colonial rule. As one of the leaders of *hul* Jharkhand, Kunjiram Tudu said,

*Mahajan*s controlled the land. If a person borrowed Rs 100, he would record it as Rs 300, three *man*[17] of rice instead of one. As the Santal had nothing in the house, they got an order from the civil court, planted a red flag on the land and confiscated the crop—half as principal, the remaining as interest. At times, they took over the land. The police and the courts supported the *mahajan*s (21 December 2000).

Between 1961–4, Kunjiram along with Sibu Murmu, who in 1972 became a Member of the Legislative Assembly (MLA), and a few leaders from the Communist Party of India (CPI), travelled through the villages of the Santal Parganas, recording stories of oppression of the Santals by the *mahajan*s. According to Dharam Marandi, the then headman of Bagdiha 'Moneylending increased from the 1930s.

[17]*Man* is a measure that equals about 40 kg.

People started losing their land. They had nothing to eat and worked as bonded labour. Many ran away to Bengal.' Detailed surveys revealed that almost each household had lost some or all of its land and depended on uncertain and low-paid wage labour for survival. People here were dispossessed due to usury.[18]

A Scheduled Caste woman narrated, 'My husband Dukhan worked in Bishto Gorain's house. He was paid one rupee a month and given one snack of *murri* during the day. We could not live on this, so went to my parent's home in Sikaripara. Flight was the only answer. We came back during the *hul* Jharkhand, and harvested our land.' The act of harvesting was carefully planned, since the fields had been planted by the *mahajan* and not themselves. The field to be harvested was identified and hundreds would gather there before dawn to start cutting, bundling and transporting the grain before the *mahajan* could find out and call the police. The grain was taken to the compound of the headman. It was divided into three parts: the first part for the owner of the field, the second for the common village fund and the third part to finance the movement. The village fund was used to set up a grain *gola* (grain bank), to provide both seed for planting and grain for consumption to those who didn't have any. This prevented them from returning to the *mahajans*. Apart from such forcible harvesting, other direct action strategies included the non-repayment of loans, thefts of grain from *mahajan*s' fields and court cases. Mass meetings were held; the word spread through the district and so did the resistance.

By and large the movement was peaceful and there was little bloodshed as compared to other 'land grab' movements by evicted tenants and the landless, fuelled by revolutionary student activists, during this period in Bihar (Das, 1993). A few violent incidents did occur, as it is often difficult to control an excited mob. On 28 February 1968, for instance, Arjun Dehri, a Paharia, apparently went to Kulapather, the village of his *mahajan*, Shankar Pal, in a drunken state, and started shouting abuses. Somehow, a house was burnt down at the same time. Arjun was assaulted and killed. Soon, the *mahajan* and his brother were both found dead. Most of the leaders of the *hul* Jharkhand, including Sibu Murmu and Kunjiram Tudu were charged

[18]Records of this movement including the surveys conducted have all been destroyed due to lack of proper storage, so it has been reconstructed from several interviews.

for murder under Section 302 of the Indian Penal Code. Several including Dharam were arrested and thrown into jail for two years. No evidence was found and ultimately they were released.

The movement peaked in 1966–7. If grain was found on a *mahajan*'s bullock cart, it was captured and unloaded; *mahajan*s were not allowed to cultivate Santal lands, no one, man or woman, went to work for the *mahajan*s. Several of the *mahajan*s burnt their *khatas* (records) and fled the villages, returning only when the movement subsided. In 1967 a coalition ministry was formed in Bihar with the support of the CPI. Though the coalition lasted only eleven months, circulars were issued in favour of the *adivasis* and the oppressed. Several of the arrest warrants were cancelled. The pressure once again increased after 1969, but the villagers remained united and carried on the struggle.

The *hul* Jharkhand was not really a rebellion (*hul*) in the strict sense of the word, but rather a movement to express discontent and demand rights and recognition as equal citizens of a democracy. Yet it drew upon the imagery of the Santal *hul* of 1855, as has the entire Jharkhand movement, evoking notions of human justice to strengthen group solidarity. A drama group put together by the local youth moved from village to village along with the leaders recounting the story of resistance to domination, of the desire for independence and political autonomy and the fight against economic oppression. Tales were told of Tirka *majhi* single-handedly attacking the Commissioner of Bhagalpur, and of the heroism of the brothers Sidho and Kanhu during the *hul*. Before each performance, which carried on through the night, people would discuss issues of exploitation by the landlords and moneylenders and the importance of regaining control over their land. Activities and strategies for the movement would also be discussed.

Women were actively involved during the *hul* Jharkhand, both in the process of planting and forcibly harvesting the fields, and more importantly, in the provisioning of food and shelter to their men, who were often on the run. Police attempts to arrest the leaders were, in most cases, foiled with the assistance of women. Once in Bagdiha, Sibu and Kunjiram, hiding in Dharam's house, heard the police come. The women of the house gave the leaders their own clothes (*lungi-panchi*) and the leaders escaped dressed as women. Sidho and Kanhu, it is believed, had also been adept at moving from village to village, avoiding capture for long periods.

Sibu's and Kunjiram's wives worked with the other women, although in the public gatherings, it was the men who were seen as leaders. The male leaders were, however, unanimous in supporting women's claims to land. Kunjiram said, 'Now beating and violence has increased. People are being misled that the girl gains rights to marital property so should not have a claim on parental property. This is wrong. Divorce is easy, so she needs the rights. If she wants, she can give it to her brother. In tradition women had rights and *hul* Jharkhand believed in this.'

In 1967, the *Hul* Jharkhand Party was registered and entered the field of electoral politics. By 1972, however, differences had emerged on strategy, financial transactions and leadership, marking the beginning of its collapse. When a movement becomes institutionalized as a political party, it tends to lose its flexibility and innovative features; it gets routinized and ceases to be a movement (Rao, 1984). Stephen Marandi, the JMM MLA from Dumka[19] explained this, 'In a political party, priorities change. Political workers are not equally motivated towards social change; often their own survival in politics becomes an issue, and thus limits them to deriving incremental benefits from the state. Social change needs a *jan andolan* (people's movement) which only a social organization can lead.' Formalization of a popular movement exposed it to oppression by the police and administration on the one hand, and charges against the leaders for using collective resources for private gains, on the other.

Soon after in 1976, Sibu Soren, who had been involved in a movement against *mahajan*s in Tundi block of Dhanbad district (Iyer and Maharaj, 1985), came to the Santal Parganas, and relaunched the *dhan katai* or forcible harvesting movement, to regain control over their land and produce. Those who had not got back their land during *hul* Jharkhand, reclaimed it now, armed with the knowledge that land was not transferable and the ownership was legitimately theirs. The struggle often turned violent, with several *adivasis* and non-*adivasis* succumbing to bullet injuries during this phase.[20] Yet the movement spread rapidly, showing a face of *adivasi* solidarity.

[19]He is presently the Deputy Chief Minister of Jharkhand, winning the Dumka seat as an independent candidate. He resigned from the JMM following a dispute with the party chief over allocation of seats.

[20]Sibu Soren was arrested in August 2004 in relation to one such massacre at Chirudih in 1978.

The difference between these two phases of the agrarian struggle in the Santal Parganas relates both to ideology and practice. Sibu Soren gave the call to the Santals to reoccupy all land that belonged to their ancestors. It was a messianic call for equality and social justice and excited the imagination of people. The execution was often violent and ended in bloodshed. Though his agrarian radicalism—the struggle against land-grabbers and usurers—was combined with a 19-point constructive agenda for social change, economic development and political decentralization including tree plantation, the setting up of grain *golas*, multi-cropping, wasteland reclamation and livestock-raising, he did not propose a practical strategy for implementation. Social themes such as the call for universal elementary education, the organization of '*baisis*' or village councils for local justice, and social reform such as prohibition were also included. Once Soren left Dumka, however, the programme collapsed. As in other peasant millenarian movements (e.g. in Sicily), while there was a commitment to a concrete set of activities, peasant leagues and associations were not organized to implement them on the ground, making the movement largely spontaneous, and also short-lived.[21]

The *hul* Jharkhand on the other hand had more limited aims, trying to reclaim land that was in their names, but over which effective occupancy had been lost. Lawyers and other professionals, who could assist with legal action and the formalization of claims, backed it, giving it a more concrete reality. There was also a constructive programme that included the setting up of grain *golas*, encouraging the cultivation of a *rabi* crop and attempting to address problems of survival and poverty. While there was a better organizational mechanism at the top, systematic grassroots organization was not adequate, here also.

Nevertheless, the widespread agrarian and anti-*mahajani* movements in the Santal Parganas and indeed, other parts of Jharkhand during the late-1960s and early-1970s, led to a spate of state action and legislation. In 1969, the Bihar Scheduled Areas Regulation was

[21]While earlier peasant movements in Europe reflected some form of village anarchist organisation, in Sicily, peasant protest was fitted into a more elaborate Marxist political framework. Soren's Jharkhand Mukti Morcha too was set up with support from the Marxist Coordination Committee in 1972–3. Like the Santal Parganas, Sicily too lagged behind other parts of Italy both socially and economically, its peasants poverty-stricken and exploited, relatively undifferentiated in their misery (Hobsbawm, 1971: 95).

passed that sought strict control over illegal transfers of land,[22] reinforcing the provisions of Section 20 of the SPTA. In 1970, Indira Gandhi, then Prime Minister of India, appointed the Ao Commission to enquire into the unrest in Dumka district. Following the report of the Commission, which acknowledged the oppression by the *mahajans*, the Bihar Moneylenders Act was passed in 1974. All moneylenders were to be registered and had to provide a report of their transactions including money due to them, within 30 days, to the state government. No reports were received. In fact most *mahajans* in the villages destroyed their records. Clearly rather than a radical land reform agenda, the state preferred a paternalistic one. When the *mahajans* ultimately returned to the villages, they altered their modus operandi considerably and set up shops and petty businesses, which sold goods on credit, rather than moneylending per se.

## GOVERNMENT INITIATIVE ON LAND DISTRIBUTION

Soon after independence, the Government of India, with a stated commitment to distributive justice, initiated a land reform and redistribution programme. But as Roy Burman (1992) has pointed out, land reform has a different meaning in the *adivasi* context, as there are not many intermediary right holders. There is also much less differentiation in the distribution of holdings by size. Further, land is not considered an economic resource alone, but is also a symbol of community, kin and male identity. Under the programme of land reforms, the government here has mainly distributed surplus land, both *bhoodan* (land-gifts, collected under the Land Ceiling Act) and those classified as government wastelands, to those who do not have land. A review of the land distribution in Dumka during 1998–9 (Table 4.3) reveals several interesting features.

Firstly, land distribution is absent in the largely tribal and forested blocks of Kathikund and Gopikandar. Here, people have reclaimed land on their own from the forests and then got it classified as government

[22]For STs the period of lease was increased to 30 years from 12 years for immovable property before a transfer was permitted. The DC could evict a transferee without payment of compensation and restore land to the ST *raiyat*. The only exception was for buildings or permanent structures on that land.

Table 4.3 Land Distribution in Dumka Subdivision, Dumka District, 1998–99

| S. No | Block | SC | | ST | | Backward | | Women | | Others | | Total | |
|---|---|---|---|---|---|---|---|---|---|---|---|---|---|
| | | No. | Acre | No. | Acre | No. | Acre | No. | Acre | No. | Acre | No. | Acre |
| 1 | Dumka | 56 | 10.4 | 129 | 102.6 | 0 | 0 | 0 | 0 | 31 | 19 | 198 | 132 |
| 2 | Jama | 4 | 1.5 | 17 | 6.3 | 23 | 13.2 | 0 | 0 | 0 | 0 | 44 | 21 |
| 3 | Jarmundi | 11 | 2.1 | 7 | 8 | 8 | 1 | 0 | 0 | 1 | 4.2 | 20 | 14.5 |
| 4 | Sariayahat | 0 | 0 | 0 | 0 | 0 | 0 | 0 | 0 | 0 | 0 | 0 | 0 |
| 5 | Sikaripara | 7 | 4.2 | 32 | 16 | 0 | 0 | 0 | 0 | 12 | 7.8 | 51 | 28 |
| 6 | Kathikund | 0 | 0 | 0 | 0 | 0 | 0 | 0 | 0 | 0 | 0 | 0 | 0 |
| 7 | Ramgarh | 0 | 0 | 15 | 6.8 | 0 | 0 | 0 | 0 | 0 | 0 | 15 | 6.8 |
| 8 | Gopikandar | 0 | 0 | 0 | 0 | 0 | 0 | 0 | 0 | 0 | 0 | 0 | 0 |
| 9 | Raneswar | 11 | 22.5 | 7 | 9.3 | 8 | 13.4 | 0 | 0 | 10 | 14 | 36 | 59 |
| 10 | Masalia | 3 | 1.2 | 0 | 0 | 1 | 0.4 | 0 | 0 | 1 | 0.15 | 5 | 1.7 |
| | Dumka SD | 92 | 42 | 207 | 149.1 | 40 | 27 | 0 | 0 | 37 | 49.1 | 369 | 263.2 |
| | Per Cent | 24.5 | 16 | 55 | 56 | 10.5 | 10 | 0 | 0 | 10 | 18 | 100 | 100 |

*Source:* Records of the Assistant Commissioner (AC) Land, Dumka.

lands at the time of registration of titles. In Chuapara, 18 households got plots of land registered in the year 1992–3. They have even been provided some material assistance (Rs 500) to make this land productive. Two anomalies emerge. On the one hand, while titles to these lands have been notified in the revenue records, with a view to enhancing settled cultivation and the generation of land revenue, a lot of these lands continue to be recorded as forest area by the Forest Survey of India. Following interim judicial pronouncements by the Supreme Court under the ongoing *Godavarman case* (Writ Petition (Civil) No. 202/95), the ambit of forests and the Forest Department has been extended to include all lands 'recorded' as forests. According to the District Forest Officer of Dumka, if any such land has been settled for other purposes after the Supreme Court judgement of 1996, then such settlement can be cancelled. But before doing so, each state government is required to prepare statements on the situation of forest-dwellers in their state. This has not been done, yet on 27 July 2002 (vide letter no. 1848), the Settlement Officer (DC, Dumka) ordered that all land that was earlier forestland, including *jhanti* (scrub and wasteland under community control as per Section 27, SPTA), *rakha* (forest under the control of the landlord/proprietor) and *sakhu* jungle (*sal* forest, usually the *jaherthan* or sacred grove) should be reclaimed for forest uses and the settlement thereon cancelled. On 4 March 2003 (letter no. 178–II), the Settlement Officer reported handing back almost 2000 acres of land to the Forest Department. The *pattas* on these lands have been cancelled, though eviction has not taken place. The order however opens the door for the harassment of *adivasis*, particularly the poorest among them, who live in remote, forest villages, and out of necessity clear and cultivate forestlands.

There is a second anomaly from the livelihood perspective. Being virgin land, converting these into paddy lands needs substantial investment of both capital and labour, which is often not forthcoming. The same is true in the case of ceiling-surplus lands, which are usually of poor quality. When talking of women's rights to land, the issue of quality, though critical, is often conveniently overlooked. To silence advocates for women's land rights, poor quality 'wasteland' is often given to women, which they find difficult to make productive.[23] Further, since the total amount of such 'surplus' or 'wasteland' available for distribution is negligible,[24] it is unlikely to influence gender or property relations in any significant way.

Secondly, while *adivasis* have received 56 per cent of the land distributed, the allotment to the category of 'others', is 0.6 acre per person more than to the *adivasis*. While constituting 10 per cent of the households, the 'others' have received 18.5 per cent of the land. Much of this is urban land, but it also includes some agricultural land. It is true that they are often landless, having come into the area as traders rather than cultivators, but they are not necessarily poor. The use of landlessness as a criterion for allocation in this particular context, apart from revealing a lack of understanding of social relations, could lead to enhanced social conflict.

Most recently, in 1994–5, in line with the Eighth Plan call to allot 40 per cent of ceiling-surplus land to women, the then DC of Dumka issued an order to prioritize women in the distribution of land. Some discussion on this seems to have taken place with a few women NGO activists, but this focus is not reflected in the land distribution data. In fact, the additional column on women only serves to highlight the lack of implementation. Government initiative in terms of redistribution then, does not seem to have touched women much in real terms, but certainly has contributed to the discourse around the legitimacy of women's land claims. Many women in Bagdiha, for instance, have used this discourse during the current settlement process, (initiated in 1978 but not yet completed), to get the land registered in their names (see Table 4.2).

The state then appears to be a socially differentiated and often uncoordinated institution, with different people and departments working with varied ideologies and understandings of both gender roles and land relationships. Some laws and policies are acted upon in the public domain and others are not. Created at fixed points in

[23]The few successful cases in India reveal considerable investments from NGOs, such as the Deccan Development Society in Andhra Pradesh, backing women's wasteland development initiatives.

[24]Agarwal (1998) has calculated that for India as a whole, surplus land is only three million hectares or 1.6 per cent of arable land.

time, these often fail to keep pace with the new meanings of land and livelihood in changing times, ending up in contradictory positions, as visible in the case of revenue and forest policies.

## MODERNIZATION AND RESOURCE CONFLICTS

Despite clear rights to forest resources, forest management seems to have been subjected to substantial local variations. It became a zone of 'exceptional administration', pointing to the controversies over types of knowledge, diversity of the region and conflicting priorities within the government (Sivaramakrishnan, 1997: 89). Most of the forests in the Santal Parganas were destroyed in the 1970s. After the *hul* Jharkhand, afraid to ask the Santals for land in lieu of debts taken, the *mahajans* insisted on cash repayment, met largely by felling trees. Villagers in and around Bagdiha noted that this was the time when the village forest was decimated. The Forest Department too was engaged in routine fellings, but as no compensatory plantation was ever done, all the forests soon disappeared. Critical as a livelihood support, for fuel wood and for providing petty cash through the collection and sale of non-timber forest produce, the 1980s saw strong resistance against forest felling and struggles over forest and water rights, neglected in the previous phases of land struggle.[25]

By the late 1980s, with state repression accompanied by ameliorative laws and policies, the project for agrarian reform went into the background, but the larger movement for political autonomy gained ground. An interesting issue in all these movements appears to be the engagement with processes of modernization and the conflicts over resources that this inevitably created. Where the movement is left to the spontaneity of the peasants as in the *hul*, the process of change is slow and at best, incomplete. But where the movement is fitted into the framework of an organization, even at the risk of losing some of its flexibility, it is transformed to make change achievable. This process is often catalysed by forces from outside, be it political parties, the Church or a revolutionary movement, which give it a voice

[25]Father Antony Murmu, a Catholic priest, led a major one in Borio block of Sahebganj district. He was shot by the Police on 19 April 1985 (PUCL, 1985).

to overcome what Huizer calls the 'culture of repression' (1986). Rituals and symbols can serve as shorthand for collective aspirations, but as the movement matures, the need for them declines. During the Santal *hul*, for instance, *sal* branches were exchanged, conveying a message of solidarity and commitment to the struggle. During the Kherwar movement, vegetarianism was promoted amongst the followers. Such symbols are no longer required today, with a general acceptance of common cause.

The Jharkhand parties in particular began to engage with modern politics and elections from the early 1970s, while keeping up the theme of political autonomy. In 1995, the Jharkhand Autonomous Area Council (JAAC) was formed within Bihar. There were several problems in its functioning, particularly as it was not adequately financed. The movement for a separate state was revived. The first government of Jharkhand, following its creation in the year 2000, was, however, formed by the Bharatiya Janata Party (BJP) and its allies, rather than the Jharkhand parties, who in one form or another, had struggled for this cause for the last 60 years.

The response of the Jharkhand government so far, to the challenges created by decades of exploitation of the *adivasis* is far from positive. The Vision 2010 document for Jharkhand clearly outlines some of the policy directions and emphases of the new state. It reveals a focus on commercialization, export orientation and market development, both in the agricultural and industrial sectors. Issues of food security, inequities in resource distribution and control and growing destitution do not seem to be priorities (Rao, 2003). To support the new industrial policy, a high-level committee under the chairmanship of the former Chief Minister, Babulal Marandi, was appointed to review the existing tenancy legislations, both the Chota Nagpur and Santal Pargana Tenancy Acts, and suggest modifications. The debate is polarized between those who favour liberalization of the legislation to allow land transfers for industrial and urban development and those who support continued protection as the only way to withstand rapid landlessness and pauperization of the *adivasis*. The debate continues, but the demands of modernization have meant that people are losing land everyday to mining, construction and infrastructure.

Stone quarrying has expanded ten-fold in Sikaripara block of Dumka district since the formation of Jharkhand, based on informal lease agreements with the owners of the land. These lands will be rendered unusable for cultivation permanently, owing to the deep pits being gouged out and the removal of topsoil. Not only this, neighbouring plots and common lands that are currently being used for dumping mud and waste, are also gradually becoming unusable. The contractors are relatively wealthy *dikus,* while the landowners are Santals, who needing cash, are leasing out their land at cheap rates. A contract has also been given for coal mining in the Pachwara region of Pakur district, noted for its coal deposits as early as the mid-nineteenth century in the correspondence from Pontet. Without any prior consultation with the villagers, the land has now been acquired by the state. In both instances, the local villagers are organizing to save their land (Rao, 2005a). While in Sikaripara, the district officials have ignored the protest so far, in Pachwara, the police force has been alerted. Finding it difficult to deal with tactics such as road-blocks and sit-ins, the state is arresting key leaders to break the protest (PUCL, 2003). With increasing alienation and virtually no restoration of land taking place, to quote Stephen Marandi again, 'soon there will be another *hul*'.

And this resurgence of *adivasi* protest movements in relation to land and forest rights seems to have emerged in the form of mobilization around the Scheduled Tribes and other traditional forest dwellers (Recognition of Forest Rights) Act, 2006, this time at the national rather than local level. There has been heated debate between environmental conservationists and forest rights and *adivasi* activists before the passage of this Act. While the former warned that such a policy would contribute to destroying India's forest cover and biodiversity, the latter argued for the correction of 'historic injustices' by legitimizing *adivasi* rights to use forest resources and land for their livelihoods. *Adivasi* people have been repeatedly displaced without adequate resettlement and rehabilitation. They have also been subject to agrarian distress resulting from cuts in public investment in agriculture alongside the opening up of agriculture to global and national corporations. While the rules for implementation of the Act have only been notified on 1 January 2008, ambiguities remain in relation to implementation and monitoring mechanisms. With the debate between environmentalists and activists still raging, one wonders if this too will become a case of 'one step forwards and two backwards'.[26]

This Act too homogenizes *adivasis* in its discourse as backward, oppressed, forest-dependent people. Nevertheless, as mentioned in the last chapter, *adivasi* women draw their identity from a range of resources, forests and forest products being a major one. Securing the rights to forest produce and stemming back the growing tide of exclusion from the forests, is then likely to help women assert their identity, perhaps more so than men.

## THE STRUGGLE CONTINUES

This historical account reveals that while protectionism was consciously made a state policy by the colonial rulers and adopted after independence, displacement has continued. It has taken various forms, whether land alienation by the landlords and moneylenders, deforestation and denial of forest rights in both colonial and post-colonial times, or the displacement by large projects—dams, mines or industries—post-independence. Though policies were made in an attempt to solve issues of economic exploitation, they were unable to do so due to a fundamental contradiction of interests within the modern state. The promotion of a particular model of development, that focuses much more on industrial and urban development and production enhancement (embedded therein is the need to enhance revenues) rather than the rural, agricultural sector or indeed social development, especially in the last two decades, has placed the government on the side of the landlords and industrial-capitalists. Hence despite the rhetoric, land has continued to pass from the *adivasis* to the outsiders, be it the local *mahajan* or the urban industrialist.

At the same time, the process of land titling, led to a growth of individualism and consequent class formation, with *majhis* often involved in the process of both land accumulation for themselves and transferring it to their kin. Individualism, in terms of competition for scarce resources, further carried with it patriarchal values, with a preference for recording

[26]Papers by Rangarajan, Bhatia, Shah and Krishnaswamy in the *Economic and Political Weekly* debate on the Tribal Rights Bill, Vol 40: 47, 19–25 November 2005, pp. 4888–901.

land titles in men's names. But alienation and displacement have not remained unchallenged, either at the individual or collective levels. The decisions of the *majhi* are openly contested through the large number of objections and appeals filed in the settlement courts, where subsistence interests of different groups including women are involved. Alongside individual protests, there have also been collective protests, accelerating in recent years, against both individual exploiters and state interventions. The *baisis* set up by Sibu Soren, for instance, can be seen not just as a body to resolve material problems, but as an assertion of their autonomous identity, and also their capacity for administration and justice.[27] Resistance has different forms—everyday forms and everyone's forms—responsive to their particular constructions of the meaning of land, livelihood and community. While Jharkhand now has political autonomy, and Sidho and Kanhu have become visible images in the district, the 'promised land' is not yet achieved, and the voices of the common people continue to be unheard. Their statues are, however, a constant reminder of the need to struggle against injustice, to protect their land and identity.

The image of the 'noble savage', constantly violated by the outsider, and who one day rises in revolt, continues to be perpetuated alongside state intervention to both protect the 'simple' tribal and maintain law and order (by preventing violent rebellion). A parallel imagery can be evoked in the case of women. Their bravery and hard work are extolled, yet they are subordinated, with traditions often being invented and re-invented for this purpose. While Santal women work independently in the fields, go to the market and migrate for work, they are also seen as naïve and sexually vulnerable, easily exploited by *diku* men with small material offerings. They are then, potential vehicles for the alienation of land to the *dikus*, in a patrilineal context, where children take the name of their father. This, then, makes them a threat to the kin-clan network justifying the denial of their right to inherit land, unless they agree to adhere to rigid norms of marital choice and control over their sexuality. These are not traditions, but are recreated

[27]The PPL (Poder Popular Local) in El Salvador during the early 1980s were seen 'as the embryo of future forms of popular local government in a liberated El Salvador and not simply as a necessary means of solving the material problems arising from the war' (Pearce, 1985: 242).

as such, in the context of certain modern reference points. While women's autonomy in the productive realm is seen as 'good', in the reproductive realm, this same autonomy becomes a 'threat' to social cohesion, hence needing to be controlled.

The traditional and the modern are then, not two opposite poles, they both offer opportunities but also carry risks; establishing complex connections not just between the local and the global, but also the past, present and future. Land symbolizes the very being of *adivasis*, women and men. Dealing with land as a technical and legal issue, in a modernist sense, has not helped achieve the goals of land policies, right from the time of their initiation, either in terms of enhancing revenues or agricultural productivity, or maintaining social stability. Rather it has shifted the balance of gender and power in profound ways. Conflicts over land reflect the persistence of ambiguities within both traditional (customary) practices and modern law, the interplay between the material and the symbolic, the negotiations of relations of power and assumptions of social propriety. Emancipatory politics for women here would mean not just asserting an individual right, but negotiating it with the privileged—men in their own communities, in state structures and other institutional sites—to gain acceptance for it as a legitimate part of their identity.

CHAPTER

# 5 Land as a Productive Resource

Livelihoods are diverse, poverty has many faces and land has many uses. The parameters for recognition of women as owners of land have perhaps been set by the formal state structures, which support individual rather than collective or lineage-based rights (recognizing the dangers to the state inherent in the collective). Nevertheless, it has led to an enhanced legitimacy for women's claims at the local level and opened the possibility for assertion. The logic however is different for women from that of the state. Rather than an isolated independent resource, the control over land is seen in terms of the linkages between their productive and reproductive selves.

There have been many debates around the value of land as an asset for the survival of poor households and individual women.[1] With growing diversification, especially in response to the decline in state investments in agriculture in the 1990s,[2] the material contribution of land to people's livelihoods and its role in alleviating poverty can be questioned. Yet the control over land continues to structure social relationships that in turn determine the incidence, severity and nature of poverty amongst different groups of people. To quote Breman, the 'ownership or non-ownership of means of production expressed in amounts of land, is a determinant for access to employment and

[1]On the basis of six World Bank African poverty assessments, Whitehead and Lockwood (2000) conclude that inadequate access to land is rarely in itself a cause for poverty.

[2]The mid-term review of the Tenth Plan identified a more or less stagnant agricultural sector as being a result of the slowing down of investment, particularly in irrigation, during the 1990s, alongside a withdrawal of input subsidies and price protection.

to the monetary yield that it offers in other sectors of the economy' (1996: 179). While there are indeed other routes to escape the hierarchies and controls of the social structure, and to exercise agency (securing a government job, for instance, as Sheela did), in Dumka, where a majority of the Santal households own land (92.5 per cent for STs in Census 2001), it is clearly the primary asset and social relations are built around landed property. The non-ownership of land thus places Santal women at a disadvantage in negotiating livelihood choices and the allocation of household resources including their own labour.

It is this larger dimension of land ownership that includes both its material and social-symbolic value that has led the Jharkhand political parties to oppose moves to liberalize clauses restricting land transfers in the SPTA. In a context of unequal power relations, they fear that if land markets are allowed to operate, the *adivasis* will rapidly be forced to sell their land and join the ranks of the landless. This is also the historical lesson learnt from the rapid land transfers that followed security of tenure in the 1880s, when land came to be used to repay usurious loans, and in fact led to the need for protective clauses.

The dispossession of women from land, however, has not been addressed. It has, in fact, been aggravated by projecting a stereotypical household model of the male provider female home-maker type, as well as the imagined unity of the community as a moral economy. Women participating in the Jharkhand movement have been accommodating the assertion of such patriarchal ideologies in the public domain. At the same time they have been engaged in everyday acts of resistance, as well as more formal contestations to reassert the centrality of their roles, vis-à-vis land, and challenge unilateral male control over resources. In this chapter, I explore further the use of land as a productive resource. What is the material value of land in people's livelihoods? What are the constraints in terms of enhancing agricultural production? How far does the ownership of land contribute to household food security, poverty reduction, and to gender equality?

## THE AGRICULTURAL SCENARIO

At present, 40 per cent of the total land area of Dumka district is agricultural land, of which, 25 per cent is lowland, 33 per cent midland and the remaining 42 per cent upland (DAO, 2000). A range of national agriculture development policies have been implemented, including the World Bank supported National Agriculture Technology Project (NATP), yet Dumka continues to be marked by low productivity (less than Rs 5000 per hectare) and very low growth rates (less than 1.5 per cent) from 1961–91 (Bhalla and Singh, 2000). Despite agriculture being the main subsistence resource, low productivity and growth are a result of the decline in irrigation and the lack of water to take a second crop during the dry season post-monsoon, as well as shifts in the macro-economic context including increased demand for agricultural labour in West Bengal in the 1980s.

The irrigated area as a percentage of gross cropped area dropped from 17.3 to 3.6 per cent in the Santal Parganas between 1931–71 (Sengupta, 1982: 23), rose to 7.5 per cent in 1991 (Bhalla and Singh, 2001) and improved further to 14.7 per cent in 2000. Following the pattern of irrigation availability, area under double cropping in Dumka district fell from 27.7 to 11.5 per cent during the period 1961–91, and improved marginally to 15 per cent in 2000 (DAO, 2000). For Bihar as a whole, on the other hand, the proportion of gross irrigated area to gross cropped area increased from 17.9 to 19.5 per cent between 1931–71 (Sengupta, 1982) and further to 40 per cent in 1991 (Bhalla and Singh, 2001). While rainfall is substantial and water could be potentially available for taking more than one crop a year,[3] rainwater needs to be stored and channeled as the monsoon is seasonal. This, however, has not happened, and explanations for this failure vary from institutional changes leading to the declining use of traditional irrigation systems (Sengupta, 2000) to sheer neglect of the region by the Bihar government (Munda, 1988). The reduction in double cropping, however, also reflects a micro-level process of struggle around the control over labour, located within a larger context of commoditization and monetization, discussed in the last section of this chapter. The criticality of labour in the production process has, in fact, become a major arena for negotiating claims to a share of the land.

Output estimates (of monsoon paddy) based on crop-cutting during 1999–2000 showed the productivity of paddy in the district varying from 2.3 tons per hectare (920 kg/acre) for high yielding varieties to

[3]The Santal Parganas has fairly good rainfall, about 1367 mm per year, based on the average from 1901–50 (Roy Chaudhary, 1965: 36). Recent rainfall data corroborates this at 1398 mm between 1994–9.

1.5 tons per hectare (600 kg/acre) for improved varieties (DAO, 2000). This is much lower than the all-India average of 3 tons per hectare in 1998–9. In my sample of 24 households the output varied between 175 kg and 1125 kg per acre, with an average output of about 477 kg per acre (280 kg in Chuapara and 546 kg in Bagdiha). Not only is this lower than the district average for improved varieties of paddy, but also the difference between the two villages and households is considerable.[4]

Apart from technical bottlenecks, there are clearly institutional and social issues involved that contribute to this huge variability. As Choti Tudu, with a dismal output of only 230 kg from her acre of land said, 'My output is low as the transplanting was delayed. We had to interrupt our own work for two weeks to engage in wage labour.' She, in fact, worked for the Hindu *pradhan* of Bagdiha, whose output was perhaps the highest in the village. With five *bighas*[5] of first class paddy land and the same amount taken on lease (*bhugat-bandha*), with capital available for investment, he uses new varieties of seeds, adequate fertilizer and hires labour for irrigation and weeding of his fields. At least half of his production is surplus, for sale in the market. The higher output here not only reflects better quality of land, but more importantly, the household's investment in the land, in terms of better quality seeds, fertilizers and labour.

Productivity is however not just a function of resources and inputs, though these are important factors, but also of differences in household structure, particularly its gender composition, capacities and social arrangements, risks and vulnerabilities. Manglu Marandi, the *majhi* of *sadhu tola* and his wife Karuna Hembrum, engage in wage labour sometimes, but invest most of their time in nurturing and improving their own land and produce. Their yield was a little more than the district average for HYV production. Figure 5.1 shows the paddy output of sample households per acre of land.

We are like birds, flitting here and there to feed our children. I go several times to the seedbed to see if the seedlings are ready for transplanting. On the way,

[4]See Annexure 3, Table 4. Though the data was collected quite carefully, a note of caution is needed. While very low output levels can be explained by factors such as delayed ploughing and planting, another explanatory factor is definitely under-reporting.

[5]Three *bighas* make an acre of land.

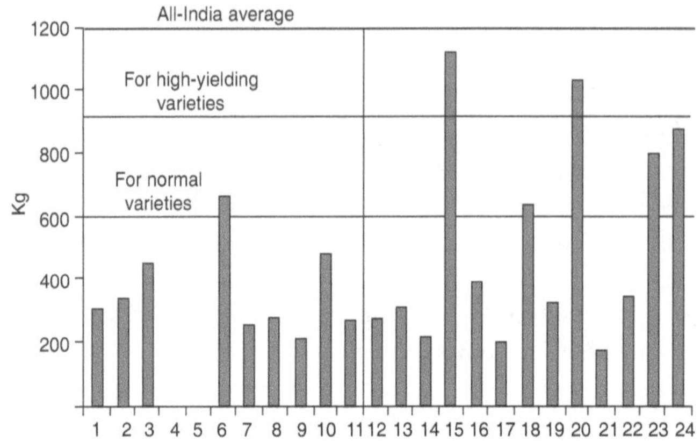


Figure 5.1: Paddy Output of Sample Households (per acre)[6]

I collect firewood and mushrooms from the jungle. This morning I took the cattle out to graze and made a mat for drying the grains. My husband and sons plough the fields, but today are repairing the field-bunds.
Karuna Hembrum, Bagdiha, 7 July 2000.

To get a full picture, each parameter affecting productivity needs to be understood separately, as also the relationship among them as a whole. One can start with the pattern of agriculture in the two villages and the classifications of land, which reflect the wider patterns of land-use in the region. To the Santal, agriculture means paddy cultivation, *khet* (field) is paddy land, and *daka* (rice) is food. However, land use and cropping patterns are much more complex than this. Five qualities of land are recorded in the land settlement. The *dhani 1* are the most prized lowlands, well-irrigated and best-suited for paddy cultivation. *Dhani 2* are the midlands, but often the distinction from *dhani 1* is merely for purposes of rent calculation. It is these two that are really considered land (*khet*) and mortgaged for purposes of taking loans and advances. *Dhani 3* are the uplands that are not irrigated, but where it is still possible to cultivate paddy. Most Santals have some paddy land and cultivate the monsoon paddy crop. *Bari 1* and *Bari 2* are superior and inferior varieties of homestead land. *Bari 1*, usually a smaller plot and close to the house, is considered a part of women's

[6]Horizontal lines mark the district averages for improved and high-yielding varieties. Households 4 and 5 did not cultivate their land.

domain, a resource contributing to the performance of women's household maintenance functions. Men's role in the *bari* is often restricted to ploughing the land.

In Chuapara, *kurram* or shifting cultivation (on forestlands), mainly practised by the Paharias, of maize in the summer (June-August) and *ghanghra* (black-eye beans) thereafter (September to December) forms an additional source of livelihood. Several Santals have also started *kurram* cultivation, paying the Paharias a sum of Rs 200 as rent, which they claim is paid to the forest guard as a bribe for the use of the hill slopes. Since *kurram* does not need ploughing, technically women can grow these crops independently. However, being in the hills, the crop needs to be guarded against monkeys and wild boars as they start to ripen. The women take most of the responsibility for this during the day, but usually it is the men who stay on the slopes at night. *Kurram* is essentially considered a woman's plot, yet its output often helps finance men's second crop, usually wheat or potato. This ensures a degree of mutuality, with men taking on some functions in the *kurram* plot while also mediating the payments to the Paharias and market arrangements. Rather than a simple segregation of gender roles, it illustrates the interdependence of men and women in farming.

While maize is for consumption, black-eye beans form a cash crop. Market prices are high, but cultivated under tied market conditions, with loan-advances from the moneylenders of Amrapara, the Paharias and Santals do not benefit from the high prices. Like all cash crops, however, this too is risky. In 1999, due to heavy rains the *ghanghra* succumbed to a pest attack and output was low. Most of the households had taken small seed loans for the crop. Few households got enough to repay the *mahajan*, and for the majority, the debts mounted. Nati and Karu had nothing to pay the lender, so they sent their daughter to work for his household instead. Like productivity, decisions on which crops to grow are also based on a complex combination of factors, such as available labour, quality of land, capital requirements, revenue regime, terms of cash advance, subsistence needs and not just the relative market prices (Datta, 1996).

## The Annual Cycle of Agriculture

June: The agricultural year starts in June with the planting of the paddy seeds. Following this, women weed the maize crop planted in

5.1: Ploughing remains a man's job.

their *bari* land. Alongside, they are busy collecting fuel wood to store for the busy monsoon months. In Chuapara, where the forests are still abundant, they also collect *sal* leaves for making leaf plates, tamarind, mango and *jamun* for consumption and possibly sale.[7] Men start planning for the next agricultural season, arranging for loans, leasing land, repairing their beds (*charpais*) and in Chuapara, selling poles in the market, to make a little extra cash.

July: Men are ploughing the fields from the crack of dawn. Women cook the food, then leave for the seedbeds to pull out the seedlings. By noon, both are back home to have a quick refreshment. While the men stay to rest, women and girls leave for the fields to transplant the seedlings they have pulled out in the morning. It is dusk by the time they return home, have a wash, and pound grain for the evening meal. Children help with feeding and cleaning the cattle, as schools are closed for the planting season. In Bagdiha, the routines are the same, although the men and women with only little land migrate to Bengal for the planting season there.

[7]See Annexure 3 Box 1 for a seasonal chart of products traded in the local markets.

August: By the middle of this month, transplanting is done and it is time to harvest the maize. For many, this is the only food for the next month, until the new paddy is harvested. It is during this time that greens and mushrooms also grow freely and are added to the diet, and in some cases, vegetables are grown in the homestead.

September: The early varieties of paddy (*sathi* or the 60-day crop) are ready for harvest by the end of this month, the maize harvest having been completed in the beginning of the month. Post-harvest cleaning and storage are major tasks, but women once again are busy making leaf plates in Chuapara to earn the little extra money needed to survive. Men are looking for other jobs, especially in Bagdiha—contracting in some instances, migration for construction work at more distant sites, in others.

October: With the clearing of maize from the *bari*, it is once again ploughed and planted with mustard, hemp or vegetables. In Chuapara, the high-value black-eye beans are planted on the *kurram* plots in the hill slopes surrounding the village. In Bagdiha, wage labour or petty trade (such as making puffed rice) are the additional activities.

November: Once again a busy month; the main paddy crop is ready for harvest. Both men and women are in the fields from early in the

5.2: Threshing paddy. Women as equal participants.

morning, cutting, bundling and transporting it to their threshing grounds, which have earlier been cleaned and prepared to receive the new crop. The signal for harvest is given by the celebration of *janthar.*[8]

December: The harvested paddy is now threshed, dried and prepared for storage. Large bins are woven together to hold the stock, and protect it from rodents and other pests. This is their food for the year. By the end of December, the mustard is harvested from the *bari* as are the black-eye beans. Mustard is used for the extraction of cooking oil, and many households in Chuapara produce enough oil for their own consumption. For those taking a second *rabi* crop of wheat or potato in Chuapara, this is also the time for preparing their fields and planting the seed. In Bagdiha, the lands are left fallow after the paddy harvest.

January: Post-harvest work continues, but it is also the time both for celebration and diversification. After the annual harvest festival of *sohrai*, large numbers of men and women in Bagdiha leave for the plains of Bengal for transplanting the late winter (*boro*) paddy crop. In Chuapara, the women focus on the collection of firewood and *sal* leaves and men on their *rabi* crop of wheat or potatoes. These have to be guarded carefully from marauding monkeys.

February: Mass migration to Bengal is the practice in a village such as Bagdiha. There is also a search for local wage-work, particularly in construction. Houses are cleaned and re-plastered. In Chuapara, leaf plates are made and sold aplenty. By the end of the month, fires are visible on the hill-slopes, clearing the forest floors in preparation for the collection of *mahua*.

March: The forests are bustling with activity from dawn, when the *mahua* flowers begin to drop and there are children and adults waiting to pick them up almost as soon as they touch the ground! By noon, they return home with their little baskets, and spread out the flowers in the courtyard to dry. These can later be eaten, brewed into liquor or sold for a good price. In Bagdiha, this is a time for relaxation; they have just returned from Bengal and will soon go back for the summer harvest. Fairs are held and weddings are arranged.

[8]A ritual to thank the Gods for the crop and seek permission for harvest, it is celebrated at the *jaherthan* (sacred grove) by the men over drinks of *handia* and liquor.

April: The *mahua* season is over, but it is time to collect *tendu* leaves (used for rolling *bidis* or Indian cigarettes) and a range of berries, both with good market value. By the middle of April, there is once again a departure from Bagdiha for the summer harvest in Bengal.

May: Preparations begin for the main crop of the year. By the middle of May, men who had migrated after planting the previous year return home to take charge of the new planting. So do the seasonal migrants from Bengal, with surplus cash to invest in their own crop (as credit for crop cultivation is hardly available). Stocks of fuel wood are built up, homes repaired and maize planted.

## LAND AND FOOD SECURITY

Five-year-old Rini was scraping the bottom of an empty vessel. Her meal that day was a handful of leftover rice, soaked in water, with a little salt added for taste. The last morsel was gone, yet her stomach was cramping with hunger. Her eyes looked sunken, but she kept quiet, and did not cry. She knew her mother had eaten nothing and still continued to breastfeed her little sister. Her father had gone to cut wood. He would carry the logs the following day to the *haat* at Durgapur and perhaps then, they would have a little more to eat. It was April, and other children like Nunka and Mistry were chewing on the dried fruit of the date-palm tree. There was nothing else they could find to eat. Their stomachs were bloated, a sign of severe malnutrition.

The importance of paddy production, however little, cannot be stressed enough in terms of household food consumption. Harvested in December, it lasts, on an average, barely four months. By March, consumption begins to tighten pointing to the onset of the days of hunger. Garma Kol said, 'After *sohrai* (harvest festival), our stomachs start becoming smaller.' Poverty here is described as hunger, the same word '*rengec*' being used for both. Even though inadequate for year-round consumption, the crop is critical in providing a few months of nutrition and respite, and a crop failure can drive the people into a vicious cycle of indebtedness, poor nutrition and illness.

Maize too is cultivated, and in Chuapara in particular, this is consumed in September-October, when most households are out of rice, as seen in Figure 5.2. Though more labour intensive in preparation,

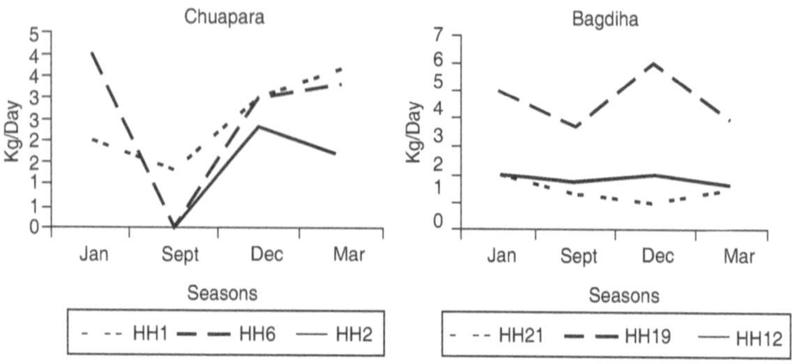


Figure 5.2: Rice Consumption during Different Seasons in Some Sample Households

maize is not considered 'food' and children especially yearn for rice. As I later learnt, one reason why Daud virtually started living with Pushpa and me, or at least joining us for one meal a day, was that we cooked rice. The consumption of rice during this period is also considered a marker of status, wealth and well-being in the village, as only those with either cash or large land-holdings can do so. In Chuapara, only Chura's household (HH1) could afford some rice throughout the year, though even for them, it was supplemented by maize during the monsoon months.

In Bagdiha, there was hardly any maize output due to the failure of the crop in 1999–2000, so people had to borrow or purchase rice for consumption. Choti Tudu's family (HH12) had a low consumption, declining further between September and December, while Panthi Marandi's (HH 19) had a more fluctuating consumption, perhaps a result of migration patterns of several members of the household, especially between December and March as discussed in Chapter 3. The monsoon was a difficult time for them too. The following year, some people did technically produce enough for consumption. Yet the moneylender was waiting to take it all away, hence the purpose of food security was not served. In the house of Panthi Marandi, during the harvest celebrations, no special food or sweets were cooked. The *mahajan* had already come and collected the grain due. 'Poor people can't save anything, so there is nothing in the house to eat. We wait to save, but how can we do it, the *mahajan* is there,' she lamented.

In terms of production itself, out of my 24 case study households, only half were able to even produce enough for their food requirements from their land; (Annexure 3, Table 4), others depended equally on livestock, wage labour and market engagement. As Lakhan Murmu of Chuapara said, 'We all grow paddy, but this is for consumption. There is never a surplus that we can sell for meeting all our needs. For this we consider our pigs and goats, and the forests as our assets' (20 January 2000). Only in six cases, did their production fulfill their food needs and contribute substantially towards other household expenses. Yet 92 per cent of the households in Chuapara and 86 per cent of Santal households in Bagdiha considered agriculture as their primary occupation. The important point seems to be the centrality of land and agriculture in shaping Santal identity as distinct from the Scheduled Castes who classify themselves primarily as labour, and the Hindu caste of *telis* who see themselves as business people.

Here the changing discourse around food security can be briefly mapped. Until the 1980s, the issue of food security was exclusively linked with food production. Following the occurrence of a series of famines in the 1970s and 1980s, Sen (1981) attempted to explain the links between people and food by focussing on a range of entitlements. These include ownership (through trade, production, own-labour or inheritance); exchange (through market-based trade or transfers from the state, such as public works, social security and food subsidies)[9] and legal entitlements. So, starvation can result from a fall in physical assets (such as land alienation), unfavourable shifts in exchange entitlements (as seen in food price and wage fluctuations) and the difficulties of implementing legal rights. Property rights in particular, are fuzzy and mediated by family and kinship ties, and hence a strict focus on legal rights can jeopardize women's rights to land and in turn, to food security.

Women's food entitlements are then, more likely, to be quasi-legal, involving common property resources and social support systems (Kynch

[9]Gladwin et al. (2001), based on a simulation of livelihood systems of women farmers in Africa found that productivity enhancing safety nets such as public employment, food-for-work, inputs-for-work, are the most beneficial strategies for strengthening women's entitlements.

1998), rather than just direct control over land and production. Male-female biases in intra-household food allocations, therefore, cannot be assumed as a corollary to non-ownership of land, they vary by region and income group. Amongst the Santals, no apparent discrimination was visible in terms of access to food, primary health and education, between girls and boys, perhaps because of high levels of poverty, and the virtual non-existence of public services, but also perhaps because both men and women are valued for their labour contributions to agriculture. This wider understanding of food security and well-being as outcomes that are not just linked to food production is particularly crucial in a context of diversification, essential both for survival and for reducing risk. What is essential is that the sectors in which women are involved do not get socially devalued and assigned a secondary status, as despite their hard work, this could potentially threaten their food security as well as identity.[10]

Stivens et al. (1994), for instance, found a growing feminization of landed property relations in rural Malaysia in the context of a general decline in the rural economy. Women's land rights in a way represented the cultural valuation of women as 'conservers' of the rural sector. Yet women's base in the community was undermined by state focus on industrial investment, massive out-migration from the rural sector, women's disadvantage in the labour market and religious revivalism. Younger women, therefore, preferred to look for socially valued work in the industrial sector, rather than staying on in the villages and tending the land. There is evidence from other parts of the world too to show that inheritance patterns can change in response to demographic pressure, occupational diversification, migration and shifts in state priorities.[11] Women's food security and control over both the product and their labour can thus not be read off in a straightforward manner from their landholding status.

[10]For a more detailed discussion on the National Agricultural Policy in India and its vision for food security, see Rao (2006). Gender wage differentials for different tasks across sectors are an example of the devaluation of women's work.

[11]De la Cadena (1995) argues that in the Department of Cuzco in the Peruvian Andes, a growing feminization of land ownership is visible and this is linked to the fact that land has lost its value as a source of income and power (quoted in Deere and Leon, 2001: 268).

## LAND AND CREDIT

While stories around the exploitation of moneylenders are well known, told and retold during resistance movements such as *hul* Jharkhand, those around formal credit are equally heart-rending. Sabu Dehri of Chuapara was sanctioned a bank loan for the purchase of two bullocks under the Integrated Rural Development Programme. Most of the village people including Sabu, unaware of bank procedures and unable to deal with the paper work independently, fall into the hands of contract-writers waiting near the bank branch. Sabu's passbook showed that he had been sanctioned a sum of Rs 11,500 for cattle, and half of this was withdrawn in the first instalment, but he received only Rs 3000. The rest was the middlemen's share, in return for their assistance in getting him the loan. Sabu was only able to secure a pair of young, somewhat sickly animals for this paltry amount. One of them died the following year, and during a visit in 2003, I found that the second one too had gone missing. The possibility of repayment of the loan was dim, so also the prospects for another loan.

The fear of losing their assets to the bank, particularly land, is high. When I first started my research in the village and was asking questions about land, Bahari asked, 'Why are you asking all these questions about our land? Do you work for the bank? Will you take away our land?' (28 June 1999). The property of a Kol household had been attached in the village a few years ago, lending some weight to this fear. Yet given the non-transferability provision embedded in the SPTA, this is not an easy process for the banks, which therefore, confine themselves to government rural development schemes with a subsidy component. Local managers have worked a way out of the problem of default on loan repayment. The second instalment of the sanctioned loan, as in Sabu's case, is often never released, but utilized by the bank in lieu of repayment, as most loans to *adivasis* carry a government subsidy of 50 per cent. While this ensures recovery for the bank, it also ensures that the amount available to the 'beneficiary' is often insufficient for his/her purpose and fails to make a real difference.

Banks are also supposed to give loans for crop cultivation, but these are hardly ever available. Statements from the lead bank revealed that during 1999–2000, actual crop loan disbursals were only 33 per cent of the target for *kharif* paddy and 17 per cent for winter or *rabi* wheat or potato. A clarification is needed here. Most people would cultivate the *kharif* crop—paddy—with or without a crop loan. If they can get a bank loan, they would probably be able to invest in better quality seeds and enough fertilizer. If not, they would fall back upon the seed stock of paddy from the previous harvest. The cultivation of the *rabi* crop, on the other hand, is entirely dependent on the availability of capital. The bank, however, calculates crop loans for both seasons jointly and gives priority to the *kharif* crop. The bank policy to favour the *kharif* crop is a major flaw in agricultural lending practice. So, while several households in Chuapara were unable to plant a *rabi* crop due to lack of funds, the bank was unable to meet its target for crop loan disbursals. It is telling that the Kuschira branch (servicing Chuapara) of the State Bank of India made no disbursal against a target of Rs 50,000, and the Gando branch (servicing Bagdiha) made a disbursal of Rs 111,000 against a target of Rs 150,000. Even in 2005–6, despite a push to improve the credit-deposit ratio in the district,[12] only a little over half of the target crop loan was disbursed.

Starting from 2000, banks have sought to make the process of accessing credit for cultivation easier through the introduction of kisan credit cards. This involves the sanctioning of a credit limit for the concerned person in line with the size of land-holding. The credit card is valid for three years and involves withdrawal of cash as per need, saving the farmer frequent paper work. In 2004–5, 45 per cent of all kisan credit cards in the district were allocated to Scheduled Tribes and Scheduled Castes, and 10 per cent to women. Though the caste or tribe status is not specified, this is still a better record than that of crop loans, gender-disaggregated data for which revealed that 3.9 per cent of all crop loans were disbursed to women in 2000–1, doubling from two per cent the previous year. While the crop loan figures are roughly in line with the proportion of land recorded in the name of women (Tables 4.1 and 4.2), the kisan credit cards seem to relate more closely to the de facto cultivation and control of land by women (roughly 11–12 per cent) (Refer Table 7.1 in Chapter 7). But it is difficult to generalize on this, without information on the number of Santal or

[12]This improved from 23 per cent in 2002–3 to 33 per cent in 2005–6.

*adivasi* women holding kisan credit cards. This is because Hindu women have a much better record of land ownership under the provisions of the Hindu Succession Act, 1956, visible in the data from Bagdiha (Table 4.2). Discussions with the managers of the lead bank seem to indicate that holding a land title (*patta*) continues to be a norm for the issue of kisan credit cards, with tenant-farmers rarely able to access these (personal interviews in 2000, 2006). By inference, with land ownership a key criterion for the sanction of crop loans or credit cards by banks, a large number of women-headed households amongst the Santals, often the poorest, are excluded from this source of credit.

An option for women, increasingly promoted by the government though NGOs, is that of self-help groups (SHGs), which links credit to the amount of savings made by the group as a whole. Given the high levels of poverty and low levels of cash availability, these groups, however, have been unable to pool large amounts of money and consequently, are unable to access credit for a higher level of investment. Further, in some of the remote areas such as Chuapara, NGOs hardly exist and as a result, neither do SHGs. In 2004–5, the total disbursement to SHGs in Dumka district was Rs 10 million as against Rs 170 million under kisan credit cards and Rs 274 million under agricultural crop loans (Annual Credit Plan 2005–6, Dumka). Women here, therefore, received less that 2 per cent of the total institutional credit. One needs to think seriously about such gender discrimination in credit access in a context where women are the principal cultivators and not petty producers or secondary earners. The differential scale of financing seems to suggest precisely this.

Credit arrangements through the formal system are planned at the district level through the Annual Credit Plan prepared by the lead bank of the district in consultation with the District Rural Development Agency (DRDA). An analysis of the credit plans and achievement levels for Dumka district reveal that priority sector lending[13] rose from 43.8 per cent to 45.3 per cent between 1997–8 and 1998–9, falling to 36.9 per cent in 1999–2000 and jumping to 62 per cent in 2004–5.

[13]'Priority Sector' refers to agriculture, small scale industry, small road and water transport operators, small business, retail trade, professional self-employed persons, state-sponsored organizations for SC/ST, education, housing, consumption loans under consumption credit schemes.

Expenditure on agriculture is however consistently below targets. As Ramachandran and Swaminathan (2005:xxviii) point out,

> At first glance, the direction in priority sector lending seems to have been reversed over the last five years. This is, however, a reversal by redefinition: 'priority sector' lending now includes advances to newly-created infrastructure funds, to non-banking finance companies for on-lending to very small units, and to the food processing industry.

To make bank credit more widely available to the Santals, recognizing that non-transferability of land had led to a problem of collateral, an amendment was introduced by section 2 (a and b) of the Santal Parganas Tenancy (Supplementary Provisions) Amendment Act 1975, which allowed Scheduled tribe *raiyats,* with the previous sanction of the DC (and non-ST without previous permission of the DC), to 'enter into a simple mortgage in respect of his holding or a portion thereof with any Scheduled Bank within the meaning of the Reserve Bank of India Act 1934, or a society or bank registered under the Bihar and Orissa Cooperative Societies Act, 1935 ....' (Prasad, 1997: 30). Further, a holding or portion thereof could be sold in accordance with the procedure laid down in the Bihar and Orissa Public Demands Recovery Act, 1914, for the realization of such loans. However, in the case of an ST *raiyat,* this could only be sold to another ST.

In practice, despite this amendment, problems have remained. First, only those with land titles can get loans, so women and other groups without land titles are ruled out. Secondly, while the banks do now issue threats to defaulters, the process of taking over and selling their land is indeed very difficult. They use the Public Demand Act to file certificate cases, and have to pay court fees, yet usually there is no recovery, so they lose both the credit given and the fees paid (see Annexure 3, Table 6). The result is hesitation by banks to engage in lending to the *adivasis.* Though theoretically accessible to both men and women, bank loans then, are rarely received by the Santals, and even when they do secure loans, they usually end up losing much of what they should receive. The long-term benefits hence elude them as they continue to depend on the moneylenders for their credit needs.

Several studies have explored the ways in which land, labour and credit markets are closely tied to each other.[14] In Chuapara, 88 per cent of the households are indebted to the moneylender. In Bagdiha, the figure is 70 per cent for all households, but 79 per cent for *adivasi* households. Except for four households in my sample, all the rest had taken loans for a range of purposes—consumption to meet seasonal shortages, treatment of illnesses, marriage expenses, seed for cultivation, and labour payments (Annexure 3, Table 5). Most loans carry an interest rate of 50 per cent (for six months) and have to be repaid after the harvest. In the case of seed-loans, the interest is doubled. Of the households who had not taken loans, one is a moneylender himself, another has a regular job, a third brews liquor on a regular basis and the last is a contractor for labour migrants to Bengal.

Most of the *mahajans*, the main source of credit, are Hindus. Before *hul* Jharkhand in the mid-1960s, almost all Santal land was being cultivated by the *mahajans* in lieu of debts taken. Yet, the debt burden never reduced and the land was virtually lost to the *mahajans*. They continue to advance small sums of cash as and when needed. At harvest time, they go to the threshing floor and take their share of grain before it is taken home. As described by Neela Tudu, the second wife of Jeevan Soren, 'They come with sacks soon after the harvest and collect the grain before we can consume it. They keep shouting "*kobe dibi*" (when will you give it), till we do.' They have also taken to contracting, to the transport business and running mills, and rarely take over land for cultivation directly. Interestingly, despite the decline in usurious money lending per se, the *mahajans* have adapted to the new order and are able to maintain their hegemony and social position.

The relationship with the moneylender is, however, not just economic, but highly personal. On the one hand, it is an essential survival strategy for consumption as well as for emergencies such as illnesses. While banks have expanded in rural areas, the red tape involved the need for numerous trips for bribes, and the inability to get consumption loans has kept the poor with the moneylenders. But

[14]The interlocking nature of land, labour and credit for the rural poor, has been discussed by economists and historians such as Bardhan (1984), Robb (1996) and others.

there are also the better off, such as Chura Marandi, who keep the debt running as an insurance against possible future misfortune. They however are better able to negotiate the terms of credit than those without other options. Repayment in cash, for instance, is considered a better repayment option than in grain and this is better than mortgaging one's land. To clarify, when grain is lent out in the hungry months it is recorded at the higher prices prevalent pre-harvest. But when repaid, it is calculated in terms of the much lower post-harvest prices, so a larger quantity of grain has to be returned. In case of cash repayments, this problem is avoided. In some instances of severe deprivation, one finds the labour of children being used for repaying debts, as in the case of Karu Tudu or Garma Kol. Karu leased in a pair of bullocks from Lakhan Murmu in summer 2000 in order to cultivate a part of his land. In lieu of the payment of Rs 400, he sent his son to work for Lakhan. His deal was '*dangra badal gidra*' (child instead of cattle). Garma's daughter was sent to work in a neighbouring household, from whom they had borrowed food, whenever needed, in the past months.

Land transactions, taking multiple forms, now mainly take place amongst the Santals and rarely with the *mahajans*. The most common form is land mortgage, locally termed *bhorna* or *miyad*. In this form, grain or money is borrowed during times of need, and a proportionate amount of land given for the crop season. The rates for *bhorna* currently are one *bigha* of land for five *kat* (144 kg) paddy or Rs 600–700 in cash. While 1.5 quintal of paddy was the average output per *bigha* in the 1999–2000 crop season, this was a year of failed crop in the village. Normally the output is higher, especially when resources are invested in cultivation; hence the effective rate of interest on a debt mortgage is also higher. Larger loans, with a longer repayment period, are now repaid through mortgaging land. Sona Tudu, for instance, mortgaged two *bigha*s of land to the lender for two years in return for the loan taken for the operation of her daughter.

In Chuapara, 27 per cent of the households were mortgaging some land in lieu of debts taken in the *bhorna* form. Of them, however, 57 per cent have mortgaged up to one acre of land, and another 36 per cent, up to three acres. Only one household has mortgaged more than three acres of land (Annexure 3, Table 3a). Interestingly, land has been leased in by 27 per cent of households, with a majority (93 per cent) taking less than an acre. This distribution in a way indicates a relative lack of differentiation on the ground, with only small amounts of land being leased in and out. In Bagdiha, on the other hand, 43 per cent of the *adivasi* households (Santal and Kol) have mortgaged some of their land in *bhorna*, with 82 per cent of them giving less than an acre. Most of the people taking this land have been other Santals, but they constitute only 17 per cent of the *adivasi* population, pointing to a higher degree of land concentration and differentiation amongst the Santals here (Annexure 3, Table 3b).

Although six *teli* and *kumhar* households have leased in land, five households from these communities have also leased out land, pointing to class differentiation even within these Hindu castes, breaking the stereotype of all *diku*s as exploiters and all *adivasi*s as the exploited in the local context. This recognition, in fact, first prompted the establishment of a broad-based political alliance of exploited groups under Sibu Soren in the early 1970s. In policy, and development discourse, however, there is still a tendency to essentialize each of these categories as internally homogenous.

The *bhorna* relationships are indicative of unequal social relations, where the lessor is usually in a weak bargaining position due to urgent need for cash or grains. Yet, taking land on *bhorna* is also seen as a moral responsibility and a way of enhancing social status by the slightly better off Santals, hence any one with even a small surplus would like to lease in land as much to increase production as to help those in deficit. Jeevan Soren has very little of his own land and this too has been divided between him and his first wife. With Rs 600 cash earned from Bengal in the summer, he however leased in one *bigha* of land for a year from Rimani Hembrum who desperately needed some resources to cultivate the rest of her land, her husband having deserted her. While contributing to material wealth, by presenting this transaction in moral terms, it also led to symbolic wealth, to a relationship of loyalty in return for generosity. Jeevan, due to such actions, repeated over several years, is now included among the village leaders, a boost to his male identity.

A second option is *bhag* or sharecropping, a more equitable arrangement than *bhorna,* used particularly to cover the temporary shortage of labour due to ill-health. The output, in this case, is divided equally, the land is the contribution of the owner, while the seeds and labour of the sharecropper. It provides an insurance against risk for the owner and an incentive to the tenant. Women like Dibri Hansdak, unable to cultivate their own land, due to ill-health or young children, turn to *bhag*, giving land to kinsmen or other close relatives.[15] A majority of women-headed households in Bagdiha have given out at least some land as *bhorna* or *bhag*. The latter particularly is a way of retaining some control over the land, while also appeasing the male kin by not only allowing them to benefit from it, but also giving the appearance that they are helping the woman concerned, often widowed or separated. Dhaki's mother engages in such a strategy for part of the land, apart from other techniques for cultivation. Women's transactions relating to land and credit are, in a majority of instances, couched in the language of social support and moral responsibility rather than being shown as straightforward economic transactions.

A third arrangement is *krishani*. Though similar to *bhag* in that both inputs and labour are provided by the tenant-cultivator, the owner of the land here gets two thirds of the output, while the tenant gets only a third. *Krishani* is only possible on *dhani 1,* the best quality and least risky paddy land. On all other kinds of land the *bhag* system operates. Unlike *bhag* however, *krishani* signifies a social relationship where the owner of the land is in a dominant position relative to the tenant. Harnath Hembrum has a lot of land and besides, is one of the village leaders, formerly the *mukhiya*. His wife Sheela has been a government primary school teacher for three decades. They are unable to cultivate their own lands, hence lease it out (*krishani*) to those with little land. It is profitable, as well as a strategy for enhancing patronage relationships, with the tenant often helping with miscellaneous household jobs. Kudhia, the tenant, a landless resident of the neighbouring village, facing chronic insecurity, prioritizes the relationship with his patrons, as this offers him short-term social protection, even though longer-term economic mobility may be restricted—a Faustian bargain, to use Wood's phrase (2003). Harnath and Sheela provide him a meal in the afternoon, a cot to sleep on, if ever required, and have also given

[15]Apart from land, there is a widespread practice in Chuapara of sharing smaller livestock, particularly pigs. The lessee household gets an equal share of the piglets when there is a litter and hence, can accumulate its own stock of animals.

him a bicycle for his use. In 1998–9, however, given the exploitative element inherent in this arrangement, the terms of *krishani* have been renegotiated in the region and changed to equal shares, at par with *bhag*.

While all the above are local arrangements, *bhugatbandha* refers to a lease of land that is legally recorded as per Section 21 of the SPTA, the maximum duration of which can extend to six years. A prominent *teli* of Bagdiha, Krishna Gorain, lost a lot of money during *hul* Jharkhand. After the *hul*, he stopped lending and started cultivating land. He has taken about 50 *bigha*s of land on *bhugatbandha*, mostly from poor *teli*s in his *tola*, who also work as wage labour on these lands. Despite the legal restriction on the number of years for which such lease is valid, one finds in practice a virtual take-over of these lands by the dominant party leasing in the land. As a poor *teli* said, 'We take loans from the *mahajan*s at an interest of 10 per cent per month. Often we give him our land on *satta* (the local term for *bhugatbandha*). If there is a dispute and we try to resolve it within the village, he will not listen to the judgment. Court is the only solution, even though it is very expensive for us. And usually, it is those with resources who get the judgment in their favour. Yet what is the option for us?' While similar to *bhorna* in form, *bhugatbandha* is almost totally restricted to Hindu groups, who are legally not allowed to acquire land in any other form.

Land offers access to credit, to labour and other exchange entitlements, and enhances bargaining power and status besides food security. Why then is production not intensified to meet the household's food needs? And despite low levels of production, why does land continue to be highly valued and its control widely contested?

## THE POLITICS OF LAND CLASSIFICATION AND CULTIVATION

While ownership is an issue, productivity enhancement and the intensification of the production process seem to be constrained also by issues of legitimate control of both land and labour. Esther Boserup (1965), a Danish economist, well-known for first highlighting women's role in agriculture and lobbying for women's recognition in economic policy, was also one of the earliest writers to propose that more intensive farming technologies tended to occur with rising population density.

Rural population growth, she held, shortens the fallow periods, increases investments in land, induces manuring to maintain soil fertility and promotes specialization in production. In this section, I examine two interlinked factors, namely, the classification and ownership of land, and the gendered control over labour and outputs, to provide some insights into why intensification has not taken place in the study area, contrary to Boserup's predictions.

As already mentioned, fields are classified into five categories in line with their quality as well as use. Paddy land or *khet* constitutes male identity, while the *bari* or homestead is accepted as being in women's control. Yet it is not considered as 'land', and has no value in exchange relationships. When I asked Dibri Hansdak why they had left so much land near their house fallow, she explained, 'All our *khet* is leased out or given on share-cropping basis, this is only the *bari*.' They were unable to cultivate it due to ill-health, yet were not able to lease it out either.

Interestingly enough, as revealed by Table 5.1, in Bagdiha, the total quantum of *bari* land has been declining, especially since the McPherson Settlement (S2) at the turn of the twentieth century, much of it apparently reclassified as *dhani*. While this does reveal the improvements made to the land over generations, and the shifts in its use, in a context where *bari* is socially accepted as being in women's domain even though men are recorded as the cultivators and rent-payers, reclassifying this as *dhani* is one way of asserting male control over landed property. It is also a way of controlling women's labour,

Table 5.1: Total Land in Acres

| Settlement | *Dhani 1* | *Dhani 2* | *Dhani 3* | Total *Dhani* | *Bari 1* | *Bari 2* | Total *Bari* |
|---|---|---|---|---|---|---|---|
| Bagdiha | | | | | | | |
| S1 | 11.32 | 14.62 | 90.15 | 116.09 | 40.28 | 259.80 | 300.08 |
| S2 | 35.16 | 56.93 | 146.49 | 238.58 | 40.76 | 87.78 | 128.54 |
| S3 | 76.71 | 48.61 | 222.77 | 348.09 | 51.60 | 99.39 | 150.99 |
| S4 | 148.26 | 248.60 | 13.02 | 404.94 | 53.88 | 59.00 | 112.88 |
| Chuapara | | | | | | | |
| S1 | 10.28 | 14.01 | 36.10 | 60.39 | 33.73 | 98.21 | 131.94 |
| S2 | 9.37 | 8.55 | 13.65 | 31.57 | 35.80 | 64.20 | 100.00 |
| S3 | 35.90 | 30.20 | 43.95 | 110.05 | 52.14 | 82.85 | 134.99 |
| S4 | 20.73 | 53.41 | 0.59 | 74.73 | 28.62 | 86.42 | 115.04 |

*Source*: Own calculations from Settlement records.

as contribution to paddy cultivation, the basic food crop, is accepted as a part of the conjugal contract. The re-classification of land can then also be seen to reflect a shift in gender ideologies, ascribing to women, subordinate roles vis-à-vis land resources, less time for other activities, and hence, a more dependent status even within marriage. Perhaps it is this stark change in land classification that has led not just to a more vocal demand by women for *dhani* land through land registrations in their name, but also the use of several strategies at the household level to protest such reclassification.

While there are a few exceptional cases of intensification of agriculture and technological improvement, rising population and a consequent decline in per-capita land holding has led to an increase in disputes around land in Bagdiha rather than intensification.[16] The value of land has increased and the inability to buy additional land has led to conflicts over interpretation of traditional rights. The desire to extend holdings has meant displacing other claimants, through reclassification of land as well as claiming the land of others, with recourse to legal courts or even violence if needed. Women are the first targets, their claims being the weakest in a male-dominated society. If extending ownership fails, other forms of controlling land are used such as leasing in land from those 'too poor to farm'. Large land-holdings provide status too, as in the case of Jeevan Soren.

Why has land use not been intensified then? Historical evidence from the District Gazetteer (O'Malley, 1910) points to the prevalence of double cropping as a rule rather than an exception. Right until the early-1980s, it was practised in Bagdiha with grain *golas* (granaries) being set up during the *hul* Jharkhand to provide seeds for the *rabi* crop. As already mentioned, while rainfall is adequate, there is no proper irrigation infrastructure—manual watering of fields from wells is too labour intensive. Yet, water was not the reason provided for the failure to intensify production. I was repeatedly told that after the *kharif* (monsoon crop) harvest, cattle are let loose and hence it is impossible to grow a second crop. Social arrangements for cattle management

[16] It remains a puzzle, however, as to why despite growing demands for land, the net sown area in the district shows a decline. Perhaps there is a shift in land management strategies in favour of creating new paddy lands, leading to the consequent abandonment of less productive uplands.

do exist during the *kharif* season, but seem to collapse during the *rabi* (winter crop).

There seems to be a gender story here. Double cropping would mean intensified work roles for both men and women, depending on the particular crop cycle. Women clearly contribute as much, if not more than men, to the production of paddy, whether in terms of direct labour or raising cash for investment therein. Despite this, the output is seen as men's contribution to the household and fulfils the latter's identity as *chasa hor* or cultivators and food providers. While land is indeed a key constituent of male identity, after fulfilling their role and responsibility through the cultivation of paddy during the monsoons, men see greater economic security in investing in off-farm income sources such as contract work or government employment, especially in a village like Bagdiha, where most of the Hindus are not cultivators, yet are generally better off in monetary terms. With cash in their hands, they are able to invest in better housing, furniture and some consumer goods, such as transistors and televisions, and sometimes, telephones and motorcycles also. Clearly then, for men, land is prized for the status it gives, the sense of identity and rootedness, and membership in the village decision-making bodies, rather than its economic value alone.

Women in joint households have no control over either the output or decision-making, and the second crop is often seen as a cash crop under direct male control, unlike paddy the staple household food. They, therefore, prefer to migrate to Bengal during the *rabi* season to earn a wage which they control or engage in local labour markets. Land was legally made a male asset with the introduction of individual titles during the McPherson Settlement, but the reclassification of land in more recent times has further intensified the 'maleness' of land. While resisting this process by attempting to register land in their names, women also perceive the need for some income under their direct control in order to retain a strong bargaining position in the household, important for claiming an equitable share of the household resources, and for ensuring future security. More so, in the context of a monetized economy, cash is important for cultivation, and also for accessing services and acquiring status. In labouring families, women contribute almost their entire income for fulfilling household food requirements in line with the 'society's view of her role and the demands of her children' (Mencher, 1988: 114), reflecting the ideology of 'maternal altruism', that mothers will not let their children starve. But they also aspire to put their incomes to other uses: the purchase of new clothes, jewellery, collecting dowries, or investing in some form of savings. While there is clearly an issue of ownership and control of land, the ability to negotiate timely labour inputs, especially the gendered allocation of labour, is critical to the production process, and in this case, a constraint to intensification.

While structural constraints to intensification do also exist, a major one being the lack of timely availability of credit and other inputs, the collapse of the grain *golas* in the 1980s, followed by the discontinuation of double cropping; the destruction of forests and a consequent rise in seasonal migration seem to reflect the playing out of power relations in a context of growing individualization of interests. In Bernstein's (1977) terms, this could also be seen as a manifestation of the resistance of peasant producers to capitalist penetration. Whatever the case, the resistance to intensification, yet the willingness to struggle for extension clearly reflects a conflict over status, over the social-symbolic meanings of land between castes, kin and genders.

In Chuapara, the availability of new land for settlement has perhaps prevented this trend. Here most of the *dhani 3* land has been reclassified as *dhani 2* in the current settlement (S4), both, however, within men's domain. The politics here is between the state and the community, with the state keen to demonstrate improvements in the quality of land through investments made as well as an enhancement, however modest, in revenue collected. Men have resisted by subverting the accuracy of the revenue records and the settlement process itself by maintaining joint, kinship-based titles rather than individual ones, as discussed in the next chapter.

The pressure on land is not as high in Chuapara as in Bagdiha, as clearing new land for cultivation is still possible. Yet, some people do take a *rabi* crop of wheat and potato, especially those with lands near the stream, which can hence be easily irrigated. Here, the constraint is essentially one of capital. Dhiru Kol was planning a wheat crop, but that year (1999) both his paddy and bean crops failed. He was already indebted, and had no cash to purchase the seeds.

Capital was not forthcoming from the bank either, so he had to give up this plan.

But the labour aspect also plays its part. During the winter months, women are engaged in the collection and sale of forest produce. They rate the returns from this activity higher than that from the labour-intensive *rabi* crop which requires constant guarding and careful nurturing. Selling forest produce also provides them with cash that is their own, rather than having to contribute their labour to the male-controlled *rabi* crop. In fact, the construction of the road and increase in the number of bicycles has prompted some men to actually help their women with the marketing of forest produce. But the women are hesitant to lose control over the marketing function and by extension, the income, even though male participation would save them labour and time. Just as land and its output provides men with a sense of identity, forests and the income earned from forest products, appear to define a domain where women are predominant. Independent control over both income and their labour is a way for them to assert their identity as individuals.

The varying patterns of intensification and extensification visible in the different sub-regions represented by my study villages reflect the diversities in livelihood responses, which though a function of the resource base, are also influenced by the political-economic context and gendered cultural valuations of work. Thus, greater political and economic autonomy of the *Damin* villages under the leadership of their headmen has meant a slower process of commoditization of both land and labour as against the plains, subject for much longer to processes of privatization and exploitation under the control of the *zamindars*. In Bagdiha therefore, while land is coveted more for its status value, in Chuapara it is still valued in addition as a productive resource, essential to food and livelihood security.

One of the major strategies for agricultural development in Dumka district is intensification through double cropping (MANAGE, 2000). Despite policy commitment to a holistic farming systems approach rather than the earlier commodity-oriented approach (Sharma, 2002), there seems to have been little attention paid to the social, gender as well as material resource issues in the field in formulating this strategy.

Technical fixes are still being sought for dealing with low productivity, such as assessment of the potential of different varieties in different agro-ecological situations and soil types, while the above discussion reveals that lack of technical information does not really seem to be the major constraint to intensification. Through years of migration, people are aware of the possibilities, new varieties of seeds, as other inputs, have indeed been introduced, yet the rich (including the policy-makers) see the poor as not cultivating because they are not interested and the fact that they become lazy once they have enough food. The NATP is based also on the premise of supporting farmers who take 'initiative' (that is, have resources) rather than delivery of services to the marginalized. It does not see the material difficulties of lack of capital and resources, or the social contestation for power and status.

Both the politics of gender and of *adivasi*/community identity are, however, embedded within a reality of subsistence and hunger, in which land is centrally implicated. Exercise of power can then be seen in simultaneous processes of subjugation of the Santals by the state and of women by men. Hunger itself is constructed by the state as a reflection of laziness and unwillingness to work hard by the Santals, hence higher taxation is seen as a way to make them work harder. Similarly, at the household level, shortfalls in food production are often seen to reflect the shirking of work by women and the inability of the man to control the labour of his wife and other women in his household. While examples of individual resistances abound, there are significant moments when these two power struggles overlap and support each other in a common struggle against subordination and marginalization, the subject of Chapter 8.

While land is important for food security, clearly land ownership is not the only constraint to food production, which includes natural risks and social uncertainty. The contribution of land to subsistence and food provisioning varies considerably across households and villages. Land, however, continues to be valued for its ability to provide security, its use in accessing credit and other social exchange transactions, and in garnering status that can in turn open other doors. In terms of both subsistence and social security, land is equally valuable to men and women. From a material viewpoint, gender does not seem to negatively influence the ability of women to use land for various purposes. Social institutions such as access to wage labour (e.g. male for ploughing), mortgaging and sharecropping offer solutions to the constraints women are likely to face in the production process. Yet women's land claims are contested. The social construction of land as a male form of property implies that men see engagement in labour markets as a loss of status, apart from signalling the improper performance of rituals to propitiate both the spirits of nature and their ancestors. I explore the issue of identity inscribed in land much more closely in the next chapter.

CHAPTER

# 6 Locating Identities

I have so far emphasized that women's role in production is recognized and valued locally and that there is a mutual engagement in the production process. Gender difference is really manifested in social transactions and discourse. So women's struggles around land represent their struggle to gain social identity as complete beings and not just *ora hor* or home-makers. In her work on the New Guinea Highlands, Marilyn Strathern (1988) makes an analytical distinction between what she calls the 'domestic domain' (which includes the sphere of production) and the 'political domain' (sphere of wider social relationships). While material production is seen as a joint enterprise in the 'domestic domain', the production of a collective identity is seen to be the task of the 'political domain', where only men as 'transactors', can convert material produce into symbolic and political capital through ritual and gift exchange. Male domination is established not by exploiting women's labour or establishing exclusive ownership over land, but rather by distinguishing between the domestic (production) and political roles, and attributing greater value to the latter. Women often support rather than contest the process of accumulation of symbolic wealth amongst their own men and kin-groups, for the status and the material rewards that it can bring them.[1] While the intention

[1] Sjoblom (1999) in her study amongst the Bhils in Rajasthan found that women were hesitant to put forward their land claims. This is because a husband who moved to a wife's village and cultivated her land did not have status and was excluded from most male decision-making bodies. In turn, the woman experienced a loss of social status, despite her ownership of land.

may not be to subordinate women, this process of gaining symbolic wealth and status amongst men does lead to the denial of women's claims to property.

Two sets of issues emerge from this premise. First, while clearly identity has a material basis, it goes beyond that, hence transferring an asset or income to women without adequate social reinforcement and shifts in attitudes, may not resolve the issue of subordination. A range of strategies from non-cooperation to violence can be deployed to thwart women's rights. Second, if gender equality goes beyond material equality, to gaining equal value as human beings, then the sources of such identity formation need to be uncovered. Do women's struggles for establishing their self-worth lie exclusively in the realm of production or do they also seek spaces in the more public and political domains? How far do these struggles symbolize the operationalization of their belief that the personal is indeed political, contrary to the distinction made by Strathern? Tinkering at the margins through special programmes and schemes for women is unlikely to resolve the issue of gender inequality. This will only happen if gender is considered as an integral component of macro-economic policies and growth processes in the public-political domain.

Land has been a highly political issue in the region—the image used in the various resistance movements right from 1855. The Jharkhand movement sought to articulate a different 'tribal' social ethic and worldview to create an identity separate from the Hindu identity, a 'great tradition', as a conscious political strategy (Orans, 1965). As the Hindus in the region were primarily traders and writers, this *adivasi* identity centred around land and natural resources. Additionally, most of the prominent *adivasi* leaders of Jharkhand insist on speaking about 'community' rights to land as opposed to 'individual' rights, whether male or female, referring not so much, to the traditional community as to one reconstructed in opposition to prevailing state focus on the individual (as enshrined in the Constitutional Fundamental Rights, for instance). As Marriott (1955) rightly argues, many features of village community including kinship structure, village layout, and modes of conflict are often responses to state policy, particularly land policies. The political context is thus crucial in reconstructing local social

Table 6.1: State versus Indigenous Constructions of Identity

| | State Construction | Indigenous Construction |
|---|---|---|
| Male Identity | Lazy, drunk, simple, noble savage | Cultivator, protector of household and community interests |
| Female Identity | Hard-working, simple, promiscuous | Home-maker, worker, producer |
| Community/ tribal identity | Backward, needing protection and affirmative action; wild, forest-dependent, yet forests to be protected from over-exploitation by them | Egalitarian culture and work ethic which is harmonious both with people and nature |

systems—there is a constant interplay between state constructed and indigenously constructed identities, with implications for the negotiation of gender identities and relations on the ground. This tension is represented schematically in Table 6.1, and is constantly called into play in everyday life, even accentuating certain features of masculinity or femininity to prove that state constructions are mistaken.

As discussed in Chapter 1, the listing of the tribes in the Constitution and providing them special status as Scheduled Tribes was both a response to mobilization by the tribes to claim recognition of their identity, and a statement by the state of their 'backwardness' and therefore, the need for special support. While the identity was recognized as distinct, it was not recognized as equal to other national identities, but in many ways inferior. They were seen as simple people, but without much initiative, and only good for labour work. While women were seen as hard working, it was their labour that was valued rather than their overall capabilities as persons. This value connotation has persisted and is visible in state policies even today as discussed in Chapter 9.

While the state seems to almost deny *adivasi* men a 'productive role', it also denies women's role within the family as a home-maker by constructing them as sexually over-active. Within local constructions, however, while both men and women are seen as producers, the status of cultivator as well as role in community affairs including dispute resolution is given only to men. At the micro-level, this exclusive representation of the 'community' by men has meant a strengthening of patrilineal kinship ties that work against women's interests by opposing their independent land claims and also excluding them from the more public, decision-making bodies of the village as well as at higher levels. There are several examples of women being denied their share of land, often with threats, and being then either forced to leave the village or live as subordinates to their brothers or other kinsmen. The idea of personal autonomy and individual rights, in this case represented through women's claims to land, is seen to be linked to the state's construction of personhood, as socially disembedded and detached from the kin-group. It is seen as a way of breaking group solidarity and cooperation, and therefore, opposed. While women contribute to the expansion of the male clan through biological reproduction, their land claims pose a dangerous penetration into the hegemony of clans and patrikin. Whenever the issue of women's rights is raised, one finds therefore an attempt to depoliticize this discourse, taking it from the public or state realm, which espouses a commitment to equal rights, into the domestic-personal arena of marriage and inheritance. The political connotations of *adivasi* solidarity and consciousness here become a hindrance to women's identities and rights as persons, seeing them only as daughters, wives and mothers. This points to an often-overlooked issue, namely, the interpenetration of models of kinship and polity and models of gender domains (Yanagisako, 1987).

If women have divergent interests, so do men. Men's well-being is primarily seen to depend on their ability to perform the 'provider' role and keep their family, especially spouse, happy. With the changing economic and policy environment, their inability to do so is creating a crisis of masculinities (Chant, 2000). Further, in the current political context, their local authority within the community is often only notional, lacking as it does both a material basis and social recognition. These men too, therefore, are struggling to reshape their identities. Several pathways are used to produce different forms of maleness, including providing support to wives and children, to wider kin and client groups, and to whole neighbourhoods; exercising control over particular physical and social spaces, or engaging in aggressive behaviour to ensure discipline (Osella et al., 2004). This diversity in the ways of expressing masculinity helps one understand why some men support women (while some women may oppose others), given their own particular positions at that point in time. Taking on particular subject-positions can then be seen as an investment in potential material, economic and social benefits, but this is also motivated by moral, emotional and sub-conscious fantasies of power and agency (Moore, 1994). The assertion of their own identities, constructed in relation to the 'Other', calls for the satisfactory performance of certain roles, not only by them, but also by women and their kinsmen.

In the next section I discuss the historical changes in land ownership patterns in the two villages and analyse the implications for changes in social relationships and hierarchies, the ways in which land works as a social resource, a tool for negotiating power and patronage and establishing 'dependence', providing a logic for contestation that extends beyond the value of land as a physical resource. The symbolic meanings of land and the notions of masculinity it projects are specifically explored.

## LAND AND IDENTITY

With the prohibition of land sales and transfers from the early-twentieth century, the major form of land acquisition in the Santal Parganas is inheritance. The land records data of the study villages provide important insights into the processes of social change and renegotiation of identities and relationships taking place during this period. Of course, as pointed out by Scott (1998: 36), by locating each plot of land at a given moment, land records and maps are really state tools, used for revenue assessment, as well as to systematize and simplify the state's understanding of society, rather than for explaining shifts in social relationships. For instance, while some plots may be controlled by women in the household, such as the *bari* plot, in the land records they are aggregated under one name, to meet official needs, thereby denying different and multiple rights. They capture a snapshot view of land-holdings, failing to recognize that the situation on the ground is constantly changing in response to social negotiation. Yet, supplemented with ethnographic material, they provide useful clues into social dynamics and identity formation.

## Chuapara: Enhancing Kinship Ties to Maintain Santal Hegemony

As already mentioned in Chapter 3, Chuapara is an entirely *adivasi* village. Until the mid-nineteenth century, there was an almost equal balance between the Kols and the Santals. By the turn of the century, however, there was a dramatic decline in the number of Kol households (by 50 per cent), the Mahlis or basket makers disappeared, and the Santals became the predominant ethnic group in the village (Table 6.2). While there is no apparent hostility between the Santals and the Kols, the dominant culture of the village is defined by the Santals. This dominance comes largely from their control over land. Presently accounting for 63 per cent of the recorded households, the Santals own 79 per cent of the village land. Of the three Kol households included in the case studies, two had very little land and were dependent on wage labour for survival.

There is only one settled Paharia household in the village, a few more scattered on the hill-slopes surrounding Chuapara, though not listed in the records. The Paharias have a relationship of both mutuality and distrust with the Santals and Kols, arising out of a long history of state policy.[2] While there is a clear hierarchy amongst the *adivasis*,

Table 6.2: Chuapara: Land Holdings by Ethnic Group during Four Settlements

| Ethnic Group | Wood (1873–79) | | McPherson (1898–1908) | | Gantzer (1924–29) | | Current (1978–Present) | |
|---|---|---|---|---|---|---|---|---|
| | No. | Acres | No. | Acres | No. | Acres | No. | Acres |
| Kol | 12 | 51.5 | 6 | 35 | 6 | 38.2 | 6 | 38.2 |
| | (41) | (31.5) | (28.5) | (26.5) | (30) | (20) | (27) | (20) |
| Mahli | 2 (7) | 1.5 (1) | 0 | 0 | 0 | 0 | 0 | 0 |
| Paharia | 0 | 0 | 1 (5) | 1.8 (1.5) | 1 (5) | 2.31 (1) | 1 (4.5) | 2.3 (1) |
| Santal | 14 | 109.9 | 13 | 94.7 | 12 | 152.1 | 14 (63.5) | 152 |
| | (48.5) | (67.5) | (62) | (72) | (60) | (79) | | (79) |
| Total | 29 | 162.9 | 21 | 131.5 | 20 | 192.6 | 22 | 192.5 |

*Note:* No. represents the number of registered titles and not the number of household units. Total includes *Pradhani Jote*, or land allocated to the headman in lieu of his services, and is presented as an additional title. Figures in brackets are column percentages.
*Source:* Land Records data for Chuapara.

[2] The reports of Mr Pontet, the Superintendent of *Damin-i-koh* from 1832–56, refer several times to the petitions of the Paharias against the Santals for cultivating on the

with the Paharias at the bottom and the Santals (self-ranked) at the top, all the tribes are marginal vis-à-vis other groups—Hindus and Muslims—who dominate the bureaucracy, trade and professions.

The process by which the Santals, and in particular the Marandi clan, gained dominance can be illustrated through tracking the historical shifts in the pattern of land ownership in the village. As the 'original settlers' of the village, the Marandis also held leadership positions here. Between 1872–80, 10 of the 28 households in the village migrated to Assam having been enticed to work on the tea plantations by British administrators and missionaries. According to the records their lands were leased out for five years, but they were given the impression that they had lost their land in the village and were thus persuaded to stay on in Assam (Transfer List, Land Records of Chuapara, Dumka Record Room, Dumka). Meanwhile, back home, the land was resettled to others, most of whom were the headman's clansmen and distant kin. This increased his personal authority while creating a support group of his own kinsmen in the village. During the McPherson settlement most of the previous informal transfers were formalized.

At the beginning of the twentieth century, out-migration to Assam stopped. Yet the Santals were able to increase their holdings by clearing jungles and making new fields for which new revenue *pattas* (title-deeds) were secured (See map 1). The current settlement shows a stagnation in the amount of land holdings, though in reality, most of the families constituting the dominant Marandi kin group had cleared and registered one or two acres of land each (a total of about 25 acres of land) in 1992–3. This was possible under the state provision to regularize and register land reclaimed for cultivation by marginal farmers (those owning less than five acres of land). Discussing the granting of *pattas* by the government to 18 households in the village, Chetan Murmu of *latar tola*, remarked, 'Chura took the leadership in getting this grant of *pattas*, but he only did so for his own kin. Our land too is shared by 10 households and each of us cultivate only a small portion, yet we did not get land.' He is not entirely correct, as five households from his kin-group also received *pattas*, yet his interpretation exemplifies the perceived role of kinship and patronage in gaining access to land.

---

slopes of their hills (1844–5, File 6) and of the Santals for being prevented from cutting the jungle.

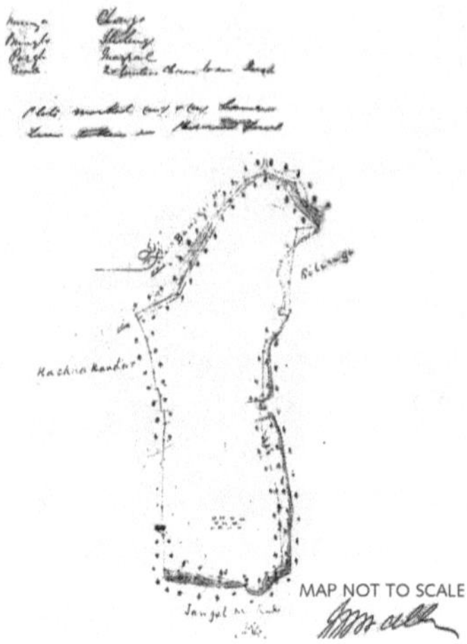


1870: During the Settlement of Browne Wood

1935: At the time of Gantzer

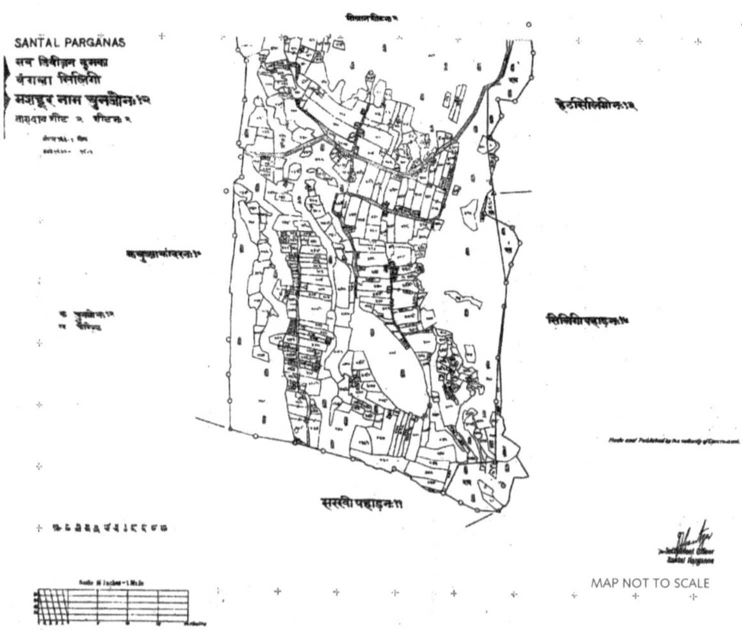


1990: A denser habitation

MAP 1

Potential benefits from kinship ties is one factor that has prevented many junior men (often younger brothers) and women from getting their rights to land recorded in the current settlement. While in terms of cooking, living and income-sharing, there are 53 household units in the village, only 21 are recorded in the land settlement.[3] In many cases, the land continues to be listed in the name of the father, often dead for several years. Dibri Hansdak, for instance, is the sole claimant to her father's property, yet she has not got the land recorded in her own name. The explanation can be both material and ideological: on the one hand, she has no resources to effect a registration in her name, on the other, she may be disinclined to do so anyway because this seems a way of retaining the kin links and the status of her father. In the case of *Jamabandi* (title number) 20, which includes 16 households, the name of Chura's elder brother Samli has replaced that of his father. A correction was made in the land record, yet none of the households got their titles recorded separately even though each conjugal unit works on clearly demarcated plots of land. While partition of families has been viewed as a normal phase in the development cycle of a household, clearly, the choice to divide and its timing can be constrained by a range of factors, including demographic changes, economic mobility and status considerations (Gould, 1968: 414).

In the case of Chura's family, although the senior-most male is now seen to control family property, this is more 'in a representative rather than a proprietory character' with the family expanding over generations to become a self-regulating 'brotherhood of relatives', the so-called 'village community' (Uberoi, 1993: 9). In Chuapara too, family power is dependent on the 'concentration of the family (read brothers) in one place, in combination with the possession of a large land-holding and a wide network of linkages outside the village' (Pettigrew, 1975: 55). The current land record is perhaps an attempt to project the image of a close-knit, self-regulating community to the outside world and to reiterate the supremacy of community institutions in a context where this authority is declining. While not controlling day-to-day land management decisions, the title-holders

[3]Yngstrom (1999: 223) finds in Mzula village, Dodoma, Tanzania, 425 had registered land while 1451 were cultivating land. She notes 'the figures from the land register can be used to establish the importance of lineage as an indicator of land-holdings.'

retain a patriarchal hierarchy and a gate-keeping role in terms of external interactions, while at the same time ensuring some collectivity in decision-making on land (including cattle management which is essential for double cropping). The kin-elders, particularly the Marandis, have been able to secure land deeds and develop an irrigation infrastructure benefitting the larger group, thus maintaining their dominance in village affairs and, at the same time, giving a new meaning to their masculinities.

This is also visible in the mediating role that the Santals have been playing in a land dispute between the Paharias and the Kols. Increasing state control and declining access to forest resources following the Forest Conservation Act 1980 made the Paharias recognize the need for settled cultivation. Chandu Grihi, a Paharia leader, had cleared a few plots of land for cultivation within the boundaries of Chuapara. The Kols staked their claim to the same land and threatened Chandu, refusing to let him cultivate. Chandu filed a complaint in the court of the SDM in mid-1997, but case hearings have been few and far between. In July 1998, under the chairmanship of a Santal *parganait* of a neighbouring cluster of villages, a community hearing was held, wherein Chandu was awarded full rights over the forestland, and the Kols over the *raiyati* (land settled for cultivation) lands. This agreement was signed by the two feuding parties and the Santal mediators with witnesses from the village. The amount of land itself is not much, 0.62 acres in all, yet a dispute such as this provides some insight into the nature of power relationships in the village. While the Kols are marginal in relation to the Santal, they are nevertheless able to exert some authority, derived from their land-holding status, over the Paharias. The Santals, negotiating the settlement, have in the process, asserted their own superiority while also indicating their clout as 'settlers of the land' to the other groups, as well as to the bureaucracy. It is another matter that legally, the land in question is under the jurisdiction of the Forest Department and not the revenue authorities, and therefore, the traditional institutions have no power to allocate it to either party.

And this is, in fact, a paradox. In a context where the traditional community authority over law and order as well as land revenue management is in decline on the one hand, and people are less dependent on land and looking for opportunities for diversification on the other, one would expect to see a decline in kinship ties. Rather, people would be expected to identify more with others in similar socio-economic positions in order to claim their rights (Pasternak et al. 1997: 263). In Chuapara, because many of the recorded households actually represent multiple households, the differentiation in terms of land-holding size is, in fact, still limited (Annexure 3, Table 1a and 3a(i)), with most households in largely similar economic positions. The strengthening of kinship ties is influenced here by the character of the economy that continues to work on the basis of patronage, taking on new roles such as accessing information and new technologies. It also appears as a resistance strategy to increasing state controls, an assertion of their own authority in the sphere of land distribution and management and a survival strategy in terms of maintaining a social security mechanism, in a context where state provision is seriously lacking. This has meant gains for certain kin-groups, clans and tribes but also exclusions for others, as the above examples have illustrated.

Kinship here subsumes both the material and ideological aspects of life, in terms of links with property and the production system, distribution of resources and the organization of work, time and space, social support, as well as status considerations in the larger context. The strengthening of kinship ties, closely connected to the isolation and marginalization vis-à-vis the state and its structures, has also led to a reshaping of masculinities, emphasizing male roles in community resource management and decision-making.

## Bagdiha: Caste Competition and Individualization of Property

While kinship is used to create a 'community' in Chuapara, it is used to openly challenge competing land claims, particularly of women, in Bagdiha. There are several reasons for this. First, Bagdiha was never a part of the *Damin* wherein headmen were given special rights of control and management over land, providing in the process, greater space for local negotiation and cooperation. Instead as a part of the Zamindari Estate, the Santals here were always subject to the collection of rent and taxes by the *zamindar* or his representatives. They had therefore historically developed strategies, both individual and collective, of dealing with the many demands placed on them. Lacking control over land management, a sense of 'community' too did not develop around it in the same way as it did in the *Damin* areas. Participation in the Santal *hul* of 1855 was similarly limited here.

A second related factor is the shift in the social composition of the village and increasing individualization of property rights during the last 130 years. While 60 per cent of the households in 1870 were Santals, this is now down to 44 per cent, the major gainers being the Hindu *telis* and the *kumhars* (Table 6.3). While still the largest group in the village, but no longer in majority, the Santals have tried to consolidate and retain their identity and position within the village by tightening their control over land. Despite differences in individual household trajectories, there has not been much change in the overall pattern, with the Santals continuing to hold about 77 per cent of the land

Table 6.3: Bagdiha: Land Holdings by Caste during Four Settlement Periods

| Caste | Wood (1873–79) | | McPherson (1898–1908) | | Gantzer (1924–29) | | Current (1978–Present) | |
|---|---|---|---|---|---|---|---|---|
| | No. | Acres | No. | Acres | No. | Acres | No. | Acres |
| Santal | 23<br>(60.5) | 316.5<br>(76) | 31<br>(42) | 293.5<br>(79) | 38<br>(50) | 415.8<br>(77) | 52<br>(44) | 414.3<br>(77) |
| Kol | 0 | 0 | 8<br>(11) | 9.7<br>(2.5) | 8<br>(10.5) | 15.3<br>(3) | 8<br>(7) | 15.3<br>(3) |
| *Kumhar* | 5<br>(13) | 30.3<br>(7) | 11<br>(15) | 25.6<br>(7) | 12<br>(16.5) | 41.4<br>(8) | 26<br>(22) | 40.4<br>(7.5) |
| *Teli* | 3<br>(8) | 41<br>(10) | 11<br>(15) | 27.2<br>(7) | 9<br>(11.5) | 36.0<br>(7) | 23<br>(19) | 42.9<br>(8) |
| SC | 7<br>(18.5) | 28.4<br>(7) | 11<br>(15) | 11.8<br>(3.2) | 8<br>(10.5) | 22.7<br>(4) | 8<br>(7) | 19.7<br>(3.5) |
| Muslim | 0 | 0 | 1<br>(1) | 4.3<br>(1.2) | 1<br>(1.5) | 7.2<br>(1) | 1<br>(1) | 7.2<br>(1) |
| Paharia | 0 | 0 | 1<br>(1) | 0.35<br>(0.1) | 0 | 0 | 0 | 0 |
| Total | 38 | 416.2 | 74 | 372.5 | 76 | 538.4 | 118 | 539.6 |

*Note:* Figures in brackets are column percentages. While there are not many Muslims in the village, and they are excluded from the caste system, it is worth mentioning that they came to the area primarily as petty traders and over time acquired a little land, largely in lieu of debt repayments.

*Source:* Land Records, Bagdiha.

over this entire period. A majority of them here have registered their rights to land in their individual names.

Amongst the Santals, the numbers of households with more than 15 acres of land has remained fairly stable (seven to nine households), but there has been a spurt in the number having less than 2.5 acres from three to 27 over the period. While a part of this can be explained by the partition of land-holdings, it also reflects a process of differentiation in terms of land-holding size, much more visible here than in Chuapara (Annexure 3, Table 1b and 3b(i)). Munshi and Dharam Marandi, belonging to the founding family of the village, claimed that they had cleared plots of *dhani* land from unoccupied wastelands. Mantu Marandi claimed one of these plots as his, but it was allotted to the former (Dispute List, Land Records of Bagdiha, District Record Room, Dumka). More than status in the kin hierarchy, it appears that Dharam's social power as a previous *mukhiya* of the village, the ability to bear the financial costs of contestation and superior knowledge of government bureaucracy and procedures helped them in claiming this land. Not legitimized in kinship terms, it is an individual claim, meant to establish power over fellow Santals, in a context where land cannot be bought or sold in the market. This becomes important as the Santals are still marginal in relation to the better off Hindus. Map 2 sharply reveals the density of settlement and disappearance of forests or any community land in Bagdiha. Yet, there is hardly any landlessness amongst the Santals. Even if their land holding does not fully meet their needs for food security, it still ensures their social identity and position as cultivators, and it is this identity as providers that is sought to be highlighted by men, in a context where the state projects them as being useless, lazy and drunk.

Land here is a major criterion for status differentiation amongst the Santals. In marriage negotiations, land is considered an indicator of the nature of the household and the work the woman would have to perform. Girls may refuse to marry boys if they do not have enough land, as this may imply migrating or engaging in other wage-work for their survival. Even young men are conscious of this, as seen in the remark of Rimani's son Vinod, 'Till I bring a wife, we will not give any land to my father, as I need to show this to my wife.' In recent years, access to a job is a criterion that has gained importance in marriage negotiations, but jobs remain few and far between. The

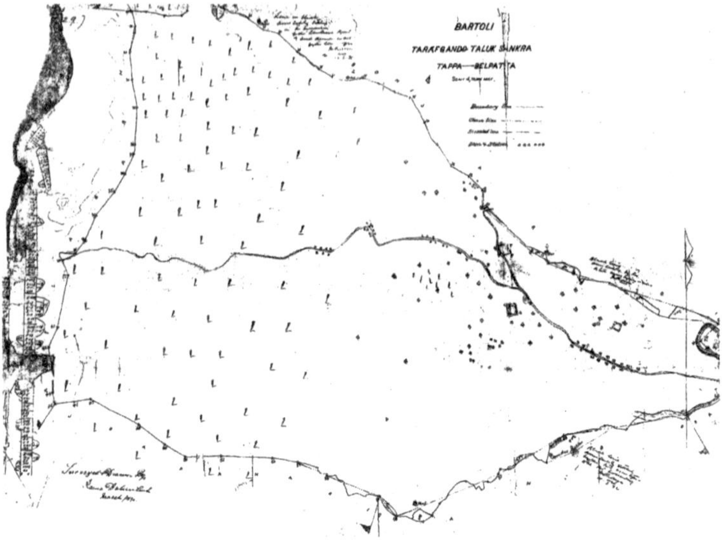


1870: The first settlement in Bagdiha

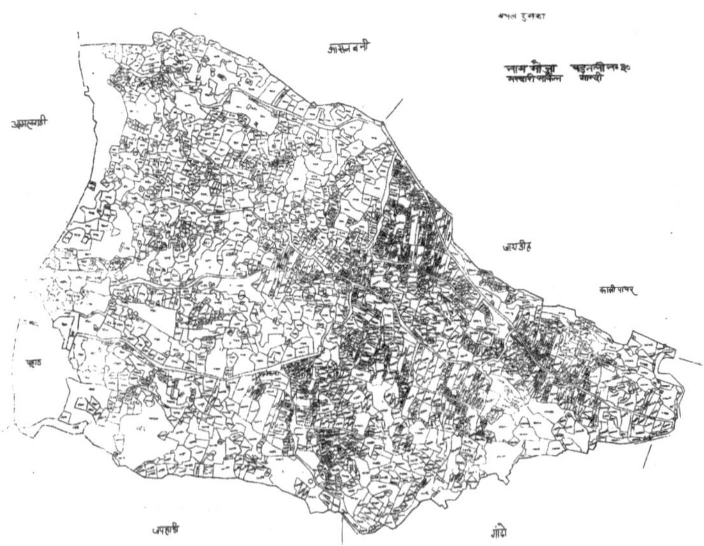

1990: The most recent settlement map

MAP 2

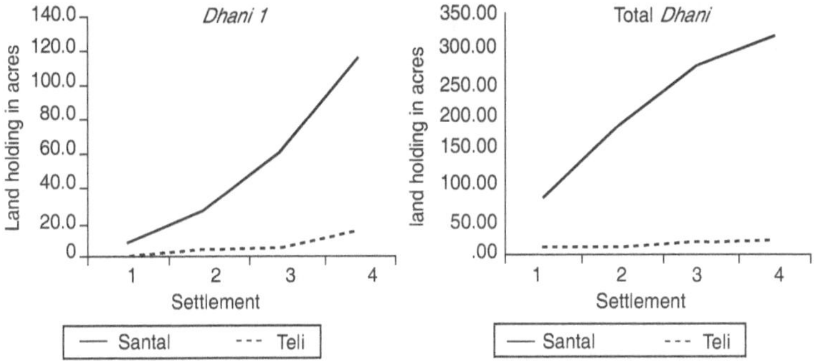


Figure 6.1: Changes in Ownership of Land by Quality: Bagdiha

competition for extending their land holding additionally reflects a symbolic means of status enhancement and challenging the economic superiority of the Hindus, whose ownership of land remains limited in a place like Bagdiha.

Amongst the *telis* and *kumhars*, differentiation in terms of land-holdings is sharper, with the presence of a few large landholders and several landless households, settled originally in the village for trade. In fact, the *teli*s have been able to increase their share of the best quality *dhani* lands in the recent past (Figure 6.1). In a study of 20 villages in Dumka district, Rao (1999) found that the *adivasi*s held only 38.5 per cent of the *dhani* lands in Dumka block, even though they constitute 50 per cent of the population. This has happened in spite of a ban on land transfers and sales for over a hundred years, as well as the land struggle (*hul* Jharkhand) against alienation in the 1960s and 1970s.

For the *teli*s, the ability to increase their holdings, largely by legitimizing illegal land transfers in the past, is a reflection of their social dominance. They have also been able to get social security and development benefits from the government, by use of both their money power and social contacts. Further, courts and lawyers, being dominated by their caste and kin networks, have generally been supportive of their interests. This clearly points to the role of political linkages and economic power that has made such claims possible.

The two villages reveal two different trajectories of change in caste and ethnic relationships, with different implications for the Santals. In a remote *adivasi* village such as Chuapara, where they are the dominant group both socio-culturally and in terms of resource control, shifting cultivators like the Paharias face an immediate threat to their livelihoods.

For the Santals, the issue is of marginalization and neglect of the entire community by the state and other external institutions. Reassertion of collective identity based on kinship (as well as lineage) is a response to the challenge to collective authority, primarily male, posed by external institutions and an attempt to better negotiate collective claims. While the land records are used by the state to understand society and social relations, the titles shown on the register seem to be at variance with the facts of possession and use. Often this reflects a conscious strategy that seeks to assert the primacy of customary tenure practices over legal property rights, rather than a mistake. But it also implies an underplaying of individual rights, especially women's rights.

In a plains village such as Bagdiha, the Hindu trader castes have gradually acquired, legally or illegally, the best quality paddy lands. Their economic prosperity, derived from their land-holdings, trading activities and enhanced access to government benefits and institutions, has had major implications for the cultural and social institutions of the Santals. Unable to assert social control, because they are not backed by material resources, real or potential, the Santals here seem much more inclined to struggle for individual claims rather than to invest in kinship networks, at least with respect to land. This competition between groups of men has, however, had contradictory implications for women's rights to land. On the one hand, while women too have the space for putting forward their individual claims, supported by a favourable policy environment, these claims are increasingly challenged, with a view to asserting male status as providers. On the other hand, given state policies that enshrine women's rights, community leaders increasingly support such claims with a view to re-establishing their own legitimacy as fair arbiters of justice and upholders of the ethic of equality. This has opened up the possibility of negotiating land claims for women within kin and community networks, in addition to legal rights. The problems confronting them may be different, but solidarity with each other helps them in their respective struggles.

## RESHAPING MASCULINITIES

A summary of the shifts in constructs of Santal male identities over time, (though equally applicable to other tribal groups in the region),

Table 6.4: Historical Shifts in the Construction of Male Identities

| Elements of Identity | 1870 (Wood) | 1900–10 (McPherson) | 1935 (Gantzer) | 1980s–90s (Contemporary) |
|---|---|---|---|---|
| Land ownership | Village boundaries demarcated, individuals used land as per need. | Guaranteed, though depended on cultivating status. | Exclusively male, no transfers allowed. | Inheritance male, but ownership threatened by pro-women state policies. |
| Social Recognition | Authority of headman recognized in return for payment of rent. | Authority of headman and community institutions recognized, though alternative state structures set up. | Community institutions recognized, but seen to be ineffective, dependence on state structures. | Community institutions lose all material power, taken over by state structures, labelled 'backward'. |
| Protection | Community responsible, and minimal state intervention. | While seeing themselves as protectors, unable to protect themselves and their property from Hindu exploiters, state takes over role of protector. | Unable to protect themselves and their property, nor does the state, so alienation of land is legalized. | Struggle to reclaim identity as protectors leading to growing conflicts and violence (*hul* Jharkhand and other agrarian unrest). |
| Self-representation | Shared production roles, decision-makers in community. | Cultivators, protectors and decision-makers at community level. | Losing control over land and decision-making, but struggle to retain it. | Active protest and reconstruction of Santal identity, language and culture. |
| Strategies for Acquisition | Smaller village units, close-knit and open discussion. | Petitions and representation to colonial state including the settlement courts. | Settlement courts, beginning of identity-based political groupings. | Court cases, political mobilization, violence, restoring community institutions, claiming benefits on the basis of distinct identity. |

through a process of negotiation between state constructed and indigenous notions of the self as represented in the land settlement process is presented in Table 6.4.

Table 6.4 highlights the fact that male identities are not static, but rather prone to change. Certain features of masculinity and male authority have been redefined over time, in relation to men in positions of authority as well as women. I discuss the changes in female identities in the context of their subject-position in the next two chapters, but here I demonstrate how male identities too shift in the ways in which they are constructed in relation to a sexual partner, a weaker person in need of protection, or an object of aggression. Ethnicity is important in this particular context, as local masculinities are constructed in opposition to the national identity of a Hindu, upper caste male. A crucial element in this redefinition is the Santal man's social-symbolic connectedness to land, which distinguishes him from both Hindu and Muslim men in the local context, and their own women. Masculinity is not static, but fluid and contestable, generated by people grappling with particular situations, acting creatively to configure new forms of gender practice at home, at the worksite or in the neighbourhood. Confronted by state policies and laws to emancipate women on the one hand, and loss of control over production relations with the opening up to market forces on the other, inheritance mechanisms are one field where male control is exercised. Another field where male control is exercised is over women's sexuality. Masculinity may be expressed in hierarchical ways, but also manifests in an egalitarian form in segregated spaces such as during the performance of agricultural rituals.

To understand gender relations, we need then to also look at the interactions and connections between different kinds of men and masculinities, and competing constructions and interpretations of identity. The implication of such analysis is wide-reaching, as what becomes clear is that women's subordination as well as violence against women may reflect male anxieties and an effort to re-establish male identity in the present time.

## The Plough, the Man and the Metaphor

Santal folktales attribute the invention of the plough to women. When people needed an implement for cultivation, they went to *thakur* (God) to help them. *Thakur* pondered all day, and finally, one morning told *thakran* (the wife) that he was going to the forest to get wood to make the implement. He came back late in the evening with a plough on his shoulder. *Thakran*, annoyed that he was late, took it from him and threw it into the air. It broke into many little pieces, as he had joined together several small pieces of wood. She then made a plough with a single piece of wood, which stayed firm even on being thrown and hit.

*Haram* was pleased and said, 'You have invented a wonderful implement, so I am blessing the entire community of women for this. Women henceforth won't touch the plough. I'm saving them from the hard work of ploughing' (Rapaj, 2000). Simultaneous with the invention, therefore, came the taboo; at the same time, this was projected as a blessing from God. This explanation, related to the intensity of work effort involved in ploughing, was given to me by both men and women in Chuapara for women not being allowed to plough. It seems women were relieved that this was one task that they were not required to do, as they were performing, often single-handedly, practically all the other agricultural operations, in addition to household maintenance tasks. Female exclusion from ploughing has, however, led to the close association of ploughing with masculinity and male identity. A man who doesn't plough is seen as inferior. Chura, commenting on Emmanuel, said, 'He doesn't plough. He doesn't have any self-respect or status. He is afraid to go to his in-laws as he will be beaten and driven out from there. Even Garma Kol, who is very poor, has taken bullocks on lease and is ploughing his land, whatever little he has' (2 July 2000). Such statements challenge the state construction of Santal men as lazy—ploughing involves hard work, and those who do not plough risk the disdain of their own kin!

While in Santal belief systems not permitting women to plough is linked with the intensity of effort involved, it has gradually, probably as a result of interaction with Hindu castes,[4] acquired the dimensions of a taboo: women *should not* plough. A parallel is seen between ploughing the land (earth is seen as female) to sow the seed (seen as male) and men injecting their semen into women's bodies. Dube (1986) sees in this seed-earth metaphor, a link between the cultural understandings of biological reproduction and the ideological basis of marriage and kinship that determine the material contexts of property and production. The act of ploughing/sexual intercourse equates the process of reproduction with production and consequently rights over children with rights over the crop. Such an explanation links back to Strathern's (1988) analysis that while women's role is recognized in the process of production (and reproduction), it is in

[4]According to the late K.S. Singh, in Chhatisgarh there is no restriction on ploughing by women among *adivasi* groups. Narayan Banerji notes that the sexual symbolism of the plough can be seen more as a Hindu influence on *adivasi* constructions (Personal Communication).

the context of social rights and identity that exclusive authority is given to the father in patrilineal descent systems. The plough metaphor is then one basis for constructing land as a male form of property, as even if physically manageable, land cannot be ploughed by women. This would almost be a sexual transgression.

In such a context, what would be the implications if women were to start ploughing? This is a particularly relevant issue in the contemporary scenario, where women particularly widows and separated women, are struggling to cultivate their land. The major bottleneck seems to be their inability to secure timely male labour for ploughing, leading to delayed sowing and a poor output. Feeding into a vicious circle of poverty and vulnerability, this ultimately prompts them to give up their lands to their male kin.

Just prior to the start of my fieldwork, in August 1998, a woman in Bagjori village, Jamtara block of Dumka district, now a separate district, ploughed her land out of sheer desperation. The rains were setting in and despite repeated requests, her husband refused to do so. The monsoon paddy crop was essential to their survival. As punishment for her act, she was yoked to the plough and beaten by the village men. A local NGO intervened, the incident was reported in the press, and an Enquiry Committee was appointed (Shekhar, 1998). The Committee allegedly took money from the village elite and denied the incident. For the sake of village peace, to hide his own failings and to ensure their future life in village society, her husband too covered up the truth.

The reactions to this incident were quite different in the two villages. In Chuapara, Santal men felt that the woman should not have ploughed, but then squarely blamed her husband for the transgression. He had failed in fulfilling his part of the production contract. Symbolically, the woman taking up the plough was a negation of interdependence not only in agriculture, but also in the institution of marriage. When talking of their own identities, they often said, 'Both land and plough are needed for cultivation, neither is helpful on its own. We each do our work' (Samli Marandi, 4 July 2000). The women reacted in almost the same way, upholding the mutuality and interdependence between men and women in both production and reproduction. This was true even of widowed and separated women, for whom the institution of marriage no longer existed. The widow Mukhi leased out her land for a few years, placed her son in someone else's house so he could learn to plough, and once he was grown up, started cultivating her land again. In Bahari's case, however, one sees kin support in operation. Theophil, married to her niece, helped Bahari with ploughing when her husband died, and she could continue cultivation even though her son was young. Ploughing was maintained as a male preserve with the back-up support of other men.

In Bagdiha, such mutuality is less visible. Men are not forthcoming in their support; instead they use their control over the plough to harass women and keep them vulnerable, until the women accept their dependent status. Given its mixed caste population, and the vulnerability of the Santal men vis-à-vis their Hindu neighbours, taboos on women appear stronger here. At the same time, it is becoming increasingly important for women to make an assertion of their identity, and refuse to be taken for granted, in a context wherein their labour is actively sought, but their personal identities are subordinated. It is a matter of losing existing ground, rather than gaining new ground. Women like Choti or Dhaki, while not taking up the plough themselves, have worked out other strategies to this end. Choti got her 13-year-old daughter married, the main purpose being to access male ploughing labour. Dhaki maintains cattle and uses this to access male ploughing labour. This is perhaps also where the struggles of Santal women vary qualitatively from the mainstream view of empowerment, which sees these women as unconscious victims of male control and to be conscientised. Instead they do have a set of possible solutions within their cognitive horizons. They struggle, and strategize at multiple levels, individually or collectively, even creating an impression of vulnerability if that is what will work for them, to meet these ends.

Culture is not static and neither is tradition. Rather, both seek to establish social-symbolic sanctions to justify certain values and rules of behaviour, in response to contextual changes. In the face of a perceived land scarcity as well as loss of status in the state and market arenas, Santal men are collectively enforcing the taboo on ploughing as a strategy to retain critical authority in the sphere of agricultural production as well as their identity as cultivators. Failure to provide the back-up support to women who lack male support, as in Bagdiha, appears to be simultaneously a strategy to reinforce the institution of marriage. Young widows like Jharna are under pressure to remarry, as are separated women, as discussed in the next chapter. There seems to be less pressure of this nature in Chuapara, where non-plough, *kurram* cultivation is still a feasible option. Ploughing then is used to enhance the maleness of landed property, shrinking the social-symbolic spaces women can use to legitimately make their land claims.

## Rootedness, Identity and Displacement

Masculinities are played out in sites of production as seen in the instance of ploughing. They are also manifested in realms of protection—a reflection of male valour. Land has to be protected for its material value, but more, for the kin, clan and social identity it provides. While women too are concerned about displacement from the land, as this would imply a total disruption of their life and livelihood, for men it is, in addition, a loss of their historical roots. Apart from the social stigma of landlessness, the fear of losing land to 'outsiders' would be seen as a failure to protect their lineage and safeguard the heritage of their forefathers. An incident in June 2000 brought to centre stage the need to protect their land from 'outside elements' including the state.

In the hot humid days of June that year, a rumour circulated that a gang of terrorists was killing people and kidnapping children. It created a tremendous wave of panic across the region but no incidents were reported in the police station. One day, in Chuapara, the villagers claimed that six people had entered the settlement, but as the women had started shouting, the people escaped into the forest. There was palpable tension in the village. That night, the women slept in groups in a few houses, while the men stood guard outside. The next day, a *sendra* (hunt) was organized to capture the *udaga* (terrorists). Men from several villages gathered with their bows and arrows. They returned home empty-handed in the evening, not having caught any *udagas*, but claiming to have driven them away. In many ways the *udaga* were picturized as *diku*s, wearing trousers rather than the *lungi* (loincloth).

According to Karu Tudu, there are rich coal deposits in this region; in fact the road was built to facilitate mining and transportation of the coal. He is not far from the mark, as in a letter dated 20 July 1844, Pontet notes that on account of the presence of coal beds near the Adjye river, 'a road should and can be made at little expense. It is well worth serious attention' (File 7). Karu's analysis of the situation runs as follows:

The King of India didn't have money, so has given this land on *bhorna* to the King of Pakistan. Five truck loads of terrorists have been brought in to drive the people away, so then they could exploit the resources. We are prepared to pay this money to the Government in the form of rent/taxes, but they should not give away our land. We will save it. (Chuapara, 2 July 2000).

The resonance of this theory in their daily lives is striking, evoking powerful images of the 'outsider' moneylender getting their lands on *bhorna* and gradually driving them to starvation and migration. Karu's two children were already mortgaged to repay his debts.

The incident can also be understood as a hopeful solution to a larger problem. In recent times, there have been challenges to collective male authority, sometimes through everyday forms of resistance. For example, Mary or Rimani find their husbands philandering and raise a hue and cry; if marriage terms are enforced on the woman, then the husband too has to fulfil his side of the conjugal contract. This demand by women for mutuality in behaviour, is in a sense, an affront to the collective psyche of men. In another development, in the panchayat neighbouring Chuapara, the process of land acquisition following a geological survey has already begun, and people are on the verge of displacement. The disregard of community institutions is a growing phenomenon, with state institutions becoming alternate centres of power and authority.

It therefore becomes important for men to re-establish their authority, to show they can maintain peace and order, that they can protect the village, their women and children from outside elements, and that they continue to be the 'providers' and 'protectors'. In June 2000, when the above incident happened, the cycle of life and work had been disrupted by the lack of timely rains. The men had been unable yet to plough their land, and uncertainty prevailed in their life and in the production cycle, sharply questioning their role as cultivators and providers. To counter this, a threat was first constructed, and then, taken care of! The men rose to that challenge to show they were in control. Some nights were spent on guard, essentially to reassert their authority as protectors and rebuild collective identity. The threat was then brought to familiar ground—the hunt. The hunt served the purpose of reasserting male authority, the men claiming to have removed the threat from the vicinity. In the narration of this incident, the image of the terrorist is that of an outsider, an unknown external threat that is ultimately chased away. Normalcy was finally restored once the rains came and the men could start tilling their land again.

## Rituals in the Agricultural Cycle

Rituals provide a way of expressing a more egalitarian form of masculinity, of establishing a 'brotherhood' of men. As in other agricultural communities, the major festivals of the Santals are all linked to the agricultural cycle. The year starts with *baha* in March to celebrate spring, praying for the new flowers and fruits, and for a good monsoon. Then comes *erok* in June-July after the first showers, marking the beginning of ploughing and the crop cycle. People are not allowed to pluck seedlings and transplant their paddy fields before the performance of *erok*. The next major festival is *janthar* in November, which is a ritual offering that signals the beginning of the harvest and threshing operations. The most important Santal festival is *sohrai*, or the thanksgiving after harvest. The celebrations are often staggered across villages, to allow kinsmen to share what they have produced. Apart from representing a period of plenty and abundance, *sohrai* honours two relationships—the married daughter or sister is always invited to her natal home, an obligation for a man that goes along with the inheritance of land. Cattle that have played a crucial role in the agricultural operations are also honoured, confirming the contribution of ploughing to agriculture and to male identity.

Ritual invocations (*bakhen*) are recited by the *naeke* (village priest) on each occasion. It must be mentioned that the *bakhen* are constantly being adapted, new lines added, depending on the context of the village. During *erok*, the following prayer is common:

Bring us rain-bearing clouds, And make our fields fit for cultivation.
With rain-waters wash away
The insects and germs that cause disease (Mahapatra, 1986: 125).

A local variation adds to this:

Drive them away—the thieves and burglars
Save us from the *Raja* (king or landlord) and *mahajan*
Release us from our loans.[5]

[5]I thank Kumar Rana for bringing this adaptation to my notice. As a woman, I was unable to directly access the *bakhen* or participate in the rituals.

The words express male anxiety about their role as producers. Even as they are about to start ploughing their fields, will their efforts bear fruit? Natural factors such as rainfall and disease are the major hazard. They also find their role as producers and providers obstructed by the activities of the landlords and *mahajans*, who take away much of their harvest. They pray to god not just for a conducive natural environment, but have also added their sources of social discomfiture and seek help for it from both the Gods and their forefathers. While the women too are anxious about crop failures, the exploitation of the *mahajans* and survival itself, it is the men who feel socially responsible for providing for the family, failing to do which, they blame themselves.

These rituals are performed outdoors, perhaps a symbolic way of dividing spaces—demarcating the outside and inside, as men's and women's spaces. As the verse indicates, however, it also seems to be a space for the admission of collective male insecurity in their role both as providers and protectors. While the issues of rain and indebtedness are discussed at the level of the individual household, collective admissions of such anxiety in front of women would be seen as undermining male authority. This could be one more explanation for the contemporary exclusion of women from the ritual space. Collective sacrifice, eating and drinking become symbolic exercises by men in demonstrating their social cohesion, strength and identity, an expression of solidarity.

It should be mentioned here that even though a majority of Santals in these villages are not Christians, Christianity has a long history in the region. Christian sects have critiqued the traditional rituals that involve faith in a range of *bongas* (animistic gods), the sacrifice of animals and poultry and the consumption of liquor on such occasions. Seen as elements of paganism, they are also construed as 'immoral'. The church building then appears as a 'cleaner' and more gender equitable ritual space, with men and women both having access to it. Rather than opening up the traditional ritual space for women, the region has seen growing tensions between Christians and non-Christians, especially as the former tend to be better educated and more easily able to access state jobs. This competition has led to a range of responses, from physical assaults to social boycott of Christian villagers. Violence has made the church, especially the Roman Catholics, go back on their strict positions and encourage its members to contribute to the traditional rituals as an exercise in social cohesion, even if not partake of the liquor and sacralised food at the end.

Those who have least to gain from the existing system and social norms are most likely to break out of it. One therefore finds more women converting to Christianity, especially those who are widowed, such as Sona in Bagdiha or Bahari in Chuapara. Excluded in any case from the traditional rituals, they seek an alternate space to meet their spiritual and moral needs. Conversion is for them an act of resistance, but at the same time it helps improve the quality of their life through both material support as in the case of Mukhi in Chuapara, who was given resources to restart her cultivation, or through education and health services. If as a result of this choice, they are better accommodated in the existing system, this can only be to their advantage. While attribution of these changes to religion per se is difficult, a package of benefits has indeed got interlinked with Christianity in the region. There are, of course, costs too, a major one being the reinforcement of patriarchal values. The enforcement of strict monogamy and a complete refusal to accept divorce makes the Church take a rather rigid position on women's land rights, seeing this as totally unnecessary if they remain good Christians, and consequently good wives. I discuss this point further in Chapter 8.

## CONCLUSION

What is clear is that land is an integral part of Santal male identities in several ways—as a producer, a provider, a protector, and bearer of community, clan and kin identity. This closeness to land gets accentuated in a political economy that marginalizes Santal men, negative stereotypes about them being widely prevalent. Several strategies are then adopted by them to assert their identity and their masculinity: highlighting collective solidarity through enhanced kinship ties is one way, controlling the autonomy, sexuality and mobility of their own women is another. I turn next to an analysis of how this process of redefining Santal masculinities impacts on women's claims to land, identifying shifts in the legitimacy of these claims through their life course as daughters, sisters, wives and widows.

CHAPTER

# 7 Women's Claims to Land

Land takes on multiple meanings in everyday lives, being simultaneously a productive resource that facilitates exchanges in cash or kind, and a symbolic resource, a marker of status and identity.* In material terms, women are as engaged with land and agriculture as men; it is in the social-symbolic realm that their rights are not just secondary, but often denied. Land is closely linked to the male identity of *chasa hor* or cultivators, with agrarian work reflecting a way of life, embedded with a moral quality and reasoning. Kinship and descent ideologies are used to justify a particular set of social rules for entitlement that emphasize belongingness to a group, even a lifestyle.[1] In a patriarchal and patrilineal society, the potential for inter-generational transfer of land out of the patriline is put forward as a justification for denying women's land claims.

Examples from different contexts across India seem to suggest that a decline in kin-group control is beneficial for women in terms of both access to productive property and control over sexuality, marriage partner, and so on (Gough, 1981, Agarwal 1994). Yet there could be a loss too, as a decline in the power of kin networks could result in a shrinking of the safety net for women.

While it is true that the breakdown of kinship and community systems of resource management has made space for women to put forward their individual claims in the land records as in Bagdiha, this does not

*A section of this chapter has been published in the *Journal of Development Studies*, 41 (3), pp. 353–75, 2005.

[1] Chopra (2004: 43) notes that agrarian work is seen by Jat male farmers in Punjab as an 'art of life'.

tell the whole story. There are many more women in de facto possession of land than are actually recorded. In some instances, not recording their rights is a conscious strategy by women to utilize claims on their kin-group for access and use rights over plots of land not in their legal share. Women often seek ways to push back the boundaries of kinship norms without renouncing them altogether through an assertion of individual rights. Further, women's reactions differ in relation to parental and marital property, pointing to the social embeddedness of land and the difficulty in treating land as a physical asset alone. The experience of life for a woman can often be one of fragmented place, kin-group and body, moving as she does both place and family at the time of marriage. Assertion of land claims can be major elements in women's search for a complete and stable identity in their marital home. Amongst the Santals, the need to secure a full identity within marriage becomes particularly important in a context where the state constructs them as sexually easy-going and not really committed to marriage.

There is an ongoing debate on the relative value of customary practices and modern law in ensuring women's rights. Agarwal argues that the 'divergence between contemporary law and actual practice stems from the continued dominance of custom. A weakening of custom and a greater adherence to prevailing laws is likely to benefit women within patrilineal settings' (1994: 291). Other writers (Scott, 1998; Toulmin and Quan, 2000) have in recent years recognized the dynamism of customary law. It may be patriarchal, but being localized, is also responsive to change. While not necessarily equitable, a review of Santal customary law as documented by W.G. Archer, Commissioner of the Santal Parganas from 1942–5, points to the recognition of the difference and hence the flexibility to adapt to changing situations. His documentation of Santal law was aimed to provide reference material for the civil courts in resolving marriage, property and inheritance disputes. The information was collected and checked in 20 centres across the Santal portions of the district by 14 local officers. He was very clear in noting that this work was not an account of customary law, rather a statement of 'present law' as practised by the Santals. Customary practices of the Kols and Paharias were not included in this exercise.[2]

[2]Submitted in 1946, the report was filed and never published. It was finally published with the support of the Indian Council of Social Science Research (ICSSR) and the Anthropological Survey of India in 1984.

The basic principle seems to have been that all members of the community, men and women, who were recognized as cultivators, got a share of land for their livelihood. As the Santals follow a patrilineal inheritance system, this meant making special provisions to justify women's land claims in different subject-positions. While the rules may differ from the practice, the intention to 'play by the rules' makes a strong case both for social prestige and legitimacy of the claim itself. When the basic principles themselves begin to alter in response to changes in the context, be it in terms of land tenure policies or general socio-economic development as discussed in the previous chapter (Table 6.4), with men too struggling to keep hold of their property and positions, the interpretations also change. One possible strategy is to define custom more rigidly, establishing rules rather than dealing with issues on a case-by-case basis. Another is to challenge custom itself by taking recourse to violence or external mediators such as the legal courts. But first, it is important to review the rules entailed by custom in relation to women as daughters, sisters, wives and widows.

## WOMEN'S RIGHTS TO PARENTAL PROPERTY

Santal law as documented by Archer seems to flatly state that a daughter has no inheritance rights in land; that the goal for every woman is supposed to be marriage and a consequent move to her husband's house.[3] After the Santal marriage ceremony, the bride puts a measure of paddy in her cloth, and at the door, she turns around and shakes this paddy out, salutes it and goes away (Bodding, 1942). This simple act is symbolic of leaving behind the grain of her father, and the land on which it is grown. She will hereafter be eating from another's land. Daughters however do have rights in movable property—in livestock, jewellery, and utensils—taken with them at their marriage.

The reality on the ground, however, is not so flat, flexibilities do exist. Seven different forms of marriage are recognized by the Santals ranging from an arranged, first marriage, just described, to an elopement.[4] In most forms of marriage the woman moves to her

[3]In practice all women and men considered adult are married, and there were no 'never married' adult women or men in the study villages. This may change, of course, in the future.

[4]Seven types of marriage practice are socially accepted. While there is a hierarchy

husband's village given the preference for village exogamy, but this is not essential, especially in some of the more informal marriages, particularly secondary alliances. While village endogamy is not socially forbidden (though intra-lineage marriage is) and exogamy is preferred, most marriages seem to be taking place between villages that are easily accessible to each other. In both Chuapara and Bagdiha, several couples belonging to the same village or adjacent villages, have lived at different points in time in different localities depending on the availability of land, household composition, as well as social negotiation.

When a Santal girl is married, she secures the rights of a wife, but also retains, in a modified form, some privileges of a daughter. If her father dies leaving no widow, sons, brothers or male agnates, for instance, she either shares his land with her sisters, or if there are no sisters, she inherits it entirely (Archer, 1984[1946]: 142). This is what happened in the case of Dibri Hansdak in Chuapara. With no siblings and no uncles, her marriage was arranged with a boy from the same village to avoid spatial dislocation and enable her to manage the land. Her husband chose to move to her home and cultivate her land, much larger than his own share in his father's property. Her right is unchallenged, yet she has chosen not to register the land in her own name.

## Protecting the Daughter: *Taben Jom*

In addition to the flexibility in marriage and residence norms, a common practice, now in decline, was to give a married woman some land in her natal village as *taben jom* (literally sufficient to eat) or maintenance by her father, brothers, or other male agnates. Not more than ten *bighas*, this gift of land was generally made out of affection, and also worked as an insurance against a bad marriage. Upon her death although her sons were allowed to use the land, the control of this property remained with her patrilyny, rather than passing on to her husband.

In Bagdiha, Binoti Kolin's father-in-law gave a plot of land to his daughter. Binoti argues:

> She is my husband's sister. Their father thought that as he had only one son, his daughter too should stay here. So he gave her one bigha of land to cultivate,

in terms of social prestige, with *dol bapla* or the standard form, the most desirable, marriage by capture, intrusion, force, intercourse, elopement and remarriage are all accepted, the rights of women being the same therein.

> but only for her lifetime. Her children should return to their father's village, where they have been share-cropping. They like this village so don't want to move. In those days, many people gave their daughters some land and asked them to stay. Now it is getting more difficult as land is scarce, but I too would like to give a share to my daughter. Her husband died and she doesn't want to get married again. Now while I am alive, it is okay. Once my son gets a wife, who knows how things will be? If my daughter has her own house and land, she can at least live on it for the rest of her life. I said to my son, if she had been a son, she would have got a share, so why not now? He is agreeable to this.

Binoti Kolin points to both the flexibility and continuity in this social practice, despite pressures to the contrary. Binoti does not argue with her sister-in-law's privilege, as she wants the same for her daughter, and can use this precedent to justify her point of view. If she displaces them now, there is a chance that when the time comes, her son and daughter-in-law may do the same to her daughter. She is consistent, therefore, in advocating for the rights of women to inherit land as daughters and sisters. This is also closely linked to the identity of the woman as a human being, with likes and dislikes, preferences and pressures. She respects her daughter's wish to remain independent and not get remarried out of necessity, and would like her to have a plot of land as a livelihood resource, a source of security and identity.

The village leaders recognize that *taben jom* is a claim that women can make on their parental property. Yet, even after two generations, they insist that the women's land claims remain temporary. While supporting women when they are most in need, this view helps men assuage both their economic anxieties in terms of maintaining and improving their material position, and their social anxieties related to control of land by a particular kin and descent group. The woman's children can never inherit this land, as by taking the name of their father, they represent a different lineage. They must inherit from *their* father; they are however entitled to use their mother's land.

*Taben jom* is a right that has clearly suffered with the process of codification of law and titling of land. Not only is it not mentioned specifically in the SPTA, but is referred to in terms of a gift that could be made to a sister or daughter with previous written permission of the Deputy Commissioner (Section 20(1))—a provision that has not been used till date. Today, in practice, when women are deserted by their husbands or end their marriage and go back to their natal home they are not automatically given a share of land as *taben jom*. This is not the case with men. Dhena, Malti's husband or Soha's husband Jadu, discussed in the next section, though having formally relinquished their land claims at the time of their wedding as *gharjawaes*, are still confident of getting a share of land if they ever go back to their village.

## The Accepted Right of a *Gharjawae*

*Gharjawae* and *ghardijawae* are two forms of marriage (in-marrying son-in-law), wherein at the time of marriage, the son-in-law officially gives up his claims on the property of his own father as long as he stays in the marriage. The girl then inherits the land on which the couple live. This is the only right that is recognized by the SPTA, Section 20(c), hence it is significant in terms of land inheritance practices. Yet it is perhaps because of this legitimacy that it has been open to a range of interpretations and challenges. Even though a relatively small part of the overall land context, I discuss the issue of *gharjawae* rights in some detail as it provides insights into the workings of social relations and negotiations, which are out of the patrilineal norm, and seek to be normalized.

The earliest description, quoting Kolean Haram in the 1880s, speaks only of the *ghardijawae*. He says, 'If the girl's parents have no son and if their daughter and their son-in-law look after them until their death, the pair will get the house, all the lands and half the cattle and goats' (Bodding, 1942: 78). Bodding clarifies the position, 'A *ghardijawae* as such is not entitled to anything more than his wife, and is not in himself an inheritor of his father-in-law's lands. Actually it is the daughter who becomes inheritor, but as she is debarred from performing certain duties in the village, she has to have a representative, who is her husband' (1920: 5).

Hence if a *ghardijawae* leaves, he loses his rights; if his wife dies, he may have a life interest. The children, particularly sons, are the real inheritors. Later the distinction between *ghardijawae* and *gharjawae* seems to have emerged, with the *ghardijawae* seen as a temporary arrangement, usually for a period of five years. The circumstances can be varied, such as the son being too young to plough, or the son-in-law being unable to pay a bride price. Once the term is completed, the couple returns to the husband's village. If the girl's father, however, wants them to continue in the village, then he could allot his daughter some land as *taben jom*. In 1928, Bodding found the idea of *gharjawae* as being 'fairly recent, a way of letting a daughter inherit the land' (Archer, [1984[1946]: 191).

Archer gives several reasons why a *gharjawae* is brought: the need for an extra man to look after the land, to keep the land in the family rather than letting it pass on to the kin, the parents' desire to fill the house with children and guard against the loneliness of old age, their love for particular daughters, the daughter being disabled or having an illegitimate child. More than one daughter could be married as *gharjawae*. This was possible even in instances where there was a son, or where a married daughter was widowed or divorced (Ibid: 205). Goody (1976) has pointed out that in contexts of intensive plough cultivation as well as individual titling linked to the commoditization of property, the desire to transmit one's property to one's direct descendants becomes strong. In the case of a failure to produce a son, alternate strategies can be used depending on the particular point in the man's lifecycle. In the Santal context, these would include allowing the daughter to inherit by gift (*taben jom*), appointing her as a social male through the formal adoption of a son-in-law (*gharjawae*) or taking more wives. While Archer's explanation, located in the context of Santal society offers a much broader view based on emotional and social bonds, it is interesting to note that it is descent that has become the major justification for challenging, rather than supporting *gharjawae*, because of intensifying intra-kin competition for property in recent years.

Through a *gharjawae* marriage, as far as her father's lands are concerned, the daughter becomes a son. Though biologically female, due to the absence of appropriate male heirs, she is transferred into the social/gender category of male. If one adds the land-holdings of

Table 7.1: Women's Land Holdings in Chuapara and Bagdiha

| | Chuapara | | | Bagdiha | | |
|---|---|---|---|---|---|---|
| | No. | Acre | Per cent | No. | Acre | Per cent |
| Title holder | 1 | 2.9 | 1.5 | 24 | 25 | 4.6 |
| *Gharjawae* | 2 | 11 | 5.8 | n.a | n.a | n.a |
| Widows | 6 | 7 | 3.7 | 21 | 42 | 8 |
| Total | 9 | 20.9 | 11.0 | 45 | 67 | 12.6 |

*Source:* Field Work.

women in *gharjawae* marriages (it was difficult to ascertain the amount of land given as *taben jom*), a different picture emerges from what the land records tell us. We find that women in Chuapara (Table 7.1) control 7.3 (Title holder + *Gharjawae*) and not 1.5 per cent of the land (13.91 acres).

At present, the only woman listed in the land records of Chuapara is Soha Marandi. Soha's father was a member of the dominant Marandi clan. An only child, Soha was married in 1981 to a *gharjawae*, Jadu Murmu of Badhniya village (about 16 km distant), when she was 11 years old. Her father had to secure the permission of the kin elders for such an alliance through a formal process of application and acceptance, sealed over several cups of rice beer (*handia*). Her father died in 1984. She and her husband cultivated their two acres of land, had three children, and were well settled. In August 1995, Soha's mother died. That year she and her husband completed their cultivation but then her father's brother's sons, Charan and Pappu, started demanding that they leave the land to them, under threats of death, so they moved to her husband's village (see figure 7.1). There is only a little land and they have to depend on wage labour for survival.

Charan and Pappu based their resistance on the claim that the land had been given for the lifetime maintenance of Soha's mother rather than as an inheritance for Soha. As they had performed the funeral rights of both her parents, they were the rightful claimants of the land. Further, if Soha inherited the land, it would then go to her sons, who, in line with patrilineal kinship descent, would take the name of their father, a Murmu, and the land would, as a result, be transferred to another clan. Believing that it is their clan that has cleared and settled the land, they argue against the descendants of another clan enjoying the fruits of 'their' labour.

In 1996, Soha returned to Chuapara to ask for her share. Charan said, 'Nothing has been cultivated on the land, so what share can I give?' The following year too, Charan refused to allow Soha and Jadu to plough the fields. A village hearing was held but no consensus was reached, for several reasons. First, in the absence of a recognized *pradhan*, the group of leaders is not fixed, hence Charan and Pappu were able to mobilize support for themselves especially among the younger generation of leaders. Fearing a potential scarcity of land (due to the legal framework that prevents sale and purchase of land

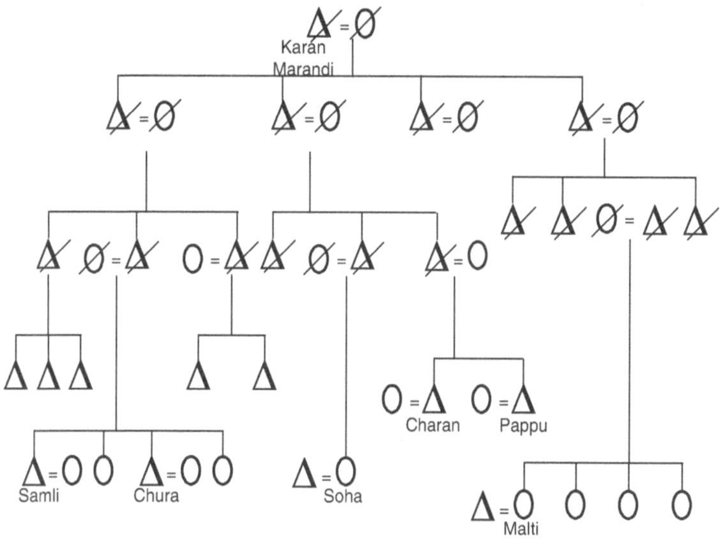


Figure 7.1: Family tree of the Marandi clan

and the forest rules that limit the clearing of forest lands for cultivation), especially in successive generations, many of them were keen to establish more rigid boundaries in order to protect their own future interests. Yet a few such as Chura and Samli, who had participated in Soha's wedding and were party to the *gharjawae* deed, supported her claim. The recognition of that marriage, in fact, was recognition of her land claims.

Finding themselves challenged, they advised her to file a case in the sub-divisional court at the district headquarters, which she did in June 1997. They also offered to accompany her there whenever required. They saw their inability to enforce her claim not only as a livelihood threat to her as an individual, but as a questioning of the very legitimacy of their authority. Fighting the case has been expensive, entailing travelling to Dumka several times a year as well as paying lawyer's fees. Although the case is still going on, it is likely to go in her favour given that, in the absence of codified Santal civil rules, *gharjawae* rights are recognized by the SPTA.

In January 1998, there was a second village hearing, following the listing of Soha's name in the new village land record. She has been officially paying the rent since 1996–7, hence Charan and Pappu agreed to take back their claim on the share of land belonging to her. Yet they continue to threaten her and do not allow her to cultivate the land. They currently have less than one and a half acres of paddy land and about two acres of *bari* each and are amongst the poorest in the village. Acquiring Soha's share of 2.1 acres of paddy land would, apart from improving their living conditions and allowing them to better perform their 'provider' roles, also enhance their social status enabling them to eventually join the 'big men' of the village. Further, the threat of violence is also a way of asserting their masculinity. In their search for prestige, status and authority, however, Soha loses an important physical asset.

In Bagdiha, unlike Chuapara, the percentage of land registered in the names of women has been steadily increasing, doubling from 2.4 per cent at the beginning of the century to 4.6 per cent at the end (Table 4.2, Chapter 4). Most of the women registered as title-holders are married to *gharjawaes*. This figure however is still likely to be an underestimation, as there are many women married to *gharjawaes* who have not got the land registered in their names. More than the amount of land per se, what is striking is the number of women who have asserted their rights to land. In contrast to 5 per cent earlier, 20 per cent of all title-holders are now women. Amongst the Santals, 11.5 per cent of title-holders are women against 5 per cent in the earlier period. While in Chuapara, women like Dibri are still prepared to socially negotiate their land claims; in Bagdiha, in contrast, more and more cases of *gharjawae* are being formalized, to ensure evidence in the event of disputes.

Yet disputes have increased, resulting even in extreme forms of violence. Munni was married to a *gharjawae*. She had three sons and two daughters. After her death in 1990, her male kin started harassing her sons attempting to drive them away from the village. The main point of dispute was whether the marriage was *gharjawae* or not and whether Munni and her husband were in cultivating possession of the land after the death of her father. The Deed of Declaration, 1960, confirmed her marriage as *gharjawae*, and the police spot report and receipts of revenue assessment confirmed their residence in the village. Yet, they tried to prove that her husband was a recorded tenant in his own village of Jaipahari, so they could use the SPTA to prove that he was not a *gharjawae*. The SPTA, following Gantzer's view, states that the *gharjawae* cuts off all connections with his father's family and for all purposes, becomes the son of his father-in-law, just like an adopted son in Hindu law. Archer, however, had shown that 'A *gharjawae* retains a son's rights in his father's land and movables' (1984[1946]: 220), while Bodding (1920) had earlier clarified that the daughter is the inheritor and not the son-in-law. This is one example where codification of custom has actually rigidified practice, working against the interests of women, as the *gharjawae*, belonging to a different lineage, has come to be seen as the inheritor rather than the daughter.

For a while, Munni's sons had police protection at least during the planting and harvesting seasons. In January 1999, when her eldest son was returning from the *haat* in Gando, Munni's male kin knifed him to death. A police case was registered, and they were arrested. Even then, one of the wives said, 'They knew they would be allowed to eat from this land only as long as their mother was alive, after that they wouldn't. We have many sons, and we are the descendants from the male line, while they are the daughter's sons. So why should we let them stay here? We have sold our cattle and mortgaged our land to fight the case. The younger women have to migrate to Bengal to earn some money. They may be winning on paper, but we will drive them out.' (Details of case in Annexure 4, Box 3).

A murder was the final straw. It clearly showed that the police or other governmental bodies could not really provide protection at the village level. After the murder, the entire village gathered, men from all the *tolas*, and the murderers' household was made outcaste—no one could interact with them, or share their *dheki* or fire. The *gudit* would not collect contributions from them for *sohrai* or other festivals. If anybody came forward to bail them out, they would be fined Rs 3000 by the village. Even the teacher, Sheela said, 'The women helped their men, handed them the swords and knives. They have small children and are having a difficult time now, but they didn't try to stop their men. They took advantage of the physical weakness and poverty of Munni's sons.'

Several tensions are apparent in these struggles, some with tragic consequences. The first tension appears to be between affinal ties and group rights with Soha's or Munni's claim (as a *gharjawae*) stressing spousal/conjugal relations over relations with siblings, in this case her male cousins. Anthropologists have noted that solidarity is weaker amongst siblings than among parents and children (Gould, 1968; Parry, 1979). Clan and village exogamy imply that women, critical to the social reproduction of the patrilyny, have to ensure their security by manipulating conjugal ties.

What is also involved here is a struggle for survival on limited resources. With each partition, the quantum of land holding shrinks. Clearly everybody cannot have enough and over the generations, selections must be made between claimants. Kinship ideologies are increasingly called into play to do this. In the face of competition, people are likely to call first on the familiar notion of unilineal kinship (that is, descent and inheritance from the father) and only to forge cross-kin associations (developing networks on the mother's side as well) when the former proves insufficient to manage the property. This is clear in both villages where, in the previous generation, women's brothers and fathers allocated them land even when they were not married in the *gharjawae* form. The rights of such women however are now being challenged.

In such a context of both marginalization and competition, and the search for male identity, women's land claims are seen as the easiest to displace, with justifications emerging not only in kinship and lineage terms, but also through the exclusion of women from the ritual space. Despite having other rights of a son, a daughter cannot perform rituals upon her father's death. Male kin use this as a bargaining point, to claim her land or at least a part of it, in return for performing the death rituals, as in the case of Munni or Soha discussed above. As far as the children are concerned, the woman has custody over them in the event of divorce. However, they take the lineage name of their father, and hence belong to another sub-clan. It is this ritual and social exclusion of women, the separation of inheritance of property from inheritance of lineage name, which brings both kinship and gender ideologies into play to counter women's inheritance claims, witnessed in increasing opposition to *gharjawae* marriages.

One, however, also finds women such as Malti Marandi (JB or Record no. 20) effectively exercising her rights to land. A Marandi and a member of the dominant kin-group in Chuapara, Malti, the eldest of four sisters, was married to a *gharjawae*, Dhena Murmu,

20 years ago (see Figure 7.1). They have one 17-year-old daughter. Even though the kin-group is now large, consisting of 16 male descendants, its members decided to give Malti an equal share of 1.75 acres of paddy land, which she has been cultivating without any challenges to her control. In fact, her husband, with knowledge of herbal medicine, is the accepted *ojha* (medicine-man) of the village and is called upon both for herbal healing and ritual incantations. When asked if they would bring a *gharjawae* for their daughter, however, the couple's reply was in the negative. Having witnessed Soha's case, they were afraid of trouble from Malti's patrikin if they did so. While not averse to the idea of getting their daughter married to a *gharjawae*, they are considering the possibility of doing so in Dhena's village.

Despite the occurrence of violent events, the social legitimacy of the land claims of women married to *gharjawaes* is recognized. A useful strategy for women is to make it a community issue and garner the support of influential men in the community. Even if not committed to the issue of women's rights per se, on account of their own life experiences and context, as well as their expected role as 'elders' in upholding social norms and practice, substantial support for the practice of *gharjawae* exists amongst the village leadership. A part of this support derives from the fact that *gharjawae* is legally recognized through the SPTA, so women could potentially bypass them to claim this right. This position is also in resonance with the larger political struggle of *adivasis*, claiming the superiority of local traditions to mainstream state policies and laws in terms of gender equality.

While some men support women's struggles for their rights, the converse is also true with some women supporting men's rights. This is because both men and women see themselves not merely as men or women, but rather within the larger social relations of a kin network in an increasingly individualized and competitive society. The wives of their male cousins, for instance, have no sympathy for Soha or Munni, but are instead, strong advocates for exclusive male inheritance rights, on account of their own contextual positioning at that point in time. Their marital as well as material interest lies in supporting their husbands and promoting the potential well-being of their children.

As Maxine Molyneux has pointed out, women have different sets of interests and one cannot assume that 'certain common interests by virtue of their gender' will always be prioritized. 'A theory of interests

... must begin by recognising difference rather than assuming homogeneity' (1985: 282–3). Such a view contradicts Agarwal's position that 'village women's strength derives not merely from the number of women seeking a change in rules and norms, but also from their willingness to act collectively in their common gender interest, over and above the possible divisiveness of caste or class' (2001: 1642). A key point that emerges is that women are conscious of their interests, and strategize to meet these interests. These strategies are diverse and flexible, involving individuals or groups, establishing solidarity with other women, or with *adivasi* men, often village leaders, short-term or longer-term, and operating at multiple levels, to solve the problem at hand.

What is also visible alongside the contestation of women's rights to inherit land is the challenge to community control both of resources and decision-making. Kinship and community transmit both identity (in terms of name) and resources. Again, it is those who do not benefit much from these institutions who are less likely to be bound by their rules and norms and more likely to subvert them. Such persons, in particular women, try to seize opportunities within the local structures to transform the rules. Post-Independence, the 'development' state has set up parallel laws and structures that undercut the material authority of the village leaders. Individual claims can be made directly to the civil and revenue bureaucracy, bypassing the hierarchies within the village and the responsibilities and norms they impose. Interestingly, one-finds village leaders also adopting such a strategy, for instance, advising Soha to go to court and supporting her by providing witness whenever required. While a tacit admission of their failure to ensure her rights, it was an attempt to use state mechanisms to legitimize their decision and bolster their authority. At the same time, a process of local negotiation continues, as without social support even a legal victory cannot realize the right. It is due to the intersecting nature of these two struggles that women often seek to 'enrol' the village leaders in their 'project' (Long, 1992), using both social negotiation and legal mechanisms to make their land claims.

One way to understand this phenomenon is to see gender, ethnicity and political status as mutually embedded. As Tsing (1993) demonstrates in the case of the Meratus Dayaks of Indonesia, there are creative intersections between these different identities, all marginal in one way or the other in relation to the mainstream state structure, with the marginal then extending not always towards the centre, but to other marginalities. The struggles of women and the struggles of the village leaders, for instance, may be different. Yet there are points of intersection where the two struggles support and legitimize each other in the larger context of power and discourse.

## WOMEN'S RIGHTS TO MARITAL PROPERTY

As a wife, a Santal woman gains a new status. It is the beginning of a new partnership between husband and wife in the running of their household. With shared responsibilities for working on the land, shared rights are taken for granted and rarely questioned as long as the marriage is stable. In Chuapara women have almost total control over the use of *bari* or homestead plots which constitute just over 70 per cent of recorded land (135 out of 189 acres). This sharing of work and responsibility involves mutuality on the part of both husband and wife, with women, though often in covert ways, asserting their identity as women and demanding that they be appreciated and valued in themselves, not just in their role-defined identities as home-makers. It is only when the marriage breaks up, or when gender relations are precarious, that the right to property becomes an issue.

### Mobility and Stability in Marriage

For men, marriage is critical for creating stability in their lives, for they are able to set up their own household and cultivate their own fields. And for women too, their interests lie in proving their commitment to marriage and the family, gaining status in their role as home-makers, as a path to gaining value as persons. At marriage, however, a Santal woman is subjected to certain new controls and rules of conduct, particularly relating to her sexuality. Pre-marital virginity is not a necessary condition for marriage in Santal society, in fact, the experience of premarital sex is seen to lay the foundation of a stable married union, but any sexual relationship outside marriage would now be considered grounds for divorce. This is a reality that diverges from state constructions of women as promiscuous. While male infidelity is acceptable, even a sign of masculinity, women are not only expected to be loyal and caring, but are also not expected to have any sexual desire outside the marriage.

Male identities in terms of love and sexuality are grounded in the control of women, with independent actions of any kind, not just infidelity, becoming sufficient grounds for separation. Yet, women too exercise agency in the case of separation. Their grievances range from 'he was a stingy man', 'they were very poor', 'he used to drink a lot' to 'he didn't care for me' or 'he didn't get me treated when I was sick'. However, one must add here that flexibility and choices for women alter with the stages in the life cycle. Negotiating gender identities is a much more complex process than a male-female binary of 'powerful' and 'powerless', as elements of love and cooperation too are implicated in this process. While it is relatively easy for women to exit a marriage in the first few years, it becomes more difficult once they have children. If the woman walks out of the marriage she is likely to lose her children. If she takes her children with her, a son may eventually be able to claim his father's land, but a daughter will get nothing. The remarriage option too gets difficult when children are involved, as illustrated in Jharna's case. While this material logic is highlighted in most discussions of divorce and separation and is valid, there is a further consideration. Often not articulated because it does not relate to a concrete practice or something legally identifiable, this consideration is about women not being a form of male property, but having identities as persons.

Married at the age of 20, widowed at 32, Jharna has two daughters aged ten and six years. After her husband's death, she moved to her parents' home in a nearby village. She earned wages through labour in order to cultivate her husband's land, one acre in all. When she returned to Bagdiha to cultivate, however, she found that this land had been ploughed over by her husband's brother and father. On being questioned, they denied her claims on grounds that she had only daughters, while her husband's brother had a son. The community leaders held a meeting and decided in her favour. She started cultivating the land, but her husband's brother and father don't talk to her. Though she is prepared to pay the full wage for ploughing her land, they ask other men in the *tola* not to plough for her. Her father-in-law belongs to the founding family of the village, and is still relatively powerful in the social hierarchy, therefore other men don't want to risk breaking that relationship for a small monetary gain. As a result, Jharna struggles every year to get her land ploughed on time.

While hearing Jharna's case, the *majhi* suggested that she get remarried, as she was still young. She however was unsure if a second husband would be prepared to accept her children. He might have other children and this could lead to conflict. If the second marriage did not work out, she would be property-less, as she would lose her rights to land in this village too. All these questions and doubts have made her struggle to keep this property in order to bring up and educate her children. Jharna sees her marital property as the only resource for her survival and for establishing her personhood.

Jharna's story reveals that women themselves treat marital and parental property differently. While fighting for her marital property, Jharna has not considered staking a claim to her parental property. Marriage is a defining institution as far as property rights is concerned; hence women like Jharna consider it appropriate to stake a claim to their marital property as long as they abide by the social rules for doing so. She does not equate widowhood with marital breakdown, hence sees no need to leave the village. Rather she wants a legitimate place in the village society. Jharna is conscious of the problems, and has chosen strategically to struggle to retain control over her marital property by not remarrying, if this is required, at least until her children are grown up and themselves married. In this struggle, she needs the support of her natal kin. It becomes important for her to maintain a cordial relationship with her brother and father.

Decisions to exit from the marriage are also influenced by the level of social protection available from the government. In the case of Naina, though she has a house in Chuapara built under the Indira Awas Yojana, the house-plot is in her husband's name. She is afraid that if he pulls down the house, she will have nothing left. The state, in granting women housing, has not thought strategically in terms of giving them the title to the house-plot. Further, while widows are entitled to pensions or ration cards, separated women are not. Women can also be insecure within marriage, constantly looking for ways to strengthen their bargaining position within the household; hence there is little or no justification for policies that limit access to benefits on the basis of marital status alone. It is only recently that equal opportunities have been established for men and women within households in manual wage work through the National Rural Employment Guarantee Programme launched in 2006.

Table 7.2: Households by Marital Status

| Marital Status | Chuapara | | Bagdiha | | Total | |
|---|---|---|---|---|---|---|
| | No. | Per cent | No. | Per cent | No. | Per cent |
| First Marriage | 28 | 54 | 158 | 67 | 186 | 65 |
| Remarried* | 14 | 27 | 35 | 15 | 49 | 17 |
| Widow/er | 9 | 17 | 36 | 15 | 45 | 15.6 |
| Separated** | 0 | 0 | 4 | 2 | 4 | 1.4 |
| N.A. | 1 | 2 | 2 | 1 | 3 | 1 |
| Total | 52 | 100 | 235 | 100 | 287 | 100 |

*Source:* Field Work.
*Note:* *Male, female or both. **Living single.

Despite the constraints, in practice there is a high level of marital mobility, separation and remarriage being acceptable for both men and women. Table 7.2 shows the number of households in which the partners are in their first marriage as well as those in which either or both are remarried. The category of separated or divorced men and women is insignificant, as most of them soon move into other relationships. In 27 per cent of the households in Chuapara, it is not the first marriage for both the man and the woman. In Bagdiha this proportion is lower because of the inclusion of the Hindu population, who believe in strict monogamy. If one only considers the Santals, then it goes up to 20 per cent.

## Coping with Co-Wives

The situation gets more complex in the event of polygyny. According to Kolean Haram, Santals 'were living satisfied with only one wife; none had two wives' (Bodding, 1942: 81). Divorce was accepted and clearly considered preferable to polygynous relationships. While this is still largely true, several instances of polygyny exist. The most frequent occasion for taking a co-wife appears when there are no children from the first marriage, as in the case of Girish Soren. In this case, he took permission from his first wife to marry Choti, and now after his death, the two wives live together in the same house. The former headmaster's wife was sickly and unable to manage the housework. He married her sister, as his second wife, to take over the management of the household. It is interesting that while the woman is expected to nurse the man if he falls sick, it doesn't work the other way around. A third reason is one of wealth or high office, where the better off Santals take co-wives in order to perform particular public or social roles. Manik Marandi, a leader of the *hul* Jharkhand, was elected Member of the Legislative Assembly (MLA) in 1969. He felt the need for an educated wife to cope with the demands of his political life, while his first wife took care of the land. A fourth cause, perhaps the most common, is friction between husband and wife, often related to extra-marital liaisons.

Usually the man attempts to seek the consent of his *badki* (first wife) for the second marriage, in return for which, she is allotted sufficient land for her maintenance as in the case of Jeevan's household. In addition to a share of the marital property, Jeevan ploughs Sevati's share of the land without charging wages and provides other support too, as and when required. If the first wife resists the entry of the *chutki* (second/younger wife), however, she is often thrown out of the house or humiliated to the point when she leaves. Dhaki said 'When he brought the second wife, he gave me my things and asked me to go. Later he said I too could stay, but I refused.'

If the situation of the *badki* is fragile, so it is with the *chutki*. Sunil's first wife refused to stay in the village, so he brought a second wife. Much later, the *badki* filed for divorce and maintenance in the court and won the case. Sunil however, refuses to pay the maintenance, because he claims that he is even now prepared to keep her. Clearly Sunil is using the Santal custom that appears to allow two wives as his frame of reference, while the *badki* has used the tenets of law that render bigamy illegal and the settlement of divorce before a second marriage can be legitimized. In this clash of the two systems, the loser appears to be his second wife Agnes, who is not formally married to him, and hence has no legal rights, though they have been together for over ten years and have two children. As long as his divorce case is not resolved in a way satisfactory to him, he refuses to marry her. This issue of how differently situated people opt for different sources of legitimacy and sites of contestation to suit their particular interests in discussed further in the next chapter.

Where the *badki*s are articulate, have voice and refuse both to leave, and to allow a second wife in the house, the conflict intensifies. Speaking of Solomon's second wife, Rimani said, 'She has come with her eyes open. Why should I give her place to stay or a share of the land? He is looking for fields here and there, when he gets fed up of going to Bengal to earn, he will come home.' She did not allow them to live in the house or work on the fields, and ultimately, her strategy paid off, as Solomon did abandon his second wife and return to her. Clearly if her sexuality is controlled, she expects a similar sexual restraint on his part. Rimani justifies her position by drawing on Christian morality, and its focus on monogamy and lifelong partnership.

Yet, given that they are still seeking to get their husbands back, first wives blame the *chutki* rather than their husbands. This keeps the door open for renegotiating the patriarchal bargain. In their resistance, they seek the support of the village leaders. Rimani managed to secure that support to keep the land, though her husband continued to harass her in many small ways such as clandestinely harvesting a part of the crop. In Rimani's case, the *majhi* said, 'He has a wife and children, by staying with him does the *chutki* think she will be a queen? Men are like that, but she should have cared more for her own husband and children.' While male sexual desires seem to be acceptable even taken for granted, women's are clearly not.

Though not discussed freely and rarely addressed directly, especially in urban middle-class settings, sexuality including sexual incompatibility is clearly a source of marital conflict. For women particularly, as home-makers and reproducers, sexuality is a key element of their identity as women. When men, bringing in a second wife, or indulging in an extra-marital affair, thwart this, resistance follows, in an effort not to lose that identity as a woman. These women have made an investment in their identities as wives and the performance of this role satisfactorily. A rejection here leads them to blame and hold responsible the person seen to be hampering or thwarting the effective performance of this role, namely, the other woman. An effort is made to break that relationship and renegotiate the mutuality expected in the marriage in the first instance rather than the woman choosing to exit the marriage. Such tensions and renegotiations are not uncommon; the middle-classes however choose to hide these from public view due to considerations of status and honour. The Santals on the other hand are more vocal about their concerns as in the absence of material comforts, relationships constitute a central element of their overall well-being.

Studies of polygyny in other cultures reveal a complex situation without any easy generalizations in terms of trends. In Indonesia, Krulfeld (1986) found it more common in 'modern' villages and negligible in 'traditional' villages, where women's central role in the subsistence economy was valued and where marital mobility was high. In Zimbabwe, on the contrary, Cheater (1984) sees it as a 'traditional' idiom of accumulation, in decline with the shift towards western behavioural models including monogamous marriages and dependence on hired rather than family labourers. While no studies of trends in polygyny amongst the Santals are available, it is interesting to note that there are still no cases of polygyny in Chuapara, but several in Bagdiha, a relatively 'modern' village.

Questions regarding the struggles over the meaning of rights and relationships, as well as differences in responses across generations and life-cycles are posed by the story of Mahani and her mother Sevati—the daughter and first wife of Jeevan Soren. Mahani was married into a poor household. Her husband sold logs for their survival. She fell very ill, but there was no money for her treatment, so her husband sent her back to her parents. The same story was repeated several times. She again came to her parents when she was expecting her first child. Her husband never even came to see his child, a daughter, but instead brought a *chutki*. Mahani felt insulted by such treatment by her husband; his total lack of care or concern hurt her sense of self-worth. Later, he asked her to come back, but she found it demeaning to live with another wife, so refused. She decided to exit from the relationship, but is now left with no share in the property. While she has parental support, they are too poor to file a case. Even if she won the case, her husband being even poorer, would be unable to pay anything. On the other hand, Mahani's mother, past her prime and with grown-up sons, has stayed on in a polygynous relationship, because she finds security in it even if she has been robbed of dignity.

Conformity to the centres of male power can lead to a sense of security but also a loss of identity. Breaking away can lead to gains in autonomy, but also increased hardship, as evident in Mahani's case. Already this is reflected in the heavy burden of work shouldered by Mahani in the household and outside. Resistance for her has meant choosing a life of struggle and hardship, but she is free from the constant feeling of rejection which would have been a part of her life had she stayed on with her husband and his second wife. Women such as Mahani and Dhaki consciously make this choice to retain their social dignity. Younger women find the practice of polygyny an affront to their identity and sexuality and not a relationship they can easily accept. By their actions they assert the importance of mutuality between husband and wife to make a marriage work. While contested extensively in everyday relations, polygyny is invisible in the settlement discussions, perhaps because it is illegal as per the law of the land.

The only option for Mahani seemed to be another marriage, not independent rights to land. One offer for marriage came soon after her return from Bengal in June 2000. The man has a wife and son, but does not want to keep her and is looking for a second wife. Mahani says, 'If I marry into such a household, who knows, one day he will drive me out too. There is no security.' There was another offer from a man with one daughter. 'This is better, as the daughter will get married outside and there would be no dispute over property.' Mahani's interest lies more in the property, in her own security, than in the man, linked interestingly to his daughter's lack of property claims. In a context of high marital mobility and intense poverty, she does not want to fall out with her natal family as she needs their support in times of distress, a stand similar to that taken by Jharna. Hence she is not staking claim to a share in her mother's property of 2.5 acres, to be divided amongst her three brothers. In 2004, Mahani did get married to this man, but he made her leave her daughter behind. This has been a source of great distress for both mother and daughter, and she is still in the process of negotiating a satisfactory agreement.

Engel's (1972[1884]) hypothesis that polygyny may be linked to the issue of economic prosperity does not explain the range of cases encountered. While economic prosperity, access to urban areas and markets can all be contributory factors for polygyny, enabling men to manage multiple lives in different locations, the linkages between marriage practices, inheritance, the nature of production and social hierarchies are much more complex. In the increasingly individualized context of Bagdiha, adding wives seems to be a strategy for ensuring direct descent by producing male heirs, rather than allowing daughters to inherit. But it also seems to be a strategy for men to fulfil their sexual desires. While men appear to accept, in most cases, their responsibility towards their first wife, patrilineal inheritance structures give them greater power than women, to exercise their choices.

Women's responses to polygyny vary, with the choice of staying in or leaving a marriage rarely being an independent, individual decision. It is influenced by the presence or absence of back-up support from the natal family, kin-group in the marital village, the presence of a son, the balance between self-esteem and material hardship and the relative valuations of women's worth in the particular context. While the exit option is not easy for women, they do challenge polygyny, often with the support of community leaders. In a mixed caste village such as Bagdiha, where the Hindus flaunt monogamy as a culturally superior trait, Santal leaders, in order to show their own culture to be both superior and fairer towards women, too oppose polygyny.

## Widows: The Legitimate Claimants

Research on widows in India has highlighted the endemic deprivation faced by them on account of their social positioning as widows. Patrilocal residence and patrilineal inheritance restrict their mobility, with implications for remarriage, employment, state and community support, as well as cultural and social isolation (Chen, 1998). Their dignity and self-respect can be threatened by rumours, accusations, sexual harassment and physical violence. Yet, it is only as widows that women appear to become legitimate claimants of land, they gain a share of their marital property, albeit on behalf of their sons, and subject to conditions that vary with region.[5] Customary law provides Santal widows a number of rights, differentiated by age, and by the sex and age of their children.

If a childless widow remarries, she severs her connection with her dead husband, his family, land and movables, and can only keep her own personal property. If a widow has children, and then remarries, the situation is more complex. If there are no other male kin, then she herself will hold the property for her sons to inherit. If there are brothers or other kin with stronger claims, they will be the

[5]In a survey of widows in seven Indian states it was found that 51 per cent women inherited a share of their marital property as widows, but only 13 per cent inherited a share of parental property as daughters (Agarwal, 1998: 22)

custodians of the property, until her sons can claim their share, and will also then, be responsible for the provisioning and marriage of her daughters. Dreze (1990) shows that while a third of widows remarry, this does not necessarily reflect freedom to remarry as most of these are levirate unions imposed upon them, as a strategy to keep the property in the family. Amongst the Santals, while levirate is not absent, I only found one case during my entire stay in the region, there is considerable pressure on younger widows to remarry and give up their property claims, as in the case of Jharna.

For a widow who does not remarry, 'She is virtually a substitute for her husband. She steps into his place, acts as his representative and exercises almost all his rights and duties ... provided the community agrees, it is immaterial whether her husband's agnates approve or object' (Archer, 1984[1946]: 171,173). If she has sons, she will act as the head of the family, until her eldest son takes over. When her sons marry, they can demand partition, but she can keep sufficient land to maintain herself.

Several young widows have been allowed to cultivate land, though often in difficult circumstances and faced by considerable harassment. Bahari and Mukhi in Chuapara were widowed when their children were still young.[6] While Bahari found support for cultivating her land from her niece's husband, for Mukhi it was more difficult and she had to wait several years, living in her natal home, until her son was a little older to restart cultivation. She then converted to Christianity and received capital and other support from her local Church for this purpose. The presence of a male heir helped these women protect their claims to the land, as the rights of a son cannot be denied.

A further problem lies in the division of social life into different domains. While in the material domain, there is considerable reciprocity, at the level of prestige or ritual exchange (symbolic capital), it is exclusively men who are the transactors, women entirely excluded.

[6] There are six widows in Chuapara, owning a total of seven acres, or about 3.7 per cent of the village agricultural lands. If added, women have control over 11 per cent of the total land (20.91 acres). There are 28 widows in Bagdiha, 21 Santal, 1 Kol, 3 *kumhar* and 3 *teli*. The 21 Santal widows have 126 *bigha*s (42 acres) or approximately 8 per cent of the village land. If this is added to the recorded land holding, then women here control about 12.6 per cent of the land (Table 7.1).

While widows and separated women do contribute to the agricultural rituals of the village in material terms, they are unable to share in the prestige it brings. Dhaki in Bagdiha said, 'We too give rice, salt and Rs 5 as our contribution for the ritual, but never get to eat the *sude* (sacralised food).' Even the teacher said, 'I don't know what will happen, but they believe that the gods will be unhappy, so don't let women go to the *jaherthan* (place of the Gods).' This exclusion from the ritual and political affairs of the community puts widows at a disadvantage even in terms of securing their material livelihoods, as they are not considered 'complete' social beings and their interests rarely considered in the making of 'community' decisions. Perhaps jealous of her independence, Bahari has been charged with a range of crimes, from petty theft to being a witch, all adding to her burdens.

Amongst older widows, one finds varying levels of dependence and independence, shifting with time and context. When his brother died, Moni's husband kept his brother's wife and started ill-treating Moni. Within a few months, Moni came back to her natal village, got her daughter married and then herself married a widower with two sons and a daughter. She looked after all the children and brought them up. When her husband was sick, she nursed him, mortgaging her share of land for his treatment, as the sons didn't help. Before her husband died, he divided the property and left her a separate share. Yet the elder son by the first wife is not allowing her to cultivate her share of the land. A village meeting was held, where he was advised to give her share to her. He refused, saying she was his stepmother and had no right. Despite the fact that Moni's second husband had earmarked a separate part of the property for her, she is unable to claim even life interest.

Malati Kisku, on the other hand, partitioned the land amongst her five sons, after her husband's death, retaining one *bigha* for her maintenance. Jeevan Soren, her elder son, ploughs the field for her, after which she employs labour and cultivates it. The produce is sufficient for her consumption. She receives a widow pension of Rs 100 per month from the state and uses it for paying for labour and other expenses. While Malati has supportive sons, and hence is able to cultivate her land, Moni has been let down by hers. In Chuapara, most of the older widows were able to negotiate their claims socially, at least for their lifetime. Some, such as Pappu's mother live with the family of their son, combining their share with that of the son. Sonless widows, such as the mothers of Soha and Dibri too, were allowed to cultivate the land until their death. For widows, what seems assured are use or maintenance rights to land for their lifetime, rather than absolute inheritance rights. They are seen to preserve and protect this right on behalf of their sons, hence do not find a separate mention in the records.

The nature of social relationships and social support mechanisms thus determine widows' ability to negotiate their land claims on the ground, though normatively they are accepted as legitimate. The village leadership is generally supportive of such claims. The support of parents or sons is however a key factor, as is external support, be it from the state (e.g. widow pensions) or missionary groups, especially in recent times. Given a context of marginality where people are increasingly required to find their own way in life, the challenge to their claims too comes from their own families—sons and male kin. While they are ensured life interest, the kin, particularly in Bagdiha, are trying different strategies—convincing them to get remarried, refusing to provide plough labour, and harassing them by calling them witches—to make them leave the village. Loopholes are identified for example in Moni's case, it was her second marriage, and in Jharna's case, the absence of sons. While it is true that in their identities as daughters and sisters, they can make claims on their parental property, they usually choose not to do so, preferring to stake claims in their marital property.

The shifts in female identities over time are summarized in Table 7.3. With male identities threatened by state constructions and policies, both in terms of social recognition and their ability to provide for themselves and protect their property, they have sought to enhance control on their own women. Women then have to struggle to maintain even their identities as producers, not just as full social members with equal entitlements, turning often to external actors to support them in this process.

## MALE IDENTITIES, ANXIETIES AND THE MAKING OF '*DAINS*'

While Santal women then have a range of customary rights to property, contextualized by their subject-position, they are also facing new

Table 7.3: Historical Shifts in the Construction of Santal Female Identities

| Elements of Identity | 1870 (Wood) | 1900–10 (Mc Pherson) | 1935 (Gantzer) | 1980s–90s (Contemporary) |
|---|---|---|---|---|
| Land ownership | Community ownership, so had an equal share | Had access and right recorded if in cultivating possession | Lost rights, rigidly excluded from land | Regaining control through use of state discourses, SPTA and community leaders' support |
| Social recognition | Equal participants in cultivation | Had rights and recognized as cultivators | With alienation of land, lost value as producers & status | Increasing controls and restrictions resulting from men's social marginality |
| Self-representation | Equal members, though excluded from community institutions | Appearance of equality, though excluded from community institutions | Economic actors & active cultivators, though excluded from political domain | Economic actors, home-makers and conscious beings, with entitlements to local resources, not just to be protected and given assets as per state's wishes |
| Strategies for acquisition | Local negotiation | Cases in settlement courts | Support to and of parents, cases in settlement courts | Cases in settlement courts and revenue courts, shaming men within community, taking recourse to state/NGO mechanisms |

challenges in realizing these claims, a reflection of growing male anxiety. The challenge to Santal male authority is coming not only from women's assertion of their rights, but from all sides, the police, bureaucrats and petty officials, traders and *mahajans*, a 'public' sphere that seems beyond their control. They are economically marginalized in relation to mainstream society, but also deprived of their social control and power in the local village domain. When something goes wrong in their lives—heavy rains or drought, sickness or death—they can only lay the blame for their misfortunes on one of their own.

Women, who, independent of male control, seem to be leading a life beyond the norm, present themselves as easy targets. Branded as witches, they are then disciplined and punished, re-establishing some semblance of male authority. The importance of 'performance' has been widely discussed in the literature on the construction of gendered identities and the negotiation of power relations (c.f. Moore, 1994, Hollway, 1984, Butler, 1990). These however are not universal, nor always a matter of choice, but adapted to local social and spatial contexts that respond to particular anxieties. The creation of witches is one such localized performance of masculinity that seeks to allay male anxieties in terms of their own social position and authority.

Kelkar and Nathan (1991) have claimed from a study of witch killings in Jharkhand that a majority of the Santal women killed as witches were widows and that the motive was to deprive them of their landed property. While harassment on a daily basis is a reality—the inability to get plough labour, rumour-mongering—killing women as witches seems to be rare, at least in Dumka district. No case of '*dain*' was registered in Gopikandar Police Station and only one in Dumka Mofussil Police Station during 2000–01. Despite the near absence of killings, the profile of women labelled as '*dain*s' does indicate that they are mostly widows, but more importantly, women who have asserted their rights to property or an independent livelihood without male support. Sona, determined to hold on to her land till her son grows up; Choti, equally determined to give her daughter a *gharjawae* marriage in the face of opposition; Mira Gorain, who has dared to expose the illegal activities of her powerful male kin have all been cast as '*dains*'. Women like Teresa, the *anganwadi* worker in Chuapara, evoke jealousy on account of their status in the public domain. Jealousy, not just related to property, but also to status, prestige and social positioning, independence and external contacts, or family disputes, also contribute to the creation of a '*dain*'.

Kelkar and Nathan (1991: 102) mention that branding a woman as a witch legitimizes violence against her, and is one way that men respond to a challenge to their authority by women. They also point out that the struggle is not between witches and witch-finders, but within clans as a whole, to establish a new male order in ritual, political and economic terms. While the ritual and political exclusion of women has more or less been established, it is their economic independence that has to be controlled. This can happen in a range of ways, the starkest being, of course, depriving them of land, a critical asset in a primarily rural context. But there are other ways too, for instance, men marketing the forest produce collected by women, or accompanying women during labour migration to West Bengal, the stated reason here being the need to protect women from sexual harassment by the *diku* traders or employers. Given the growing dominance of the non-*adivasi*, primarily Hindu trader caste groups in the public/economic domain, who follow rigid gender norms, Santal men too are trying to re-establish their spheres of control, starting with the domestic realm to compensate for what they have lost in the public.

Clearly there is a shift in the basic principles underlying gender relationships here. I started the last chapter with a statement that women are recognized as equal partners in the domestic domain, their subordination lies in their exclusion from the more public and ritual domains. What one finds now are subtle and not-so-subtle shifts to control women's labour in the domestic domain as well, a result of male anxieties in relation to their own position in the public realm. Rather than an intention to subordinate women per se, the particular manifestations of local masculinities can be understood as a reaction to several extraneous factors: state policies that are pro-women and treat all *adivasis*, particularly the men, as backward and lazy; an increasingly Hinduized public sphere which entails restricting women to the domestic sphere as a reflection of male valour and honour and the growth of consumer capitalism in which Santal men are unable to adequately participate. Conscious of this shift, women have to choose their strategies carefully, compromising when needed, yet ensuring that their identities are not completely trampled over. Weaving their way carefully through both state constructed and indigenous identities, gives Sona, Rimani and so many other women like them the courage to say 'No'.

Attacks on women become necessary only where they have authority and assert it, not where their status is already low or patriarchy firmly established. Violence itself then, '*dain*' harassment being one form, is a reflection of male anxiety about their own roles and an attempt to maintain certain notions of power and identity, a response to the challenge to masculinity by women's assertion, rather than a sign of women's victimhood. Violation of the social and sexual norms and principles they have set up to establish male authority is used to justify violent sanctions against women. It points to the crisis in the gender order, as a legitimate hierarchy would have less need to intimidate. This is clear from the fact that instead of accepting such violence passively, women use different sites and discourses to upturn the '*dain*' accusations against them. So while Choti accompanies her male kin to the *ojha* and gets her name cleared, Sona goes to the local panchayat for support and Mira to the police. It is a public process of negotiating their rights and identities as members of the community, reasserting their equal status in the domestic domain.

In 1999, the Prevention of Witchcraft Act was passed by the Indian Parliament. It has been presented as a legislation to protect *adivasi* women's life and rights against their men. While it can be seen as a gender-progressive legislation, by viewing witch-killing as a result of superstition and illiteracy rather than as a response to economic and regional marginality resulting in a struggle to renegotiate gender relationships, it ignores the economic and social relations and anxieties underlying this phenomenon.

Now that the state and police are quick to record and investigate '*dain*' cases, Santal men use this provision in their own struggles against their male kin, as in the case of Chetan in Chuapara, or for gaining benefits from the government. In a village near Bagdiha, Juna Hansdak brought a charge of '*dain*' against his daughter-in-law, with the support of a Hindu moneylender. While dispossessing her from her share of the property was one aim, another was to use the state discourse of 'backwardness' of the *adivasis*, to secure contracts and benefits—securing more resources for their 'development'. It seems to confirm Tsing's (1993) thesis that cultural difference is both a sign of exclusion from the centre, and a tool for destabilising central authority. Santal men like Juna use the '*dain*' discourse in the official realm to secure benefits, and in turn, some authority, for themselves. Clearly the issue of '*dains*' in the contemporary context reflects a larger power struggle for status, prestige and resource control amongst different castes, classes, ethnic groups and genders.

## CONCLUSION

Land is important for women to fulfil their household maintenance functions within marriage. It is even more crucial in the event of widowhood or marital breakdown, when they have to take on the full role of 'provider'. Realizing that male anxieties have increased in a context where they are constantly being devalued by state and market institutions, to resist male pressure and garner their support, women therefore often claim weakness and vulnerability, or the lack of happiness. The feeling of being valued and needed by their women becomes an affirmation of male identity. This has however led to renewed efforts to seek legitimacy for their authority, by reasserting their collective kin and lineage identity vis-à-vis the outside environment but also rigidifying gender ideologies at home. Despite women's efforts to appease men, these contests over power and authority between different groups of men end by denying women their rights. At the same time, women use state constructed identities of themselves and the pro-women policies advocated by the state, to make gains in their indigenously constructed identities. While their strategies can at times expose them to violence, they also offer lessons on how notions of mutuality and interdependence can be established even in contexts that are largely hierarchical.

Valuations of different types of action or indeed the constituents of mutuality are not hard and fast rules, but are negotiated, and change over the life-course, influenced by the different sub-cultures and livelihood trajectories, land tenure arrangements and political history. This is reflected in the different response patterns in the two villages, the different sites of contestation and the range of legitimizing discourses prevalent therein that I turn to in the next chapter.

CHAPTER

# 8 Custom and the Courts
## Bargaining with Modernity

Contests over property reflect and shape relationships between people over a period of time, as much as they do between people and resources.[1] They also reflect competing representations of these relationships and notions of the 'community' in specific political-economic contexts (Li, 1996). Women occupy a disadvantaged position in terms of property rights within traditional social structures, and as a result, in contexts of scarcity, their rights are likely to be the first to be challenged. But the claims for women's rights to landed property also represent the struggles over institutions, status, identities, roles, rules and practices, not just between men and women, but between different groups of men as well.

I have previously indicated that both women and men hold differentiated views on property depending on their particular subject-positions. Gender does not, however, override other identities, say, of class or caste in relation to land. Women do often take forward projects of masculinity in furthering the material interest and prestige of their own household unit. Men too support the claims of their wives as daughters, and senior men, of destitute women in general, when they see gains in such a position. In this chapter, I discuss the multiple arenas in which women's land claims are contested and negotiated. What are the ideological bases for different positions and how far do women's land claims get established as legitimate in these different arenas?

[1] A large part of this chapter has been published in *Development and Change* 38(2), pp. 299–319, 2007.

Following the Convention on the Elimination of All Forms of Discrimination Against Women (CEDAW) and the UN Women's Decade, laws and administrative policies in India have tended to favour women,[2] a major victory being the amendment in August 2005 to the Hindu Succession Act (1956), providing equal inheritance rights to all daughters, including married ones. While this provides women opportunities to claim their share of land through judicial and revenue courts, there is a gap in practice (see Agarwal 1994 for a detailed discussion). The reason for the gap can be found in the social embeddedness of land and the relational aspects of gender, which however are largely ignored by the statutory codes that treat all people as equal, autonomous individuals (Basu, 1999).

The failure to ensure property rights to women, has, in recent times, led to a decline in agricultural productivity in the context of men migrating in search of non-farm employment. This has pushed policy-makers at both national and international levels towards a consideration of more locally negotiated land management systems (Toulmin and Quan, 2000, Gopal, 1999). This is also driven by the asymmetrically gendered formal court processes, with women not having equal access to courts due to lack of time, resources, mobility and judicial bias. Yet local institutions too can be hierarchical and highly iniquitous, and the 'resurgence of policy interest in various local and informal mechanisms and institutions for land management', alongside the emphasis on developing land markets, have also been identified as threats to poorer women being able to access land on a secure basis (UNRISD, 2005: 13). A key question that arises in this context is one of interpretation—how is law interpreted, and by whom?

Faced with such a choice, feminist lawyers and their networks, such as the Lawyer's Collective in India (c.f. Jaising, 1996, Kapur and Cossman, 1996) or the Women and Law in Southern Africa (WLSA) a network in seven countries of southern Africa, continue to uphold legal reform as the way forward for ensuring women's rights (Knowles, 1991). In India, feminist researchers such as Bina Agarwal (1994, 2003) and NGO collectives such as the Working Group on Women's

[2]Apart from the Five Year Plans, a key policy statement for women is the National Policy for the Empowerment of Women 2001.

Land Ownership (WGWLO) in Gujarat or the Gender, Livelihood and Resources Forum in Jharkhand also repose greater faith in legal and policy reform than in changing customary value systems that are largely patriarchal. This has led them to adopt additional strategies of raising awareness within the community and providing support on the ground when required. While a legal framework is undeniably crucial in enabling women to make land claims, the role, scope and limitations of such legitimization systems also need to be recognized, as does the problematic of separating the material from the social-symbolic realms with respect to land.

Also, the concept of a right to land itself needs unravelling. Does it refer to ownership as embodied in a legal title and registration in the record of rights, or is it the ability to access and use the land with varying levels of control, which could be seen as stages in the process of empowerment? While striving towards legal control with a proper land title, there is a simultaneous need to work on issues of social legitimacy, drawing on custom, if needed, to ensure access and use. Legal ownership in an individual, can in fact, curtail relations between people, 'owners can exclude those who do not belong' (Strathern, 1996: 529). Seeing the process of claiming absolute rights in land as a process of exclusion provides some insight into why women themselves may not claim exclusive rights; inherent in such a step is the danger of excluding male support for land-related and other enterprises in the future. Such an understanding raises the issue both of inclusive, perhaps collective rights and of collective interpretations of individual rights as forms of social protection, particularly in indigenous communities, marginalized from the mainstream.

Examining theories of social praxis in conjunction with theories of jurisprudence becomes necessary as 'rules of the game' include elements of state law as well as norms and rules evolved from social life and practice. If law is seen as a social process, one cannot dichotomize between the modern and the traditional. Yet this dichotomy continues to dominate global discourse. Apart from the IFAD Rural Poverty Report, the World Bank's landmark Land Reform Policy Paper of 1975, recommended land titling, the abandonment of communal tenure systems and the promotion of land markets as preconditions of modern development. Even though the Bank's policy document of 2001 argues for legal recognition of customary tenure, in practice, it continues to finance large-scale land titling and registration projects (Whitehead and Tsikata, 2003), with the majority of the land being titled to men (World Bank, 2005). The issue then is to recognize the temporal and political situatedness of 'law', and the processes that allow a legal right to be actualized, by providing social recognition and validity. Women use different arenas from the extended household and kin-group to outside agencies (the courts) to make their claims, the choice of arena depending on access, legitimacy and available resources, as well as their own expectations of social support or lack of support.

## WHAT DOES LAW REALLY MEAN?

In order to reverse the prevalent social and economic inequalities, the democratic state in independent India has sought to plan the core development sectors of the economy. While policies may be centralized, governments are not monolithic entities. State policies are interpreted by individual bureaucrats at different levels according to their own ideologies as social actors. Bureaucrats, lawyers and judges in Dumka, for instance, mostly Hindu men, bring into play their own ideas of what is appropriate and what is not, for men and women. Their own male biases have often led them to treat women as 'dependents' rather than independent actors, muting in the process, both women's voices and claims. Thus, even though the new land reform guidelines prioritize women in all land distribution programmes, no woman has actually received land in the last few years. Still, the existence of policies can be used as leverage in political struggles for resources.

In the last decade, the state has been pulling back from the economy in line with processes of liberalization and the operation of global markets. Perhaps there is also a recognition of the limits of the centralized state and the need to include local and customary knowledge for effective administration. A process of decentralization through local self-government or *Panchayati Raj* institutions has followed this, though not yet operational in Dumka district (as other parts of Jharkhand state). While decentralized governance and the use of local and customary practices should not be romanticized, it is important to note that these too are not static but are constantly adapted and reinvented in the process of interaction with state authority.

Parallel to the development state, the legal system, both customary and modern, is embedded in society and social relations. Drawing on the human rights discourse, modern law is seen as a government-enforceable tool that is impartial to individuals in the maintenance of a stable social order, while customary law is seen as a set of binding practices of local peoples. Considerable literature on the interlocking of the personal and political dimensions of disputes indicates that such a dichotomy may not be entirely valid, as every interaction may contain a range of alternatives. An individual may be subject, at the same time, to rules of the family, kinship and community networks, religion and to those of formal state and market organizations including international treaties and even project practices. Each of these can be seen as 'semi-autonomous social fields', with an intermeshing of legal and non-legal norms that may be generated internally, but are also subject to rules and decisions emanating from the larger external world (Moore, 1978: 55).

People may also behave differently in the private and public realms, and this reflects a way of accommodating traditional and modern forces. For example, while an upper caste person may not generally eat with a scheduled caste in his or her personal life, he may be forced to do so in a more public, political space (Rudolph and Rudolph 1967: 122), like the workplace. If there is an expectation that this behaviour should be replicated in the private realm, there is a greater likelihood of conflict and resistance. This appears to be particularly true in relation to property rights, seen as an essential element of kinship systems, yet now sought to be governed by statutory law. In response to overly simplistic models of both statutory law and customary practice, Moore has pointed out: 'In reality boundaries were not always clear, that mixed systems and intermediate types were commonplace, that transformation and transition were ubiquitous, and that conflict and contradiction were inherent in social life and human thought' (1986: 4).[3]

[3] O'Rourke (1995) shows how despite the passing of the Land Act in 1963, in Tanzania, the Chagga in Mount Kilimanjaro continued to determine land rights through the local lineage-neighbourhood complex.

Rules and laws thus include ambiguities and are open to a range of interpretations. In the present context, what happens is that rather than operating as separate fields, the main actors seek to make connections between the two. Hybrid systems of jurisprudence begin to emerge, with village leaders often using the state systems to legitimize their viewpoint and vice versa, rather than trying to assert the superiority of one or the other. An account from Papua New Guinea (Demian 2003) demonstrates how custom is invoked as a legal tool in the courtroom, and is seen to have moral weight, and therefore, better able to fix responsibility. What happens at the village level often follows the statutory code, which being more distant, evokes more fear and hence compliance.

Seeing the statutory and customary as two parallel rather than interconnected systems implies that the basic principles of the two systems differ. While there appears to be an underlying singularity in terms of fairness, justice and equity in the two systems, what differs is the morality which sets up the framework of interpretation. Modern law, based on universalist generalizations about social reality, tends to deny the collective interpretation of the individual's rights and needs, as shaped by her or his social positionality, which forms the practice of the customary systems. This is because in modern law, the individual is treated as an autonomous entity rather than as part of a larger social domain, embedded simultaneously in community relationships and rules. Universalism and individualism appear to be the cornerstones of the modernist project as opposed to context-specificity and social embeddedness within the local systems.

While the dichotomy in legal systems may be more of a myth in practice, it persists in discourse; and plays a major role in shifting the relative bargaining positions of people dealing with one another. As Meinzen-Dick and Pradhan note, 'multiple legal frameworks also provide flexibility for people to manoeuvre in their use of natural resources' (2002: 2). In the Jahaly Pacharr irrigated rice scheme in the Gambia, for instance, men used the discourse of tradition to maintain control over land rights and women's labour (Carney, 1988). On the other hand, in Kenya, women disguised their acts of resistance in the authorized vocabulary and discourse of the state, such as using the *harambee* ideology of self-help groups to withdraw labour from their household plots controlled by men, and use it instead for paid wage work (Mackenzie, 1990). The selective use of the available and recognized legal discourses is visible in the case of Santal women too. Soha, Sona, Munni are all attempting to claim recognition and rights under the rubric of national policies that provide for equal rights to women, while simultaneously trying to manipulate customary law to their advantage. The very diversity of practices gives them room for manoeuvre.

Much of the debate around legal pluralism today is really about the nature of the state in the context of globalization—how far does the state acknowledge diverse social fields within society or seek collaboration with non-state social fields for the implementation of its laws and policies (Moore, 2001: 107), and what is the distribution of power between these different actors? Rather than pluralism, this reflects a move towards hybridization, the picking of different rules and norms from different fields to construct a new code of practice, changing in response to the context. Apart from the recognized fields of the family, economy and the state, Nancy Fraser points to the presence of a relatively open, societal arena as a site of discourse about people's needs, particularly problematic needs, which were earlier considered 'private' matters (1989: 156). Village men and women may be unable to participate directly in this 'social' arena but their views do shape and are shaped by discourse here, through the overlapping identities of the concerned 'publics'—be they lawyers, activists, missionaries or political leaders.

## LAWS IN PRACTICE

I turn now to the practice in resolving disputes in daily life and the ways in which it operates at different levels, from the household to the courts. I focus particularly on women's inheritance rights through marriage to a *gharjawae* as this is one customary practice that is recognized in the statutory law governing land relations, namely, the Santal Pargana Tenancy Act (SPTA), 1949, Section 20(2) (Prasad, 1997).

### The Household and Kin Group

The considerable literature on households and intra-household relationships that discusses power and negotiation within the household, based on the relative resources that men and women are able to command (Hart, 1997, Whitehead, 1981), sees law as one such resource in struggles over land. Yet different resources have very different potentials for enhancing women's voice within the household. Access to land, waged employment or education, for instance, can lead to distinct outcomes in terms of critical life choices for women, in varied social contexts. One needs also to remember that women may exercise their agency in tune with their particular subject-positions, and not as women per se. So they may be more vocal in highlighting their roles as mothers vis-à-vis their children, rather than as wives in conjugal relationships; and widows may contest their claims to their husband's property on behalf of their sons (or daughters), rather than for their own survival.

Amongst the Santals, the *gharjawae* is a social mechanism set up to enable a daughter to inherit her father's land. Her father negotiates this arrangement with his male kin and gains acceptance through a ritual village feast. While Archer (1984 [1946]) has pointed to the flexibilities in customary law in the case of a *gharjawae*—it can be performed by the widowed mother, a second marriage can be performed to a *gharjawae*, more than one daughter can be married to *gharjawaes*—these flexibilities are now being strongly contested. More so because the SPTA, 1949, does not take note of such instances, but recognizes the rights of a *gharjawae* only in the absence of a male heir. So, we have a situation where a customary practice is absorbed into state legal practice, but with differing underlying assumptions and this makes negotiation difficult.

The struggle at this level then, is not within the nuclear household, but within the patrilineage. Women have adopted several strategies for negotiation, to build up the legitimacy for a claim: getting a daughter married to a *ghardijawae* (Choti Tudu), seeking support from married daughters and their husbands (Sona Tudu), maintaining cattle to negotiate plough labour (Dhaki Marandi), or filing complaints with the panchayat or police, when the harassment threatens to get violent. Their preference seems to be to negotiate solutions within the household, using 'authority from outside' only to strengthen their voice. The discourse here focuses on the material value of land as a key subsistence resource, and hence its criticality in both men's and women's lives.

The most successful negotiation of claims to land by women at the household level seems to be within the marital relationship. In the case of both Jeevan Soren and Girish Soren, once the man had decided to enter a polygynous relationship, the usufruct rights in the property were divided by mutual negotiation, as the *badkis* refused to stay in the same house with a second wife. While leading, no doubt, to control over the land, this narrative tends to sustain the 'maleness' of property. Widows' claims to their husband's land, while seen as legitimate, still have to be negotiated. Those with sons have found it easier to do so than those without. While younger widows cannot be displaced from the land directly, pressure has been brought to bear on them by their husband's male kin in many ways—to get remarried, or to live jointly with them and cultivate the land together, and finally, to prevent them access to plough labour. In some cases, harassment has been physical, starting with accusations of being a '*dain*' and going on to physical threats.

As women's claims to land directly affect the material interests of the male agnates, in a context of scarce resources, it appears difficult for these to be successfully contested within the arena of the household or kin group. At best, temporary solutions can be reached, but situated within long-term processes of competition, these tend to ultimately work against the interests of the women concerned. The contestation then invariably spills into the more public arenas, at both the village and state levels.

## The Village Council

When negotiations fail within the household or kin group, the case is taken to the village council. In the case of Munni Murmu of Bagdiha or Soha Marandi of Chuapara, the village leaders tried several times to resolve the dispute locally. Yet when the male kin refused to comply with the decision and turned to violence, the case was referred to the police and courts. *Gharjawae* cases are more likely to be referred to the courts, as they have legal backing.

In the case of a sister's claim, the village council can request a brother to accept it, but cannot force him to do so. The brother often argues that he is keeping his sister in his house, feeding her and maintaining her in all respects, thus challenging the legitimacy of her claim to a share of the land. The village leadership too are often of the view that a sister's rights are temporary in nature, and that she should claim her permanent rights in her marital property.

Cases relating to wives and co-wives seem to predominate in the village arena. Noni's husband Shyam, in Bagdiha, brought a *chutki*, in spite of her resistance. He was unwilling to give Noni a share of the land. She went to the *majhi* and explained her case, and a time was fixed for the village meeting. Then Noni went around the *tola* to the houses of several of the male elders, speaking to them directly or in their absence, to their wives, telling her own story. She managed to secure their support and thus successfully negotiate a share of the resources, both land and other assets. In the case of Rimani, discussed in Chapter 7, the *majhi* wanted her to share the land with her husband, but she refused. The *majhi* did not see this as a struggle over property, but rather as a struggle over a man. Rimani used the land as leverage to get the man back, as without land, his male identity was incomplete. For the *majhi*, both the competing parties were women, and the man and his property the object of struggle. In the legal arena, the only resolution would be through a formal process of divorce. This would lead to the granting of maintenance in cash. In a situation of subsistence, where survival depends on both cultivation and labour and the social linkages of both men and women, it is unlikely that a man could provide this maintenance. Even a well-off man like Sunil is unable to do so; as for Dhaki or Mahani, they have never expected to receive any compensation from their husbands, often worse off than themselves. Gender, property and marriage are closely interlinked and it is difficult to deal with any one of them in isolation from the others, as the courts tend to do; hence if women want land, the village arena seems the more appropriate one.

Women are not represented in the village council,[4] nor are they present in the courts at the district level as officials, lawyers or judges. Yet legally they have equal access to the state institutions, while their participation in village meetings is restricted. In the words of the *majhi* of Bagdiha,

[4] A woman can become a *majhi* if her husband is *majhi* and dismissed for improper conduct or her father was *majhi* and she is the only child. If a woman is *majhi*, then she can collect revenue and *bheeja* (ritual offerings) during festivals, but cannot participate in the village justice process or outdoor rituals.

When a case involves women, they will narrate everything from the beginning, so it becomes embarrassing for the men. They have to turn their heads away in shame. Women don't participate in the *kulhi durup* (village meeting), as their presence will embarrass their male relatives even further. If a case involves a man, he can be told to cut it short, but with a woman she can't (31 May 2000).

Women articulate the nuances of social relationships in great depth, recounting little details that may seem insignificant, but are 'embarrassing' to the male leadership and a threat to their masculinities. As in the account of ritual space, men here appear fearful of their dignity being challenged, hence exclude women from this space. While Noni was not allowed to speak in the village meeting, much of the background work had already been done through her informal conversations before the formal meeting.

Despite the formal exclusion, a majority of women who have effectively claimed land have done so through negotiation at the village level. This is particularly true for widows, abandoned wives and women in polygynous relationships, for whom in fact, there is no clear recognition in the statute. Despite being male bastions, community institutions do appear more responsive to competing discourses, having as they do, a direct knowledge of the local context and relationships, responding on a case by case basis, rather than through universal policies. Judgments of the village council are also more likely to be followed by the parties in question because of the focus on consensus and maintaining dignity for both parties, rather than identifying winners and losers.

## The Settlement Courts

The settlement court is an intermediate institution set up during the second land revenue settlement in the Santal Parganas, supervised by McPherson from 1898–1908, to hear and resolve disputes in the process of land titling and settlement of rents. The very process of settlement, by providing the space to raise objections, presented an arena for negotiating and contesting rights to land. Hearings were conducted in local camps, seen as cheaper, quicker and more accessible than the formal courts, yet following a set of universal norms of fairness in opposition to the traditional structures. During this settlement, many of the cases filed in the settlement courts related to title claims, disputes over who had cleared the land and in whose name it should be registered. These contestations were usually between men.

During the next settlement, supervised by Gantzer (1925–37), the nature of disputes began to change. While still predominantly between men, they now related to issues of inheritance within kin groups as well as disputes on tenancy agreements. During the current settlement period from 1980 onwards, we find an intensification of inheritance and tenancy disputes. The relatively new trend is the preponderance of *gharjawae* registrations, given also its legal recognition, and the contestations around this (See Annexure 4, Boxes 3 and 4 for examples). Women have realized the importance of such registration during their lifetime in order to avoid conflicts, even violence, in the future, as happened in the case of Munni's son. In the event of a woman's claim being challenged, a notice is sent and a hearing held to decide the case. Women attempt to secure the support of other women in their position, and of key men in the village as witnesses. The village leaders are generally supportive of these women, wanting to project their society as fair and just, as opposed to the more patriarchal and restrictive Hindu society.[5] Further, the *majhi* of one of the *tolas* of Bagdiha, himself a *gharjawae*, championed this cause with the other leaders. Women's claims in their other roles as sisters, wives or widows, are not brought to the settlement courts, as legally, the SPTA accepts them as gifts (or concessions) rather than rights.

In addition to the Settlement Officer, the land settlement process involves two other functionaries, who play a key role in influencing the adjudication process: the *amin* who measures the land, and the *karamchari* who is responsible both for rent collections and the evaluation of social security claims such as pensions for widows and the aged. The latter maintains copies of the rent receipts, which form crucial evidence in terms of rival claims to land. While there are differences in the attitudes of these petty bureaucrats, based on their own personal histories and positions,[6] we do find, in general, a tendency

[5]With a large Hindu population in Bagdiha, comparisons and inter-community one-upmanship is continuous. In the economic realm, the Hindus have the upper hand, so one way for the Santals to establish their superiority is through their social and cultural practices.

[6]While there are almost an equal number of Santal and non-Santal *amins* and *karamcharis*, as one moves up the hierarchy, the majority of the officers are non-Santals.

to support *gharjawae* rights in an attempt perhaps to appear 'modern' and above their local caste or ethnic prejudices in line with the national legal framework. As Panthi Marandi narrated, 'the *amin* of Guhiajori took me to the settlement camp. He asked me to get my name registered.' Such persons, with knowledge of state policies and legal procedures, then replace local mediators, significant in moulding opinion at the village level, as people do continue to fear the written word, especially as represented by officialdom. Villagers also try to establish closeness with those with access to the records, using this as leverage in local power struggles, gaining as a result, not just materially, but also in status and prestige.

The settlement courts present a good example of processes of hybridization, of local and national discourses feeding into each other, to legitimize and strengthen women's land claims. When disputes threaten to get violent, however, the only recourse is to the courts of law, both civil and criminal. While the former lie in the purview of the Revenue Department—the courts of the Sub-Divisional Officer (SDO), Assistant Collector (AC) and District Collector (DC), the latter cases are normally filed through the police stations and go directly to the courts of the Sub-Judge and District Judge. Administratively, the former are part of the Executive, while the latter are governed by the rules and norms of the Judiciary. In both cases, their distance from the village and 'perceived authority' creates fear in the minds of the opponents, much more than the diktat of the village leadership. Yet, to uphold their own moral authority, leaders of the village council, usually support women's claims in the courts, through establishing informal linkages, contacts and arrangements with the 'legitimate' institutions of state, and also formal presentation of evidence in the court where the case is being tried.

## Revenue and Civil Courts

There are perhaps a hundred revenue cases of various types registered in the civil courts of Dumka each month, 75 per cent of them relating to issues of demarcation, tenancy and inheritance. According to the Registers of the Sub-Divisional Court, 12–15 per cent of the cases in this category have involved women in the last decade (See Annexure 4, Tables 1–3). Oral evidence seems to suggest that contestation has increased since the early 1980s; longer-term court data were not available to confirm this.

The first point of reference for the civil courts is the SPTA which seeks to protect *adivasi* land from alienation by prohibiting all land transfers (Section 20), but has provided for women's rights as exceptions to the rule. In the case of a sister, daughter, widowed mother or wife, it provides for gift or grant with the written permission of the Deputy Commissioner (Section 20(1)). Only in the case of a *gharjawae* is it considered a legitimate right (Section 20(2)). However, following Gantzer, the SPTA has represented the *gharjawae* as an adopted son-in-law who inherits the land, rather than the daughter. By thus splitting descent group from property inheritance, it opened the space for objections from the woman's male natal kin.

Archer had hoped to record as case law the flexibilities in Santal law with respect to women's rights. His report was however rejected by the government of independent India. In the absence of such a body of case law, the civil courts draw on the advice of the village leaders in deciding cases. Despite the change in form, social and kin relationships thus continue to play a role in determining access to land. Yet, the legalization of their voice, through the SPTA and the court process, gives it a 'public constituency' (Crook, 2001: 43) rather than being an exclusive privilege of elite 'insiders' (Khadiagala, 2001), as has often been the charge against customary institutions. If the village leaders fail to reach a consensus, then the court draws upon the Hindu Succession Act (HSA), 1956, which provides equal inheritance rights to the widow, sons and daughters, in the event of a man's death. In most cases, however, the mere possibility of such recourse to Hindu law paves the way for a negotiated decision!

The key difference between the settlement courts and the civil courts is the intervening role of the lawyers in the latter. This is one reason why the Santals often stop attending regularly even the cases they themselves have filed in the court, as they begin to find the lawyers' fees, payable over a period of several years, burdensome. Women often file cases as government suits, implying a waiver of legal fees. However, non-payment of fee completely robs the lawyers of the motivation to argue or resolve the case, and often such cases drag on for many years. The only woman in Bagdiha who has filed such a case and pursued it is the widow Mira Gorain, belonging to the group of Hindu *telis*. While eking out a meagre existence by making and selling *murri* (puffed rice), she is sure of an ultimate resolution in her favour, as per the HSA, 1956.

While I have not pursued the relationship of Hindu women with land in any detail in this book, a brief comment is needed at this point. While land is perhaps as important to Mira as to any of the Santal women as a source of subsistence, she does not cultivate it directly, but leases it out, mainly to the Santals. She has an alternate source of earning, even though it is not hugely profitable, and hence can afford to wait for the court decisions. Without generalizing about all Hindu women, it must be said that the relationship of the *mahajan* and *teli* women in Bagdiha with land is more indirect, a mere step in the ladder of upward mobility in the caste hierarchy. For a majority of Santal women, on the other hand, inability to cultivate would, in all probability, lead to migration from their homes. They cannot wait several years for a court decision, and prefer an immediate decision through social negotiation.

The differences between the Santals and the Hindus in using the courts takes us back to the issue of culture, institutions and the construction of identities in relation to land. While the *telis* see land mainly as an economic resource, drawing their basic identity from their skills in trade and commerce, for the Santals, land is the basis of their identity, culture and rituals, as well as their fears and aspirations. The historical associations of land make it as much a matter of concern for the collective as for the individual. There is hence a greater willingness to negotiate alternate claims at the local level, as the pressure to find a satisfactory solution is high.

When cases are filed in the courts, however, it falls upon the judge (the SDO, AC or DC), usually a non-Santal, to reach a decision. In cases where witnesses are called, the *karamcharis*, *amins* and village leaders do play an influencing role. But as Moore (1978) has pointed out, while laws are seen as rational and systematic norms by the state, they are open to different interpretations to accommodate the complexities of social life, and in keeping with the different social positionings of the state personnel themselves. While evidence in terms of marriage registration and rent receipts are produced where

8.1: The revenue court. Waiting to be heard.

available, these too are challenged, and land cases are argued mainly on the basis of genealogies and migrations, with claims resting on historical, often oral knowledge. Production of oral history being competitive, some voices carry more weight than others, owing to their social position, and as Dhagamwar (2003) points out, courts have often ended up giving judgements in favour of dominant interests. It is no surprise then that the poor, particularly women, see the state as allocating land to and supporting the 'big' people, those able to 'feed' them (Goheen, 1988: 298) and hence, prefer the customary courts.

While NGOs have been active both in advocating for women's legal rights to land and in the struggle of *adivasis* and other oppressed groups against the *mahajans*, they have not often engaged directly in the legal arena. More recently, some NGOs have been providing legal aid and helping *adivasis* file cases for reclamation of alienated land in the local courts. Despite lack of information and access, legal support is adding authority to women's voice and strengthening their land claims. They may even stop attending the hearings, as in the case of Soha, yet recognize the value of the courts as a site for the reinterpretation of their claims at the local level.

## Criminal Courts

Criminal cases range from minor beating (Section 107) and breach of peace (Section 144), to robbery (Section 394) and murder (Section 302). A police complaint is filed and the case proceeds according to the normal legal process. The court fixes dates for hearings, lawyers are appointed and the case is argued. While there is an attempt to resolve minor cases within a period of 60 days, most others go on for years.

In the case of Munni, for instance, the case grew out of the questioning of a woman's inheritance. Before the murder of her son, the kin adopted a range of strategies from verbal threats to petty thefts and robberies in order to frighten their cousins and make them give up claims on the property of their mother, the inheritor. For a decade, a range of cases, both civil and criminal were filed, police protection was sought at different points, yet the murder could not be averted (Annexure 4, Box 3). The core of the dispute was material with competing claims for a scarce resource, justified by the use of kinship and descent ideologies. Munni's cousin brother had performed the funeral rites for her father. As the next in line in the descent group, his sons now claimed the land as legitimately theirs. Her marriage to a *gharjawae* too was challenged in the process.

While both sides are now in a precarious position, struggling to survive, neither side is prepared to give in. Gender is incidental in this context—a convenient justification for claiming the inheritance with women of the accused household supporting their men in the struggle. Realizing that it was easier to contest the rights of an inheriting daughter than an inheriting son, they brought in notions of appropriate roles and conduct for women: 'Good women should not claim a share in the inheritance. Even if there are no brothers, the daughter should give up her claims in favour of the male agnates.' Such notions of female identity, the ideologies of a good daughter and a dependent wife, articulated by the women, both meet their own gender interests at that particular moment, and serve to, once again, reinforce the notion of land as a male resource.

Unlike the discourse in the settlement courts or even the revenue courts, that lay much greater emphasis on customary law and practice, and are hence perceived as more accessible by Santal men and women, the discourse in the criminal courts is couched in the language of the

Indian Penal Code. It relies much more on reports from the police than the viewpoints of the local leaders. The police do consult village leaders before making their report, but are easily influenced by bribes, often turning a blind eye to crucial evidence. The normative basis of criminal justice is thus a universal one, rather than dependent on local contexts.

The use of legal terminology enhances the dependence on lawyers, and makes the role and motivation of lawyers critical. Mostly non-Santal, they tend to look down on their clients. Several interviews with both Muslim and Hindu lawyers in Dumka revealed that they construct Santal men as constantly drunk, good for nothing and getting themselves into unnecessary trouble, and Santal women as hard-working, yet ignorant and promiscuous. They are not really concerned about the long-term outcomes of the case, for instance, the political implications of securing bail for the killers of Munni's son. If lawyers are progressively motivated, however, they can play a major role in positively influencing the judicial process on behalf of the marginal, as during the agrarian struggle in the late 1960s.

Unlike the issue of title registrations in the settlement courts, the number of cases brought to the civil and criminal courts by Santal women remains limited, for reasons of time, resources and legitimacy. Village leaders support women in the settlement and lower revenue courts but discourage them from going to the higher courts. Their voice is hardly heard there and they see this as an affront to their prestige. Instead they try their best to resolve such disputes locally. Further, while distance from the village does evoke a sense of fear, exclusion of local discourse, especially from the criminal courts, makes it difficult for them to influence the final outcomes.

Law can thus be both empowering and disempowering, depending on the particular perspective from which it is viewed. Titling is not necessarily better than the flexible rights ensured by customary practice, as these are legitimized by a sense of social responsibility, not fully encapsulated in the legalities of land rights. One needs to accept that social relationships, particularly of gender, embrace elements of conflict and competition, as well as cooperation and mutual support.

Legal pluralism, according to Benda-Beckman (2001: 48), is an acknowledgement of 'the theoretical possibility of more than one legal order, based on different sources of ultimate validity and maintained by forms of organisation other than the State'. It does not imply a normative preference for one or the other, as the choice of the arena for contestation is ultimately a political one, determining as it does the access to resources. In practice however, there is an interpenetration of state and customary laws, and a complex relationship between ethnicity, a struggle for identity and these plural systems of law, with the boundaries often blurred.

## THE 'SOCIAL' CONTEXT

A range of actors—Santal men and women, village leaders, lawyers, petty and higher bureaucracy, judges—participate in the formal arenas where women's claims to land are contested. Others, such as missionaries, NGOs or political party leaders may not directly intervene here, yet representatives of these groups, in their roles as village men or women, carry these views into their other subject-positions. The point to note is not only the presence of multiple actors and multiple arenas for contesting rights, but also the overlapping of different identities in these arenas. On account of their particular political affiliations at different moments in history, lawyers, for instance, have been critical in influencing social outcomes. *Adivasi* lawyers have often opposed Santal women's rights, seeing themselves as political activists or professional elite, rather than lawyers alone.

Engaged in development interventions, NGOs on the other hand, firmly support women's land claims, though reaching this position from different perspectives. While some work with a feminist stance, others have participated in the land and forest struggles amongst *adivasi* communities, and still others on livelihood issues. Badlao Foundation, for instance, in a survey conducted in 60 villages of Jamtara, found 165 cases of abandoned women, facing a crisis of livelihoods in the absence of land (1998). They therefore initiated advocacy in favour of women's inheritance of natal property as daughters. However, this ended up diverging from the views of the women, both in terms of content and strategy. While women at the village level seem to prefer staking claims in marital property, as the cases discussed earlier reveal, NGOs (and the state) have focused on the inheritance of parental property; and while women seem to prefer social negotiation at the local level in the first instance, NGOs emphasize legal reform. Progressive from a rights-based perspective to women's equality, the NGOs assume that women do not have rights in customary law. Further, power relations in the 'modern' institutions of state are not questioned, nor the institutional and cultural biases that prevent women from making their claims.

A gradual shift is however visible in this perspective. The Jharkhand Mahila Mukti Morcha (JMMM), a network of indigenous women's groups in Jharkhand, seems to come closer to the view of the village women. Some of the groups in the network felt that law and legal reform would not necessarily solve the problem, given the social character of land. Instead, issues of property and identity need to be considered within a holistic framework. Customary law accords unmarried daughters rights in her father's land; while maintaining this demand, the JMMM is more concerned with marital property. Their position is that, along with a man, his wife's name too should be registered in the land records (Abhiyaan, 1999). If the man wants to separate, then he has to give his wife a share of the land. While largely feminist in their outlook, these groups recognize the embeddedness of property and inheritance in marriage and kinship structures and the need to negotiate therein. This view helps build bridges with male leaders and thus garner support for women's land claims more easily than a position based on the decontextualized principle of equal rights for men and women.

The NGOs as well as political leaders often blame missionaries for destroying community solidarity and institutions, by dividing the Santals into Christians and non-Christians.[7] The roots of this hostility lie in the complex role of missionaries in the history of the Santal Parganas and Chota Nagpur. As part of their 'civilizing mission', they not only set up numerous educational institutions and provided medical services, even in remote areas where the government failed to reach, but also played an active political role. They helped *adivasis* represent their grievances first to the colonial government and post-

[7]The only written text that forms the basis of Santal custom—*Mare hapram ko reak katha* or 'Traditions and Institutions of the Santals'—is that recorded by the Norwegian missionary Skresfrud.

independence, to the Indian nation-state. Jaipal Singh, the founder-leader of the Jharkhand Party in 1939, was educated in Oxford with missionary support. N.E. Horo, often referred to as the 'grand old man of Jharkhand', held a position in the Gossner Evangelical Lutheran Mission (GEL) till he went into politics full-time. In the 1980s, Father Antony Murmu organized the *adivasis* against the *mahajans* in the Banjhi area of Sahebganj district, on the issue of forest and water rights. A majority of NGO workers, Santal professionals and elite have, in fact, been educated in mission schools—the only source of decent education in the region, and women like Sona and Bahari have converted to Christianity only recently to access reliable health care. While materially leading often to an improvement in their quality of life, ideologically the missionaries construct the *adivasi* as the 'noble savage', and continue to see them as ignorant and exploited people in need of protection and direction.

The hostility against the church organizations has manifested itself in the rising instances of physical violence—Anthony Murmu was shot and killed in Banjhi in 1985.[8] Reports of attacks on both nuns and priests have been frequent in the press in the last decade. Several of the recent attacks appear to be supported by right-wing Hindu nationalist groups, keen to 'Hinduize' the *adivasis*—integrating them however at the bottom of the caste hierarchy. While portraying the Christians as tools of western imperialist control, and consequently decrying conversions, they fear a threat to their own position of power and hegemonic social control over the *adivasi* masses from missionary activity, in particular education. Far from being 'innocent dupes of the missionaries' (Hardiman, 2000: 1), the Santals, particularly women, however, have used Christianity as a means of breaking out of the exploitative social order as well as securing material and emotional support, whenever they required it. Conversion for them becomes an act of resistance, a way of securing a more equal social position. Despite this 'perceived threat' from Christian missionary efforts, it is interesting to note that Christian Santals only form 4.2 per cent of the Santal population in Dumka district (Census, 1991), hence are

[8]Anthony Murmu was elected to the 6th Lok Sabha from Rajmahal (ST) on a Janata Party ticket.

hardly a real threat to Santal solidarity. However, being educated, they do tend to be better represented and more vocal in public arenas.

While the missionaries support women's education, enhancing their capacity to earn and for independent thought through exposures of different kinds (religious films on Jesus Christ were the only films seen by several people in Chuapara, still unexposed to the cinema or DVDs), most were opposed to the demand for land by Santal women. They held the view that given rights to land, women would marry the economically better off *dikus*, leading to a growing penetration of the *dikus* into Santal territory, a view also promoted by the major political party (JMM). More important, however, Christian morality advocates loyalty and mutuality between husband and wife, in a lifelong, monogamous relationship. Women are seen as the primary bearers of this morality across generations. Interestingly, women are seen as active agents in that their behaviour and morality is questioned rather than that of men. In a recent case involving Mary and Chura, after Chura had beaten her badly, she left home, vowing not to come back. On the pleas of her young son, she agreed to go to the Church for arbitration. A date was fixed, but Chura failed to turn up. The priest then accompanied her to the village and conducted a hearing there. While Chura was let off lightly, with a promise not to get violent again, Mary was given a long lecture about loyalty and responsibility towards her husband and children. Another ritual emphasized by the Church is pre-marital training for the couple, where they attend classes on behaviour and morality for a week prior to getting permission from the Church for their marriage. In this framework, claiming independent rights to land, or the possibility of a livelihood apart from the husband, is not easily supported. With divorce frowned upon, in fact impossible in a Roman Catholic context, such independent rights are also seen to be unnecessary. So while in some respects the physical rituals of Christianity are more inclusive, the symbolism inherent within this discourse reinforces gender inequality.

*Adivasi* leaders have used the shift in the discourse from property to marriage, emerging in different ways from both the NGOs and missionaries, to deny women's land claims. The leading political party in the region, the JMM, although constructed on the premise of agrarian change and development, and while supporting gender equality in a broad sense, opposes formal land rights to women, including that of *gharjawae*, fearing 'alienation' of land through mixed marriages. In a patrilineal society, though the mother may be a Santal, the effective control of the land is seen to pass out of the lineage and to 'other castes', as the children take the name of the father. While mixed marriage has perhaps been one method of alienation, particularly near major towns, its magnitude does not as yet seem significant (Thakur, 1977), and is definitely not the only reason for alienation.

Santals themselves, like the JMM leaders, acknowledge the central role of Santal women in the land economy. While they understand that *adivasi* women are attracted to *diku* men in seeking a better life, as the latter are generally economically better off, they present this as an exploitation of simple women by *diku* men. The solution is seen in controlling women's sexuality and restricting their marital choice. This obsession with women's marriage with *dikus* has to be interpreted in the context of their own economic poverty and social and political marginalization vis-à-vis the dominant Hindu groups. In such a context, women's rights to land are seen as divisive and opposed. Where resources are scarce and everyone's needs cannot be met, politics becomes strategic in terms of projecting the needs of particular groups over others. In negotiating *adivasi* rights more broadly and the identity of the society as whole, in a context of exploitation, impoverishment and dispossession from resources, the specific rights of *adivasi* women are put on the back-burner. Yet the leaders are now willing to negotiate more specific rights in marital property, though linked to restrictions on marital choice—the condition is marriage to a Santal man.

While there are divisions and differences within each of these categories, in the larger policy discourse they appear as sharply opposing voices—one an advocate, another an opponent of the legitimacy of women's land claims. Nancy Fraser points out that at least three competing types of discourse exist for talking about women's needs. One is the 'oppositional' discourses led by women and men supporting women's land claims and the other the 'reprivatization' discourses led by the political parties, elite Santal men and missionary groups, seeking to retain the status quo. Given this sharp divergence in views, the third group of 'experts' led by some development NGOs, welfare administrators and policy planners (the service providers), seek to build bridges 'which mediate the relations between social movements and the State' (Fraser, 1989: 11). To do so, they translate politicized needs into a series of generalized and depoliticized administrative projects such as tree plantation, wasteland development, savings and credit. The nuances relating to women's land claims in marital and natal property, in different environmental contexts and subject-positions, then do not find adequate reflection in State policy and hence bely implementation, as demonstrated in the next chapter.

The meanings of land to different groups of men and women are constructed on the basis of their material reality as well as symbolic moorings, and hence competing claims to land are contested in both the local customary village councils and the legal courts. From the perspective of the development administration, in a context of limited resources, it is essential to fix one social reality and reach an authoritative definition and hierarchy of needs and mechanisms for implementation. Perhaps, the way forward could be the pursuit of hybridity—allowing for the co-existence of a range of alternatives, and giving legal recognition to socially validated rights as a step forward in the movement towards gender equality.

CHAPTER

# 9 Development Interventions

## Does One Size Fit All?

Hand in hand with women's struggles for land—an attempt to repoliticize their rights and demonstrate that the personal is indeed political—there is a movement towards a negotiated political consensus, albeit conditional, with respect to women's rights in marital property. The rights of an in-marrying daughter or a separated sister in her parental property continue to be sharply contested. The state is a key player in this process of contestation and mediation, both through its legal justice system, and its administrative policies. One of the aims of public provisioning by the state is to pre-empt resistance by promoting welfare. At the same time, absolute commitment to gender equality cannot be taken for granted given the state's views of *adivasi* women as promiscuous even though simple, starved and hardworking, the 'maleness' of landed property and the ideologies of *adivasi* leaders, professionals and missionary groups, all groups wielding influence in one way or another. The state, therefore, seeks to protect, but also to extract surplus from the labour of *adivasi* women.

A key question is the effectiveness of the state as a service provider, in responding to and satisfying the needs of the poor, in this case Santal women. As Dreze and Sen comment, 'much depends on what issues are politicised and which deprivations become widely discussed and electorally momentous' (1999: 374). Redistributive measures, including land reform, have been hard to implement in most of India, with the exceptions of the Left ruled states of Kerala and West Bengal as the privileged, who dominate the political process and state bureaucracies, have an interest in resisting them. The state, far from being a neutral body, is embedded in local social relations, ideologies and hierarchies, all reflected in its practice.

In her analysis of the U.S. social welfare system, Nancy Fraser notes that the state treats highly contested interpretations of people's needs as unproblematic and given. It then redefines them as 'system-conforming satisfactions', based on what it can offer, moving away from the question of 'who interprets social needs and how?' (1989: 156). In this process, it misses the inter-connectedness of needs claims, the 'chains of "in-order-to" relations' that lie behind any need claim (Ibid: 163). Women's need claims to land are related not just to security of food and shelter, but also to their bargaining position within the household, with creditors, with banks and agencies of the state, their need to strengthen social support mechanisms through reciprocation and gifts, to enhancing status, to providing for their children, but most important, to gaining recognition as equal and valued members of the society. These needs, politicized continuously through their struggles, in daily practice as well as in the available public spaces, cut across the boundaries between the political, economic, domestic and personal spheres of life.

In material terms, the demand for land rights by women represents a demand for secure livelihoods at the minimum, thus implying, in addition to land titling, a bundle of other interventions that can operate synergistically across a range of fronts. These could include supporting production through the independent provision of credit, irrigation facilities, training and extension services (seeds, fertilizers and other inputs), strengthening market interactions and wage employment in the slack agricultural seasons. In addition, measures to ease household maintenance tasks by the provision of safe drinking water, food in periods of shortfall, and childcare would be necessary. Finally, social security in the form of access to housing, dependable health services and quality education are essential for ensuring livelihood security.

Yet their demand for land rights is not just material. Had this been the case, then given the problematic nature of land and the intense competition for it, a possible solution could have been to replace rights to land with rights to employment, for instance. Several rehabilitation schemes in India, in fact, assure a job to one member of the household, usually the male, to compensate for the loss of land. A study of these resettlement projects, however, reveals a grim tale of alienation, social breakdown and steep decline in women's status (Das, 2001). Needs are, therefore, inter-related, but not necessarily fungible, with land essential to give stability to women's lives, in all senses. As reflected in Sheela's case, however, a well-paid and respectable government job to the woman herself, with work-linked entitlements, rather than her husband, can perhaps form an alternative to land. Such public employment opportunities are however not just limited in the local context, but shrinking.

While integrated initiatives are often planned, in practice, these often fail. The sectorization of programmes, with division of labour and resources amongst different departments of the state, often uncoordinated, is one reason, the absence of public pressure, another. A major reason is, however, the labelling of people, especially women, as 'dependents' or 'beneficiaries', and responsible for the performance of particular roles. It follows a 'deficit model' in seeing people as lacking and needing help, rather than as active agents in the development process, with needs and rights often beyond their role-defined identities.

Fraser has pointed to the ideological underpinnings of 'dependency' as an increasingly feminized, racialized and individualized term, in the contemporary welfare state (1997: 134). The problem is seen to lie with particular people, who need support of different kinds to overcome the problem, rather than with the structures of state and society. Power and domination are missing from this welfarist discourse of dependency, and history is all but forgotten. It is generally stigmatized as an undesirable condition, as a drain on state resources. There, however, remain forms of 'good' dependency, relating mostly to female nurturers, dependent on those for whom they care. Widows, who have served their husbands and nurtured their children, are one such group.

It is important to have public policies and a legal framework that address issues of inequality. Yet in broad and general terms, for the sake of administrative convenience and efficiency, interventions are often based on simplistic assumptions, and as a result, fail to achieve their objectives. Chapter 4 illustrated how using the criteria of 'landlessness' for land distribution in Dumka district, meant that a larger proportion of land was given to non-*adivasis*, often not poor or even dependent on land for their living. To take another example, the

National Policy for the Empowerment of Women, officially adopted in March 2001, recognizes that the lack of property rights has contributed to the subordinate status of women. It therefore aims 'to encourage changes in laws relating to ownership of property and inheritance *by evolving consensus* in order to make them gender just' (Paras 2.2 and 2.3: 8, emphasis mine). Yet such 'consensus' is usually an illusion and 'lack of consensus' then becomes an excuse for inaction. The policy further calls for 'concentrated efforts (to) be made to ensure that benefits of training, extension and various programmes will reach them (women) in proportion to their numbers' (Para 5.5: 10). Such well-meaning statements are useful in terms of asserting intent, and creating a facilitative environment within which women can claim their rights. They do not, however, easily translate into practice, as they fail to acknowledge the political, institutional and cultural reasons that have excluded women in the first place, despite recognition for several decades now, of their central roles in the land economy.[1]

Apart from the problems of simplification and generalization, informal power relations, individual ideologies and behavioural practices also mediate the translation of policies into practice (Goetz, 1997). With a divided discourse on women's land claims, the servicing of needs seems to be emerging from the histories of institutions, the preconceptions of the bureaucracy, and the social identities of its officers. Most of the local bureaucracy, being non-Santal men, is influenced by Hindu notions of appropriate gender roles, seeing women primarily as home-makers. Development policies are perhaps 'not *deliberately* designed to be biased in favour of men, but their lack of explicit consideration of gender relations means that in practice this is what happens' (Elson, 1991: 253, emphasis in original). Yet, 'local discretion proves kinder than the official guidelines' (Subramanian and Harriss-White, 1999: 35) as noted in the case of Panthi Marandi, where the *amin* facilitated the registration of land in her name. Creative bureaucrats have been known to address local needs in key livelihood sectors, whether it is the development of water resources to facilitate double cropping, or making credit available for petty commodity

[1] Different international statements as well as time use studies have been claiming that women's contribution accounts for 50–70 per cent of agricultural production (IFAD, 2001; Boserup, 1970).

production. Despite differences in interpretation, a supportive policy framework does contribute to strengthening women's claims in direct contestation; it is a back-up that they can call upon in garnering the support of local officials and leaders. The following sections examine some of the key development policies being implemented in the Santal Parganas, and analyse how far they respond to women's need claims. The discussion is divided into two parts based on the implementing agency—the Land Revenue Department and the Community Development Block—the former administering programmes of the state government and the latter national-level programmes. The division of functions is based on administrative criteria rather than a logical chain of inter-related needs and their satisfaction.[2] Notably, women are treated more sympathetically by the development bureaucracy than the revenue bureaucracy, perhaps because the national rhetoric of gender equality (that governs development interventions) is stronger than the local ideologies of hierarchy and rights, or due to the social legitimacy for women as dependent clients and development beneficiaries, rather than as cultivators in their own right.

## THE REVENUE CIRCLE: CONFLATING LAND AND DEVELOPMENT

Apart from dealing with land settlement, land distribution, the collection of annual rents and minor irrigation schemes, the Revenue Circle also deals with the social security benefits administered by the state—employment assurance, pensions for widows and the aged, maternity benefits and food provisioning through the public distribution system (PDS). In this list of programmes, there seems to be, at first sight, considerable sensitivity conceptually to the linkages of land with social security, food security and production security. On the surface, it seems to pay attention to women's need claims by referring specifically to pensions for widows and maternity benefits, irrespective of their poverty status. Women in virtuous roles such as mothers or widows are seen as vulnerable and needing support, though the same

[2]The subjects under the jurisdiction of state and central governments are laid down by the Constitution; the budgetary sources are also different.

does not apply to separated women. There is an underlying gender ideology that seeks to support women as dependents, and in particular roles, excluding in the process, women seen as independent agents.

In India, the pressure of the women's movement to recognize women's rights to land (Mazumdar, 1997), and the legitimization of their demands in the Sixth Five Year Plan (1980–5), created a fertile ground to take forward this agenda. The Eighth Plan (1990–5) highlighted the need to change inheritance laws to give women equal shares on the one hand, and called upon state governments to allot 40 per cent of ceiling surplus land to women, the rest being in joint titles, on the other (Thakur, 2001). With the added impetus of the Supreme Court directions on women's claims to land as an essential component of the Right to Life in the *Madhu Kishwar v. State of Bihar* case, and the more recent amendment to the HSA in 2005, both inheritance of land by and its distribution to women became the rhetoric of the Revenue Department. This was further encouraged by the pro-women stance of the DC of Dumka during the period 1993–6. Despite the hype, however, nothing was formalized and not much changed in terms of state action. While there is an additional column entitled 'Women' in the monitoring formats used for land distribution, this is quick to reveal that no land has actually been distributed to women since 1994 (Table 4.3, Chapter 4 and Table 2, Annexure 3). While the total amount of land distributed is not much, nevertheless the complete exclusion of women reveals an inherent bureaucratic bias, a deep-rooted social valuation of women as home-makers rather than cultivators.

However, when it comes to the inheritance of private land, there has been support for women in *gharjawae* marriages, seeking to legalize their claims in their parental property, by the revenue bureaucracy—*amins, karamcharis* and the Circle Officers. Based perhaps on the recognition of this right in the SPTA, it is not backed up, however, by any other systemic support for women as cultivators. While social benefits and programmes are largely targeted at women as widows and mothers, there are no moves to include such women in the land records, currently in the process of revision. The ideology of monogamy, a wife's dependence on and loyalty to her husband, seems to make such provision unnecessary. The claims of separated women, though sharply contested in practice, are totally ignored in the policy process.

While land distribution to women has been virtually absent and titling limited to those married through *gharjawae*, there has been an attempt to address women's need claims through limited social security as well as non land-based development interventions. The problem seems to lie in the construction of women as dependents and supplementary earners. Rather than conceding equal rights, therefore, the identification of women's entitlements translated into administrative programmes, remains selective, fragmented and mediated by gender ideologies.

## Pensions and the Public Distribution of Food

As part of its social security package, the government assures old people (both men and women over 65 years of age) and widowed women (of any age) a monthly pension of Rs 200.[3] In Chuapara, while seven women were eligible for pensions, and they had applied on many occasions, none of them had actually received one (Table 9.1). In

Table 9.1: Pensions for Widowed Women in Chuapara and Bagdiha

| Caste | Chuapara | | | Bagdiha | | |
|---|---|---|---|---|---|---|
| | Total HH | Eligible for pension | Received pension | Total HH | Eligible for pension | Received pension |
| Santal | 39 (75) | 7 (18) | 0 | 143 (61) | 20 (14) | 3 (15) |
| Kol | 11 (21) | 0 | 0 | 9 (4) | 2 (22) | 0 |
| Paharia | 2 (4) | 0 | 0 | 0 | 0 | 0 |
| Rajwar/SC | | | | 2 (1) | 0 | 0 |
| *Kumhar* | | | | 46 (19) | 6 (13) | 4 (66.7) |
| *Teli* | | | | 28 (12) | 2 (7) | 2 (100) |
| Others | | | | 7 (3) | 0 | 0 |
| Total | 52 (100) | 7 (13) | 0 | 235 (100) | 28 (12) | 9 (32) |

*Source:* Social Security Records, 2000.
*Note:* Figures in brackets are percentages.

[3]This was increased from Rs 100 per month in 2002, following the formation of Jharkhand.

Bagdiha, out of 28 eligible widows, nine are receiving pensions, most of them *teli* and *kumhar* women. Access in this case is clearly not determined only by material conditions, or the status of a widow or elderly person, but by kinship, ethnicity, patronage and monetary links. Further, those who are closer to Dumka, and can follow up their cases directly with the bureaucracy as in Bagdiha, are better able to access their claims than those in remote villages like Chuapara.

Pensions for widows are allocated by the central government on the basis of quotas calculated on overall demographic trends. In 1991, widows formed 8 per cent of the total female population of India. But if one considers only the ever-married population, then the proportion of widows is close to 15 per cent. The above table shows that this is a reasonably accurate calculation. However, with the exception of Kerala, where the pension scheme seeks universal coverage of widows, different states in India have varying restrictions based on age, residence and social support available. It is unclear on precisely what basis the funds have been allocated in Dumka district. Yet drawing upon Prasad's (1998: 294) illustration of Tamil Nadu, it seems that obtaining state assistance for a destitute widow can be a daunting task, given the rigid procedural orientation and scope for patronage. Though an entitlement, it cannot be taken for granted as a reliable source of support.

The pension can make a significant difference both socially and economically to Santal widows. Malati Kisku of Bagdiha, for instance, uses her pension—a cash resource—to buy labour or fertilizers to cultivate her small plot of land. The bureaucracy, however, views the amount—too small for subsistence—as pocket money for additional expenses. The assumption seems to be that widows are looked after by their sons, and do not live and cultivate independently. The distribution is not regular and when released, has to be collected from the Block Office. Obviously then, it is not accessible to older widows unable to travel the distance. When the need for cash is urgent and the pension not forthcoming, Malati ends up making and selling liquor, too old to go out for wage labour. Although aware of the active role of Santal women in the production system, the dominance of patriarchal gender ideologies is clearly in evidence here.

The PDS in India was set up with the goal of providing food security to the masses. It was a universal entitlement, providing basic food grains at subsidized rates, meant particularly to benefit the poor and vulnerable. In 1997, with the strengthening of the processes of liberalization, the concept of targeted PDS was introduced, whereby only households below the poverty line were to receive subsidized food grains.[4] Swaminathan (2000: 32) has shown that although only 37 per cent of the population are classified as income-poor by the state, 80 per cent suffer from calorie/food deficits. Using poverty lines fixed at near-destitution levels as the criteria for inclusion or exclusion, has, thus, led to the exclusion of a large number of vulnerable households from the PDS, more so in the tribal areas. In Chuapara, while a few households may be marginally better off than others, they are all equally vulnerable to shocks and crises; a majority of children (also adults) are severely malnourished, hence prone to illness. Yet, only 29 households in Chuapara and 60 in Bagdiha have received ration cards under the targeted PDS (Table 9.2). Out of the seven widows in Chuapara, four have received ration cards. In Bagdiha, out of 28 widows, eleven (eight Santal and three *teli*) have received ration cards.

Table 9.2: Caste-wise Distribution of Employment and Ration Cards

| Caste | Chuapara | | | Bagdiha | | |
|---|---|---|---|---|---|---|
| | Employment card | Ration card | Total HH | Employment card | Ration card | Total HH |
| Santal | 4 (10) | 21 (54) | 3 (75) | 55 (38.5) | 28 (20) | 143 (61) |
| Kol | 0 | 8 (73) | 11 (21) | 0 | 0 | 9 (4) |
| Paharia | 0 | 0 | 2 (4) | 0 | 0 | 0 |
| Rajwar/SC | | | | 0 | 0 | 2 (1) |
| *Kumhar* | | | | 10 (22) | 24 (52) | 46 (19) |
| *Teli* | | | | 1 (3.5) | 2 (7) | 28 (12) |
| Others | | | | 1 (14) | 6 (86) | 7 (3) |
| Total | 4 (8) | 29 (56) | 52(100) | 67 (28.5) | 60 (26) | 235 (100) |

*Note:* Data refers to the year 1999–2000. Figures in brackets are percentages.

[4]Despite asserting the multi-dimensionality of poverty, priority is given to the income/consumption indicators (Razavi, 2000). The price adjusted poverty line based on the monthly per capita total expenditure (MPCTE) was calculated as Rs 335.05 (rural) and 451.09 (urban) for 1999–2000 (Sundaram and Tendulkar, 2005).

The coverage is better in Chuapara, due to recognition by the state of widespread, near universal, poverty in the entire block.[5] Alas, having a ration card in itself is not very meaningful, since rations are never available in the area. As elsewhere, dealers are required to make advance payments to the State Food Corporation for the grains requisitioned. There is substantial time lag between payment and the receipt of stocks, and as several of the *adivasi* dealers in Gopikandar block complained, they themselves were poor and could not afford to block capital for long periods. So they gradually stopped stocking food grains. While this may be true, several women in Chuapara and surrounding villages claimed that the dealer, in fact, sold the grains meant for the PDS, in the open market. Women from a neighbouring village publicly protested against the particular dealer, exposing him to the authorities by demonstrating that while there were no entries in their ration cards showing that they had not received any rations, he had all the time been acquiring and selling grains. The dealer, furious at their audacity, took away the women's ration cards the following month, and refused to return them. In Bagdiha, a disproportionately higher proportion of *kumhar* households appear as recipients of ration cards. As in the case of pensions, this could be attributed to the fact that the *mukhiya* (official headman) of the village was a *kumhar* and clearly sought to help his own caste group.

A further process of targeting was under way in 1999–2000, in the form of two new schemes, *Antyodaya* and *Annapurna*. Of the poorest, 15 per cent were to be included under *Antyodaya*, entitling them to food grains at a fourth of the current price, and 1 per cent of the poorest, mainly destitute women, would be the target group for *Annapurna*, which would entitle them to grains free of cost.[6] The remaining BPL

[5]The DC mentioned that 60 per cent of the population of the district and 75–80 per cent of the *adivasi* population lives below the poverty line (Interview, 15 July 1999, Dumka). Meenakshi et al. (2000) show a Head Count Ratio of Poverty for Bihar as 62.4 per cent, but 75.7 per cent for STs.

[6]

| | Wheat | Rice | Entitlement |
|---|---|---|---|
| Lalcard (TPDS) | Rs 5/kg | Rs 6/kg | 12 kg wheat and 8 kg rice/card |
| *Antyodaya* | Rs 2/kg | Rs 3/kg | 25 kg/card |
| *Annapurna* | free | free | 10 kg per individual |

Table 9.3: Targeting: Excluding the Poor or Including the Rich?

| Ration cards | TPDS | *Annapurna* | *Antyodaya* |
|---|---|---|---|
| District | 116,729 | 2,659 | 18,617 |
| Dumka block | 13,767 | 409 | 2,057 |
| Gopikandar block | 4,821 | 90 | 784 |

*Source:* District Food and Civil Supplies Officer, Dumka, 2000.

households would no longer be entitled to subsidized food grains. Table 9.3 presents the target number of households, calculated at District Headquarters, for each of these categories of food provisioning. It is clear that instead of following even the conceptually faulty criterion of the existing poverty line, these percentages based on national estimates, have no relationship with the contextual reality in the district. In the whole of Gopikandar block, for instance, only 784 households were to be identified for *Antyodaya* and 90 for *Annapurna*. The identification was done, but given the small numbers, it invariably went to more accessible villages and better connected people. In Chuapara alone, at least five households live in conditions of abject poverty, with not more than a single meal a day even at the best of times. Yet none of them possess a ration card.[7]

Progressive targeting is likely to have mixed gendered effects. Since on the one hand, there is a mention of women-headed households as the most economically vulnerable and needy of support under *Annapurna*, some women, particularly widows, might benefit. Separated women, though extremely vulnerable, are seen as deviants and not even considered a legitimate category for access to the PDS. However, given a very tight targeting frame (1 per cent of population) and a much larger number even of widows (12–13 per cent of population), there is likely to be intense competition for designation in this category. Rules and norms are formulated for selection of the 'beneficiaries', but given the limited resources available, these are manipulated by those with social contacts. Acquiring a card becomes

[7]Dibri Hansdak, Pappu Marandi, Karu Tudu, Sabu Dehri, Chutka Kol, acknowledged by the entire village community as being amongst the poorest households in the village, all lack ration cards.

a costly business, excluding the poorest, who have no resources to pay the bribes. Dibri Hansdak, one of the poorest in Chuapara, said, 'We do not bother to meet the Village Level Worker, as we would have to pay Rs 100 just for filling the form. We do not have the money' (1 July 2000). In a context of widespread deprivation, it would then seem appropriate to have a more broad-based system of entitlements based on citizenship, giving equal rights to all people, rather than a narrow one, based on need or desert, as the costs of exclusion could mean a threat to survival. A universal system would also prevent the labelling and stigmatization of particular groups of people as a drain on state resources.

While pensions and public distribution categories such as *Annapurna* are particularly targeted at 'good' dependents, mainly widows, who have performed their roles as reproducers, but are presently without support and protection, other state programmes are, in fact, targeted more widely at 'poor' households. Poverty is increasingly seen by the state as an individual deviance, a negative moral trait, rather than as a structural problem. There is a hidden assumption that the poor are poor because they do not work hard, are lazy and ignorant. I have referred in passing to such remarks by several officers, but the playing out of this assumption in programme implementation is evident particularly in the case of the Employment Assurance Scheme (EAS), subsumed in 2006, by the National Rural Employment Guarantee Programme (NREGP).

## Employment Schemes

With a complete record of the ownership of land by different households in every village of the Circle, the Revenue Department is in a strong position to estimate the livelihood shortfalls and needs of households within the Circle. Most of the small and marginal farmer households could, thus, be seen as eligible for additional wage or employment support. Under the EAS, and now the NREGP, any registered person would get priority in terms of wage employment in public works programmes to the tune of at least 100 days of work per annum. While the earlier programme was restricted to one member per eligible household, giving priority implicitly to men rather than women, the NREGP has the additional provision that all household members demanding work have a right to work. Several recent studies have, in fact, noted that over 50 per cent of workers on many of the NREGP worksites are women.[8]

While in the land records, several households related by kin are registered jointly, for the purpose of employment cards, each is registered as an independent unit. Where immediate consequences for daily living, including accessing state support are concerned, the reality of individual households is presented rather than the imagined unity that is closely associated with land. The differential representation of the household in relation to land and other resources highlights, once more, that land, unlike labour or other resources, signifies something more than a material, wealth-generating resource to the Santals.

The caste-wise distribution of entitlements in the two villages (Table 9.2) confronts one with a host of apparent ad hoc practices in the process of selection and distribution. While 190 of the 235 households in Bagdiha are recorded as BPL,[9] only 67 of them received employment cards. Of the 28 widowed households, only seven have labour cards.[10] Thus neither being BPL nor being a woman-headed household seems to be a sufficient criterion for the allocation of a labour card, but rather the construction of Santals as 'labour' in relation to the other caste groups. This was confirmed by personal conversations in Bagdiha in February 2006 during the registration process for the NREGP. Several Hindu youth, despite being poor, quite openly said that they were unwilling to undertake manual work, and hence would not register under this programme. Even some of the Santal youth with a few years of schooling, although registered for the programme, complained that it offered only manual labour work, rather than providing them more skilled, entrepreneurial work.

Amongst the seven women-headed households in Bagdiha, only one woman had received the labour card under the EAS, in her own name. From the same *tola,* Jamin Marandi reported that though they

[8]See CBGA (2006), ILO and ISST (2006), Bhatia and Dreze (2006) on implementation of NREGA in different states of India.

[9]Enumeration of BPL families is done by the functionaries of the District Rural Development Agency (DRDA), but registration for employment cards is done by officials of the Revenue Circle. Panchayats and Block Development Officers have been responsible for the enumeration under the NREGP.

[10]None of those with a labour card receive the pension. These figures refer to EAS and not NREGP, where the numbers may have risen, but the patterns are roughly similar.

have labour cards, they get only 10–15 days work annually on public works. Checking the records, I found that the average days of work during 1994–5 and 1995–6 were between 25 and 50 days, no one getting the minimum assured 100 days of work. While theoretically there are no gender wage differentials, in practice, wage calculations were linked to quality of work and outputs, leading generally to lower payments for women (Rs 25 for women and Rs 30 for men). As only one person from a household was eligible for employment, this would usually be the man, as a strategy to secure a higher wage.

Due to its linkage with manual labour, EAS self-selected the poor (as does the NREGP), but distributed on a household basis, and carrying within it an inherent male bias, the programme, by and large, excluded women from the benefits. Few widows and fewer separated women had access to it. While these biases against recruitment of women have been removed under the NREGP, by inclusion of all household members in the card, gender wage differentials remain alongside lack of adequate work (ILO and ISST, 2006). The Ministry of Rural Development in its report for the year 2006–7 on NREGP admitted that the fund utilization ratio remained as low as 51 per cent even after the completion of one full year of operation, and was lower still in the poorer states due to problems of both implementation and funding.

In Chuapara, 48 households lie below the poverty line, seven of them headed by widows. Unlike Bagdiha, however, less than 10 per cent of the population here has employment cards. This low priority for wage employment reflects the patterning of livelihoods around land and forests rather than wage-work as discussed in Chapter 3. Timely and adequate credit provision could contribute more to securing livelihoods here than uncertain assurance of employment, yet no attention seems to have been given to this.

Coming back to the notion of 'dependency', it becomes clearer why employment cards are offered in preference to, say, credit provision by the state. As Herring and Edwards note in their analysis of the Employment Guarantee Scheme in Maharashtra, such employment schemes carry within them an inherent assumption of a 'non-working culture of the rural areas', of lazy clients, in whom there is need to 'instil the values of hard work, regular discipline, and productivity-linked payment' (1983: 587). It is also a tool for social control and allows the rural elite (usually appointed as the supervisors and contractors of such work) to 'manage, reinforce and legitimate (their) hegemony' (Ibid: 587). While the NREGP promises payment of a daily unemployment allowance in cash if adequate employment is not provided, there is no evidence of the implementation of this clause to date. But more, a study on the implementation of NREGP in four states, namely, Andhra Pradesh, Madhya Pradesh, Chhatisgarh and Jharkhand in May-June 2006, reported supervisors justifying underpayment of wages to the *adivasis* on grounds that they were inefficient, often came to work in a drunken state and hence were not able to complete the task assigned to them (CBGA, 2006: 58). The images of the lazy and drunken *adivasi* seem to persist, justifying both underpayment and the need to control them, despite the existence of egalitarian and secular policy narratives.

Productive use of credit, on the other hand, carries the assumption of independent action, of self-employment and self-motivation, but the state is often not prepared to trust the 'poor', in particular *adivasis*, or their capacities to work without supervision. It does not acknowledge that lack of access to resources other than their own land and labour, could in itself, be a constraint, as evident in Chuapara. In terms of production-related support, what it does provide is broad-based and community-oriented irrigation schemes, but with no coordination with other inputs and services, the utility of these remains questionable.

## Production Support

*Jaldhara*, literally translated as the 'flow of water', seeks to enhance agricultural productivity by assuring water for irrigation. Apart from land distribution, it is the one scheme of the Revenue Circle that is directly related to strengthening agrarian livelihoods by promoting more intensive utilization of the land. It involves support for tanks, ponds, check-dams and wells, depending on the ecology and natural resources of the village concerned. Such irrigation schemes are now likely to be undertaken through the NREGP.

In Bagdiha, lying in the plains, the scheme has involved the digging of wells. Fifteen wells were allocated in the year 1990–1.[11] Thereafter,

[11]The then Collector sought to develop the irrigation infrastructure of the district through groundwater use, hence sanctioned and got constructed several thousands of wells in the district. He also travelled extensively, motivating people to use these wells to grow a second crop.

in 1997–8, one well was allocated to a non-Santal, Nirmal Gorain, a *teli* by caste. None of the women-headed households have been allocated wells. Clearly, the allocation of wells has been linked to landholdings and, therefore, secured by those men who have both title and access to the bureaucracy. Amongst the Santals, these are the village leaders and kin elders. In Chuapara, topographically hilly, with a stream flowing along the western boundary of the village, a check-dam was built in the year 1995–6. Though the construction contracts were given to men, this intervention is more communal in its benefits, as it can irrigate all the land lying beside the stream. To that extent it does not discriminate on the basis of ethnicity or gender. Unlike Bagdiha, which is unable to take to double cropping because of a failure of social institutions for cattle management and labour negotiation (Chapter 5), in Chuapara, the major hindrance to double cropping is the lack of financial resources. During 1998–9 and 1999–2000, the rain-fed paddy crop failed, leaving people with neither surplus to invest, nor bargaining power to negotiate a loan for investing in the second *rabi* crop.

If irrigation is seen as a means to promote double cropping and strengthen livelihoods, one would assume that it would be a part of

9.1: Digging a well. A typical employment generation scheme.

a package of inputs. Staudt (1985) has shown in the case of Kenya, where three or more agricultural services were provided jointly to women, the response was dramatic and performance much better than that of jointly managed households. Credit is an obvious need. Unlike in the case of paddy, people do not store seeds for the *rabi* crop, but consume it during periods of extreme hunger. Further, both *rabi* wheat and potato require the application of fertilizers in order to produce yields that make cultivation worthwhile. Credit is, however, nowhere on the agenda of the Revenue Circle, nor is the distribution of seeds and fertilizers. Incidentally, the latter is undertaken by the Block Agricultural Officer, attached to the Development Block. At most times, however, the seed is not only of poor quality, but either not available or available too late to be of any use. The problems with bank credit and crop loans have already been discussed in Chapter 5.

While theoretically complementary in nature, co-ordination on the ground seems next to impossible. This partly emerges from the fact that implementation, even within the Revenue Circle, appears adhoc. Neither BPL lists so laboriously prepared by the Block Development Office, nor operational land-holdings, the records of which are in the Circle Office, are systematically used as criteria for providing benefits; rather it is money, social contacts and patronage that seem to play a decisive role. So while claims to gender equality are rampant in state discourse, including that of land reform and land settlement, these remain largely in word rather than deed. Practice reveals little evidence of concrete support to women as cultivators, but in parallel, there is also little attention to the needs of *adivasis*, with a bulk of benefits, especially social security benefits, going to the non-*adivasis*.

## COMMUNITY DEVELOPMENT BLOCK: TOP DOWN OR BOTTOM UP?

The Development Block is the primary channel for the implementation of national rural development programmes targeted specifically at the 'poor', such as the Indira Awas Yojana (a housing scheme), or the Integrated Rural Development Programme (IRDP), renamed the Swarnajayanti Gram Swarozgar Yojana (SGSY) in 1990–2000. With national-level guidelines, allocated quotas and overall limits for disbursements, only limited flexibility is possible in terms of actual implementation. Further, all these programmes describe the poor as 'beneficiaries' rather than legitimate claimants, reflecting a hidden subtext of hierarchy and 'dependency'.

## Indira Awas Yojana (IAY)

Indira Awas Yojana has been one of the few programmes that has learnt lessons from past mistakes. In the early years, the state would construct single-room houses, usually closely set in rows and facing the main road, which were then allocated to 'beneficiaries'. Unable to meet the living needs of the 'clients', rarely were these houses lived in. From 1996–7 onwards, the money is directly provided to the 'beneficiaries', who then construct the house on their own homestead plots and with some flexibility in terms of the design. Through a circular letter dated 14 July 1995, the central government asked the states to give women preference in allotment of IAY.[12] Thereafter, IAY houses have been allocated to women, undoubtedly a positive step.

The contextual reality of land rights and land ownership in the Santal Parganas has, however, been overlooked, and in so doing, much of the transformatory potential of this intervention is lost. Naina's arguments reveal the criticality of the house-plot as much as the house in the real life context of desertions and abandonments. For the period of my field work I had rented her house, as her husband Som was away in Assam. During the rains, the roof was leaking. I asked her to repair it, offering an advance rent payment for the same. She refused. Som had left after a fight. If he didn't want to stay with her after his return, he could throw her out of the house. If she protested, all he needed to do was pull down the house, as the land was his. Without assuring rights to the plot on which the house is constructed, allocation of the house in the woman's name becomes meaningless, failing to provide secure shelter or play the role of an asset that can effectively enhance her bargaining power within the household. There has been no move to get the house-plot (*vaastu*) registered in the woman's name alongside granting her the house under IAY.

[12]This was both in response to the Eighth Plan commitment, as well as the pressure building up on account of the fourth World Women's Conference at Beijing.

That the allocation of houses to women is viewed as just a formality is also visible in the attitude of the petty bureaucracy. The Block Development Officer justified it by saying, 'Women stay in their senses and are not drunk', rather than seeing it as a tool for strengthening women's material and social condition. While the woman has to sign the papers to secure the release of the funds for house construction, thereafter, this formality too is dispensed with. The money is released to the husband, or any other man acting on her behalf. When the Block workers and engineers visit the village to review the progress of house construction prior to the release of the next instalment, they prefer to talk to the men. While distance, lack of mobility and other practical constraints of women are used to explain their exclusion at the Block level, this excuse cannot be used for explaining the lack of contact with the women at the village level. Santal women do not observe *purdah* (veiling or seclusion) and do not hesitate to talk to outsiders. As Charan's wife in Chuapara said once in great anger,

> The contract for my house was first taken by Dhiru, then Lala, now Theophil. None of them have completed it. I threatened Theophil that I would complain about him in the Block. He said, 'Please don't say anything, I will complete it.' I can complete the house on my own, I am not afraid of anyone, only I don't know how to speak (in Hindi). I can even speak to the big *sahebs* (officers) without fear. Our house is about to collapse, it is very cold, yet we have to sleep outside (9 December 2000).

Clearly the ideological biases of the petty bureaucracy, most of them Hindu men, as well as their inability to speak or understand Santali language, seem to lead unconsciously to minimal interaction with women, bolstering in the process, the larger stereotype of the dependent and helpless, though hard-working woman. Staudt (1985) in Kenya also found this, hence her strong recommendation for recruitment of female extension staff as the only way of correcting the male bias in practice.

Unlike social security benefits, IAY has been better able to cover households in remote areas such as Chuapara (Table 9.4). Specifically targeted at the Scheduled Tribes (ST) in the district, there has been a greater allocation of resources to the ST-dominant blocks and villages. While 70 per cent of Chuapara's population has received house-

Table 9.4: House Allotment in Chuapara and Bagdiha

| Caste | Chuapara | | Bagdiha | |
|---|---|---|---|---|
| | Received | Total hhs | Received | Total hhs |
| Santal | 24 (61.5) | 39 (75) | 42 (29) | 143 (61) |
| Kol | 11 (100) | 11 (21) | 0 | 9 (4) |
| Paharia | 2 (100) | 2 (4) | 0 | 0 |
| Rajwar/SC | | | 0 | 2 (1) |
| *Kumhar* | | | 3 (6.5) | 46 (19) |
| *Teli* | | | 0 | 28 (12) |
| Others | | | 0 | 7 (3) |
| Total | 37 (71) | 52 (100) | 45 (19) | 235 (100) |

*Source:* Records of the BDO, Gopikandar and Dumka blocks, 2000.
*Note:* Figures in brackets are percentages.

grants under IAY, the figure is less than 20 per cent for Bagdiha as a whole, or 30 per cent for its *adivasi* population. Allocations for IAY in Dumka block from 1997–8 onwards do confirm overall allocation to *adivasis* proportionate to their numbers in the population.[13]

There is however a fear, real or imagined, that this would not be the case in future. Allotment of 30 IAY houses was expected in Bagdiha in January 2001. The *kumhar* and *teli* women were preparing to stake their claims. Many Santal women, desperate for a roof, were willing to forego their migration for the *boro* planting in West Bengal and the lump sum income to be earned, in order to be present in the village when the decision on allotments was made. While there is no official shift in policy, the experience of all benefits being cornered by the Hindu castes in the last few years, due to the links of the *mukhiya* with the bureaucracy, has aggravated this fear. Santal women seemed quite aware that provisioning is not in response to need, but rather relates to the social negotiation and political manoeuvring that one is able to engage in.

## Integrated Rural Development Programme (IRDP)

The IRDP has been one of the most important rural development programmes in the country. Under its overall umbrella, it has covered

[13]The district-level report for the year 2000–01 shows that of a total of 5332 IAY houses during the year, 564 were allotted to SCs, 2784 to STs and 1984 to others.

both credit-based programmes for the creation of assets and employment-generating programmes. In Dumka district, a large number of households have availed of loans for the purchase of cattle and goats. In plains villages such as Bagdiha, several people have also got loans for pump-sets. From the mid-1980s, IRDP included a women's component called Development of Women and Children in Rural Areas (DWCRA), based on access to a Revolving Fund to be used collectively by a women's group. Several evaluations of DWCRA have shown that the groups, based as they were on the assumption that women's earnings formed a source of secondary income, often excluded the poorest women, dependent on regular labour for survival. Further, while they prioritized petty commodity production for the markets, women's groups were unable to engage successfully in market processes in order to generate profits, without marketing and infrastructure support. As the Assistant Project Director of the DRDA said, 'Over five hundred DWCRA groups were formed and provided with a Revolving Fund of over Rs 10 million in the last five years. Yet nothing has changed, all this money is lost' (31 May 2001).

In 1998–9, IRDP, DWCRA and a few other schemes were combined and launched as the Swarnajayanti Gram Swarozgar Yojana (SGSY or Golden Jubilee Rural Self-Employment Scheme). SGSY has been conceptualized as a group-based programme, building on the concept of SHGs. On the basis of their own savings (Rs 3000), each group would be eligible first for a Revolving Fund of Rs 25,000 from the state. Successful utilization would make them eligible for financing of larger projects from the banks. Key activities have been identified for each block in Dumka; however, SGSY is facing problems, similar to DWCRA earlier.[14]

First, living in extreme poverty and often forced to migrate in search of employment, it has not been easy to organize groups that can adhere to the SGSY norms. Related to this, of course, are the limits on the capacity to save. In Chuapara, for instance, and in a large part of Gopikandar block, people still survive with very little cash income.

[14]The SGSY progress report for 2000–01 reveals that in Dumka district, 68 groups have been formed (six each in Dumka and Gopikandar blocks), yet the Revolving Fund has been released to only 16 of them to date, five in Dumka block, but none in Gopikandar (SGSY Report: 2000–01, DRDA, Dumka).

Where wage labour is scarce and the cash economy has not penetrated deeply, it can take years to save Rs 3000. After a whole year, a women's group organized by an NGO in a village near Chuapara had managed to save Rs 800. It is disheartening that they may have to wait another two years to reach the established criteria. Third, in forested blocks such as Gopikandar, SGSY has now rightly identified the making of leaf-plates as a key activity to be financed. If one looks at leaf-plate making as an economic enterprise in the locality, what are the investments needed? Essentially it is the labour required for the collection of leaves from the forest and the making of the leaf-plates. The women carry them in head-loads to the local *haat*. The lack of infrastructure—accommodation and storage at the market-place as well as transport facilities for moving the products—is a major constraint faced by the women sellers in enhancing their bargaining position vis-à-vis the male traders. SGSY has a provision for infrastructure support, however, this comes only after the group is well established, has a concrete project and has secured bank financing. In the above case, this infrastructure can actually be vital in terms of enabling the project to take off successfully, hence rather than coming last, infrastructure support should be provided first. Such flexibility, however, is not forthcoming; women are not trusted as business or financial managers. Central guidelines are a further constraint, based on a deep-rooted ideology of controlling, supervising and disciplining the poor.

As the SGSY report for 2000–01 reveals, expenditure on infrastructure in the district has been low, with no expenditure in Gopikandar block, where the need seems to be the greatest. Two-thirds of the resources have gone to Jamtara, Jarmundi and Saraiyahat blocks—all in the plains, with *adivasis* constituting less than 25 per cent of the population. The non-*adivasis* here, though also poor, have more varied sources of income, there is a greater penetration of the cash economy and, hence, a higher propensity to save. Interpreted as a sign of successful 'self-help' and 'hard work', they receive further state support. SGSY is thus biased in favour of the economically better off, unintentional as it may be. It also seems to favour those with better social access to the state mechanisms, rather than the poorest and most vulnerable, who fail to display signs of adequate self-help, as gauged in cash terms.

Group processes are undeniably important and so is self-help. In moving from IRDP to SGSY, there however seems an ideological shift from treating poverty as a structural problem requiring public support, to poverty as an individual condition to be addressed by the individual's own effort, albeit through group processes. But, at subsistence levels, access to resources is essential even to prepare the conditions for self-help.

## Integrated Child Development Services (ICDS)

The ICDS, coordinated by the development machinery with support from the health services, is a programme targeted specifically at women as mothers and their children. Started in eight blocks of the district in 1990 with support from the World Bank, it is now operational throughout the district. Designed as an integrated programme with educational, health and nutritional components, the ICDS, in a large part of the district, has become a feeding programme. Food supplements are provided to children as well as pregnant and lactating mothers. Despite problems of pilferage, this still remains one of the most positive interventions, particularly in times of scarcity. The village *anganwadi* centre has also played a key role in terms of the national immunization programme—pulse polio for children and tetanus for pregnant women. However it does not pay attention to the general health needs of women.

Apart from nutritional support and immunization, women expect the centre to provide literacy for themselves and their children as well as some childcare. There are several reasons why this has not happened. First, the *anganwadi* workers are only paid a stipend of Rs 300–500 per month depending on their qualifications.[15] Mostly poor women, this amount is insufficient to free them from the responsibility of making a livelihood, whether through agriculture or labour. Naturally, they want to minimize the time they spend in the centre. Second, in many remote villages including Chuapara, where the status of women's literacy is low, the *anganwadi* worker may have completed primary schooling, yet be virtually illiterate and not in a position to teach young children or their mothers. She has neither the skills nor the time to meet expectations in terms of educational and childcare

[15]This had increased to between Rs 800 and Rs 1200 by 2004–5.

needs. Developed to respond to and support women's nurturing role, the ideology of the ICDS then does not allow it to support women adequately as workers. By defining itself strictly within the context of the reproductive role of women, the programme is unable to transcend its boundaries to bridge the gap women face between raising children and making a living, although the two remain deeply interconnected in women's lives.

## CONCLUSION

The agendas of the Revenue Circle and Development Block appear to be in tune with the needs of women and the 'poor', yet a closer look reveals major flaws in both conceptualization of the programme and mechanisms for its implementation. While the process of rent collection gives the Revenue Department a fairly good idea of the village situation, operational holdings and production capacities of different households in the village, this knowledge does not seem to be applied consistently in its other programmes. Women's inter-related need claims for land titles, capital for agriculture, market infrastructure, food and employment security, is clear. While women may be granted houses in their names, there is no attempt to transfer to them the homestead plot on which the house is constructed. There is no certainty that a widow will simultaneously receive a pension, ration card, housing and bank credit, though such consolidated support could contribute fruitfully to livelihood security, by meeting a chain of 'in-order-to' relations.

Further, in a cultural context of high marital mobility and women's key role in the economy, women need to be recognized and supported at the individual level, and not just the household level. Yet ration cards, employment cards and irrigation facilities are allocated to men, though women are known to be the major users. While the conceptualization of the policies and programmes does appear to carry within it the potential to satisfy women's need claims, they are biased in favour of women in virtuous roles, rather than separated or (increasingly) abandoned women who are constructed as deviants. There seems to be an implicit institutional ideology of male producers and female home-makers that dominates state provisioning. Even in this limited sense, however, implementation leaves much to be desired, contingent as it is on social identity, access, political circumstances and patronage relations, rather than the official criteria. In Bagdiha particularly, government schemes are seen by the *adivasis*, not just women, as benefiting the 'haves'—those who have jobs and regular incomes get the widow pensions, scholarships and loans. There is a clear ethnic divide here; the Santals have applied several times, but have received little. Over-represented amongst the poor, this makes them doubt the intentions of the government to help the 'poor'.

From a historical perspective, notions of poverty and dependency seem to be changing within state policy. The move towards even greater targeting in the PDS or the suspension of EAS in Bihar in 1999–2000 (of which Dumka was a part) is reinforced by and, in turn, reinforces the attitudes of the local petty bureaucracy, mostly non-Santal men, who blame the poor for their poverty. 'The Santal men don't work hard and cultivate their land, but go away frequently to Bengal' was a remark I heard often from the bureaucracy across levels and departments. They see the 'poor', a majority of them Santals, as a drain on state resources. Motivation for effective implementation is thus low, and this seems obvious to the Santals.

Inaugurating the meeting of the Jharkhand Development Council on 9 July 2001, the Chief Minister identified infrastructure development, particularly roads, power and irrigation, and education, as the development priorities for his government. This fits in well with the neo-liberal agenda of providing infrastructure support to facilitate individual enterprise. Will the market logic of 'survival of the fittest' take over or will the state as 'provider' still attempt to respond to women's need claims, create a level playing field and provide the requisite support and trust for enterprise? Will the roads link the local markets to the villages or the urban centres? Will irrigation be directed at the small and marginal farmers, particularly *adivasis* and women-headed households or the 'enterprising' Hindu farmers? Will education improve at the level of the village school? Where do the 'needs' for land titles, financial capital and social security for women fit in this development scheme? The trends so far are not promising.

Illiteracy takes the major share of the blame for the under-development of the region. Both politicians and civil servants use it to explain poverty and exploitation. In a world that works through the written word, illiteracy is seen as a source of powerlessness, and literacy, a means of social mediation and control, and thus, a pathway to access a better life. In this scheme, illiterate women are seen as incapable of dealing with the state. The only woman with a labour card was a literate one, further vindicating the view of literacy as development! It is also the reason for not trusting women or their groups with credit and infrastructure that could indeed facilitate enterprise. Yet despite improved access, the quality of education has hardly improved in the last decade, as discussd in Chapter 3.

A second target for blame is the consumption of liquor, used by political leaders, the bureaucracy, missionaries and even Christian villagers. But as several of the Santal men in the villages said, 'Drinking is part of our culture, but we are not drunks. We do our work. In every society, there are a few drunks, and it is the same in ours.' While many men drink regularly, only a few were constantly drunk. In these few households a large part of the family budget does go into the purchase of liquor, but this is not the case for the majority. The image of 'lazy' and 'drunk' Santal men, however, continues to be widely prevalent amongst the bureaucracy. It is used to blame them for their poverty and justify the progressive curtailment of state welfare support, whether in terms of subsidized food or guaranteed employment.

Even this image of Santal men, however, is insufficient to challenge still more deeply ingrained gender ideologies. If it were taken seriously, one would expect a greater channelization of responsibility and opportunity to women. Irrespective of the local culture and context, and the images of *adivasi* men, rigid patriarchal values and principles persist in the interaction of the bureaucracy with women. They prefer, at all times, to interact with the male 'heads of households', though the de facto control is with the women. Apart from exclusion from land titles (except in the case of *gharjawae*), married women are not issued employment cards, or provided crop loans (linked to land titles). Divorce is considered morally wrong and there is an attempt to invisibilize the group of separated women, perhaps an attempt to wish away the 'problem'. While the liberal rhetoric of state policies does provide a site for freedoms, bureaucratic practice often makes them a source of 'non-freedoms'.

State bureaucracies however are not monolithic entities. Bureaucrats at different levels do interpret needs differently and respond accordingly. So while one DC of Dumka focused on irrigation, another took up literacy and credit for women. The problem here seems to be one of continuity and follow-up. Yet, overall, employment generation has been more successful than credit provisioning, revealing a particular ideological construction of the service recipient. Involving manual labour with external supervision, rather than individual entrepreneurship, employment-oriented programmes are not just based on an ideology of the 'lazy poor', but also the vested interests of people involved in running the programme. These interests are both material (corruption and rent-seeking) and symbolic (status and power). Sibu Soren, leader of the JMM, pointed out that development should start at the village level, with a clear focus on agriculture and irrigation (3 August 2000). Agriculture, sadly, seems to have dropped out from the agenda of the present Jharkhand government. While the centre promotes enterprise, the local *adivasis* are not trusted or seen as capable enough to be entrepreneurs. This leaves them in the role of unskilled manual labour, servicing the needs of other groups.

Development practice then reveals a process wherein material needs, even if recognized, are set aside in favour of institutional norms, legitimating ideologies and the desire to discipline the slackers, based on notions of gender, ethnicity and 'dependence'. The clearest evidence of this is found in the gaps between the discussion of women's rights to resources, or the *adivasi* rights to self-determination, and practice. Development here is not a benign process, but a highly political struggle, for re-negotiating power relations between genders and amongst different social groups.

CHAPTER

# 10 Reframing the Debate
## Challenges and Dilemmas

You may write me down in history
With your bitter, twisted lies,
You may trod me in the very dirt
But still, like dust, I'll rise.
Did you want to see me broken?
Bowed head and lowered eyes?
Out of the huts of history's shame, I rise
Up from a past that's rooted in pain, I rise

Maya Angelou, 'Still I Rise'

Choti and Sona, both widows who could be classified as illiterate agricultural labour, retaliate against being branded witches by going to the panchayat or the police. Soha is now a construction worker. This does not stop her from going to the courts in Dumka to fight her case, or coming to the village to assert her claims locally. She may not have money, but when I visited her in her husband's village, she was generous in her hospitality. She was touched that I had sought her out, as a person, a woman, interested in the story she had to tell.

The examples are endless, of ordinary women rising against injustice, refusing to be broken. These women may be malnourished; district officials may label them 'simple' and 'oppressed'; their material hardships remain, yet they carry on. Nati has lost three children since I have known her and two before that. Part of the blame for this could be put on poverty and malnutrition. She now has three surviving children, whom she loves unconditionally. She does not fear hard work nor standing up to obstacles. Dibri was young and had already lost a child when I first met her. Her five-year-old son did not go to school. She was admitted to hospital and was not discharged as they could not pay the hospital fees. One of the poorest in the village, she hesitated to invite me to her house. In 2007, I met a transformed Dibri, actively engaged with the school and its activities, cooking the mid-day meal, and speaking confidently.

History records the lives and views of the dominant; the everyday struggles of women are almost totally bypassed. Subaltern historians too, while seeking to provide the views of the subordinate classes and groups, do not generally record women's versions as distinctive from the homogenized class discourse. Maya Angelou's life, in an echo of these women's lives, was one of intense struggle, rejection, hard work and exploitation. Such struggles are a part of ordinary women's lives, across space and time. Yet they are routinely overlooked, more so within development programmes and interventions. Almost 15 years ago, Diane Elson, a feminist economist, wrote about male bias in the development process. Much water has flowed under the bridge, but nothing much has changed on the ground.

If we ask ourselves why, we find it is not a result of male bias alone. It is also a problem with the theoretical frameworks that inform development policy. A framework that is based on the patriarchal paradigm of domination and subordination cannot but fail to understand the complexities of the land issue amongst the Santals in particular, or social life and development more generally. A theoretical shift is required to a paradigm that rejects binary classifications of all sorts: between the modern and the traditional, men and women, production and reproduction, even state and society, but rather seeks out the linkages and interactions between them. It needs to accept the reality of individual agency, of basic human self-respect. One could perhaps call it a paradigm of 'personhood'.

## A PARADIGM SHIFT

One cannot deny the existence of competition, conflicting interests and even discrimination. There are the landed and landless, educated and illiterate, winners and losers. Yet if one focuses on these distinctions alone, one may fail to find solutions to the development problem. Giving land to the landless, for instance, in the case of Dumka, has meant that the non-*adivasi*, not-so-poor groups of people, often the Hindu traders, have benefited disproportionately from land distribution. Dhaki has five acres of land, yet is next to destitution and desperately requires support, but because she is technically above the poverty line and does not fit the 'widow' category, she is deprived of any kind of support.

While the material distinctions are undeniable, other outcome indicators of well-being such as health, education and incomes too, are an insufficient basis for assuming subordination. While declining sex ratios in Dumka, for instance, might lead one to conclude that women's status is declining, other indications like the continuing exercise of marital choice, women's ability to exit from an unsuccessful marriage, to challenge male authority, both in public and private arenas to ensure reciprocity in conjugal relations, are evidence of women's agency and power. It is, therefore, important to look at processes as well, before drawing conclusions on women's well-being and power, or deciding what interventions they most need. 'Indicators of well-being, while necessary for revealing bias, disclose nothing about their social meanings or about the social processes giving rise to gender differentials. In the absence of information on causality, policies can easily be restricted to specific interventions in the areas revealed by the indicators to show gender difference, to the neglect of underlying determinants' (Saith and Harriss-White, 2000: 83). Women's everyday struggles and forms of backstage negotiation are important indicators of women's needs and demands, and of the processes of bias underlying these outcomes.

Understanding relationships should therefore be the focus rather than binary and materialist distinctions alone. A major implication of this paradigm shift is that it moves beyond the role-ascribed identities of men and women to see them both as persons, with different roles, interests and identities, but with scope for overlaps, sharing and cooperation as well. It helps one think beyond the stereotypical images of the lazy, drunken, *adivasi* man and the hard-working, illiterate and sexually free *adivasi* woman, to see them as people, struggling to survive and making the best of their lives. Support needs to be provided in more creative ways, rather than along standardized assumptions of what is good for one or the other. This is important, as we all carry multiple identities within ourselves, and these are played out in different contexts in our everyday lives. In relation to the state, for instance, collective *adivasi* identities are often projected, rather than individual male or female ones, articulating the needs of an entire group rather than the micro-needs within it. In struggles for land, however, played out in multiple mutually interacting arenas of contestation, one finds in the foreground the contradictions between self-images and externally-constructed ones, as well as between elements of multiple identities based on gender, ethnicity and political status. Outcomes and processes of these struggles have implications for material circumstances, household livelihoods and well-being.

Such a relational framework, based on a notion of personhood, has methodological implications too. While I was clearly an outsider, there were commonalities between my experience of being a woman and theirs. The issues were different, so were the strategies, but the emotions and the struggles were often not, the underlying message being one of asserting one's personhood. Consider the contrasting examples of Sheela or Rimani. Sheela did not give up her job as a teacher even though this proved really burdensome in the early years. She showed herself to be a good mother and a good wife, and also as a social person with an identity of her own. Rimani on the other hand directly challenged the male authority of both her husband and the village leaders by drawing on Christian morality to her advantage. Denial of sexual rights and walking out of non-caring marriages are other strategies for asserting identity. Commonalities with our own lives as middle-class women are unmistakeable, exposing the hollowness of notions of backwardness or progress.

This alternate framework does not exclude men and masculinities, rather sees men as integral to women's project of gaining an equal position in society. The vision is of a society where hierarchies of birth and ascription are not important. Despite the existence of some hierarchy, like that of merit, everyone gets an equal chance and even if one is low in the hierarchy, basic rights and identities are not denied. To attain this, a certain degree of denigration too is often accepted, seen as a step towards a new strategy. One example is Sona, who continued to cultivate the land after her husband's death, not giving in to the demands of his brother. Then, she was branded as a *'dain'* and harassed daily. Ultimately, she decided to go with her husband's brother to a local *ojha* and performed the ritually prescribed cleansing ceremonies. But at the same time she reported the harassment to the local government leaders, who as upholders of citizens' rights, issued a warning to her brother-in-law. In retrospect, her apparent adherence to social norms and subscribing to her brother-in-law and his family's wishes not only seems to have been a strategy to retain control over the land, but additionally, to assert her identity as a member of the family, and therefore, entitled to its resources. Women are not mere victims, and domination and control are not one-sided; bargaining and negotiation is ongoing.

But clearly there are structures of inequality that also prevail, not least in the state domain. Despite narratives of equality, state practice remains male biased. While women may be technically given the housing projects, it is men who are contacted during field visits to check on progress. Women are only trusted with small projects, and even this is dependent on their having proven their ability to manage resources, something not often asked of men. Micro credit has been hailed as a key tool for women's empowerment, with more than 80–90 per cent beneficiaries of micro credit being women. This is the problem with it—the money is small, the vision is small, non-governmental organizations are increasingly left to manage this process rather than mainstream institutions like the banks and women first have to save substantial amounts of money before they even receive this micro credit. There was a time after the Beijing conference in 1995, when gender mainstreaming became the stated objective, to ensure that women's rights and claims were given serious consideration across development sectors, alongside men, and not just restricted to small projects for women. Gender desk officers were appointed across Ministries, gender sensitization trainings organized for bureaucrats at high levels and gender budget analysis were initiated. Yet, mainstreaming is hard to practice without a major ideological shift, as both the activities and the outcomes involved are less tangible. Gender mainstreaming seems all but abandoned now and we are back to small, targeted projects for women. These invariably continue to fail, as this is not what women want—they want to be equal in mainstream society, they have similar needs and aspirations, they do not want to be enclaved in marginal fields.

Of course there are differences between women themselves, as between women and men. The aspirations of different categories of women are different, as of those in different subject positions. Their sense of selfhood may be different, so is their relationship to property. Mahani is entitled to *taben jom* in her parental home, yet she does not want to claim this from her father. Rather, being still young, her aspiration is to make a good marriage. Her mother, on the other hand, is happy with her share in her husband's property. With three grown-up children, she did not want to shift base when her husband brought a second wife. In our own lives too, we react differently at different stages, as the factors to be taken into account change. Children make a lot of difference to the decisions made, but so do the existence of state social security, family social support, and education.

A major part of the problem with state policy is the absence of such understanding, of a thinking that treats *adivasis,* and *adivasi* women in particular, as homogenous, and indeed subordinate or backward. One of the reasons that development fails is because the state or even NGOs have their own ideologies and constructs of *adivasi* identity, which often run parallel to people's own constructions of themselves and their needs. In many ways, it denies them both agency and voice. For example, the policy focus continues to remain on manual employment rather than credit provision, contrary to local needs and perceptions. Takers may then not always be there, and at the end of the day there is an under-utilization of funds. Similarly, while educated *adivasis,* young women and men, aspire to skilled work, all that they are offered is manual labour.

If the ultimate objective is gender equality, the gaining of an equal position in society, then the solution may be found in the creation of an enabling environment for women, one in which they can establish and assert their identities as equal persons, rather than objects of charity. Solutions to land problems may not necessarily lie in the area of land reform or redistribution. If women's access to land is denied on account of the failure by men to fulfil their provider roles, for instance, then greater attention may be needed to improve agricultural support and infrastructure in general, to enable men to perform their roles, and at the same time, provide women direct support through strengthening the subsidized food distribution systems. A separate state of Jharkhand was created in November 2000, with the hope that this is precisely what it would do, what the previous Government of undivided Bihar had neglected to do.

Statues of *adivasi* leaders have been installed in public places, yet the content of policy has not changed, nor the state constructions of *adivasis*. The Strategic Research and Extension Plan for Dumka district of the World Bank-funded National Agricultural Technology Project, for instance, continues to identify the *adivasis*' lack of education and liquor consumption as the major 'social constraints' to agricultural development (MANAGE, 2000: 20). It lays emphasis on user fees for accessing extension services, seen as a reflection of interest, commitment and self-help, rather than the structural problems confronting the majority. While Santali has been added to the constitutional list of national languages, there has been no effort to provide mother tongue education in the local primary schools or even develop a curriculum for the same, steps that could eventually help children escape the label of educational backwardness and illiteracy. Children who do not even understand Hindi are taught classical Sanskrit, rather than Santali, dooming them to educational failure. While paying lip-service to the marginalization of the *adivasis*, the policies of the new state have focused on commercialization, export orientation and market development, drawing in foreign capital investment, rather than food security or the inequities in land distribution faced by *adivasis* in the remote rural areas (Rao, 2003).

The political leaders are now *adivasis*, but the bureaucracy continues to be dominated by Hindu men from the northern states of Bihar and Uttar Pradesh. Stereotypical gender images of the hard-working Santal woman and lazy Santal man continue to prevail, yet these have not translated into enhanced support for women as economic or social actors. The struggle for Jharkhand seems to have strengthened a particular notion of indigeniety, with an emphasis on community control and management of resources, represented of course by men in the public domain. In the 2004 Lok Sabha elections, for instance, the JMM contested in nine out of fourteen seats in

Jharkhand, but put forward only one woman candidate, who lost. Interestingly, of the thirteen women who contested this election, six were independents (Election Commission of India, 2004: 188–9).

Even when policy is formulated, its implementation is not necessarily responsive to contextual particularities, but tends to reflect the ideological biases and preconceived notions of the implementers. The context here seems to suggest an apparent decline in women's status, but despite this, perhaps because of this, one finds a continued assertion by women of their land claims, a struggle to re-politicize their needs and entitlements as equal members of the 'community', and as active agents strategically responding to given situations rather than passive and ignorant clients. Without a shift in the ideologies underlying development practice, and recognizing women, and in fact, *adivasis*, as full persons, gender equality, or social equality more broadly, will be hard to achieve.

## REFRAMING THE GENDER AND PROPERTY DEBATE

To have a chance of practical success, the gender and property debate needs to be reframed from a theoretical perspective based on notions of personhood, a move away from binary oppositions, to a more relational and inclusive perspective, which sees personal struggles too as essentially political. Critical themes of the debate include: recognizing the theoretical distinctions made between different kinds of property in relation to their control and management; interrogating the assumption that land as a physical asset is equally valuable to all people; and finally, paying adequate attention to the existence and use of a range of strategies, overt and covert, by men and women, to negotiate land claims on an ongoing basis.

### Notions of Individual and Community in Resource Relations

Agricultural lands and non-agricultural ones, including forests and common property resources, are seen as a mutually supportive continuum within the local landscape. They complement and supplement each other in shaping local livelihoods, both subsistence and market-oriented. They are, however, defined as distinct categories in both state parlance and academic analysis. This definitional separation is then followed by further divisions in terms of spheres of control and management. Thus agricultural land is seen as individual property under individual or familial control, while forests and non-agricultural land are seen as community property, with control shared between the state and the local community in differing degrees. While forests were categorized as 'village land' in earlier settlements, for instance, they are labelled as 'government land' in the latest settlement. Agricultural land is seen to serve private, everyday needs, while common property is often required to serve the 'public good', which may even be against local interests. Increasing work burdens of women as a result of closure of forests for purposes of protection are a clear testimony to this.[1] Given the dominance of state power and the resulting legitimacy accorded to its definition of resources, their control and use, one finds several contradictions in local practice, created by these binary categorizations of land and property as agricultural or forest, individual or community. To take just one example, while the state system is used to stake individual claims to revenue land through the process of titling in order to ensure individual security, state hegemony is also challenged by using common land too to secure individual and household livelihoods (e.g., *kurram*). With people thus simultaneously acting in different, often conflicting ways, the understanding of land relations gets further complicated.

The definitional boundaries create at least two levels of tensions: one between the individual and the community, and the second between the state and society (inclusive of both the individual and the community). The first tension is clearly visible in the discourses and actions of the Jharkhand movement in relation to land. In their struggle for political autonomy, the leaders claimed a notion of 'community' that would be responsible for the livelihood security of its members and consequently determine the utilization of land, water and forest resources. This holistic conception of resources lays emphasis on community control and denies the legitimacy of any individual rights. It was used by the leaders of the movement to oppose the 1996 Supreme Court judgment in favour of land rights to women. While cooperation in the community does exist in the sharing of

[1] See also Sarin, 1997, on this point.

certain kinds of resources and assets such as the *dheki*, or even labour, differentiation in landholding is clearly visible between kin and clan-groups and between genders. Distribution of agricultural land amongst households and individuals does not always reflect need, as is the claim, but rather power and status. Community institutions are often weak and unable to enforce the ideas of 'community control' on the ground, leading to the dominance of senior men, generally the legal title-holders. Junior men have struggled against senior kin and women too have tried in different ways to stake their claims to land. While there has been no comment on male claims, women's claims have been opposed by the political leaders who see them as divisive and opposed to the ideology of their larger struggle. So while men's individual rights are accommodated within the notion of 'community', women's individual rights are seen as disruptions of the 'community' and hence opposed. This comes from women's differential positioning within kinship and family structures.

A second tension relates to the struggle over defining the spheres of control of the state and community with respect to non-agricultural land. Taking an integrated approach to land provides some insights into why state policies seeking community control selectively (in relation to some types of land resources and not others) do not necessarily work. In Gopikandar block of Dumka district, for instance, the Santal leadership rejected community resource management programmes such as Joint Forest Management, imposed by the government, claiming that property belonged to the village and not the state, and that they could manage their village forests without state supervision. They were asserting indigenous definitions of both land and the community. Consistent with this position, they have also thwarted efforts at individual titling through the settlement process, by presenting a picture of kinship-based control. In a sense, their attempt is to actualize through a kin and village-based approach, a more holistic system of resource management that includes the continuum of landscape, both agricultural and forestlands. While maximizing the range of control of male village elites, seen as representatives of the 'community', this security in their own authority also makes them grant women some rights.

Ignoring this continuum of landscapes and the porousness of boundaries between agricultural and non-agricultural land can also be seen as part of a process of socially labelling people as 'settled cultivators' or 'forest-dwellers', with connotations for individual versus community control, but also carrying ideologies of development and backwardness. The debate around the Scheduled Tribes (Recognition of Forest Rights) Act, 2006, put the spotlight on this process of land classification, use and control. Scheduled Tribes, though often constructed as forest-dwellers, are projected as being incapable of managing the forests, or understanding its importance for environmental stability and sustainability. Their progressive marginalization and alienation from parts of land classified as forests, without adequate compensation in other types of land classified as agricultural, which could have resulted in poaching and unsustainable practices, is hardly mentioned. Chandu Grihi and the other Paharias of Chuapara are a good illustration of this process. They have been forced to cut and use forest lands often in unsustainable ways, due to the lack of alternate livelihood resources, including agricultural land. The problem for them is worse confounded because of the split in jurisdiction of these different types of land between different departments within the government—the Forest and the Revenue Department—themselves in competition with each other for control of these resources and the consequent power it provides them.

In terms of community control, in contexts where the Santals have lost both forests and their socio-cultural dominance, as in Bagdiha, they appear to have given in to this statist ideology. Closer scrutiny of the struggle over women's land claims, however, reveals a strategy by the leadership to use state mechanisms to reassert their own authority at the local level, drawing simultaneously on the government rhetoric of community management and control to support such claims. One can then see how *adivasi* men, women and communities use and manipulate state-constructed identities in an effort to establish the efficacy of local, indigenous constructions in relation to resource management and control.

Notions of both 'individual' and 'community', and within this, masculinity and femininity, are thus being redefined in the larger context of state domination and control over both resources and services, yet are often overlooked by the debates around women's land rights. Re-establishing the superiority of community authority can result in enhanced control over women, but also carries the potential for increased freedom for women, by decentralizing control over resources and bringing the arena for negotiation closer home. Understanding the state of flux in the basic ideological assumptions about relationships between people and resources is critical to the formulation of gendered land and indeed resource policies.

## Land as a Resource: Does One Size Fit All?

A second problem with the gender and land debates is their almost exclusive focus on land as an important physical asset for women that can ameliorate poverty and ensure gender equity. Advocating for equal rights for women in land, this view overlooks the complexities of *how* land produces well-being for women as gendered subjects. While lamenting the failure of implementation, it continues to argue for further reform, not taking note of the larger context that often creates a set of social relations that resist implementation. The underlying assumption of approaches focused on the value of land as a physical asset is that land is good for women, as it is for men.

Land is undoubtedly a key physical asset for Santal women (as for men), although the link between the quantum of land held and women's well-being is not clear. Dibri Hansdak has land, yet is unable to use it for making a living. Amongst the women-headed households in Bagdiha, all of whom controlled some land, one was able to break even, the remaining three faced food deficits. The use of land is mediated by a host of other social relations; hence the output and consequent food and livelihood security is related not to land-holding per se, but their ability to negotiate its use socially. So Jharna or Dhaki are denied male labour to plough their land and Sona and Choti are branded as witches, reducing their output even compared to other households with similar land-holding positions but headed by men. Apart from its material value, land has a symbolic meaning that extends beyond the individual, and even the household. It is a social resource that represents the history of the community and lineage (represented by men), hence women are unable to act as autonomous individuals in relation to land. But it is precisely because of these social and status considerations that claiming land becomes one way for women to claim full personhood within their society.

Women themselves see their land claims as different from those of men, mediated by the particular subject-positions they are in and the cooperation or non-cooperation these positions entail. For a Santal woman, marriage is seen as a necessary and perhaps inevitable aspect of adult status. As much of the literature on the household reveals, intra-household relations are not just about bargaining and conflict, but also about mutuality and interdependence. Strathern (1988) and Sharma (1980) have both pointed out that as wives in successful marriages, rather than feeling excluded, women find their own prestige in taking forward notions of masculinity and male prestige. Fairness is conceptualized in terms of equal outcomes in critical areas of life rather than exactly equal divisions of labour, responsibilities or assets. As long as their marriage is successful, they share common interests and prestige with their husbands. Yet when things go wrong, they are not passive victims, but adopt a range of strategies to assert their claims. This can happen in the event of widowhood, separation or a polygynous arrangement, when women have to take on the full role of 'provider'.

Rights are customarily ensured to all these groups of women so long as their continued ownership will not disrupt lineage calculations or challenge power relations. While levirate is not common amongst the Santals, the male kin would prefer the widow to depend on them for maintenance, rather than lead her own life. Similarly, women who choose to exit from polygynous relationships are seen to be challenging male authority. Women's land claims imply recognizing the independent status of once 'dependent' women, posing a challenge to male authority as 'providers' and 'protectors' internally, in a context where they are already marginalized externally. The back-up support of parents and natal kin becomes critical in enabling women to negotiate their status and position as well as land claims within marriage and with marital kin. So, despite the existence of customary provisions, women are themselves unwilling to stake claims in their parental property, but prefer to do so in their marital property.

But the interpretation of opposition is different in the two instances. While claims in marital property pose a challenge to individual male identity, women's claims in parental property are seen as a collective challenge to male kin and clan authority. Despite its social legitimacy, especially in the absence of male heirs, the *gharjawae* husband, for instance, is still seen as dividing kin solidarity and hence, opposed. As resources become scarce, competition inevitably causes greater male kin solidarity, since in the absence of effective protection from the state, this is the only way to compete. Within the larger context of regional marginality, where non-land resources are concentrated in the hands of the non-*adivasi* groups, the attempt to retain control over land leads to the strengthening of male solidarity as evident also in the rhetoric of the 'community'. While subordination of women is not the objective, it is nevertheless an outcome of such processes of competition over resources.

Highlighting the basic disjuncture between inheritance of property and inheritance of the lineage name in a patrilineal society in the interpretation of the *gharjawae*, for instance, indicates that ideological constructions can also have a logic of their own. One finds contradictions between what is done and what is said. While in practice, several women married to *gharjawaes* are in full control of their land in Bagdiha, with or without registration, the talk around this indicates sharp contestation. It reflects men's imaginings and aspirations of the world as they would like to see it, influenced by their political affiliations and cultural representations, which also constitute an essential part of their realities. Men too are gendered subjects and take differentiated positions based on their own life experiences and needs, including the competition for symbolic wealth and prestige amongst men and kin-groups, across generations. Thus while men and women are not always opposed to each other in the struggle over land, but often support each other in their respective projects, both support and opposition have to be understood within a larger context of competition and marginalization, rather than as drunken men violating and killing their wives and widows. The methodological challenge, of course, has been to constantly attempt to find the links between material livelihoods and discursive contestations, rather than choosing one in preference to the other.

Universal rights have value as a broad normative framework clarifying the intentions of the state, yet women's demand is for the recognition of particular, contextualized rights by the state, as a back-up to their struggles for securing their identity as persons and strengthening their relative bargaining power. The Santal Pargana Tenancy Act as a piece of state legislation is a good illustration. Specifically mentioning *gharjawae* rights has made it easier for women in this position to secure their rights, despite its rigid interpretation of the institution of *gharjawae* itself. This view is further confirmed by the fact that in the last two years there is a new initiative by women's groups in the Santal Parganas to push for codification of customary law.

Dealing with land as a purely technical or legal issue is clearly futile, as it is a bearer of social identities and gender ideologies framing particular notions of masculinities and femininities. Variations of course do exist across locations, in response to differences in the ecological context, the history of land tenure policies and the socio-political development of different regions. Land thus has different meanings even in the two contexts of the study villages—an individual, status-giving resource versus a shared, livelihood-supporting resource. This has implications for processes of contestation, the availability of social and kin support and hence on gendered access and use, challenging also the stereotypes of *adivasi* homogeneity both as individuals and communities. What also becomes clear is that asset interventions that strengthen the position of poor men need not have the same impact on poor women.

## Strategies of Assertion and Resistance

The third major element of the debate relates to the strategies used by women to assert their land claims. Strategies can be diverse and range from the macro-political to the micro-individual. For instance, the politics of the *hul* Jharkhand, a people's movement against land alienation and money lending in Dumka district in the 1960s and 1970s, was quite influential in improving material conditions. In Bagdiha, a majority of the households were able to reclaim their land, which they had been unable to do legally. Both men and women participated in the movement, but class and ethnic identities rather than gender identities marked the public assertion.

Around the same time, one finds a growing assertion by women, particularly those married in *gharjawae* form, to get their marriages registered in the civil court and hence ensure the legitimacy of their land claims. This is particularly interesting in the light of my field data that reveals that customary institutions, even though entirely male, have generally supported women's claims. As male elders, they see themselves as 'protectors' of all members of the community. What seems to be happening is that with the decline in the real power of these institutions, individual male rights as legitimized by the state land-titling process have been publicly asserted. This has reduced local flexibilities in land use and distribution and led to a reinforcement of patriarchal controls. Women's assertion becomes essential even to hold on to their present identities, not necessarily seeking an expansion in their spheres of control.

At the micro-level, women take recourse to everyday forms of resistance that include social negotiation through village institutions, returning to the natal home, organizing male labour through *gharjawae* or *ghardijawae* arrangements, sharing a part of their property with male marital kin or using narratives to outsiders to denigrate their kin, as a source of power. They have also publicly challenged male control by drawing upon the authority of legal and state mechanisms. This is more to reinforce their claims in the event of a threat or act of physical violence. Often more than one strategy is adopted simultaneously, the objective being to 'play by the rules' and gain social support on the one hand, while asserting the legitimacy of their claims on the other. One-upmanship is not the purpose of their resistance, but emphasizing that equality to them means being respected in their own right.

Women's land claims can succeed on account of their own struggles, but they can also be met as a result of negotiation amongst male kin (perhaps in response to women's struggles). The institution of *gharjawae* itself emerged in 1916 following a meeting of male elders in Dumka, that, in seeking to ensure lineage property retention, legitimized inheritance by women. Thus, while women may face subordination in the face of male solidarity, they can also benefit from the competition between men of different groups. Women thus struggle in many different ways; legal rights too have to be socially negotiated and accepted before they can change practice, including state practice.

## POWER, IDEOLOGY AND CULTURE IN REALIZING ONE'S IDENTITY

There are two elements to realizing one's identity as a woman—one is the meeting of material or practical needs that help improve the performance of objective roles as women. The second relates to the subjective valuation and recognition of women as equal social persons. In a context of scarce resources, all needs are politicized and contested in multiple institutional sites between different social actors. Different ideologies and notions of society and social relations are brought into play in these contestations. While survival cannot be easily denied, equality of status is much more sharply contested, justified by particular constructions of masculinity and femininity, and indeed of the community itself.

Women are central to the Santal land economy and to that extent one might imagine their claims to land to be strong. The approach here is essentially a role-defined one, so as cultivators of land, women should also be given ownership of land. Why then does this not happen as easily? What is missed by most research and policy is that land is used also as a discursive resource in the negotiation of power between genders as well as between different groups of men in society. This was particularly visible in the discourse of the Jharkhand movement that centred on the control over natural resources—land, forests and water. Despite the fact that in reality, large sections of the people were unable to meet their livelihood needs from these resources and were largely dependent on selling their labour locally or elsewhere. The struggle for land signified much more than a struggle for an economic resource, a deeper struggle over cultural, ideological, moral and political questions. Following Gramsci, power is not exclusively economic or ideological, but is constructed in relation to both. Ideological victory too can result in material benefits, as much as the recognition of the material need itself.

And this is where the struggle for land comes in. Successful claims can give women full social membership, yet it is in establishing this as a legitimate need-claim that women seem at a disadvantage. The trump card for men is the legitimacy of 'provider' expectations, which locally signify an indisputable need. And the symbolic construction of land as a male form of property supports this claim. A shift to individualism, which women's land claims are seen to signify, would imply an ideological disruption of the very basis of their society and relationships therein. Contestation over land is then driven not only by physical need but also by the ideological construction of gender roles and responsibilities.

One example is the articulation of the image of a 'good woman', as one who accepts the diktats of the father, husband, brother or son. The presence of both Hindu neighbours and Christian missionaries, with their emphasis on monogamy and a strict sexual morality, has had a major role to play in the construction of this image. A '*dain*' is then presented in opposition to this image of a 'good woman'—one who is assertive and sexually free, not a good mother or a good wife, and a threat to processes of both production and reproduction. Women, however, resist such accusations by taking the help of other village women and men, escaping the accusations by shifting the cultural frame, for example, moving to their parental home or even changing the paradigm of discourse by bringing in the modern legal system. The increase in contestation and disputes, even violence, is an indicator of the unwillingness of women to accept this new identity being imposed on them. It is not a sign of weakness or victimhood.

This image of the 'good woman' however also underlies the construction of 'dependency' in state policy. So while women in virtuous roles, fulfilling the expectations of their particular gender roles, such as widows who have served their husbands but are now destitute are seen as worthy of state social security and support, divorced or separated women, seen as deviants, are not. The schemes targeted at women are widow pensions and maternity benefits, housing and group-based credit. While the first two are directed specifically at women as wives without husbands and as mothers, the latter two see women essentially as home-makers caring for their families. Their income needs are seen as secondary rather than primary, hence excluding women who are, in fact, the main providers from such group activities. State support ends up bypassing women within marriages, especially those who are 'providers' like Nati, an entirely neglected category in an ideological structure that unquestioningly accepts the completeness of male provisioning. So while policies do conceptually recognize the inter-related needs raised by women's land claims, the processes of implementation often ignore the meanings implicit within these demands.

Another vulnerable group are the 'poor'; women are over-represented in this group, and a range of development policies are targeted at them. While state policy reflects simultaneous and sometimes contradictory core assumptions about the causes of poverty, ranging from those embedded in structural inequities, to those resulting from individual failings, particular strands of thinking become significant at particular points in time. In the present national discourse, based on principles of market orientation rather than socialist redistribution, poverty is seen more as an individual failing, rather than of structural and systemic failures by many sections of the state. It is, therefore, stigmatized as 'bad'. Rather than focusing on the development of agriculture and irrigation, the current focus is on the generation of employment, manual and often arduous, reflecting a particular construction of *adivasis* as providers of labour rather than independent actors and entrepreneurs. The strategy is to make the poor work harder and to control their labour. The National Rural Employment Guarantee Act, 2005, passed under the pressure of the Left parties, recognizes structural inequities, and seeks to guarantee minimum employment if it is to make a difference in the lives of the poor. Its implementation in Jharkhand to date has been far from satisfactory. What is clear, however, is the struggle for power and ideological hegemony both in the prioritization of policies and their implementation on the ground.

By ignoring structural constraints and focusing on individual and collective self-help initiatives, closely monitored by the state, development practice and support has unfortunately moved further away from the poorest. It is important to understand the basis for entitlement—is it citizenship (universal), deserts (work) or need (means-tested)? (Fraser, 1997: 50) While citizenship is the most broad-based right and in a context of widespread poverty perhaps the most appropriate, 'deserts', being employment-linked, are inherently biased against women. In a largely rural context like Dumka, where not many Santals are in public sector employment, it is also limited in scope. The third category of entitlement based on 'need', includes the 'poor' and 'women'. Underlying this, however, are both patriarchal gender ideologies as well as neo-liberal ideologies of who is deserving of support. By denying public responsibility, such constructions serve to depoliticize the causes of both poverty and gender inequality.

While the state tends to see development as a linear path, from the traditional to the modern, from 'assetlessness' to asset ownership, from have-not to have, this is not necessarily a straightforward and unidirectional process. Similar interventions have produced different outcomes in different contexts. Not all state structures are enabling, not all community institutions restrictive—their mutual interactions produce sites for freedoms as well as challenge those freedoms. While proclaiming the principles of equity, state benefits have often enhanced inequities, through provisioning that is riddled with corruption and patronage. Customary institutions while enforcing ritual exclusions and patrilyny on women have also supported their claims in a range of circumstances. This, in some sense, exposes the sterility of positions that are either pro- or anti-state, customary law or titling per se. Social change seems to result from an interplay between endogenous and exogenous factors, a process of negotiation and the adjustment of cultures. Solutions too cannot be found in a dichotomized manner. A universal state law need not necessarily be superior to customary law, which is often flexible, socially negotiated and hence more practicable. It can, however, provide a back-up support to customary institutions struggling to enforce women's claims or act as an essential protection from abuses of customary law by the locally powerful.

Development itself is a highly political process. It is as much a struggle for negotiating identities, power relations and ideological dominance between genders and other social groups as about improvements in material conditions. The Jharkhand movement, though grounded in the reality of material marginalization, was also a struggle over the meanings of state and society. The struggle over women's land claims is similarly not just a struggle over a physical asset, but also a struggle over identities, notions of masculinity and femininity, poverty and marginality, authority and prestige. Recognizing that the personal is political not just for women, but for other actors too, can itself point to possible solutions to land problems, that may well lie beyond land redistribution alone. To arrive at that implies adopting a differentiated and context-sensitive, yet inclusive and integrated approach to resources as well as gendered identities and relationships.

# Annexure 1

# Profile of Sample Households

| HH | Fam. size | Members of household (with approximate ages) | Occupational status | Land holding* (in acres) | Literacy of adults (Grade) |
|---|---|---|---|---|---|
| C1 | 6 | Mary Tudu (Wife, 38) | Agriculture, helped at the *anganwadi*, domestic work. | *Dhani*: 2.5<br>*Bari*: 0.66 | 5 |
| | | Chura Marandi (husband, 42) | Agriculture, government contractor. | | 7 |
| | | Sheila (daughter, 18, married in 2000) | Agriculture, forest produce and marketing, domestic work. | | 3 |
| | | Sanju (daughter, 12, married, 2004) | Grazing cattle, student. | | 3 |
| | | Santosh (son, 10) | Grazing cattle, student. | | 2 |
| | | Naina Marandi (husband's sister, 40, separated from first husband, second one ran away to Assam) | Agriculture, domestic work, forest produce and marketing. | | – |
| C2 | 6 | Nati Hansdak (wife, 35, second marriage) | Wage labour, forest produce and marketing, *kurram* and *bari* cultivation. | *Dhani*: 2.5<br>*Bari*: 0.5 | – |
| | | Karu Tudu (husband, 38, third marriage) | Gudit or village messenger, land all leased out. | | – |
| | | Detmai (daughter, 13, married in 2003) | Domestic work, forest produce, care of younger siblings, working for another household. | | |

*(contd.)*

| HH | Fam. size | Members of household (with approximate ages) | Occupational status | Land holding* (in acres) | Literacy of adults (Grade) |
|---|---|---|---|---|---|
| | | Saheb (son, 10, died in 2000) | | | |
| | | Nunka (son, 7) | Grazing cattle, helping grandmother | | |
| | | Mistri (son, 4, died in 2001) | | | |
| | | (baby boy born in 2003) | | | |
| C3 | 2 | Chutki Kolin (wife, 22) | Wage labour, little cultivation. | *Dhani*: 0.5<br>*Bari*: 0.16 | –<br>– |
| | | Chutka Kol (husband, 25, second marriage) | Wage labour, little cultivation, selling poles in the market. | | |
| C4 | 5 | Dibri Hansdak (wife, 25, *gharjawae*) | Domestic work and care of children, have leased out land. | *Dhani*: 2.66<br>*Bari*: 1 | –<br>2 |
| | | Mantu Marandi (husband, 27) | Wage labour, sale of poles and some forest produce. | | |
| | | Mithu (daughter, 5) | | | |
| | | Babu (son, 3) | | | |
| | | Munna (son, new born) | | | |
| C5 | 4 | Minu Dehri (wife, 28) | Domestic work. | *Dhani*: 1.5 | – |
| | | Sabu Dehri (husband, 35) | Wage labour, agriculture and construction, sale of poles in the market. | *Bari*: 0.16 | –<br>– |
| | | Mitu (daughter, 9) | | | |
| | | Sona (son, 5, died in 1999) | | | |
| | | Babu (son, 1) | | | |
| C6 | 7 | Marangkudi Hansdak (wife, 30) | Domestic work and care of children, some cultivation. | *Dhani*: 1.0<br>*Bari*: 0.5 | – |
| | | Pappu Marandi (husband, 35) | Cultivation and sale of forest produce in the market, wage labour. | | – |
| | | 4 children (two sons and two daughters all below 6 years) | | | – |
| | | Jhumri Murmu (blind mother, 58) | | | – |

*(contd.)*

| HH | Fam. size | Members of household (with approximate ages) | Occupational status | Land holding* (in acres) | Literacy of adults (Grade) |
|---|---|---|---|---|---|
| C7 | 4 | Bitia Kolin (wife 38, second marriage) | Cultivation, domestic work. | *Dhani*: 0.5<br>*Bari*: 0.16 | – |
| | | Garma Kol (husband, 40, third marriage) | Wage labour, a little cultivation. | | – |
| | | Hirulal (son, 15) | Wage labour. | | – |
| | | Sundari (daughter, 13) | Working for another household. | | – |
| C8 | 6 | Arti Hembrum (wife, 25, second marriage) | Agriculture, forest produce collection, *kurram* cultivation, domestic work. | *Dhani*: 2.0<br>*Bari*: 0.5 | 2<br>5 |
| | | Ramu Marandi (husband, 32, second marriage, children from first wife who died when youngest son born) | Agriculture, brewing liquor. | | 5 |
| | | Mukesh (son 13) | Studying in Susni Mission. | | 2 |
| | | Hira (son 10) | Grazing cattle. | | 1 |
| | | Moti (son, 8) | Grazing cattle and school. | | – |
| | | Shikhar (son, 4) | | | |
| C9 | 3 | Sita Kolin (wife, 36, second marriage) | Cultivation, domestic work. | *Dhani*: 3.0<br>*Bari*: 0.5 | –<br>– |
| | | Dhiru Kol (husband, 40) | Cultivation, government contracting work. | | – |
| | | Ravan (son, 15) | Cultivation, wage labour. | | – |
| C10 | 14 | Mani Soren (wife, 28, second marriage) | Cultivation, domestic work | *Dhani*: 1.66<br>*Bari*: 0.33 | – |
| | | Chetan Murmu (husband, 33, second marriage, first wife left him when charged with rape) | Agriculture, some contracting work for government. | | 5 |
| | | Baburam (son, 3) | | | |
| | | Pitho Murmu (Chunu'smad brother, 25) | | | |

*(contd.)*

| HH | Fam. size | Members of household (with approximate ages) | Occupational status | Land holding* (in acres) | Literacy of adults (Grade) |
|---|---|---|---|---|---|
| C11 | 4 | Bahari Murmu (widow, 35) | Cultivation, wage labour, domestic work. | *Dhani*: 1.0<br>*Bari*: 0.5 | – |
| | | Baburam (son, 14) | Some cultivation (learning to plough), wage labour. | | – |
| | | Pahi (daughter, 12) | Domestic work, forest produce. | | – |
| | | Chuna (son, 8) | | | 1 |
| B1 | 4 | Choti Tudu (second widow of Girish Soren, 45) | Cultivation, seasonal migration, wage labour, brewing liquor. | *Dhani*: 1.0<br>*Bari*: 0.16<br>*Dhani*: 1.0 | – |
| | | Munni Hansdak (first widow, 55) | Domestic work, some cultivation. | | – |
| | | Sharmila (daughter, 14, married in 2001) | Studying in school, domestic work. | | 6 |
| | | Mita (daughter, 10) | Studying in school. | | 4 |
| B2 | 9 | Mitya Rajwar (wife, 28) | Cultivation, domestic work. | *Dhani*: 2.0<br>*Bari*: 0.5 | –<br>– |
| | | Harilal Rajwar (husband, 32) | Cultivation, wage labour. | | |
| | | 6 children, 4 daughters and 2 sons between ages 10 and 6 months | (This is a Scheduled Caste household and not Santal) | | |
| | | Manno (widowed mother of Harilal, 60) | | | |
| B3 | 2 | Shaniwari Murmu (mother, 50, widow) | Cultivation, little wage work. | *Dhani*: 1.5<br>*Bari*: 0.16 | |
| | | Dhaki Marandi (daughter, 30, separated when husband took second wife) | Grazing cattle, domestic work. | | – |
| B4 | 4 | Agnes Hembrum (wife, 30) | Cultivation, domestic work. | *Dhani*: 2.66<br>*Bari*: 0.25 | 9<br>10 |
| | | Sunil Marandi (husband, 40, second marriage though not officially married) | Farm management (including hiring labour), money lending, ex-serviceman. | | |
| | | Two young sons (6 and 2) | Elder son studying in Dumka with Nirmala's parents. | | 1 |

*(contd.)*

| HH | Fam. size | Members of household (with approximate ages) | Occupational status | Land holding* (in acres) | Literacy of adults (Grade) |
|---|---|---|---|---|---|
| B5 | 4 | Sona Tudu (widow, 44)<br>3 married daughters fourth daughter died in 1999 | Agriculture, wage labour, domestic work. Son-in-law ploughs her land. | *Dhani*: 2.5<br>*Bari*: 0.16 | 2 |
| | | 2 daughters, aged 12 and 6 | Studying in school. | | 5, 3 |
| | | David (son, 8) | | | 2 |
| B6 | 3 | Rimani Marandi (mother, separated from husband who left with another woman) | Cultivation, wage labour, seasonal migration to Bengal, domestic work. | *Dhani*: 2.0<br>*Bari*: 0.5 | – |
| | | Vinod (son, 15) | Studying in Dumka high school. | | 9 |
| | | Ritu (daughter 11) | Studying in local primary school. | | 4 |
| B7 | 2 | Neela Tudu (wife, 38, second marriage) | Cultivation, seasonal migration to Bengal, domestic work. | *Dhani*: 0.5<br>*Bari*: 0.16 | 2 |
| | | Jeevan Soren (husband, 50, second marriage, first wife lives in an adjacent house with children) | Cultivation, seasonal migration to Bengal, raising buffaloes for milk. | | – |
| B8 | 12 | Panthi Marandi (widowed mother, gharjawae, 70) | | *Dhani*: 2.0<br>*Bari*: 0.33 | |
| | | Jivan (son, 45, remarried after death of first wife) | Cultivation. | | 5 |
| | | Hamir (son, 40) | Cultivation. | | 5 |
| | | Sonamati Kisku (Hamir's wife, 32) | Cultivation, domestic work, seasonal migration to Bengal. | | |
| | | Sonoti (daughter, 38, separated from husband, was a second wife) | Wage labour, seasonal migration to Bengal. | | 4 |
| | | Jitan (son, 30) | Cultivation, seasonal migration. | | 7 |
| | | Panbati (Jivan's daughter, 16) | Domestic work, seasonal migration to Bengal. | | 4 |
| | | Raju (Jivan's son, 12) | Student. | | 5 |

*(contd.)*

| HH | Fam. size | Members of household (with approximate ages) | Occupational status | Land holding* (in acres) | Literacy of adults (Grade) |
|---|---|---|---|---|---|
| | | Sabita (Hamir's daughter, 7) | Student. | | 2 |
| | | Ramu (Hamir's son. 4) | | | |
| | | Nirojani (Sonoti's daughter 13) | Student, domestic work. | | 6 |
| | | Sarojini (Sonoti's daughter 10) | Student. | | 4 |
| B9 | 6 | Karuna Hembrum (wife, 45) | Cultivation, domestic work. | *Dhani*: 3.33 *Bari*: 0.33 | – |
| | | Manglu Marandi (husband, 50) | Cultivation, village *majhi*, hence dispute resolution work. | | – |
| | | Nimbulal (son, 28) | Cultivation. | | 7 |
| | | Mita (Nimbulal's wife, 25) | Domestic work. | | 6 |
| | | Jito (son, 25) | Cultivation, wage labour. | | 8 |
| | | Mini (Jito's wife, 20) | Domestic work. | | 10 |
| B10 | 3 | Binoti Kolin (widow, 60) | Cultivation, brewing liquor, domestic work. | *Dhani*: 2.66 *Bari*: 0.33 | – |
| | | Maku (daughter, 35, separated, now remarried) | | | – |
| | | Bina (daughter, 30 married) | | | 5 |
| | | Jaboti (28, remarried and widowed) | Wage labour, seasonal migration to Bengal. | | 3 |
| | | Diwan (son, 25) | Migrant to stone crusher. | | 5 |
| B11 | 3 | Shanti Marandi (wife, 35) | Cultivation, domestic work, wage work. | *Dhani*: 0.83 *Bari*: 0.16 | – |
| | | Phagu Baskey (husband, 40) | Unwell, little cultivation. | | 10 |
| | | Binti (adopted daughter, 10) | Student. | | 3 |
| B12 | 6 | Sevati Tudu (mother, 50, husband Jeevan living with second wife, B7) | Foot injured, presently invalid. | *Dhani*: 2.5 *Bari*: 0.16 | – |
| | | Jitu (son, 32, married) | Lives with wife in another village. | | 7 |
| | | Mahani (daughter, 28, separated) | Seasonal migration, domestic work. | | 5 |

*(contd.)*

| HH | Fam. size | Members of household (with approximate ages) | Occupational status | Land holding* (in acres) | Literacy of adults (Grade) |
|---|---|---|---|---|---|
| | | Jeevan (son, 24) | Cultivation. | | 6 |
| | | Balli (son, 20) | Cultivation. | | 8 |
| | | Babita (daughter of Maku, 6) | Student. | | 1 |
| B13 | 3 | Sheela Hansdak (wife, 58) | Primary school teacher, domestic work. | *Dhani*: 4.5 *Bari*: 0.33 | 11 |
| | | Harnath Hembrum (husband, 62) | Farm management, settling disputes. | | 10 |
| | | Varsha Tudu (female niece, 35) | Working on fields, domestic work. | | – |
| | | Mona (married daughter, 33) | All the children are away. | | Graduate |
| | | Rita (married daughter, 29) | | | 10 |
| | | Rajesh (married son, 26) | | | Graduate |

* *Dhani* land includes lowland (*baihar*), midland (*sukhda*) and upland (*tandi*), hence all of it is not equally productive.

# Annexure 2

# Regional Demographic Indicators

Table 1: Population Trends in the Santal Parganas

| Census year | Population | Total ST | Percent ST to total |
|---|---|---|---|
| 1901 | 18,04,526 | 6,70,535 | 37.2 |
| 1911 | 18,77,486 | 6,60,847 | 35.2 |
| 1931 | 20,50,258 | 7,54,804 | 36.8 |
| 1951 | 23,22,092 | 9,82,170 | 42.2 |
| 1981 | 37,17,528 | 13,67,869 | 36.7 |
| 1991 | 45,91,092 | 14,63,937 | 31.9 |
| 2001 | 55,92,405 | – | – |

*Source:* Various Census publications.

Table 2: Rural Work Participation Rates, 1991 (in million)

| | India | | | Bihar | | | Bihar STs | | |
|---|---|---|---|---|---|---|---|---|---|
| | M | F | Total | M | F | Total | M | F | Total |
| Total Population | 321 (51.5) | 302 (48.5) | 623 (100) | 39 (52) | 36 (48) | 75 (100) | 3.11 (50.5) | 3.04 (49.5) | 6.15 (100) |
| Main Workers | 166 (26.6) | 56 (9) | 222 (35.6) | 18.9 (25.2) | 3.9 (5.2) | 22.8 (30.4) | 1.65 (34) | 0.70 (14) | 2.35 (48) |
| Marginal Workers | 2.3 (0.4) | 24.7 (4) | 27 (4.4) | 0.14 (0.2) | 1.96 (2.6) | 2.1 (2.8) | 0.03 (0.7) | 0.5 (10.3) | 0.53 (11) |
| Non-Workers | 153 (24.5) | 221 (35.5) | 374 (59) | 20 (26.7) | 30.1 (40.1) | 50.1 (66.8) | 1.1 (22.5) | 0.9 (18.5) | 2 (41) |

*Source:* Census 1991, B Series, Government of India, New Delhi.
*Note:* Figures in brackets are percentages.

Table 3: Occupational Status in the Santal Parganas by Gender (1911–91)

| Year | Total Pop | Rentiers | Cultivators | Agri Labour | Livestock | Trade | Industry | Services | Non-worker |
|---|---|---|---|---|---|---|---|---|---|
| 1911:M | 933425 | 1316 | 429300 | 61627 | 93141 | 8627 | 5066 | 10841 | 694318 |
| F | 949548 | 495 | 368307 | 74146 | 18779 | 6149 | 11514 | 5784 | (M+F) |
| 1931: M | 20,51,472 | 8607 | 565014 | 41304 | 9741 | 13880 | 16845 | | |
| F | (M+F) | 32 | 397529 | 56350 | 3245 | 6640 | 12152 | | |
| 1951:M | 1172,594 | 4990 | 945664 | 79396 | | 28674 | 24431 | 44374 | |
| F | 1149,498 | 5290 | 939152 | 80509 | | 25326 | 21173 | 34105 | |
| 1961:M | 1351,149 | | 551652 | 66427 | 39659 | 22171 | 41373 | 60325 | 545074 |
| F | 1324,054 | | 481787 | 57969 | 12159 | 3020 | 26786 | 14035 | 726863 |
| 1971:M | 1627014 | | 569038 | 189967 | 15607 | 24020 | 26099 | 35733 | 733761 |
| F | 1559894 | | 61174 | 74503 | 1263 | 682 | 5521 | 3457 | 1411189 |
| 1981:M | 1899,410 | | 627918 | 176694 | | | 35207 | 169149 | 849009 |
| F | 1818,118 | | 347893 | 79442 | | | 11217 | 24085 | 1355481 |
| 1991:M | 765002 | | 271397 | 65315 | 2953 | 16397 | 11226 | 22424 | 349427 |
| F | 730707 | | 213518 | 36888 | 403 | 547 | 4572 | 3406 | 470732 |

*Source:* Census of India for Bihar and Orissa, 1911 and 1931 and Census of India, District Census Handbook for Santal Parganas from 1951 onwards.

*Notes*: 1: Industry figure for 1911 includes food and textile industry, women predominate in the former.

2: Livestock refers to forestry, livestock, fishing, mining, wood etc.

3: 1961 onwards industry refers to household industry.

4: 1981 data under services refers to trade, services, livestock, mining etc.

5: 1991 data refers to Dumka district.

6: In 1961, an attempt was made to account for family labour, by defining work to include participation as well as production of economic goods or services for consumption, sale or exchange. Hence we find one of the highest enumerations of women as cultivators in the history of the Census operations.

Table 4: Literacy Rates in the Santal Parganas and Other States (in per cent)

| Year | India | Bihar | Santal Parganas | | | |
|---|---|---|---|---|---|---|
| | | | Total | Male | Female | Gender Gap |
| 1901 | 5.35 | | 2.5 | 4.7 | 0.2 | 4.5 |
| 1911 | 5.92 | 3.9 | 3.2 | 6.13 | 0.32 | 5.81 |
| 1931 | 9.5 | 4.37 | 2.9 | 5.3 | 0.5 | 4.8 |
| 1941 | 16.10 | 9.19 | 7.18 | 12.75 | 1.57 | 11.18 |
| 1951 | 16.67 | 11.5 | 8.26 | 11.68 | 4.76 | 6.92 |
| 1961 | 24.02 | 12.4 | 10.07 | 16.84 | 3.24 | 13.6 |
| 1971 | 29.45 | 19.9 | 15.93 | 25.02 | 6.44 | 18.58 |
| 1981 | 36.23 | 26.2 | 22.25 | 33.5 | 10.5 | 23 |
| 1991 | 42.84 | 37.5 | 26.0 | 37.26 | 14.0 | 23.26 |
| 2001* | 55.30 | 47.53 | 44.03 | 57.82 | 29.25 | 28.57 |

*Note:* * Refers to population over 7 years of age.
*Source:* Figures for Jharkhand and All India from Census 2001, for others from Census of Bihar and Orissa, 1911 and 1931, District Census Handbook of Santal Parganas for other years.

Table 5: Population Sex Ratios in Selected States: 1901–2001

| Year | India | Bihar | Jharkhand | Dumka* | STs in Santal Parganas | Chhatisgarh | Kerala |
|---|---|---|---|---|---|---|---|
| 1901 | 972 | 1061 | 1032 | 1019 | | 1046 | 1004 |
| 1911 | 964 | 1051 | 1021 | 1017 | 1010 | 1039 | 1008 |
| 1921 | 955 | 1020 | 1002 | 1007 | | 1041 | 1011 |
| 1931 | 950 | 995 | 989 | 1000 | | 1043 | 1022 |
| 1941 | 945 | 1002 | 978 | 993 | | 1032 | 1027 |
| 1951 | 946 | 1000 | 961 | 986 | | 1024 | 1028 |
| 1961 | 941 | 1005 | 960 | 985 | | 1008 | 1022 |
| 1971 | 930 | 957 | 945 | 967 | | 998 | 1016 |
| 1981 | 934 | 948 | 940 | 968 | 982 | 996 | 1032 |
| 1991 | 927 | 907 | 922 | 955 | 973 | 985 | 1036 |
| 2001 | 933 | 921 | 941 | 961 | n.a | 990 | 1058 |

*Source:* Census of India 2001, Series 1, Provisional Population Totals, Paper 1 of 2001. Census of India 2001, Series 21, Jharkhand.

Table 6: Juvenile Sex Ratios

| Year | All India | Dumka* | Bihar | Jharkhand | Chattisgarh | Kerala |
|---|---|---|---|---|---|---|
| 1991 | 945 | 985 | 953 | 979 | 984 | 958 |
| 2001 | 927 | 976 | 938 | 967 | 975 | 963 |

*Source:* Census 2001.

Table 7: Infant Mortality (0–5 years)

| | 1981 | | 1991 | |
|---|---|---|---|---|
| | Male | Female | Male | Female |
| Dumka | 148 | 157 | 86 | 85 |
| Bihar | 131 | 153 | 75 | 104 |
| India | 147 | 157 | 91 | 101 |

*Source:* Registrar General of India, Occasional Paper No. 1 of 1997, New Delhi.

# Annexure 3
# Land and Production

Table 1: Distribution of Land Holdings by Size, Class and Caste over Four Settlement Periods

(a) Chuapara

| Size in Acres | Santal | | | | Kol | | | |
|---|---|---|---|---|---|---|---|---|
| | 1 | 2 | 3 | 4 | 1 | 2 | 3 | 4 |
| 0–1 | 1 | 2 | 1 | 1 | 1 | 1 | 1 | 1 |
| 1–2.5 | 0 | 2 | 0 | 0 | 2 | 1 | 0 | 0 |
| 2.5–5 | 3 | 1 | 1 | 3 | 6 | 1 | 2 | 2 |
| 5–10 | 6 | 5 | 4 | 4 | 2 | 2 | 1 | 1 |
| 10–15 | 3 | 2 | 3 | 3 | 1 | 1 | 2 | 2 |
| 15–25 | 1 | 1 | 1 | 1 | 0 | 0 | 0 | 0 |
| Over 25 | 0 | 0 | 2 | 2 | 0 | 0 | 0 | 0 |
| Total | 14 | 13 | 12 | 14 | 12 | 6 | 6 | 6 |

(b) Bagdiha

| Size in Acres | *Adivasis* (Santal & Kol) | | | | Hindu (*Teli* & *Kumhar*) | | | |
|---|---|---|---|---|---|---|---|---|
| | 1 | 2 | 3 | 4 | 1 | 2 | 3 | 4 |
| 0–1 | 1 | 10 | 8 | 18 | 0 | 8 | 7 | 32 |
| 1–2.5 | 2 | 6 | 6 | 9 | 0 | 5 | 3 | 6 |
| 2.5–5 | 3 | 4 | 5 | 5 | 1 | 5 | 5 | 5 |
| 5 – 10 | 3 | 9 | 5 | 8 | 6 | 4 | 4 | 4 |
| 10 – 15 | 5 | 3 | 12 | 11 | 0 | 0 | 2 | 2 |
| 15 – 25 | 6 | 4 | 7 | 7 | 0 | 0 | 0 | 0 |
| Over 25 | 3 | 3 | 2 | 2 | 1 | 0 | 0 | 0 |
| Total | 23 | 39 | 45 | 60 | 8 | 22 | 21 | 49 |

*Note:* 2.5 acres is 1 hectare. According to Indian classifications, cultivator with less than 2.5 acres (1 hectare) is a Marginal Farmer, with 2.5–5 acres (1–2 hectare) a Small Farmer, with 5–12.5 acres (2–5 hectare) a Medium Farmer, and above that, a Large Farmer.

Table 2: Distribution of Wastelands in Dumka District: 1994–1997

| Year | Paharias | | Santal | | Scheduled Castes | | Total | |
|---|---|---|---|---|---|---|---|---|
| | No. | Area | No. | Area | No. | Area | No. | Area |
| 1994–95 | 564 | 465.98 | 6673 | 9405.5 | 18577 | 21752.6 | 45259 | 58805 |
| 1995–96 | 117 | 88.14 | 350 | 186.45 | 27 | 21.78 | 546 | 383.2 |
| 1996–97 | – | – | 1233 | N.avail | 64 | N.avail | 1299 | 973.8 |
| Total | 681 | 554.12 | 8256 | | 18668 | | 47104 | 60162 |
| Per cent | 1.5 | 1 | 17.5 | 16 | 40 | 36 | 100 | 100 |

Table 3a(i) Chuapara: Land Holding by Caste

| Caste | Upto 1 acre | 1–3 acre | 3 –5 acre | Above 5 acres | Total |
|---|---|---|---|---|---|
| Santal | 18 | 16 | 3 | 2 | 39 |
| Kol | 7 | 1 | 3 | 0 | 11 |
| Paharia | 0 | 2 | 0 | 0 | 2 |
| Total | 25 | 19 | 6 | 2 | 52 |

Table 3a(ii) Chuapara: Land Leased Out

| Caste | Upto 1 acre | 1–3 acre | Over 3 acre | Total leased out | No lease out | Total |
|---|---|---|---|---|---|---|
| Santal | 5 | 2 | 1 | 8 | 31 | 39 |
| Kol | 3 | 1 | 0 | 4 | 7 | 11 |
| Paharia | 0 | 2 | 0 | 2 | 0 | 2 |
| Total | 8 | 5 | 1 | 14 | 38 | 52 |

Table 3a(iii) Chuapara: Land Leased In

| Caste | Upto 1 acre | 1–3 acre | Over 3 acre | Total leased in | No lease in | Total |
|---|---|---|---|---|---|---|
| Santal | 10 | 1 | 0 | 11 | 28 | 39 |
| Kol | 3 | 0 | 0 | 3 | 8 | 11 |
| Paharia | 0 | 0 | 0 | 0 | 2 | 2 |
| Total | 13 | 1 | 0 | 14 | 38 | 52 |

Table 3b(i) Bagdiha: Land Holding by Caste

| Caste | Upto 1 acre | 1–3 acre | 3 –5 acre | Over 5 acres | Total |
|---|---|---|---|---|---|
| Santal | 69 | 51 | 14 | 9 | 143 |
| Kol | 1 | 8 | 0 | 0 | 9 |
| Rajwar | 1 | 1 | 0 | 0 | 2 |
| *Kumhar* | 41 | 3 | 0 | 2 | 46 |
| *Teli* | 20 | 6 | 1 | 1 | 28 |
| Others | 6 | 1 | 0 | 0 | 7 |
| Total | 138 | 70 | 15 | 12 | 235 |

Table 3b(ii) Bagdiha: Leasing Out of Land

| Caste | Upto 1 acre | 1–3 acre | Over 3 acre | Total leased out | No lease | Total |
|---|---|---|---|---|---|---|
| Santal | 49 | 10 | 2 | 61 | 82 | 143 |
| Kol | 4 | 0 | 0 | 4 | 5 | 9 |
| Rajwar | 2 | 0 | 0 | 2 | 0 | 2 |
| *Kumhar* | 0 | 0 | 2 | 2 | 44 | 46 |
| *Teli* | 2 | 0 | 1 | 3 | 25 | 28 |
| Others | 5 | 1 | 0 | 6 | 1 | 7 |
| Total | 62 | 11 | 5 | 78 | 157 | 235 |

Table 3b(iii) Bagdiha: Land Leased In

| Caste | Upto 1 acre | 1–3 acre | Over 3 acre | Total leased in | No lease | Total |
|---|---|---|---|---|---|---|
| Santal | 22 | 3 | 0 | 25 | 118 | 143 |
| Kol | 1 | 0 | 0 | 1 | 8 | 9 |
| Rajwar | 0 | 0 | 0 | 0 | 2 | 2 |
| *Kumhar* | 1 | 2 | 0 | 3 | 43 | 46 |
| *Teli* | 0 | 2 | 1 | 3 | 25 | 28 |
| Others | 0 | 0 | 0 | 0 | 7 | 7 |
| Total | 24 | 7 | 1 | 32 | 203 | 235 |

Table 4: Paddy Output and Consumption of Sample Households

| HH | Name of Title-Holder | Total Output (kg) | Consumption Requirement (kg) | Surplus | Output Value | Total Income | Output/ Income (per cent) |
|---|---|---|---|---|---|---|---|
| 1 | Chura Marandi | 960 | 908 | 52 | 3360 | 11522 | 29 |
| 2 | Karu Tudu | 170 | 360 | –190 | 595 | 4652 | 13 |
| 3 | Chutka Kol | 95 | 220 | –125 | 1332.5 | 3665 | 36 |
| 4 | Dibri Hansdak (F) | 240 | 479 | –239 | 840 | 2045 | 41 |
| 5 | Sabu Dehri | 0 | 214 | –214 | 0 | 3309 | 0 |
| 6 | Pappu Marandi | 1000 | 967 | 33 | 3500 | 6190 | 57 |
| 7 | Garma Kol | 202 | 270 | –68 | 2707 | 6475 | 42 |
| 8 | Ramu Marandi | 650 | 657 | –7 | 2275 | 2570 | 89 |
| 9 | Dhiru Kol | 850 | 780 | 70 | 2975 | 5620 | 53 |
| 10 | Chetan Murmu | 800 | 630 | 170 | 2800 | 3625 | 77 |
| 11 | Bahri Marandi (F) | 175 | | | | | |
| 12 | Choti Tudu (F) | 230 | 662 | –432 | 805 | 4215 | 19 |
| 13 | Hari Rajwar | 864 | 1214 | –350 | 3024 | 4900 | 62 |
| 14 | Shaniwari Murmu(F) | 288 | 243 | 45 | 1008 | 1650 | 61 |
| 15 | Sunil Marandi | 6000 | 303 | 5697 | 21000 | 21000 | 100 |
| 16 | Sona Tudu(F) | 720 | 971 | –251 | 2520 | 3860 | 65 |
| 17 | Rimani Marandi | 300 | 669 | –369 | 1050 | 1390 | 76 |
| 18 | Jeevan Soren | 640 | 653 | –13 | 2240 | 4065 | 55 |
| 19 | Panthi Marandi(F) | 640 | 1731 | –1091 | 2240 | 6135 | 37 |
| 20 | Karuna Hembrum(F) | 2074 | 1122 | 952 | 7259 | 8000 | 91 |
| 21 | Binoti Kolin(F) | 175 | 531 | –356 | 612.5 | 4782 | 13 |
| 22 | Shanti Marandi(F) | 230 | 511 | –281 | 805 | 2695 | 30 |
| 23 | Sevati Tudu | 2000 | 1183 | 817 | 7000 | 7905 | 89 |
| 24 | Harnath Hembrum | 3800 | 990 | 2810 | 13300 | 93300 | 14 |

Table 5: Ownership of Assets and Indebtedness of Sample Households

| HH No | Name of Title-Holder | Land Holding *Dhani* | Land Holding *Bari* | Cattle | Small Livestock Goats | Small Livestock Pigs | Small Livestock Chicken | Indebt-eness (in Rupees) |
|---|---|---|---|---|---|---|---|---|
| 1 | Chura Marandi | 2.5 | 0.66 | 5 | 2 | 6 | 4 | 595 |
| 2 | Karu Tudu | 2.5 | 0.5 | 0 | 0 | 2 | 0 | 450 |
| 3 | Chutka Kol | 0.49 | 0.16 | 0 | 0 | 1 | 1 | 300 |
| 4 | Dibri Hansdak(F) | 2.66 | 1 | 0 | 0 | 5 | 7 | 900 |
| 5 | Sabu Dehri | 1.5 | 0.16 | 2 | 0 | 1 | 2 | 12520 |
| 6 | Pappu Marandi | 3 | 0.5 | 2 | 0 | 6 | 8 | 415 |
| 7 | Garma Kol | 0.49 | 0.16 | 2 | 0 | 1 | 3 | 1100 |
| 8 | Ramu Marandi | 2 | 0.5 | 6 | 0 | 2 | 15 | 0 |
| 9 | Dhiru Kol | 3 | 0.5 | 4 | 0 | 1 | 8 | 785 |
| 10 | Chetan Murmu | 1.66 | 0.33 | 3 | 2 | 1 | 3 | 240 |
| 11 | Bahari Marandi(F) | 0.66 | 0.50 | 1 | 0 | 0 | 3 | 200 |
| 12 | Choti Tudu(F) | 2 | 0.16 | 0 | 2 | 1 | 3 | 440 |
| 13 | Hari Rajwar | 1.99 | 0.5 | 1 | 0 | 1 | 2 | 1050 |
| 14 | Shariwari Murmu(F) | 1.5 | 0.16 | 5 | 0 | 0 | 0 | 520 |
| 15 | Sunil Marandi | 2.66 | 0.25 | 3 | 0 | 4 | 5 | 0 |
| 16 | Sona Tudu(F) | 2.5 | 0.16 | 1 | 0 | 1 | 2 | 1500 |
| 17 | Rimani Marandi | 2 | 0.5 | 0 | 0 | 1 | 0 | 910 |
| 18 | Jeevan Soren | 0.5 | 0.16 | 7 | 4 | 4 | 0 | 0 |
| 19 | Panthi Marandi(F) | 2 | 0.33 | 5 | 0 | 8 | 10 | 120 |
| 20 | Karuna Hembrum(F) | 3.33 | 0.33 | 5 | 0 | 4 | 10 | 4000 |
| 21 | Binoti Kolin(F) | 2.66 | 0.33 | 0 | 0 | 1 | 6 | 680 |
| 22 | Shanti Marandi(F) | 0.83 | 0.16 | 0 | 0 | 1 | 1 | 880 |
| 23 | Sevati Tudu | 2.5 | 0.16 | 0 | 0 | 1 | 10 | 475 |
| 24 | Harnath Hembrum | 5.0 | 0.33 | 3 | 0 | 0 | 0 | 0 |

Table 6: Certificate Cases

| | Cases pending: 1.4.01 No. | Cases pending: 1.4.01 Amount | Cases filed after 1.4.01 No. | Cases filed after 1.4.01 Amount | Total disposed 2001–2 No. | Total disposed 2001–2 Amount |
|---|---|---|---|---|---|---|
| Banks | 3666 | 2.60 crore | 1357 | 62.02 lakhs | 468 | 93.19 lakhs |
| Total | 4992 | 3.95 crore | 1654 | 1.48 crore | 546 | 1.01 crore |

*Note:* Of the cases settled: within 5 years: 272 cases, within 5–10 years: 129 cases.

**Box 1: Seasonality of Products Traded in the Local Markets**

| Month | Products traded |
|---|---|
| January | Paddy, rice, chicken, goat, leaf plates, wood, *ber*, roots, beans |
| February | Paddy, rice, chicken, goat, leaf plates, wood, *ber*, roots, beans |
| March | *Mahua, tendu* leaf, paddy, rice, fuelwood, coal, chicken, potato |
| April | *Mahua, tendu* leaf, fuelwood, coal, *kurthi*, rice |
| May | Mango, *jamun*, tamarind, leaf plates, *mahua*, chicken, pig, goat, mats, beds (*charpai*), fuelwood |
| June | *Jamun*, jackfruit, mango, leafy vegetables, fuelwood, leaf plates |
| July | *Jamun*, jackfruit, chicken, goat, pig, fuelwood, coal, rice, wild vegetables, mushrooms |
| August | Maize, rice, greens, bitter gourd, *ghanghra*, mushrooms, vegetables |
| September | Custard apple, *kurthi*, rice, leaf plates, fuelwood, coal |
| October | Pumpkin, gourd, greens, beans, guava, leaf plates, fuelwood, coal, paddy |
| November | Mustard greens, paddy, tubers (sweet potato) |
| December | Paddy, rice, chicken, goat, guava |

# Annexure 4
# Types of Land Disputes

Table 1: RM Cases

| Year | Number | March | April | May | June | Sept | Oct | Dec |
|---|---|---|---|---|---|---|---|---|
| 1990–91 | Total | 37 | 31 | 37 | 27 | 26 | 16 | 50 |
| | *Adivasi* | 12 | 11 | 12 | 6 | 9 | 4 | 10 |
| | Women: | 0 | 8 | 5 | 5 | 1 | 0 | 5 |
| | *Adivasi* | 0 | 2 | 2 | | | | 2 |
| | Non-*adivasi* | 0 | 6 | 3 | | | | 3 |
| 1995–96 | Total | 45 | 21 | 15 | 24 | 45 | 22 | 36 |
| | *Adivasi* | 21 | 5 | 6 | 6 | 19 | 11 | 19 |
| | Women: | 6 | 0 | 2 | 2 | 8 | 0 | 2 |
| | *Adivasi* | 3 | | 1 | 2 | 2 | | 1 |
| | Non-*adivasi* | 3 | | 1 | 0 | 6 | | 1 |
| 2000 | Total | 32 | 29 | 35 | 60 | 19 | 12 | 68 |
| | *Adivasi* | 12 | 14 | 11 | 13 | 5 | 3 | 13 |
| | Women: | 5 | 2 | 8 | 10 | 1 | 1 | 8 |
| | *Adivasi* | 0 | 0 | 2 | 2 | 0 | 0 | 1 |
| | Non-*adivasi* | 5 | 2 | 6 | 8 | 1 | 1 | 7 |

*Note*: RM (Revenue Miscellaneous) cases are related to demarcation, tenancy and inheritance issues and constitute about 75 per cent of all cases.

Table 2: SR Cases

| Year | No. | March | April | May | June | Sept | Oct | Dec |
|---|---|---|---|---|---|---|---|---|
| 1990–1 | Total | 29 | 17 | 13 | 27 | 19 | 25 | 51 |
| | *Adivasi* | 13 | 11 | 9 | 6 | 5 | 10 | 19 |
| | Women: | 2 | 3 | 0 | 3 | 2 | 3 | 6 |

*(contd.)*

| Year | No. | March | April | May | June | Sept | Oct | Dec |
|---|---|---|---|---|---|---|---|---|
| | *Adivasi* | 1 | 3 | | | 1 | 1 | 2 |
| | Non-*adivasi* | 1 | 0 | | | 1 | 2 | 4 |
| 1995–6 | Total | 21 | 6 | 14 | 14 | 31 | 9 | 32 |
| | *Adivasi* | 6 | 2 | 3 | 7 | 8 | 3 | 12 |
| | Women: | 0 | 0 | 1 | 1 | 4 | 0 | 4 |
| | *Adivasi* | | | 0 | 0 | 1 | | 4 |
| | Non-*adivasi* | | | 1 | 1 | 3 | | 0 |
| 2000 | Total | 29 | 14 | 25 | 23 | 15 | 10 | 27 |
| | *Adivasi* | 9 | 2 | 0 | 5 | 5 | 0 | 9 |
| | Women: | 3 | 4 | 1 | 1 | 3 | 1 | 3 |
| | *Adivasi* | 1 | 1 | 0 | 0 | 1 | 0 | 1 |
| | Non-*adivasi* | 2 | 3 | 1 | 1 | 2 | 1 | 2 |

*Note*: SR (Settlement Raiyat) cases are related to the allotment and settlement of land.

Table 3: RE Cases

| Year | No. | March | June | Sept | Dec |
|---|---|---|---|---|---|
| 1990–1 | Total | 12 | 8 | 13 | 8 |
| | *Adivasi* | 0 | 1 | 2 | 1 |
| | Women: | 0 | 1 | 0 | 0 |
| | *Adivasi* | 0 | 0 | 0 | 0 |
| | Non-*adivasi* | 0 | 1 | 0 | 0 |
| 1995–6 | Total | 9 | 7 | 7 | 8 |
| | *Adivasi* | 2 | 1 | 1 | 1 |
| | Women: | 2 | 2 | 2 | 2 |
| | *Adivasi* | 0 | 1 | 1 | 0 |
| | Non-*adivasi* | 2 | 1 | 1 | 2 |
| 2000 | Total | 6 | 11 | 3 | 5 |
| | *Adivasi* | 1 | 2 | 1 | 1 |
| | Women: | 2 | 3 | 2 | 0 |
| | *Adivasi* | 0 | 0 | 0 | 0 |
| | Non-*adivasi* | 2 | 3 | 2 | 0 |

*Note*: RE (Raiyati Eviction) cases are those of encroachment.

**Box 1: Reaching the High Court**

Jadav Gorain, the husband of Manoda Sundari Dasi, died before the McPherson Settlement. She brought her brother to help manage her 100 bighas in the three villages of Bagdiha, Jaradih and Gando. He died in 1937, then his son helped her. For their service and love, she gave her properties in Jaradih to Tinkori Gorai, his sons and descendants (including Mira).

Manoda died in 1943 and thereafter, a family dispute erupted on property. As she didn't have children, her husband's cousins claimed the land and refused to give Mira a share. Trouble started with her in 1972. Ramapada Gorain s/o Manindra Gorain, complained to the court that he had grown paddy in the Jaradih plots in 1972. The accused, Shiblal Murmu, Barka Marandi, Subda Hembrum, and wives of Panchanan (Phuru bala), Gopal (Saratbala) and Chandi (Mira) were ploughing these lands and destroying the seed. He went to the *mukhiya*, but he was on their side. The case went in favour of the accused.

He then filed a title-suit for declaration of right, title and interest on 13–7–10 *bighas* of land, out of which 11–9–18 was *dhani* and 1–17–10 was a *nala* (gully) in JB 31 and 24 of Jaradih. He claimed that a widow who dies intestate, has limited interest in the properties and could not part with it in favour of Tinkori or others. So a 'family arrangement' had been made in favour of Tinkori's wife for her lifetime. He however lost the case and in 1982, Mira was given possession by the District Judge Dumka PS no. 36–1976/8–1982. He again challenged it in the High Court, but order no. 420 of 1984 of Patna High Court, confirmed this judgement.

More recently, in 1999, Mira has filed a case in the CJM's court, dated 13.10.99, GR No. 82/99, relating to harassment as '*dain*' by her kin. The Inspector came to the village for a spot enquiry, but Dharam's daughter-in-law had died, so the Santals were busy. Her kin bribed the police and gave the other villagers food to eat, so no one spoke in her favour. The case is still ongoing.

**Box 2: Killing of a '*Dain*'**

Case 23/95, section 448,302/34, case registered on 9 December 1995, village Chuapara, accused: Lala Murmu; Shivla Murmu, Lakhan Murmu and Lakhan's mother, filed by Chetan Murmu s/o late Luthru Murmu.

*Box 2 (contd.)*

On Sunday, 8 October 1995, Chetan had gone to Gopikandar. His younger brother Hopna is mad and stays outside the house. At 10 am, he went to the Bengali's shop to bring tea and sugar. His mother, Mani Hansdak was at home. On returning home half an hour later, he found her dead on the *charpai* (bed), her neck swollen. On enquiry, their neighbour Shivlal Murmu and his brother's son, Luthru Murmu, said that Shivla, Lakhan and Lala had entered the house. Lakhan's 8-year-old daughter had died during the paddy transplantation period of illness. During Dussehra, they had gone to the *ojha* at Amrapara, who identified Chetan's mother as the '*dain*', responsible for their daughter's death. At that time, Chetan gave Rs 750 as fine, Rs 500 for the *ojha* and Rs 250 for the village. The issue had ended there, as far as he was concerned. Yet these people had entered the house and killed his mother. They chased him with an axe; somehow he hid and ran to the police station.

The case was investigated, but adequate evidence could not be found. Later Chetan admitted that his mother had been sick for a long time. Many witnesses were examined in the village and they all said that Mani Hansdak had been sick, she had not been treated properly as Chetan was in jail for a rape case and hence she died. She was not killed. Chetan has not given any objection to this evidence through his letter dated 9 March 1998. The judge has therefore ordered for a finalization of the case diary on 12 May 1999, to be submitted at the next hearing on 18 August 1999.

### Comment:

The wife of one of the accused said, 'Chetan returned home drunk one evening and found his mother dead. He was drunk, so went and filed a case against his brothers. The village people tried to stop him, but he just ran off. The police came and made enquiries. They found out that his mother had died of illness, this was confirmed by the post-mortem report as well. Yet Lakhan and his two brothers were kept in custody for three days and then released. At that time, we had just got a loan sanctioned for bullocks and brought the money home. So we could immediately pay Rs 1000 each to secure the release of the three brothers, as well as the fares of the village people for travelling to Dumka to provide witness in the case. We had to feed them and provide *handia* (rice beer) as well. A lot of expense was incurred.' Chetan wants to close the case now, but he has no money to file an affidavit to this effect.

*(contd.)*

*Box 2 (contd.)*

The *parganait* claimed, 'The case was false, so I got it stopped from the court. This involved an expense of Rs 500. It is better to resolve cases locally, with the help of *chowkidars* (village watchmen), to avoid any problem. Courts are expensive—it is difficult to avoid the "black coat" —they involve a lot of time and justice too is often denied. When I had the power, I would record the case details and if necessary submit copies to the *thana* and SDO court.' He was however unwilling to show me the records, the source of his power.

**Box 3: A Decade of Legal Intervention: Contested Claims to Land**

Jagu Marandi brought Bariyad Hembrum as *gharjawae* for his daughter Munni. By the Deed of declaration made on a stamp paper of Rs 3.75 on 8 April 1960, he gave all his land in JB no. 51/21 (7.2 acres *dhani* and 1.07 acres *bari*) and 53/22 (1 acre *dhani*), to his daughter. Jagu's brother has a son Jhangal Marandi. Jhangal has four sons, and Munni three.

Soon after Munni's death fighting started. As a precaution, her sons filed a title suit (Misc Case no. 910) and got an order in their favour from the SDO's court on 1 November 1994. The cousins were enraged and started harassing them. The first case was registered on 29 November 1994 itself, against 6 persons, Jhangal Marandi and his sons, Munshi, Ishwar, Thambun, Shibrat, and grandson Bhagan. The proceedings under Sec 144 Cr. PC were based on a police report from Dumka Mofussil thana (FIR No. 7/94). The main pointed contested in this case was the marriage of Munni as a *gharjawae* and whether she was in cultivating possession of Jagu's land after his death.

The court found that JB no 51 and 53 were registered in the name of Bhatur Marandi and Jagu Marandi in the Gantzer settlement. The first party are the sons of the daughter of Jagu, while the second party are descendants of Bhatur. The first party claimed that Munni was married to Bariyar as *gharjawae*, so inherited her father's property. They have lived and worked here ever since, and produced both the registered deed of 1960 and rent receipts in their favour. The second party claimed that it

*(contd.)*

*Box 3 (contd.)*

was an ordinary marriage, so they as co-agnates are the real heirs of this property. Also that the first party were never in possession of the disputed land. They produced rent receipts and the settlement receipt of Jaipahari to prove that Bariyar was recorded as a tenant there.

According to the Indian Evidence Act, a document of over 30 years is presumed to be correct, so the *gharjawae* marriage was confirmed. Also the first party was paying rent and living in Bagdiha. The police confirmed this in their spot report, so the first party's possession was confirmed. The second party then produced the *khatiyan* (record) of settlement no. 28, *khata* 4 of Jaipahari, where Bariar Hembrum is mentioned. The court however observed that while the right of inheritance amongst Santals is guided by customs and practices, variations can occur, and a 'family arrangement' could have led to the inclusion of Bariar in Jaipahari. This does not falsify the evidence of inheritance in Bagdiha. The order was issued in favour of the first party.

But this did not solve the matter. PCR No. 255 of 1994 u/s 379/149 and 339 IPC was filed soon after by Bejun Hembrum vs Munshi, Ishwar, Bhagun, Dabu, Shibrat, Phulmuni w/o Munshi, Lukhi w/o Ishwar, Sonmati w/o Bhagun, Fulin w/o Dabu and Jhangal Marandi, who died thereafter. They had illegally entered the land and cut the grain. Then they forcibly entered the house with weapons (*lathis, tangi, kulhari*), began to abuse and asked the family to leave, otherwise they would be done to death. The complainants left the house out of fear. When he later went to Dumka *Mofussil* (rural) Police Station for information, Bejun found the accused talking to the ASI. They had used their money power to gain the support of the police and prevent them from following up the case.

Soon Munni's sons had to file a dacoity case against their cousins. This was criminal case no 828 of 1995 under Sec 144: Bejun Hembrum vs Munshi Marandi and nine others (men and their wives), *mofussil thana* s.no 5/95. According to the police report, the accused had stolen jackfruit from their tree and robbed their house. Bejun Hembrum complained that from JB 51, plot no. 207, the second party took jackfruit on 11 June 1995. They had been cultivating this land since the last 35 years. They won a case the previous year and now wanted to cultivate their land, but the second party threatened them with *lathis* and axes. They entered their house and stole the silver, utensils and all other articles. All the

*(contd.)*

*Box 3 (contd.)*

accused were arrested including the women. The latter were released after four days. The women however denied taking anything.

There are now five cases against the second party—under sections 144, 107 and 188. The last was the murder case—Dumka *Mofussil* PS case no. 3/99, *State v. Ishwar Marandi, Munshi Marandi, Gopal Marandi, Dabu Marandi, Bhagun Marandi and Sivrat Marandi* u/s 147/148/307/324, FIR registered on 6 January 1999. Sec 302 IPC added by the I.O on 17 February 1999.

In January 1999, Bejun was walking down the road to the *haat*, when the accused caught him and beat him badly. He was rushed to the hospital in Dumka, but died on the fourteenth day. The assault was wilfully done. One of the accused was arrested, the others had run away, but when they heard that they would be beaten if they didn't surrender, they did so, and are now all in jail. Bejun's family have again asked for police protection, as the women are now threatening to use *goondas* (thugs) to kill them. According to an earlier order, the *thana* had helped them to harvest grain. Now after the brother's murder, they are afraid, so have again requested help for cultivation.

Comment:

According to the lawyer for the accused, the accusation that sword, tangi and bow and arrows were used was not found in the post-mortem report. Further, as section 302 added on to the case after 46 days, this could be a possible ground for bail for the accused. Two of the women went to Dumka, for the hearing in the dacoity case. The men were handcuffed and brought to the court. The first party has died, and there were no witnesses, so the second party had to sign and take another date. The lawyers too did not come to the court, as apparently their fee of Rs 100 had not been paid. One of the lawyers said to his colleague, 'I have so many cases. Just yesterday I have met the accused, I can't be meeting them everyday. If the witness comes, the clerk will call me.' The wives of the accused have now mortgaged all their land to the *mahajans*, as a lot of money is needed for fighting the case, yet they are unrepentant. The men have threatened to kill the remaining two brothers as soon as they are released from jail.

**Box 4: Contesting Settlement Claims**

Objection 1: Manglu Marandi s/o Safu Marandi has a *gharjawae,* Boyla Hembrum. Boyla says, 'I was married to Manglu's daughter Tulsi Marandi in court. Now her father is dead, and his share should be registered in the name of Tulsi. Bejun Marandi, her male kin, objected that none of Manglu's daughters were married as *gharjawae.* The marriage papers dated 5 July 1977 were produced. Later Boyla left Tulsi and married someone else. Bejun said that Tulsi was now no longer *gharjawae,* so couldn't inherit. However, as Tulsi stayed on in the village, she was allotted a share.

Objection 54: Bhatu Kisku's daughter Rasodi Kisku was married in *gharjawae* form. When her father died, she wanted her name entered in the settlement records. Durga Kisku and Lobin Kisku objected that they didn't consider her husband as a *gharjawae,* as he didn't stay here or plough the land. She produced a letter from 18 October 1965 validating her marriage in *gharjawae* form and rent receipts from 1983–4 to 1987–8. Dharam Marandi, the former *panchayat mukhiya,* testified that she had a *gharjawae* marriage. The settlement went in her favour.

*Source*: Transfer and Dispute list, 1988–97, Settlement Records, Settlement Office, Dumka.

# Bibliography


Abhiyaan, 1999, *Jharkhandi mahilaon ki davedari, satta mein aadhi bhagedari* (Hindi), Abhiyaan, Madhupur.

Agarwal, B., 1994, *A Field of One's Own: Gender and Land Rights in South Asia*, Cambridge University Press, Cambridge, UK.

———, 1998, 'Disinherited Peasants, Disadvantaged Workers: A Gender Perspective on Land and Livelihood', *Economic and Political Weekly*, 33, 13 March, pp. A2–14.

———, 2001, 'Participatory Exclusions, Community Forestry, and Gender: An Analysis for South Asia and a Conceptual Framework', *World Development*, 29(10), pp. 1623–48.

———, 2003, 'Gender and Land Rights Revisited: Exploring New Prospects via the State, Family and Market', *Journal of Agrarian Change*, 3(1&2), pp. 184–224.

Agnihotri, S. B., 2000, *Sex Ratio Patterns in the Indian Population: A Fresh Exploration*, Sage Publications, New Delhi.

Agrawal, A. and K. Sivaramakrishnan (eds.), 2000, *Agrarian Environments: Resources, Representation and Rule in India*, Duke University Press, Durham and London.

Anderson, B., 1983, *Imagined Communities: Reflections on the Origin and Spread of Nationalism*, Verso Books, New York.

Andersen, P., 2005, 'Sagram Murmu: Authorship and Resistance', Paper presented at 'Reinterpreting Adivasi Movements in South Asia' Conference, University of Sussex, 24 March 2005,

Appadurai, A., 1991, Afterword, Appadurai, A., Korom, F. J. and M.A. Mills, *Gender, Genre, and Power in South Asian Expressive Traditions*, University of Pennsylvania Press, Philadelphia, pp. 467–76.

Archer, W.G., 1984 [1946], *Tribal Law and Justice: A Report on the Santal,* Concept Publishing Company, New Delhi.

Arendt, H., 1958, *The Human Condition,* University of Chicago Press, Chicago.

Athreya, V.B., G. Djurfeldt and S. Lindberg, 1990, *Barriers Broken: Production Relations and Agrarian Change in Tamil Nadu,* Sage Publications, New Delhi.

Badlao Foundation, 1998, *Adivasi betion ke adhikaar* (Hindi), Alekhan, Patna.

Banuri, T. and F.A. Marglin, (eds.), 1993, *Who will Save the Forests? Knowledge, Power and Environmental Destruction,* Zed Books, London.

Bardhan, K., 1984, 'Work Patterns and Social Differentiation: Rural Women of West Bengal', Binswanger, H.P. and Rosenzweig, M. R. (eds.), *Contractual Arrangements, Employment and Wages in Rural Labor Markets in Asia,* Yale University Press, New Haven and London, pp. 184–207.

Bardhan, P.K., 1984, *Land, Labour and Rural Poverty: Essays in Development Economics,* Columbia University Press, New York.

Barthes, R., 1977, *Image Music Text,* Fontana Press, London.

Baviskar, A., 1995, *In the Belly of the River: Tribal Conflicts over Development in the Narmada Valley,* Oxford University Press, New Delhi.

Benda-Beckmann, F. von, 2001, 'Legal Pluralism and Social Justice in Economic and Political Development', *IDS Bulletin,* 32(1), pp. 46–56.

Beneria, L. and G. Sen, 1981, 'Accumulation, Reproduction and Women's Role in Economic Development', *Signs,* 7, pp. 279–98.

Bernstein, H., 1977, 'Notes on Capital and Peasantry', *Review of African Political Economy,* 10, pp. 60–73.

Berry, S., 1993, *No Condition is Permanent: The Social Dynamics of Agrarian Change in Sub-Saharan Africa,* University of Wisconsin Press, Madison, Wisconsin.

Béteille, A., 1991, *Society and Politics in India: Essays in a Comparative Perspective,* The Athlone Press, London.

Bhalla, G.S. and G. Singh, 2001, *Indian Agriculture: Four Decades of Development,* Sage Publications, New Delhi.

Bhatia, B and J. Dreze, 2006, 'Employment Guarantee in Jharkhand: Ground Results', *Economic and Political Weekly,* 41(29), 22 July.

Bodding, P.O., 1920, *Some Remarks on the Position of Women among the Santals,* Santal Mission Press, Benagaria.

Bodding, P.O., L.O. Skresfrud et al., 1994 [1942], *Traditions and Institutions of the Santals,* Bahumukhi Prakashan, New Delhi.

Boserup, E., 1965, *The Conditions of Agricultural Growth: The Economics of Agrarian Change under Population Pressure,* Aldine, Chicago.

Boserup, E., 1970, *Woman's Role in Economic Development*, Allen & Unwin, New York.

Bourdieu, P., 1977, *Outline of a Theory of Practice*. Cambridge University Press, Cambridge.

Bradley-Birt, F.B., 1909, *The Story of an Indian Upland*, Smith, Elder, London.

Brass, T., 1984, 'Permanent Transition or Permanent Revolution: Peasants, Proletarians and Politics', *Journal of Peasant Studies* 11(3), pp. 108–12.

Breman, J., 1996, *Footloose Labour*, Cambridge University Press, Cambridge.

Butegwa, F., 1991, 'Women's Legal Right of Access to Agricultural Resources in Africa: A Preliminary Inquiry', *Third World Legal Studies–1991*, pp. 45–57.

Burman, B.K.R., 1992, 'Historical Process in Respect of Communal Land System and Poverty Alleviation among Tribals' Chaudhuri, B., (ed.), *Tribal Transformation in India, Vol 1,* Inter-India Publications, New Delhi, pp. 131–61.

Butler, J., 1990, *Gender Trouble: Feminism and the Subversion of Identity,* Routledge, New York.

Byres, T.J., 1977, 'Agrarian Transition and the Agrarian Question', *Journal of Peasant Studies* 4(3), pp. 258–74.

Carney, J., 1988, 'Struggles over Crop Rights within Contract Farming Households in a Gambian irrigated Rice Project', *The Journal of Peasant Studies* 15(3), pp. 334–49.

Carney, J. and M. Watts, 1990, 'Manufacturing Dissent: Work, Gender and the Politics of Meaning in a Peasant Society', *Africa,* 60, pp. 207–41.

Carstairs, R., 1935, *Harma's Village: A Novel of Santal Life,* The Santal Mission Press, Pokhuria, Manbhum.

Caulfield, M.D., 1979, 'Participant Observation or Partisan Participation?', Huizer, G and B. Mannheim (eds.), *The Politics of Anthropology: From Colonialism and Sexism Towards a View from Below,* Mouton Publishers, The Hague/Paris, pp. 309–18.

CBGA, 2006, Draft report on implementation of NREGA in Andhra Pradesh, Chhatisgarh, Jharkhand and Madhya Pradesh in May and June 2006, Centre for Budget and Governance Accountability, New Delhi.

Chant, S., 2000, 'Men in Crisis? Reflections on Masculinities, Work and Family in North West Costa Rica', *The European Journal of Development Research,* 12(2), pp. 199–218.

Chaudhuri, B.B., 1996, 'The Process of Agricultural Commercialisation in Eastern India during British Rule: A Reconsideration of the Notions of "Forced Commercialisation" and "Dependent Peasantry"', P. Robb (ed.), *Meanings of Agriculture: Essays in South Asian History and Economics,* Oxford University Press, New Delhi, pp. 71–91.

Cheater, A.P., 1984, *Idioms of Accumulation: Rural Development and Class Formation among Freeholders in Zimbabwe*, Mambo Press, Harare, Zimbabwe.

Chen, M.A., (ed.), 1998, *Widows in India: Social Neglect and Public Action*, Sage Publications, New Delhi.

Chopra, R., Osella, C. and F. Osella, (eds.), 2004, *South Asian Masculinities: Context of Change, Sites of Continuity*, Kali for Women, New Delhi.

Corbridge, S., Williams, G., Srivastava, M. and R. Veron, 2005, *Seeing the State: Governance and Governmentality in India*, Cambridge University Press, Cambridge.

Crook, R.C., 2001, 'Cocoa Booms, the Legalisation of Land Relations and Politics in Cote d'Ivoire and Ghana: Explaining Farmers' Responses', *IDS Bulletin* 32(1), pp. 35–45.

DAO, 2000, Land Use and Production Data, Dumka, District Agriculture Office.

Das, A., 1993, 'Agrarian Change from Above and Below: Bihar, 1947–78', R. Guha, *Subaltern Studies Vol II: Writings on South Asian History and Society*, Oxford University Press, New Delhi.

Das, V., 2001, 'Struggle for Land and Forest Rights: Tribal Women's Perspectives', Paper presented at the Workshop on Women's Empowerment, Policy and Natural Resources: 'What Progress?', New Delhi, 18–19 May.

Datta, K., 1988, *The Santal Insurrection of 1855–57*, University of Calcutta, Calcutta.

Datta, R., 1996, 'Peasant Production and Agrarian Commercialism in a Rice-growing Economy: Some Notes on a Comparative Perspective and the Case of Bengal in the Eighteenth Century', P. Robb, *Meanings of Agriculture: Essays in South Asian History and Economics*, Oxford University Press, New Delhi, pp. 92–131.

de Haan, A., 1999, 'Social Exclusion: Towards a Holistic Understanding of Deprivation', Social Development Department, Department for International Development, London, p. 18.

Deere, C.D. and Leon, M., 2001, *Empowering Women: Land and Property Rights in Latin America*, University of Pittsburgh Press, Pittsburgh.

_____, 2003, 'Women's Land Rights and Rural Social Movements in the Brazilian Agrarian Reform', *Journal of Agrarian Change*, 3(1), pp. 257–88.

Demian, M., 2003, 'Custom in the Courtroom, Law in the Village: Legal Transformations in Papua New Guinea', *The Journal of the Royal Anthropological Institute*, 9, pp. 97–115.

Department of Women and Child Development, 2001, *National Policy for the Empowerment of Women, 2001*, Ministry of Human Resource Development, Government of India, New Delhi, p. 20.

Dirks, N., 1997, 'The Policing ofTradition: Colonialism and Anthropology in Southern India', *Society for Comparative Study of Society and History*, pp. 182–212.

Dhagamwar, V., 2003, 'Invasion of Criminal Law by Religion, Custom and Family Law', *Economic and Political Weekly*, 38(15), pp. 1483–92.

DRDA, 2001, SGSY Report, Dumka, 2000–01, Dumka, District Rural Development Agency.

Dreze, J., 1990, *Widows in Rural India*, London School of Economics, London.

——— and A. Sen, 1995, Introduction, Dreze, J. Sen A. and A. Hussain (eds.), *The Political Economy of Hunger: Selected Essays*, Clarendon Press, Oxford, pp. 13–45.

———, 1999, 'Public Action and Social Inequality', Harriss-White, B. and S. Subramanian (eds.), *Illfare in India: Essays on India's Social Sector in Honour of S. Guhan*, Sage Publications, New Delhi, pp. 374–401.

District Statistical Office, 1986, *Dumka District at a Glance 1986*, District Statistical Office, Dumka, Government of Bihar.

Dube, L., 1986, 'Seed and Earth: The Symbolism of Biological Reproduction and Sexual Relations of Production', Dube, L., Leacock, E. and S. Ardener (eds.), *Visibility and Power: Essays on Women in Society and Development*, Oxford University Press, New Delhi, pp. 22–53.

Election Commission of India, 2004, *Statistical Report on General Elections 2004 to the 14th Lok Sabha*, New Delhi.

Ellen, R.F., 1984, *Ethnographic Research: A Guide to General Conduct*, Academic Press, London.

Ellis, F., 2000, *Rural Livelihoods and Diversity in Developing Countries*, Oxford University Press, Oxford.

Elson, D., (ed.), 1991, *Male Bias in the Development Process*, Manchester University Press, Manchester.

Engels, F., 1972[1884], *The Origin of the Family, Private Property, and the State*, Pathfinder Press, New York.

EPW, 2005, 'Groundbreaking Legislation', *Economic and Political Weekly*, 40(41), pp. 4487, 15 October.

Evans, M., 1987, 'Engels: Materialism and Morality', Sayers, J., Evans, M. and N. Redclift (eds.) *Engels Revisited: New Feminist Essays*, Tavistock Press, London.

Fernandes, W. and M. Paranjype, 1997, *Rehabilitation Policy and Law in India: A Right to Livelihood*, Indian Social Institute, New Delhi.

Foucault, M., 1990[1976], *The History of Sexuality*, Penguin, London.

Francis, E., 2000, *Making a Living: Changing Livelihoods in Rural Africa*, Routledge, London and New York.

Fraser, N., 1989, *Unruly Practices: Power, Discourse and Gender in Contemporary Social Theory*, Polity Press, Cambridge.

Fraser, N., 1997, *Justice Interruptus*, Routledge, New York.

Gadgil, M. and R. Guha, 1992, *This Fissured Land: An Ecological History of India*, Oxford University Press, Delhi.

Gadgil, M. and R. Guha, 1995, *Ecology and Equity: The Use and Abuse of Nature in Contemporary India*, Penguin, New Delhi.

Gantzer, J.F., 1936, *Final Report on the Revision Survey and Settlement Operations in the District of Santal Parganas, 1922–35*, Patna, Superintendent, Government Printing.

Gautam, M.K., 1977, 'The Santalization of the Santals', K. David (ed.), *The New Wind: Changing Identities in South Asia*, Mouton Publishers, The Hague/Paris, pp. 369–81.

Geertz, C., 1968, *Agricultural Involution: The Processes of Ecological Change in Indonesia*, University of California Press, Berkeley.

Giddens, A., 1990, *The Consequences of Modernity*, Polity Press, Cambridge.

Gladwin, C. H., Thomson, A.M., Peterson, J.S. and A.S. Anderson, 2001, 'Addressing Food Security in Africa via Multiple Livelihood Strategies of Women Farmers', *Food Policy*, 26, pp. 177–207.

Goetz, A.M., (ed.), 1997, *Getting Institutions Right for Women in Development*, Zed Books, London and New York.

Goheen, M., 1988, 'Land Accumulation and Local Control: The Manipulation of Symbols and Power in Nso, Cameroon', Downs R.E. and S.P. Reyna (eds.), *Land and Society in Contemporary Africa.*, University Press of New England, Hanover and London, pp. 280–308.

Goody, J., 1976, *Production and Reproduction: A Comparative Study of the Domestic Domain*, Cambridge University Press, Cambridge.

Gopal, G., 1999, *Gender-related Legal Reform and Access to Economic Resources in Eastern Africa*, The World Bank, Washington, D.C..

Gordon, C., (ed.), 1980, *Michel Foucault: Power/Knowledge, Selected Interviews and Other Writings 1972–7*, Harvester Wheatsheaf, New York.

Gough, K., 1981, *Rural Society in Southeast India*, Cambridge University Press, Cambridge.

Gould, H.A., 1968, 'Time-dimension and Structural Change in an Indian Kinship System: A Problem of Conceptual Refinement', Singer, M. and B.S. Cohn (eds.), *Structure and Change in Indian Society*, Aldine Publishing Company, Chicago, pp. 413–22.

Government of India, 1991, *Census of India*, Series 4 Bihar, Part II-B (i), Bihar, Directorate of Census Operations.

Grown, C. and J. Sebstad, 1989, 'Introduction: Towards a Wider Perspective on Women's Employment', *World Development* 17(7), pp. 937–52.

Guha, R., 1983, *Elementary Aspects of Peasant Insurgency in Colonial India,* Oxford University Press, New Delhi.

Habermas, J., 1987, *The Theory of Communicative Action, Vol 2: Lifeworld and System,* Polity Press, Cambridge.

———, 1989, *The Structural Transformation of the Public Sphere,* Polity Press, Cambridge.

Hardiman, D., 1987, *The Coming of the Devi,* Oxford University Press, Oxford.

———, 1996, *Feeding the Baniya: Peasants and Usurers in Western India,* Oxford University Press, New Delhi.

———, 2000, 'Christianity and the Adivasis of Western India: 1880–1930', Paper Presented at the 16th European Modern South Asian Studies Conference, Edinburgh.

Harriss, J., 1982, *Capitalism and Peasant Farming: Agrarian Structure and Ideology in Northern Tamil Nadu,* Oxford University Press, New Delhi.

———, 2001, *Depoliticising Development: The World Bank and Social Capital,* Leftword Books, Delhi.

Hart, G., 1997, 'From Rotten Wives to Good Mothers: Household Models and the Limits of Economism', *IDS Bulletin* 28(3), pp. 14–25.

Hauser, W., 1995, *Swami Sahajanand and the Peasants of Jharkhand,* Manohar, New Delhi.

Heggenhoughen, K., 1992, 'The Inseparability of Reason and Emotion in the Anthropological Perspective: Perceptions upon leaving "The Field"', P. R. DeVita, *The Naked Anthroplogist: Tales from Around the World,* Wadsworth Publishing Company, Belmont California, pp. 244–52.

Herring, R.J. and R. Edwards, M., 1983, 'Guaranteeing Employment to the Rural Poor: Social Functions and Class Interests in the Employment Guarantee Scheme in Western India', *World Development* 11(7), pp. 575–92.

Hobsbawm, E. and T. Ranger, (eds.), 1983, *The Invention of Tradition,* Cambridge University Press, Cambridge.

———, 1971, *Primitive Rebels: Studies in Archaic Forms of Social Movement in the 19th and 20th Centuries,* Manchester University Press, Manchester.

Hollway, W., 1984, 'Gender Difference and the Production of Subjectivity', Henriques J., Hollway W., Urwin C., Venn C. and V. Walkerdine (eds.), *Changing the Subject: Psychology, Social Regulation and Subjectivity,* Methuen, London, pp. 228–52.

Huizer, G., 1986, 'Women in Resistance and Research: Potential against Power',. Dube, L., Leacock, E. and S. Ardener (eds.), *Visibility and Power: Essays on Women in Society and Development,* Oxford University Press, New Delhi, pp. 235–51.

Hunter, W.W., 1996 [1868], *The Annals of Rural Bengal,* Government of West Bengal, Calcutta.

IFAD, 2001, *Rural Poverty Report 2001: The Challenge of Ending Rural Poverty*, Oxford University Press, Oxford.

Iyer, G.K., and R.N. Maharaj, 1985, 'Agrarian Movement in Tribal Bihar (Dhanbad) 1972–80', A. R. Desai (ed.), *Agrarian Struggles in India after Independence*, Oxford University Press, Delhi, pp. 330–61.

ILO and ISST, 2006, 'Social Protection for Informal Home-based Women Workers in South Asia (2004–2006)', Institute of Social Studies Trust and Home Net South Asia, New Delhi.

Jaising, I., (ed.), 1996, *Justice for Women: Personal Laws, Women's Rights and Law Reform*, The Other India Press, Mapusa, Goa.

Kabeer, N., 2000, *The Power to Choose: Bangladeshi Women and Labour Market Decisions in London and Dhaka*, Verso, London.

Kannabiran, V. and K. Lalita, 1990, 'That Magic Time: Women in the Telengana People's Struggle', Sangari, K.and S. Vaid (eds.), *Recasting Women: Essays in Indian Colonial History*, Rutgers University Press, New Brunswick, pp. 180–203.

Kapadia, K., 1995, *Siva and her Sisters: Gender, Caste and Class in Rural South India*, Westview Press, Boulder, Colorado.

Kapur, R. and B. Cossman, 1996, *Subversive Sites: Feminist Engagements with Law in India*, Sage Publications, Delhi.

Karlekar, M., 1995, 'Gender Dimensions in Labour Migration: An Overview', L. Schenk-Sandbergen (ed.), *Women and Seasonal Labour Migration*, Sage Publications, New Delhi, pp. 23–78.

Kelkar, G. and D. Nathan, 1991, *Gender and Tribe: Women, Land and Forest in Jharkhand*, Kali for Women, New Delhi.

Khadiagala, L.S., 2001, 'The Failure of Popular Justice in Uganda: Local Councils and Women's Property Rights', *Development and Change*, 32(1).

Kishwar, M., 1997, 'Yes to Sita, No to Ram: The Continuing Hold of Sita on Popular Imagination', *Manushi*, Issue 98.

Knowles, J.B., 1991, 'Women's Access to Land in Africa', *Third World Legal Studies–Special Edition*, pp. 1–14.

Krulfeld, R., 1986, 'Sasak Attitudes towards Polygyny and the Changing Position of Women in Sasak Peasant Villages', Dube, L. Leacock, E. and S. Ardener (eds.), *Visibility and Power–Essays on Women in Society and Development*, Oxford University Press, New Delhi, pp. 194–208.

Kynch, J., 1998, 'Famine and Transformations in Gender Relations', Jackson, C. and R. Pearson (eds.), *Feminist Visions of Development: Gender Analysis and Policy*, Routledge, London and New York, pp. 108–34.

Li, T.M., 1996, 'Images of Community: Discourse and Strategy in Property Relations', *Development and Change*, 27, pp. 501–27.

Long, N. and A. Long, (eds.), 1992, *Battlefields of Knowledge: The Interlocking of Theory and Practice in Social Research and Development,* London and New York, Routledge.

Lukes, S., 1974, *Power: A Radical View,* Macmillan, London.

MacDougall, J., 1985, *Land or Religion? The Sardar and Kherwar Movements in Bihar, 1858–95,* Manohar, New Delhi.

Mackenzie, F., 1990, 'Gender and Land Rights in Murang'a district, Kenya', *The Journal of Peasant Studies,* 17(4), pp.: 609–43.

MacPhail, J.M., 1922, *The Story of the Santal with an Account of the Santal Rebellion,* Thacker, Spink and Company, Calcutta.

Mahapatra, S., 1976, 'The Insider Diku: Boundary Rules and Marginal Man in Santal Society', *Man in India,* 56(1), pp. 37–49.

Mahapatra, S., 1986, *Modernisation and Ritual: Identity and Change in Santal Society,* Oxford University Press, Calcutta.

Man, E.G., 1983, *Sonthalia and the Santhals,* Mittal Publications, Delhi.

MANAGE, 2000, *Strategic Research and Extension Plan of Dumka District,* National Institute of Agricultural Extension Management, Hyderabad.

Manimala, 1984, 'Zameen Kenkar? Jote Onkar!', Kishwar, M. and R. Vanita (eds.), *In Search of Answers,* Zed Books, London, pp. 149–76.

Marriott, M., 1955, 'Little Communities in an Indigenous Civilisation', M. Marriott (ed.), *Village India: Studies in the Little Community,* The University of Chicago Press, Chicago.

McPherson, H., 1909, *Final Report on the Survey and Settlement Operations in the District of Santhal Parganas, 1898–1907,* Bengal Secretariat Book Depot, Calcutta.

Meenakshi, J.V., R. Ray and S. Gupta, 2000, 'Estimates of Poverty for SC, ST and Female-Headed Households', *Economic and Political Weekly* 35(31), 29 July, pp. 2748–54.

Meinzen-Dick, R. and R. Pradhan, 2002, 'Legal Pluralism and Dynamic Property Rights', *CAPRI Working Paper 22,* IFPRI, Washington D.C.

Mencher, J., 1988, 'Women's Work and Poverty: Women's Contribution to Household Maintenance in South India', Dwyer, D. and J. Bruce (eds.), *A Home Divided: Women and Income in the Third World,* Stanford University Press, Stanford, California, pp. 99–119.

Mishra, S., 2003, *Casting the Evil Eye: Witch Trials in Tribal India,* Namita Gokhale Editions, New Delhi.

Molyneux, M., 1985, 'Mobilisation without Emancipation? Women's Interests, the State and Revolution in Nicaragua', *Feminist Studies,* 11, pp. 227–54.

Moore, H., 1988, *Feminism and Anthropology,* Cambridge University Press, Cambridge.

_____, 1994, *A Passion for Difference*, Polity Press, Cambridge.

Moore, S.F., 1978, *Law as Process: An Anthropological Approach*, Routledge and Kegal Paul, London.

_____, 1986, *Social Facts and Fabrications: 'Customary' law on Kilimanjaro, 1880–1980*, Cambridge University Press, Cambridge.

_____, 2001, 'Certainties Undone: Fifty Turbulent Years of Legal Anthropology, 1949–1999', *The Journal of the Royal Anthropological Institute*, 7, pp. 95–116.

Munda, R.D., 1988, 'The Jharkhand Movement: Retrospect and Prospect', *Social Change*, 48(2), pp. 28–58.

Murray, C., 2001, *Livelihoods Research: Some Conceptual and Methodological Issues*, Development Studies Association Annual Conference, 10–12 September, University of Manchester.

O'Malley, L.S.S., 1910, *Bengal District Gazetteers: Santhal Parganas*, Bengal Secretariat Book Depot, Calcutta.

Oppong, C. and K. Abu, 1987, *Seven Roles of Women: Impact of Education, Migration and Employment on Ghanaian Mothers*, International Labour Office, Geneva.

Oldham, W., 1930, *Journal of Francis Buchanan kept during the Survey of the District of Bhagalpur in 1810–1811*, Government Printing Bihar and Orissa, Patna.

Orans, M., 1965, *The Santal: A Tribe in Search of a Great Tradition*, Wayne State University Press, Detroit.

O'Rourke, N., 1995, 'Land Rights and Gender Relations in Areas of Rural Africa: A Question of Power and Discourse', *Social and Legal Studies* 4(1), pp. 75–97.

Parry, J.P., 1979, *Caste and Kinship in Kangra*, Routledge, London.

Pasternak, B., C.R. Ember, et al., 1997, *Sex, Gender and Kinship: A Cross-cultural Perspective*, Prentice Hall, Englewood Cliffs, N.J.

Pearce, J., 1985, *Promised Land: Peasant Rebellion in Chalatenango, El Salvador*, Latin America Bureau, London.

People's Union for Civil Liberties, 1985, 'The Banjhi Massacre', People's Union for Civil Liberties, Delhi.

Pratichi Trust, 2005, *Pratchi Health Report*, Pratichi Trust, Shanti Niketan, Kolkata.

PUCL Enquiry Report, 2003, Pachwara Coalmining Project, Conducted by P.A. Chacko, Anant Hembrom, Md. Rehman and B.N. Upadhyaya, People's Union for Civil Liberties.

Pettigrew, J., 1975, *Robber Noblemen: A Study of the Political System of the Sikh Jats*, Routledge and Kegal Paul, London and Boston.

Prasad, B.M., 1997, *Santal Parganas Tenancy Manual*, Malhotra Bros., Patna.

Prasad, K.V.E., 1998, 'The Pension Scheme for Widows in Tamil Nadu', Chen, M.A (ed.) *Widows in India: Social Neglect and Public Action*, Sage Publications, New Delhi, pp. 283–95.

Ramachandran, V.K. and M. Swaminathan (eds.), 2005, *Financial Liberalisation and Rural Credit in India,* Tulika Books, New Delhi.

Ramazanoglu, C., 1989, *Feminism and the Contradictions of Oppression,* Routledge, London.

Rao, M.S.A., 1984, *Social Movements in India*, Manohar, New Delhi.

Rao, N., 1999, *Owning their Land: Rights of Santhali Women,* Friedrich Ebert Stiftung, New Delhi.

———, 2003, 'Vision 2010: Chasing Mirages', *Economic and Political Weekly,* 38, pp. 1755–8.

———, 2005, 'Questioning Women's Solidarity: The Case of Land Rights, Santal Parganas, Jharkhand, India', *The Journal of Development Studies* 41(3), pp. 353–75.

———, 2005a, 'Displacement from Land: Case of Santhal Parganas', *Economic and Political Weekly*, 40 (41): 4439–42.

———, 2006, 'Land Rights, Gender Equality and Household Food Security: Exploring the Conceptual Links in the case of India', *Food Policy,* 31, pp. 180–193.

———, 2007, 'Custom And The Courts: Ensuring Women's Rights To Land, Jharkhand, India', *Development and Change,* 38(2), pp. 299–319.

Rapaj, T.K., 2000, 'Jharkhand reak' itihas—casbas reak', *Natun Ganatantrer Janya* (in Bengali), 11 November, Calcutta.

Razavi, S., (ed.), 2000, *Gendered Poverty and Well-being,* Blackwell Publishers, Oxford.

Robb, P., (ed.), 1996, *Meanings of Agriculture: Essays in South Asian History and Economics*, Oxford University Press, New Delhi.

Rorty, R., 1989, *Contingency, Irony, and Solidarity*, Cambridge University Press, Cambridge.

Rudolph, L.I. and S. H. Rudolph, 1967, *The Modernity of Tradition,* University of Chicago Press, Chicago.

Russell, R.E., 1938, *Report of the Santal Parganas Inquiry Committee,* Superintendent of Government Printing, Patna.

Rustagi, P., 2002, 'Gender Development Indicators: District level Analysis for the Eastern Region', *Occasional Paper No. 36,* Centre for Women's Development Studies, New Delhi.

Sacks, K., 1974, 'Engels Revisited: Women, the Organisation of Production, and Private Property', Rosaldo, M.Z. and L. Lamphere (eds.), *Woman, Culture and Society,* Stanford University Press, Stanford, pp. 207–22.

Saith, R. and B. Harriss-White, 2000, 'The Gender Sensitivity of Well-being Indicators', S. Razavi (ed.), *Gendered Poverty and Well-being*, Blackwell Publishers, Oxford, pp. 57–88.

Saradamoni, K., 1983, 'Changing Land Relations and Women: A Case Study of Palaghat district, Kerala', Mehra, R. and K. Saradamoni (eds.), *Women and Rural Transformation: Two Studies*, Concept Publishing Company, New Delhi,

Sarin, M., 1997, 'Gender and Equity concerns in Joint Forest Management', Rao, N. and L. Rurup (eds.), *A Just Right: Women's Ownership of Natural Resources and Livelihood Security*, Friedrich Ebert Stiftung, New Delhi, pp. 267–336.

Scott, J.C., 1976, *The Moral Economy of the Peasant*, Yale University Press, New Haven.

_____, 1985, *Weapons of the Weak: Everyday Forms of Peasant Resistance*, Yale University Press, New Haven, CT.

_____, 1990, *Domination and the Arts of Resistance: Hidden Transcripts*, Yale University Press, New Haven.

_____, 1998, *Seeing like a State: How Certain Schemes to Improve the Human Condition have Failed*, Yale University Press, New Haven and London.

Sen, A., 1981, *Poverty and Famines: An Essay on Entitlement and Deprivation*, Clarendon Press, Oxford.

_____, 1990, 'Gender and Cooperative Conflicts', I. Tinker (ed.), *Persistent Inequalities: Women and World Development*, Oxford University Press, New York, pp. 123–49.

Sengupta, N., 1982, 'Background of the Jharkhand Question', *Fourth World Dynamics: Jharkhand*, Authors Guild Publications, Delhi, pp. 3–39.

_____, 1988, 'Reappraising Tribal Movements' (in five parts), *Economic and Political Weekly*, 7, 14, 21, 28 May, 4 June, pp. 943–5; 1003–5; 1054–5; 1111–2; 1153–4.

_____, 2000, 'Negotiation with an Under-informed Bureaucracy: Water Rights on System Tanks in Bihar', Bruns B.R. and R.S. Meinzen-Dick (eds.), *Negotiating Water Rights*, ITDG Publishing, London, pp. 137–61.

Sharma, R., 2002, 'Reforms in Agricultural Extension: New Policy Framework', *Economic and Political Weekly*, Review of Agriculture, 27 July.

Sharma, U., 1980, *Women, Work and Property in North West India*, Tavistock Publications, London.

Shekhar, 1998, *Bailki jagah joti gayi Santal aurat* (Santal Woman Yoked to the Plough), Aaj, Patna.

Shivaraman, M., 1973, 'Thanjavur: Rumblings of Class Struggle in Tamil

Nadu', Gough, K. and H. P. Sharma (eds.), *Imperialism and Revolution in South Asia,* Monthly Review Press, New York, pp. 246–64.

Simon, R., 1982, *Gramsci's Political Thought: An Introduction,* Lawrence and Wishart, London.

Singh, K.S., 1966, *The Dust-storm and the Hanging Mist,* Firma and K.L. Mukhopadhyay, Calcutta.

Sinha, S.P., 1991, *Santal Hul,* Bihar Tribal Research Institute, Ranchi.

Sivaramakrishnan, K., 1997, 'A Limited Forest Conservancy in Southwest Bengal, 1864–1912', *The Journal of Asian Studies* 56(1), pp. 75–112.

Sjoblom, D., 1999, 'Land Matters: Social Relations and Livelihoods in a Bhil Community in Rajasthan, India', Phd Thesis, School of Development Studies, University of East Anglia, Norwich, UK.

Skaria, A., 1999, *Hybrid Histories: Forests, Frontiers and Wildness in Western India,* Oxford University Press, New Dehi.

Soren, S.K., 1999, *Santalia: Catalogue of Santali Manuscripts in Oslo,* Nordic Institute for Asian Studies, Copenhagen.

Srinivas, M.N., 1962, 'The Study of Disputes in an Indian Village', *Caste in Modern India and Other Essays,* Asia Publishing House, Bombay.

Staudt, K., 1985, *Agricultural Policy Implementation: A Case Study from Western Kenya,* Kumarian Press, West Hartford.

Stivens, M., C. Ng, et al., 1994, *Malay Peasant Women and the Land,* Zed Books, London and New Jersey.

Strathern, M., 1988, *The Gender of the Gift,* University of California Press, Berkeley.

______, 1996, 'Cutting the Network', *The Journal of the Royal Anthropological Institute* 2(3), pp. 517–35.

Subramanian, S. and B. Harriss-White, 1999, Introduction, *Illfare in India: Essays on India's Social Sector in Honour of S. Guhan,* Sage Publications, New Delhi, pp. 17–43.

Sundaram and Tendulkar, 2005, 'NAS-NSS estimates of private consumption for poverty estimation: a further comparative examination' Deaton, A. and V. Kozel (eds.) *The Great Indian Poverty Debate,* Macmillan India, New Delhi, pp. 119–35.

Supreme Court of India, 1996, Letter to State of Bihar with Judgment in Writ Petition No. 219 of 1986 and No. 5723 of 1982, Supreme Court of India, New Delhi.

Swaminathan, M., 2000, *Weakening Welfare: The Public Distribution of Food in India,* Leftword Books, New Delhi.

Thakur, I. N., 1977, 'Bihar', Dubey S. N. and R. Murdia (eds.), *Land Alienation and Restoration in Tribal Communities in India,* Himalaya Publishing House, Bombay, pp. 153–79.

Thakur, S.G., 2001, 'Women and Land Rights: Policy and Practice', Paper presented at the workshop on women's empowerment, policy and natural resources 'What progress?' 18–19 May, New Delhi, Write-Arm: 16–26.

Thompson, E.P., 1978, *The Poverty of Theory: Or an Orrery of Errors,* Merlin Press, London

Toulmin, C. and J. Quan, (eds.), 2000, *Evolving Land Rights, Policy and Tenure in Africa,* DFID/IIED/NRI, London.

Tsing, A., 1993, *In the Realm of the Diamond Queen,* Princeton University Press, Princeton.

Uberoi, P., (ed.), 1993, *Family, Kinship and Marriage in India,* Oxford University Press, New Delhi.

UNRISD, 2005, *Gender Equality: Striving for Justice in an Unequal World,* Geneva, UNRISD.

United Nations, 1980, *Report of the Second World Conference on Women,* Copenhagen, United Nations.

Visaria, P., 1996, 'Structure of the Indian Labour force: 1961–94', *Indian Journal of Labour Economics,* 39(4), pp. 725–40.

White, G., 1993, 'Towards a Political Analysis of Markets', *IDS Bulletin,* 24(3): 4–11.

White, S.C, 1992, *Arguing with the Crocodile: Gender and Class in Bangladesh,* Zed Books, London.

Whitehead, A., 1981, "I'm hungry mum':The Politics of Domestic Budgeting', Young, K., Wolkowitz, C. and R. McCullagh (eds.) *Of Marriage and the Market:Women's Subordination in International Perspective,* Routledge and Kegan Paul, London, pp. 93–116.

Whitehead, A., 1984, 'Women and Men, Kinship and Property: Some General Issues', R. Hirschon (ed.), *Women and Property—Women as Property,* Croom Helm, London and Canberra, pp. 176–92.

Whitehead, A., 2000, 'Continuities and Discontinuities in Political Constructions of the Working Man in Rural Sub-Saharan Africa: The 'Lazy Man' in African Agriculture', *The European Journal of Development Research,* 12(2), pp. 23–52.

Whitehead, A. and M. Lockwood, 2000, 'Gendering Poverty: A Review of Six World Bank Poverty Assessments', Razavi, S. (ed.) *Gendered Poverty and Well-being,* Blackwell, Oxford, pp. 115–44.

Whitehead, A. and D. Tsikata, 2003, 'Policy Discourse on Women's Land Rights in Sub-Saharan Africa: The Implications of the Re-turn to the Customary', *Journal of Agrarian Change,* 3(1&2), pp. 67–112.

World Bank, The, 2001, *World Development Report 2000/2001: Attacking Poverty,* Oxford University Press, New York.

———, 2005, *Gender Issues and Best Practices in Land Administration Projects: A Synthesis Report*, The World Bank, Washington.

Yanagisako, S., 1987, 'Mixed Metaphors: Native and Anthropological Models and Kinship Domains', Collier, J. F. and S. Yanagisako (eds.), *Gender and Kinship: Essays towards a Unified Analysis*, Stanford University Press, Stanford, pp. 86–118.

Yngstrom, I., 1999, 'Gender, Land and Development in Tanzania: Rural Dodoma 1920–1996', University of Oxford, D.Phil, Oxford.

Young, K., C. Wolkowitz, et al., (eds.), 1981, *Of Marriage and the Market: Women's Subordination in International Perspective*, CSE Books, London.

# Glossary

| | |
|---|---|
| *Adat* | Customary |
| *Adivasi* | Scheduled Tribe |
| *Aman* | Name for monsoon crop in West Bengal |
| *Amin* | Land Assessor |
| *Anganwadi* | Child care centre |
| *Badki* | Elder (first) wife |
| *Baha* | Flower (spring) festival |
| *Baisi* | Community meeting |
| *Bakhen* | Ritual Invocations |
| *Bari* | Homestead plot |
| *Benami* | Proxy |
| *Bhag* | Share |
| *Bhoodan* | Land gifts |
| *Bhorna* | Mortgage |
| *Bigha* | Measure of land (three acres) |
| *Boro* | Late winter crop in West Bengal |
| *Bund* | Embankment |
| *Chasa* | Cultivation |
| *Chuin* | Stream |
| *Chutki* | Younger (second) wife |
| *Dain* | Witch |
| *Dal* | Lentils |
| *Dalit* | Scheduled Caste |
| *Damin* | Region in the Santal Parganas reserved for the Scheduled Tribes |
| *Dehri* | Priest |

| | |
|---|---|
| *Desmanjhi* | Leader of group of villages |
| *Dhan Katai* | Paddy harvest (forcible) |
| *Dhani* | Paddy land |
| *Dheki* | Hand pounding device |
| *Diku* | Outsider-trader (one who gives trouble) |
| *Diwani* | Revenue jurisdiction |
| *Ferari* | One who is absconding |
| *Ghanghra* | Black-eye beans |
| *Ghardijawae* | Husband resident in wife's home for a limited time period |
| *Gharjawae* | Husband resident in wife's home (house son-in-law) |
| *Gola* | Granary |
| *Gudit* | Community messenger |
| *Haat* | Market |
| *Handi* | Rice beer |
| *Hor* | Person |
| *Hul* | Rebellion |
| *Jaago Behena* | Awake, sisters! |
| *Jaherthan* | Sacred Grove |
| *Jal* | Water |
| *Jamabandi* | Rent fixation (refers to title record number) |
| *Jamin* | Land |
| *Jangal* | Forest |
| *Jhumli* | Measure for heads of corn |
| *Jote* | Land/plough |
| *Karamchari* | Revenue clerk |
| *Kath* | Poles |
| *Kendu leaf* | Leaf used for making *bidi* or hand-rolled cigarettes |
| *Kharif* | Monsoon crop |
| *Khas Mahal* | Government estate |
| *Khas* | Administered by government for revenue purposes |
| *Khet* | Field |
| *Kumhar* | Caste of potters |
| *Kurram* | Shifting Cultivation |
| *Lobir* | Highest (literally, mountain) |
| *Lungi* | Loincloth |
| *Magh* | Name of month (February) |

| | |
|---|---|
| *Mahajan* | Moneylender |
| *Mahila Samiti* | Women's Group |
| *Majhi* | Headman |
| *Mukhiya* | Elected headman of local government |
| *Murri* | Puffed Rice |
| *Mutt* | Hindu monastery |
| *Naeke* | Village priest |
| *Ojha* | Traditional healer |
| *Ora* | House |
| *Pai* | A measure used for paddy and other grains |
| *Panch* | 'Five', refers to the community elders |
| *Panchayat* | Unit of local government at village level |
| *Parganait* | Leader of group of villages |
| *Patta* | Land Title-deed |
| *Pradhan* | Headman |
| *Pradhani Jote* | Land allocated to headman |
| *Purdah* | Veiling or seclusion |
| *Rabi* | Winter crop |
| *Raiyat* | Cultivator |
| *Raja* | King |
| *Saheb* | Officer |
| *Sahukar* | Moneylender |
| *Sal* | *Shorea Robusta,* leaf used for making plates |
| *Sapha hor* | Santal revivalists |
| *Sarkar* | Government |
| *Sendra* | Hunt |
| *Sohrai* | Harvest festival |
| *Sude* | Sacralized food |
| *Taben Jom* | 'Right to eat' or maintenance |
| *Teli* | Caste of oil-pressers |
| *Thakur* | God |
| *Thana* | Police station |
| *Tola* | Hamlet |
| *Udaga* | Terrorist |
| *Van panchayat* | Forest council |
| *Zamindar* | Landlord |

# Acronyms

| | |
|---|---|
| AC | Assistant Commissioner |
| ANM | Auxiliary Nurse Midwife |
| BDO | Block Development Officer |
| BJP | Bharatiya Janata Party |
| BPDP | Bihar Plateau Development Project |
| BPL | Below Poverty Line |
| DAO | District Agriculture Office |
| DC | District Commissioner |
| DRDA | District Rural Development Agency |
| DSO | District Statistical Office |
| DWCRA | Development of Women and Children in Rural Areas |
| EAS | Employment Assurance Scheme |
| HSA | Hindu Succession Act, 1956 |
| IAY | Indira Awas Yojana |
| ICDS | Integrated Child Development Services |
| IRDP | Integrated Rural Development Programme |
| JAAC | Jharkhand Area Autonomous Council |
| JB | *Jama Bandi* |
| JFM | Joint Forest Management |
| JMM | Jharkhand Mukti Morcha |
| JRY | Jawahar Rozgar Yojana |
| MLA | Member of Legislative Assembly |
| MP | Member of Parliament |
| NATP | National Agriculture Technology Project |
| NGO | Non Governmental Organization |

| | |
|---|---|
| PDS | Public Distribution System |
| PHC | Primary Health Centre |
| PMRY | Prime Minister's Rozgar Yojana |
| RBI | Reserve Bank of India |
| SC | Scheduled Caste |
| SDO | Sub Divisional Officer |
| SGSY | Swarnajayanti Gram Swarozgar Yojana |
| SHG | Self Help Group |
| SPTA | Santal Pargana Tenancy Act, 1949 |
| ST | Scheduled Tribe |
| TOI | Times of India |
| TPDS | Targeted Public Distribution System |

# Index


Abhiyaan, 11, 251
Agarwal, B., 25, 114, 201–2, 214, 233
Agnihotri, S.B., 66, 70
agrarian reform (*see also* land reform),
  Bhoodan, 136
  government land distribution, 23, 26, 112, 136–9, 185, 235, 260–2, 285, 289
  social change and inequality, 22–3, 28, 134–5
  welfare state, 28, 258
agricultural rituals, 45, 87, 192, 198–9, 225
alcoholism (*see also* drunkenness), 10, 40
*aman* crop, 96–7
Anderson, B., 121, 125
*anganwadi* worker, 54, 73, 228, 278, 303
Archer, W.G., 59, 75, 130, 202–4, 207, 211, 224, 239, 245
Auxiliary Nurse Midwife (ANM), 51, 67, 71
Assam, 40, 84, 125, 128, 181, 273,
autonomy,
  cultural, 8
  political, 9, 13, 133, 140–4, 291

Badlao Foundation, 250
Bagdiha,
  *mukhiya*, 92, 166, 187, 265, 275
  Hindus and Santals, 38, 92, 94, 103, 125, 163, 170, 176, 181, 187, 212, 246
  livelihood resources, 23, 36, 79, 81, 94, 205, 293
  paddy cultivation, 5, 43, 55, 65, 76–7, 88, 91, 98–102, 105, 125, 138, 148–55, 160, 169–70, 194, 198, 213
  *sohrai*, 102, 154–5, 198, 211
Bansloi river, 54, 118
Bardhaman, 96–7
Baviskar, A., 7, 119
Below Poverty Line (BPL), 29, 82, 264–5, 268, 272
Benda-Beckman, F. von, 249
Bengalis, 73, 86, 118–19, 120, 123
Béteille, A., 9, 28
Bhagalpur, 117, 133

Bhatia, B., 143, 268
Bihar Plateau Development Project (BPDP), 55–7
Bodding, P.O., 122, 129, 203, 206–7, 211, 218
Boserup, Esther, 167–8
British , 40, 58, 95, 117, 181
bureaucracy,
access to, 44, 103
attitude to Santals of, 29, 181, 184
attitude to women of, 39, 115, 250
development, 29, 39, 48, 106, 260, 274, 280
implementation of reform by, 259, 289
revenue, 34, 48, 125, 187, 214, 260–1
Buchanan, Francis, 57, 122
Burman, Roy, 130, 136

Carney, J., 237
caste,
identity, 9, 12, 95–100
movement, 18
Catholics, 199, 253
Census, 61–9, 124, 147, 252
*Chasa hor,* 2, 40, 170, 201
Chhatra Yuva Sangharsh Vahini, 115
childcare, 16, 20, 49, 89, 257, 278
Christian(ity), (*see also* church)
conversion to, 30, 71, 73, 224, 252
influence of, 59, 124, 251
marriage, 35, 199–200, 253, 257
morality of, 5, 199–200, 220, 253, 281, 286, 300
Syrian, 11
Church, 17, 35, 140, 199–200, 224, 252–3
Chuapara,
drinking water, 47, 50, 76, 82, 88, 102, 257
Kol, 73, 93, 96, 159, 165, 180, 184, 202
*majhi*, 74–6, 80, 93, 122–4, 129, 143–4, 149, 217, 220, 241
*majhi-parganait* system, 75, 243
school, 66–9
mid-day meal, 67, 69, 284
medium of instruction, 69, 289
Paharia, 40, 73, 78, 92, 94, 117, 121–2, 132, 151, 180–1, 184, 186, 189, 202, 293
teachers, 57, 67–9, 93
citizenship, 28–9, 111, 267, 310
colonial, 7–8, 23, 58, 75, 87, 112, 116, 118–31, 143, 251
Community Development Block,
Integrated Rural Development Programme (IRDP), 272, 275–8
Indira Awas Yojana (IAY), 39, 77, 217, 272–5
Integrated Child Development Services (ICDS), 278–9
National Rural Employment Guarantee Programme (NREGP), 267–70
self help groups (SHG), 161, 276
social security benefits, 24, 29, 157, 173, 185, 189, 243, 157, 260–2, 272, 280
Swarnajayanti Gram Swarojgar Yojana (SGSY), 272, 276–8
Constitution, 10–11, 28, 69, 176–7, 289
Corbridge, S., 30

corruption, 29, 282, 302
cooperative, 114, 162
credit, 23, 36, 82, 123, 136, 159–64, 171–3, 255, 257, 269–72, 281–2, 287–8

*dain* (*see also* witch), 4, 13, 16, 41, 226–30, 240, 287, 300, 322–3
*Damin-i-koh*, 54, 57, 107–9, 117, 180
Das, Arvind, 110, 132, 258
Datta, K., 118
decentralization, 18, 25, 135, 294
Deere, C.D., 12, 24–5, 114
development discourse,
  gender and property, 20–6, 290
  production relations, 8, 21, 192
  feminist, 15, 20–1, 25, 31, 36, 115, 233, 250–1, 284
  Millennium Development Goals, 24
*dheki*, 76, 88–90, 103, 211, 292
*diku*, 11, 94
  relations with *adivasis*, 85–6, 92, 124–7, 142, 165, 196
  with *adivasi* women, 144, 229, 253–4
displacement, 7–8, 23, 49, 57, 75, 143–4, 196
domestic labour, 21, 69, 88–90, 104
Dreze, J., 18, 24, 224
Dube, L., 193

economy, political, 18, 40, 59, 200
Elson, D., 259, 284
Ellis, F., 87, 129
emancipation, 17, 20, 116, 145, 190 (*see also* empowerment)
Employment Guarantee Scheme, 217, 267, 269, 301
empowerment, 3, 15, 25, 37, 90, 195, 234, 249, 259, 287
endogamy, 203
Engels, F., 20, 222
ethnography, 30, 33, 47, 179
equality, gender, 6–7 , 10, 20–9, 120, 147, 176, 254–5, 260, 272, 288–90
Evans, Mary, 20, 21
exogamy, 204, 212

food security, 6, 22, 52, 59, 141, 147, 155–8, 167, 173, 187, 260, 263, 289
  government policy on, 22, 141, 260, 263
  land and, 6, 155–8, 167, 173, 187, 289
forests
  deforestation, 8, 143
  forest guard, 8, 106, 151
  forest produce, 65, 72, 79–81, 83, 100, 105–8, 117, 140, 143, 172, 229
  mahua, 79, 124, 154–5, 319
Foucault, M., 14, 17
Fraser, N., 18, 29, 41, 238, 254–8, 301

Geertz, C., 65
Giddens, A., 112, 118
globalization, 7, 112, 238
Goetz, A.M., 30, 259
*Gogo hor*, 2
Gough, K., 113, 201,
Grain Golas, 132, 135, 169, 171
Guha, R., 119, 121

*haat*, 40, 58, 101, 118, 277

Durgapur, 54, 57, 81, 155
Gando, 95, 99–101, 211, 326
Habermas, Jurgen, 16, 26
Hardiman, D., 10, 84, 252
Harriss, John, 14, 46, 87
Harriss-White, Barbara, 259, 285
health,
doctors, 51, 71, 77
malaria, 50–1, 71, 77, 84, 90
*ojha*, 71, 213, 230, 287, 323
Primary Health Centre (PHC), 71–2
quack, 51, 71–2
hegemony, 17, 118, 163, 178, 180–5, 270, 291, 301
Hindi, 38, 67, 86, 274, 289
Hindu,
interaction with tribals, 7, 43–4, 91–2, 163–7, 252
bureaucrats, 29, 274–5, 289
morality, 218, 223, 259, 300
women's status, 161, 229–30
domination, 170, 176, 185–94, 254, 285
Hobsbawm, Eric, 60, 111, 125, 135
home-maker(s), 2, 6, 14, 64, 215, 220, 227, 259, 279
honour, 16, 220, 229
Human Development Indicators, 61
Hunter, W.W., 7, 116, 121

identity (ies), 2–5, 8, 11–16, 20, 26–7, 37–9, 44–7, 51, 93, 107, 112, 176, 179, 246, 286–7, 298–300
*adivasi*, 5, 9–10, 18, 30, 37, 41, 59, 125–6, 143–4, 157, 173, 176–7, 186–8, 194–5, 199, 214, 231, 250–1, 254, 288
class, 4, 17, 20–1, 64, 87, 92, 105, 113–14, 119, 126, 143, 165, 214, 220, 232, 284
collective, 9–10, 18, 23, 125, 175, 190, 196–7
female/women's, 19, 32, 60, 72, 81, 105, 130, 143, 158, 175–7, 194, 201–2, 212, 215, 220–2, 227, 230, 248, 295–6
male (*see also* masculinity),
devaluation of, 10, 33, 177, 191–9, 231
land as determinant of, 64–5, 95, 135, 165–70, 201, 212, 241, 295
negotiation of, 14, 32, 41
independence, economic, 66, 81, 225, 229
Indonesia, 214, 221
interdependence, 17, 32, 151, 194, 231, 295
International Fund for Agricultural Development (IFAD), 25, 234, 259
invisibilization (*see also* visibility), 23, 63, 120, 281

Jharkhand,
education, 38, 40, 125, 135, 251, 278, 280
Education Officers, 50, 68
leaders of Jharkhand movement, 112, 114, 223, 292
literacy rates, 62–3, 66, 108, 278
Mahila Mukti Morcha (JMMM), 12, 251
Mukti Morcha (JMM), 60, 134, 253–4, 285

Sibu Soren, 60–1, 112, 134–5, 144, 165, 282
state, 18, 31–2, 60, 235
Joshi, Sharad, 115
justice,
social, 110, 135
distributive, 29, 136, 256

Kelkar, G., 228
Kenya, 105, 237, 272, 274
Kerala, 256, 263
Khadiagala, L.S., 245

labour, division of, 20, 88, 103, 114, 258
Lakra, Juliana, 10
land records, 33, 79, 94, 128, 179–90, 251, 261, 268
landowners, 95, 124, 142
landless, 95, 124, 132, 139, 141, 147, 187, 196, 258
as cultivators, 64, 166
non-tribal, 23–4, 105, 284–5
land reform, 23, 96, 110, 114, 136, 234–5, 256, 272, 288
transfers, 65, 127, 141, 147, 189, 245
land rights,
collective, 6, 10, 14, 234
community, 11–12, 116–17, 125, 138
cultivating, 12, 123
first struggle for women's rights, 114–16
individual titles, 23, 33, 129, 170
property, 6, 20–1, 72, 87, 157, 183–5, 190–4, 202–3, 232–3, 236, 259
struggles, 113, 140
women's interest in, 12, 23, 176–8
land types,
*bari*, 73, 78, 83, 108, 150–4, 168, 179, 209, 215, 303–9, 318, 324
*dhani*, 83, 98, 150, 166, 168–70, 187–9, 303–7, 318, 322, 324
*kurram*, 78, 83, 117, 151, 153, 196, 291
land survey and settlement,
Bihar Scheduled Areas Regulation Act, 135
Gantzer Settlement, 70, 128–30, 180, 227, 324
McPherson Settlement, 122–3, 127–9, 168, 170, 180–1, 186, 227, 242, 322
Permanent Settlement of Bengal, 117
Raiyati land, 127, 184
Santal Pargana Inquiry Committee, 130
Wood Settlement, 123, 126, 180, 186, 191, 227
laws (*see also* legislation),
inheritance, 6, 11, 16, 27, 47, 72, 127–9, 178, 191–2, 203–7, 212–13, 226, 238, 261
customary, 11, 25–7, 202, 223, 226, 236, 238–9, 247–51, 295–7, 302
daughters, 32, 129–30, 202–4, 222, 232–3, 245, 250–1
favouring women, 129, 245, 259, 261
Hindu Succession Act, 1956, 27, 161, 233, 245, 261
Santal Pargana Tenancy Act, 1949, 74, 130–1, 136, 138, 147, 159, 167, 205–6, 209–11, 213, 227, 238–9, 243, 245, 261
statutory, 25–6, 236, 238

separated women,
lack of, 94, 217, 256, 261, 289
widows, 129, 223–6, 228, 243
laws in practice,
*amins* and *karamcharis*, 122, 243, 246, 261
criminal court, 123, 244, 248–9
kin group, 16, 37, 129, 178, 181–5, 201–2, 212, 223, 238–40, 296
legal pluralism, 238, 249
oral evidence, 244
revenue/civil court, 119, 130–1, 202, 214, 227, 233, 244–5, 248–9, 297
settlement court, 48, 129, 144, 242
settlement officer, 79, 123, 127, 138, 243–9
village council, 1, 129, 135, 240–3, 255
lawsuits/litigation, 10, 91
*Madhu Kishwar v. State of Bihar*, 10, 116, 261
legislation, 8, 28–9, 110, 135, 141, 230, 297
legitimacy, social, 203, 213, 219, 234, 260, 296,
Leon, M., 12, 25, 114
liberalization, 18, 29, 87, 141, 235, 264
literacy, 22, 32, 38, 59, 61–3, 66–7, 107, 278, 281–2
Long, N., 214
Lukes, S., 113

MacDougall, J., 119, 122, 124
*mahajans* (*see also* moneylenders),
movements against, 109, 119, 131–6, 140, 247, 252
oppression by, 70–1, 104, 118–19, 123, 126, 163, 167, 199
relative prosperity of, 91
Mahapatra, S., 86, 198
maintenance, 1, 11, 22, 219, 225–6, 231, 241, 295
malnutrition, 24, 40, 65, 70, 77, 155, 283
Marandi, Babulal, 141
Marandi, Stephen, 134, 142
marginalized, 8, 14, 28, 33, 112, 173, 215, 227, 234, 295
market orientation, 25, 87–8, 91, 103, 125, 130, 141, 235, 276, 280, 289–90, 301
marriage, 12, 16, 45, 60, 82, 88, 105, 115, 127, 169, 187, 193–7, 201–12, 215–24, 253–4, 288, 300, 324–7
between Santals and non-Santals, 45, 201, 254
failed, 3, 285–6
registration of, 243, 246, 297
remarriage, 204, 216, 218, 223, 226, 239
masculinity, 30, 95, 100, 129, 136, 178–9, 191–3, 198–200, 210, 215, 228–31, 293, 295, 299, 302
materialist, 22, 24, 285
middle-class, 2–3, 27, 32, 115, 220, 286,
migration, 96–100, 107, 125, 173, 181, 196,
seasonal, 97, 152–6, 171,
men's, 22, 99, 153, 233,
women's, 96–9, 102, 158, 170, 211, 229, 246–7, 275
missionaries, 34, 48, 119–22, 125, 181, 226, 238, 250–6, 281, 300
moneylender (*see also* usury), 83, 91, 116–24

land alienation by, 8, 122–3, 131–3, 143, 189–91
power of, 55, 86, 109, 136, 156
customary role of, 82, 84–5, 151, 162–3, 230
monogamy, 5, 200, 218, 220, 223, 261, 300
Moore, H., 21, 179, 228, 236, 238, 246
*mukhiya*, 1, 92, 166, 187, 265, 275
Munda, R.D., 148
Muslims, 11, 67, 93, 109, 128, 181, 186, 192, 249

National Policy for the Empowerment of Women, 233, 259
National Family Health Survey, 36
National Rural Employment Guarantee Programme (NREGP), 217, 267
National Sample Survey, 23
New Agricultural Policy, 22
NGOs,
as service providers, 41, 104, 161, 287–8
as mobilizers, 75, 194, 233–4, 247, 250–5, 277,
nutrition, 22, 155, 278

Oldham, W., 57, 123
*Ora hor* (*see also* home-makers) 2, 90, 175
Orans, M., 30, 119, 176
O'Malley, L.S.S., 40, 79, 119, 169,

panchayat,
as arbitrator, 2, 41, 230, 239
as benefactor, 68, 85, 92
Panchayati Raj, 235
Panchayati Raj Extension to Scheduled Areas Act, 75
paradigm shifts,
debate around Scheduled Tribes, 7–13, 59–61, 142, 177, 293
reframing the gender and property debate, 290–3
subaltern historians, 9–10, 284
Parliament, 29, 60, 230
paternalistic, 39, 136
patrilineage, 26, 239
patronage, 29, 166, 179, 181, 185, 263, 272, 280, 302
pauperization, 141
Pearce, J., 124, 144
pensions, 217, 226, 243, 260, 262–3, 267, 280, 300
pluralism, 238, 249
politicization, 18, 92
Prasad, B.M., 162, 238, 263
privatization, 29, 110, 172, 254
property, landed, 5, 7, 10, 72, 158, 168, 196, 228, 232, 256
family, 25, 183
marital, 27, 134, 202, 215–26, 241, 250–5, 295
polygyny, 108, 218, 221–3
Public Distribution System (PDS),
*Annapurna*, 265–7
*Antyodaya*, 265–6
Targeted PDS, 264–6, 268

Quan, J., 201, 233

race, 9, 28, 117, 118, 121
Ramachandran, V.K., 162
Ranger, T., 60, 111
Rao, N., 6, 57, 105, 141, 142, 158, 189, 289
redistribution (*see also* inequality), 7, 12, 28–9, 136, 139, 288, 301
reform, land, 23, 96, 110, 114, 136, 234–5, 256, 272, 288

relationships,
agrarian, 9–10,
gender, 15, 20, 26, 31, 33, 60, 73, 91, 112–13, 114–16, 128, 139, 177–8, 192, 213–15, 228–30, 259
hierarchical, 12, 28, 65, 86, 105, 191, 230–1, 233
marital, 3, 239
social and cultural, 34, 105, 214–16

reproductive,
rights, 24, 145, 193–4
role, 26, 90, 177, 215, 220, 279, 284
resources,
redistribution of, 7, 12, 28–31, 136, 139, 288, 301–2
common property, 10, 157, 290
Revenue Department/Circle, 260, 267–70, 272, 279
Employment card, 268–9, 279, 281
production support, 270–1
revivalist, 34, 158

Santal *Hul*,
aftermath of *hul*, 121–30
*marang buru*, 125
Norwegian missionary accounts, 119–21, 251
Santal archives, 59, 121
Sidho and Kanhu, 109–13, 116, 119–21, 125, 133, 144
women's role, 9, 58
*zamindars*, 119–20, 122–3, 172, 185
Santal men,
drunkenness, 29, 56, 76, 132, 187, 270, 281, 296
landlessness of, 64, 124, 139, 141, 187, 195
unemployment of, 40, 270
Scheduled Areas, 8, 75, 135
Scheduled Castes, 28, 93, 96, 104, 132, 157, 160, 236
Scheduled Tribes, 10, 32, 59, 61, 66, 142, 160, 177, 274, 293
education, 32, 38, 59–60, 67, 69, 93, 124
girls' education, 69, 158, 253
Recognition of Rights Act, 59, 79, 113, 142, 293
Scott, J.C., 25, 119, 179, 202
self-worth, 4, 38, 42, 176, 221
Sen, A., 18, 21, 24, 157, 256
Sengupta, N., 148
sensitization, 287
sex ratios, 32, 61–3, 70, 72, 106, 285
sexuality,
assertion of, 3, 5
control of, 121, 144, 192, 200–1, 215–16, 220–3, 254
Shetkari Sangathana, 115
Silingi, 54, 57, 58, 67, 71, 75, 85
Sivaramakrishnan, K., 8, 140
Skaria, Ajay, 10, 30
Strathern, Marilyn, 45, 175, 176, 193, 234, 295
status, social, 8, 106, 165, 210
Staudt, K., 272, 274
subaltern studies, 9, 284
Swaminathan, M., 162, 264

Thakur, I.N., 254, 261
tenancy, 106, 130, 141, 162, 238, 243–4, 296
Tenth Plan, 22
Thompson, E.P., 18
Toulmin, C., 202, 233
Tsing, A., 17, 214, 230

Uberoi, P., 183
usury, 7, 123, 132

virginity, 215
visibility, 22, 63

watersheds, 37–8
welfare state, 28, 258
West Bengal, 72, 96–7, 148, 211, 220–2, 229, 256, 275
West Singhbhum, 61
White, G., 81
Whitehead, A., 4, 19, 146, 235, 239
widows,
  conversion to Christianity of, 30, 200
  customary rights of, 37, 95, 129, 207, 223–6, 239–46
  empowered, 3, 100, 102, 115, 194–5, 217–18, 295–6
  Hindu, 93, 101
  negotiation of rights, 240, 242, 283, 300
  pensions for, 92, 100, 217, 225–6, 243, 260–9, 279–80, 300
  vulnerability of, 19, 96, 105–6, 228–30
witch, 2, 4, 74, 95, 101, 106, 122, 225–30, 283, 294
women,
  abandoned, 41, 44, 94, 105, 220, 234, 242, 250, 273
  groups, 23, 36, 113–14, 251, 276, 281–2, 297
  headed households, 90, 106, 161, 166, 266, 268, 271, 280, 294
  single, 95, 218
women's rights to marital property
  co-wives, 218–19, 241
  conjugal relations, 52, 212, 215–17, 239, 285
  male anxieties, 192, 199, 228–31
  male infidelity, 215–16
  marriage breakdown/divorce, 134, 200, 207, 212, 215–16, 218–19, 241, 281, 300
  mobility in marriage, 13, 108, 200, 215, 221–3, 279
  Prevention of Witchcraft Act, 1999, 74, 230
  widowhood, 217, 231, 295
women's rights to parental property,
  *gharjawae*, 95, 98, 206–13, 238–40, 243–5, 248, 254, 261–2, 281, 296–8, 324–7
  in-marrying daughter, 206, 256

  land registered in women's names, 128, 139, 210
  *taben jom*, 27, 204–8, 288
World Bank, 22–3, 56–7, 148, 234–45, 278, 289

Yanagisako, S., 178

FSC
www.fsc.org
MIX
Papier | Fördert gute Waldnutzung
FSC® C083411

Kolibri 360 GmbH
Ferdinand-Jühlke-Straße 7
99095 Erfurt, Deutschland
produktsicherheit@kolibri360.de